A
BRIDGEPOINT
BOOK

BridgePoint,
an imprint of
Baker Academic,
is your connection
for the best in
serious reading
that integrates
the passion of
the heart with
the scholarship
of the mind.

Renewing the Center

*Evangelical Theology
in a Post-Theological Era*

Stanley J. Grenz

A BridgePoint Book

Baker Academic

A Division of Baker Book House Co
Grand Rapids, Michigan 49516

Published by BridgePoint Books
an imprint of Baker Academic
a division of Baker Book House Company
P.O. Box 6287, Grand Rapids, MI 49516-6287

Printed in the United States of America

Library of Congress Cataloging-in-Publication Data

Grenz, Stanley, 1950–
    Renewing the center : evangelical theology in a post-theological era / Stanley J. Grenz.
        p.   cm.
    "A BridgePoint book."
    Includes bibliographical references and indexes.
    ISBN 0-8010-2239-8 (cloth)
    1. Evangelicalism. 2. Theology, Doctrinal. I. Title.

BR1640 .G75 2000
230′.04624—21   00-057923

For information about academic books, resources for Christian leaders, and all new releases available from Baker Book House, visit our web site:
                      http://www.bakerbooks.com

Contents

Preface   7
Introduction: Evangelicalism in a Time of Transition   11

1. The Gospel and Awakening Evangelicalism   25
2. Scripture and the Genesis of the New Evangelicalism   53
3. The Shaping of Neo-Evangelical Apologetic Theology   85
4. The Expansion of Neo-Evangelical Theology   117
5. Evangelical Theology in Transition   151
6. Evangelical Theological Method after the Demise
   of Foundationalism   184
7. Theology and Science after the Demise of Realism   218
8. Evangelical Theology and the Religions   249
9. Evangelical Theology and the Ecclesiological Center   287
10. Renewing the Evangelical "Center"   325

Scripture Index   353
Author Index   355
Subject Index   361

To Prof. Kermit Ecklebarger,

a celebrative, hopeful evangelical scholar,

in recognition of his retirement from the deanship

of Denver Seminary

Preface

North American evangelical theologians are a gloomy, pessimistic group, or so it often appears from the books, articles, and papers that gain widespread attention among us. Every several years we hail a new jeremiad that bemoans the state of evangelicalism or anticipates its imminent demise. At meetings of our learned societies, we give rousing applause to speakers who chide us for our theological waywardness. And we seem to find it necessary to be constantly on the lookout for those within our ranks who we sense might be drifting uncomfortably close to the theological "edge." In short, we so often give evidence that our guiding dictum is—to parody that of a well-known television series from the 1980s—"to cautiously go where everyone has gone before."

Yet evangelical theologians have every reason to be celebrative in the present and hopeful about the future. By proudly bearing a designation derived from the Greek word for "gospel," we of all people ought to glory in the realization that the God who in Christ has reconciled the world to himself has invited us to be heralds of good news, which is ultimately a message of reconciliation. Our eighteenth-century evangelical forebears knew this. Consequently, they faced a time of upheaval and far-reaching transition with forward-looking confidence borne from a trust in the convincing power of the Spirit-endued gospel. The great Baptist leader Isaac Backus—to cite one example—refusing to be boxed in by the fortress mentality that characterized the religious establishment of his day, declared optimistically, "Truth is great and will prevail."

This volume seeks to follow in the spirit of people like Backus and offer a hopeful appraisal of evangelical theology in the time of upheaval in which we are living. I am convinced that it is "for such a time as this" (Esther 4:14) that God has placed us in the world to be a gospel people in the

7

midst of the current generation and our particular culture. Consequently, this is a glorious time to engage in the crucial task of theology on behalf of, and for the ministry of, the church. We ought therefore to be celebrative and hopeful in our theological endeavors.

At the same time, I must admit that I am the reluctant author of this book. The genesis of *Renewing the Center* lies in the initiative of Bob Hosack, the visionary acquisitions editor at Baker Book House. In 1997, he raised the question with Mickey Maudlin of *Christianity Today* as to what books needed to be written. High on Mickey's list was a piece that would offer an irenic assessment of the state of evangelical theology at the dawn of the new millennium. Moreover, Mickey suggested that I was the person for the job. With Mickey's recommendation in hand, Bob approached me with the idea. Initially I was not convinced that I could, or should, take on such a daunting challenge. But Bob persisted, and through subsequent conversations I came to see that such a project fit well with the trajectory that my writing had been taking over the last decade. Especially since publishing my programmatic book *Revisioning Evangelical Theology* in 1993, I have been keenly interested in the shape of evangelical theology in the contemporary context, as is evident in my theological "trilogy," *Theology for the Community of God* (1994, 2000), *Created for Community* (1996, 2d ed. 1998), and *What Christians Really Believe . . . and Why* (1998), as well as in *A Primer on Postmodernism* (1996), which perhaps provides the clearest backdrop for this volume.

In many ways, *Renewing the Center* marks a watershed in my literary output. These pages entail a distillation of my work in recent years in several areas of theological reflection, while at the same time suggesting avenues that I hope to explore in the coming years. Chapter 6 offers a synopsis of my thinking in the crucial area of theological method, which has already taken book-length form in a volume coauthored with John R. Franke, *Beyond Foundationalism: Shaping Theology in a Postmodern Context* (Louisville: Westminster John Knox, 2000). The chapter itself is adapted from the revision and expansion of a paper delivered at the fall theology conference held at Regent College in October 1999, published as "Articulating the Belief-Mosaic: Theological Method after the Demise of Foundationalism" in *Evangelical Futures: A Conversation on Theological Method*, ed. John G. Stackhouse, Jr. (Grand Rapids: Baker, 2000). The substance of the chapter appears likewise in my essay, "Conversing in Christian Style: Toward a Baptist Theological Method for the Postmodern Context," *Baptist History and Heritage* 35, no. 1 (Winter 2000). An invitation from Prof. David Williams at Colorado Christian University to deliver a Templeton Lecture in March 1999 offered the occasion to work out my call for a renewed understanding of the engagement between theology and science, an issue that has been at the heart of evangelicalism throughout its history. This essay was subsequently published in *Zygon* 35, no. 2 (June 2000), and it forms the basis for what I develop in chapter 7. I had given attention to the question of Christianity and the religions in "Toward an Evangelical Theology of the Religions" published in the *Journal of Ecumenical Studies* 31, no. 1–2 (1994), which served as the beginning point for the fuller treatment of this topic in chapter 8. I gratefully acknowledge the permission of these publishers and journals in allowing me to use materials from these works in this volume.

As these literary acknowledgments indicate, in writing *Renewing the Center* I owe a debt of gratitude to many people. Some provided more tangible assistance to me in this project. In addition to Bob Hosack, many other folk at Baker have had a hand in this volume, including Brian Bolger, who was responsible for shepherding the manuscript through the editing process, and Kirsten Malcolm Berry and Andrea Boven, whose artistic giftedness is responsible for the cover design. I must likewise mention the competent work of teaching assistants Marcus Tso and Kris Peters, who took on the important task of tracking down and confirming a host of footnote references, and of Hella Strothotte, who offered her Latin language skills. I acknowledge as well the assistance of the helpful staff at the Regent-Carey library. I appreciate the willingness of Gary Dorrien to read an earlier draft of the manuscript, and I profited from the helpful suggestions he offered. And I ought not to overlook the important contribution of Carey Theological College, which for a decade now has provided a hospitable academic home for me and which also granted me a sabbatical leave in the fall of 1999, when I composed the initial draft of the book.

My indebtedness extends to many supportive Christians, some of whom are unknown even to me, who uphold my writing efforts through prayer. I was reminded of this rarely acknowledged, seemingly intangible, but no less important contribution through an incident that occurred during the days of intense work on this volume. Since participating in a six-week course on the theology of prayer that I offered at my home church (First Baptist Church, Vancouver, B.C.) some years ago, Carol Blyth has occasionally inquired about the progress of my various writing projects. In response to one of her queries, I had shared with her the nature of this particular work early in the process. After the Sunday morning service on October 3, 1999, Carol handed me a note that she had sensed a compulsion to write. It read: "I felt the Lord wanted me to share something further with you concerning the present writing endeavour you are engaged in. The verse Eccles. 11:5 came to mind, that we 'do not know the path of the wind . . .' and that as you wait upon the Lord in your writing He will add even more insights, fresh depths and layers of meaning, and that this will require a more profound trust in the Holy Spirit even than you have had before to bring together into a cohesive whole the elements of this book. I also felt that your 'right brain' will come more into play, resulting in a fundamental shift in your creative process. This won't be a catastrophic change, but as gentle as the opening of a flower." Carol's gracious note occupied a prominent place right above my computer throughout the subsequent days that I worked on this project. It stood as a silent reminder both of the prayers of supportive persons like Carol and of the sacred trust that I have received as a writing theologian.

When I arrived on the campus of Denver Seminary as an incoming M.Div. student, I was placed in the advisory group of Kermit Ecklebarger, who had recently joined the faculty as professor of New Testament. In the classes I had with him, Prof. Ecklebarger showed himself to be a celebrative, hopeful evangelical scholar who was not afraid to consider ideas and explore avenues that were not necessarily the standard positions of the tradition in which he himself stood. In so doing, he gave his students permission to pursue truth wherever it might be found. Later in my student days, he encouraged me to try my wings as a theological educator in a very tangible way, namely, by inviting me to work with him in leading the laboratory aspect of his hermeneutics class. Then in June 1976, just after my seminary graduation, he delivered the sermon at my ordination service at Northwest Baptist Church in Denver. Since those years, Prof. Ecklebarger has continued to encourage me in my attempts to be faithful to my calling, even as he has been faithful to his. In gratitude for his mentorship and in recognition of his sixty-fifth birthday as well as his retirement from the deanship at my alma mater, I dedicate this volume to Kermit Ecklebarger, who is indeed a celebrative, hopeful evangelical scholar.

Introduction

Evangelicalism in a Time of Transition

The future of evangelicalism is in doubt. At least this is the assessment of many of today's evangelical pulse-takers, prognosticators, and prophets. Writing on the eve of the year 2000, the editors of the premier neo-evangelical magazine, *Christianity Today*, took stock of the current state of the movement. They cited Billy Graham's diagnosis delivered at the founding of the magazine over four decades earlier. On that occasion Graham concluded, "We seem to be confused, bewildered, divided, and almost defeated in the face of the greatest opportunity and responsibility, possibly in the history of the church."[1] Nearly forty-five years later, the editors sensed that the evangelist's depiction remained essentially accurate. "Though the specifics may have shifted since Graham's 1955 speech," the *Christianity Today* editorial pined, "evangelicals are still confused about their role in society, divided as a body, and even bewildered about what *evangelical* means."[2]

Moreover, viewing the future from their vantage point as the fashioners of this trend-setting, trend-following publication, the *Christianity Today* editors found little reason to anticipate that consequential change would come anytime soon. One especially debilitating problem that evoked this sobering judgment was the leadership crisis they perceived to be looming on the horizon. The editors pointed to the central role personalities such as Graham and John Stott had played throughout the previous decades of neo-evangelical history: "When asked what an evangelical was, we pointed

---

1. "*CT* Predicts: More of the Same," *Christianity Today* 43, no. 14 (December 6, 1999): 36.
2. Ibid., 37.

11

to our leaders." But, the editorial then added, "the upcoming leaders of evangelicalism do not seem to have the rallying effect our elder statesmen . . . have had for half a century."[3]

A variety of other prophetic voices could be added to the chorus that emanated from the *Christianity Today* building in Carol Stream, Illinois. Some of these seers are certain that the looming crisis in the leadership of the movement as a whole pales in comparison to what is occurring in evangelical ranks. According to their prognosis, evangelicals today are adrift. Some churches are restructuring congregational life in a manner that, perhaps even unbeknown to them, takes its cue more from the nation's business schools than from the Bible. Others are blindly and unquestioningly catering to the contemporary consumerist mentality. Many evangelicals have substituted therapy for salvation, thereby "exchanging the language of Scripture for the language of *Psychology Today*," to cite Donald McCullough's disquieting appraisal.[4] But above all, evangelicals today are falling prey to wholesale cultural accommodation.

Critics claim that ironically the movement's phenomenal success over the past fifty years has occasioned its impending demise. Timothy Phillips and Dennis Okholm note that engagement with culture marked neo-evangelicalism's great tactical innovation when it initially developed out of the isolationism of its fundamentalist forebears. Their history lesson reads,

> During the 1940s key fundamentalists questioned this separatistic, anti-intellectual stance and called for Christians to engage culture. Evangelicalism emerged from the isolated cocoon of fundamentalism with a strikingly different strategy and mission in the world. For the last five decades evangelicalism worked through the intellectual and social structures of American life to engage and transform it from within.[5]

Yet in the estimation of the two Wheaton College theologians, viewing the situation from a vantage point fifty years later leads to the conclusion that this strategy has become evangelicalism's "quagmire."[6]

Theological physicians such as David Wells offer a parallel, yet somewhat different, diagnosis. As evangelicalism grew numerically and in stature in society, he claims, its fundamental ethos shifted from antagonism

---

3. Ibid.

4. Donald W. McCullough, *The Trivialization of God: The Dangerous Illusion of a Manageable Deity* (Colorado Springs: NavPress, 1995), 40.

5. Timothy R. Phillips and Dennis L. Okholm, "The Nature of Confession: Evangelicals and Postliberals," in *The Nature of Confession: Evangelicals and Postliberals in Conversation*, ed. Timothy R. Phillips and Dennis L. Okholm (Downers Grove, Ill.: InterVarsity, 1996), 9.

6. Ibid.

toward culture to adaptation of culture. Wells laments this shift in ethos in his offering for a collection of essays edited by Reformation and Revival Ministries founder, John Armstrong, ominously titled *The Compromised Church*. He complains,

> But if we have much, I believe that we now also have little—too little of what is true and right. Our appetite for truth, as well as for what is morally right, is being lost. Evangelical abundance on the surface, and boundless evangelical energy, conceals a spiritual emptiness beneath it.[7]

Echoing Wells's dirge, Phillips and Okholm report that "popular indicators" suggest "that evangelicalism's unique moral and theological inheritance has been traded for a bowlful of spiritual junk food that feeds the contemporary appetite."[8] In Wells's estimation, these various developments are symptoms of a deeper and more troubling disease that has eaten away the solid theological moorings at the heart of the evangelical faith. He thus continues his lament: "The character of contemporary evangelicalism is changing because of its unwitting entanglement with a culture that, in its postmodern configuration, has the power to eviscerate the doctrinal substance of that faith."[9]

Other voices rue that the future of evangelicalism is clouded by the numbers of their co-religionists who have left the movement. Not only have some erstwhile evangelicals—such as John Hick, to cite one prominent example—rejected the label in the wake of undergoing a shift in their personal beliefs, but a growing number are forsaking evangelical churches for a variety of new ecclesiastical sanctuaries, even while holding on to a basically conservative theological perspective. The refuges of choice for such ecclesiastically disquieted evangelicals range from magnificent cathedrals to charismatic storefronts, but in either case the shift in worship venue marks a move that to a previous generation of evangelicals would have been tantamount to apostasy. The lure of the liturgical churches has been enhanced by the influential precedent set by prominent former evangelicals who have not only set out on the Canterbury Trail but, more significantly, have walked the Roman Road (e.g., Thomas Howard) or traversed the Highway to Constantinople (e.g., Franky Schaeffer). Taken together, this plethora of developments indicate to some observers that evangelicalism is, in the words of Phillips and Ok-

---

7. David F. Wells, "Introduction: The Word in the World," in *The Compromised Church: The Present Evangelical Crisis*, ed. John H. Armstrong (Wheaton: Crossway, 1998), 22.
8. Phillips and Okholm, "Nature of Confession," 8.
9. Wells, "Introduction," 14.

holm, "fragmenting and collapsing" and the movement is in a state of "dissolution."[10]

Not only does evangelicalism face a cloudy future, the future of evangelical theology is also in doubt. At least this is the verdict of many of those who chart today's theological waters.

Typical of the various warnings of impending demise is an essay published in *Christianity Today* in the late 1990s. This assessment of "the future of evangelical theology" argued cogently that a division within the ranks of evangelical theologians is threatening "to end our theological consensus," to cite the editors' characterization of the essay's thesis.[11]

To fears of an imminent theological schism could be added other distressing developments that bode ill for the future of evangelical theology. Today's theological voices are beset by uncertainty as to the sine qua non of evangelical theology, the nature and role of doctrine, and the proper relationship of divine revelation in Scripture to evangelical confession in the world.[12] Some keepers of the theological watch have concluded that the task of sorting out the various teams competing on the evangelical theological intramural playing field is now so hopelessly confused that the label itself has become meaningless, even to the point that integrity demands a moratorium on the use of the term "evangelical."[13]

Fears for the future of evangelicalism in general and evangelical theology in particular are exacerbated by the unsettling sense that we are living in a transitional time, that society around us is abandoning the familiar landscape of modernity for uncharted territory. The advent of the postmodern condition raises a host of questions that lay well beyond the purview of previous generations of evangelicals. In short, evangelicals are living at a time when the opening line from Dickens's *A Tale of Two Cities* is no longer cliche. The present is in many ways "the best of times" and "the worst of times." Above all, however, the current point in history offers an occasion to take stock. For evangelicals, "taking stock" involves reviewing where we have come from, so that we might gain clarity as to where we should be headed.

Laced throughout the process of taking stock, however, is the difficult yet unavoidable definitional question. The postmodern condition has heightened, rather than lessened, the significance of defining communi-

---

10. Phillips and Okholm, "Nature of Confession," 8.

11. Roger E. Olson, "The Future of Evangelical Theology," *Christianity Today* 42, no. 2 (February 9, 1998): 40.

12. Phillips and Okholm, "Nature of Confession," 8.

13. One of the earliest statements to this effect came from Donald Dayton in 1991. See Donald W. Dayton, "Some Doubts about the Usefulness of the Category 'Evangelical,'" in *The Variety of American Evangelicalism*, ed. Donald W. Dayton and Robert K. Johnston (Downers Grove, Ill.: InterVarsity, 1991), 251.

ties. The December 1999 *Christianity Today* editorial noted this. With their prognosticator hats firmly in place, the editors predicted, "As Christianity sees a rise in cultural and ethnic contextualizations, defining our terms and core principles will become of prime importance. We are already seeing a push to define evangelicalism. It may be a precursor to a larger battle over defining Christianity worldwide."[14] The quest to define evangelicalism, however, immediately confronts all would-be dictionary contributors with the basic methodological question: How do we go about the task of defining a phenomenon as seemingly amorphous as the evangelical movement? Not surprisingly, even this issue has become a source of division among evangelical scholars and scholars of evangelicalism.

Perhaps the simplest method is to define the movement sociologically. Viewed from this perspective, evangelicalism constitutes a loosely structured coalition of persons who share certain religious and cultural symbols, participate in a somewhat readily identifiable number of institutions, look to a changing yet discernible group of leaders, and through these associations gain a corporate self-consciousness as well as a sense of identity as belonging to a particular group. Another, more eclectic approach is David Bebbington's widely cited schema, which draws from sociological, historical, and theological considerations. Based on his study of evangelicalism in Britain from its genesis in the eighteenth century to its resurgence in the late twentieth century, Bebbington concludes,

> There are four qualities that have been the special marks of Evangelical religion: *conversionism*, the belief that lives need to be changed; *activism*, the expression of the gospel in effort; *biblicism*, a particular regard for the Bible; and what may be called *crucicentrism*, a stress on the sacrifice of Christ on the cross. Together they form a quadrilateral of priorities that is the basis of Evangelicalism.[15]

In keeping with the goal of reviewing the past for the sake of charting the way forward for evangelical theology, the following chapters treat evangelicalism as a theological phenomenon and therefore draw from the particularly theological character of the movement's historical trajectory. This trajectory leads to a crucial differentiation between the older evangelicalism that finds its genesis in the awakenings of the 1730s and the neo-evangelicalism that emerged in the mid-twentieth century as an attempt to move beyond the constraints of fundamentalism. At the same time, a blurring has occurred in recent years, as many persons and groups

14. "*CT* Predicts," 37.
15. David Bebbington, *Evangelicalism in Modern Britain: A History from the 1730s to the 1980s* (Grand Rapids: Baker, 1992), 2–3.

whose historical and theological roots lie with the former have increasingly come to sense affinities with the latter.

My own background exemplifies this tendency. I grew up in a confessional tradition (the North American Baptist Conference) that did not go through the modernist-fundamentalist controversy. Yet, by the time of my birth, this ecclesiological group, like several others that likewise do not share the post-fundamentalist character of neo-evangelicalism, had come to align itself with the neo-evangelical movement. Thus, I was nurtured in an environment that readily identified with the various neo-evangelical organizations and neo-evangelical leaders. I recall as a preteen regularly sending part of the tithe from my allowance and meager earnings to M. R. DeHaan's *Radio Bible Class* in the form of a dime and a nickel taped to a sheet of paper on which I had written a short letter explaining the nature of the contribution.

Theological history, therefore, marks the beginning point of the following study of evangelicalism. This telling of the foundational theological story of the movement spans the first four chapters and spills over into chapter 5. The pattern of the story in the opening chapters reflects the consensus of historians that the roots of contemporary evangelicalism lie in three concentric circles. So widely held is this approach that William J. Abraham can state matter-of-factly, "the term 'evangelical' embraces at least three constellations of thought: the Reformation, led by Luther and Calvin, the evangelical revival of the eighteenth century as found, say, in Methodism, and modern conservative evangelicalism."[16] Consequently, some groups that share central theological characteristics and commitment with evangelicalism and therefore are "evangelicals" in the broad sense (most notably certain groups among the sixteenth-century continental Anabaptists) do not figure into the theological narrative recounted in this volume simply because they did not participate directly in the trajectory that gave rise to the evangelical awakenings or to the emergence of neo-evangelicalism.

In keeping with the concern to look at the specifically *theological* roots of contemporary evangelicalism, the first two chapters sketch the theological trajectory that led first to the evangelical awakening in the eighteenth century and then to the birth of the neo-evangelical movement out of fundamentalism in the 1940s. More specifically, assuming the "received" accounting of the genesis of the movement but following the lead of those who speak about a formal and a material principle, I explore the two central theological interests that lie at the heart of the contemporary evangel-

16. William J. Abraham, *The Coming Great Revival* (San Francisco: Harper and Row, 1984), 73.

ical ethos: the maintaining of the true biblical gospel (chapter 1) and upholding of the Bible as the inviolate theological authority (chapter 2).

After the fashion of most evangelical historiography, chapter 1 begins with the Reformation. Although they see themselves as heirs of the Reformers' rediscovery of the gospel, today's evangelicals are not merely propagating "Luther pure and simple." Rather, they read the gospel of "justification by faith" largely through lenses colored with the retrieval of the quest for sanctification inaugurated by Calvin and augmented by the concern of both the Puritan and the Pietist movements for a personal conversion experience, sanctified living, and assurance of elect status. As these concerns coalesced in the context of a church that had grown comfortable with the outward forms of the faith, the result was the great awakenings in Britain and the American colonies during the middle third of the eighteenth century, which marked the birth of the evangelical movement in its "classic" expression. The emerging evangelicalism was characterized by convertive piety, the vision of the faith that sees a personal experience of regeneration through the new birth coupled with the transformed life, rather than adherence to creeds and participation in outward rites, as the essence of Christianity. Evangelical theologians, in turn, took up the crucial questions that the focus on convertive piety evoked, and as a result evangelical theology became a salvation-centered discipline with a highly practical component.

The emergence of convertive piety in the eighteenth century provided the clearest defining moment marking the genesis of the evangelical movement as a whole. Nevertheless, in addition to upholding the gospel principle, evangelicals today see themselves as a people committed to Scripture and, with it, to biblical doctrine. Chapter 2 argues that the contemporary evangelical understanding of the great Reformation principle of *sola scriptura* was not shaped solely by Luther nor for that matter by the line running from Calvin, through the Puritans and Pietists, to the early evangelical reverence for the Bible as a practical book. Instead, the character of the Scripture focus among many evangelicals today is also the product of the approach to bibliology devised by the Protestant scholastics, which transformed the doctrine of Scripture from an article of faith into the foundation for systematic theology. The nineteenth-century Princeton theologians appropriated the scholastic program in their struggle against the emerging secular culture and a nascent theological liberalism. Drawing from this legacy, turn-of-the-twentieth-century fundamentalism elevated doctrine as the mark of authentic Christianity, transformed the Princeton doctrine of biblical inspiration into the primary fundamental, and then bequeathed the entire program to the neo-evangelical movement. Concerned to bring classical Christianity once again into dialogue with a world infatuated with naturalism, neo-evangelical theologians sought to provide a cogent response to competing alternatives that challenged what they saw as the central commitments of biblical faith. As a result, the neo-evangelical movement cast theology in an apologetic mode.

This understanding of the theological nature of contemporary evangelicalism sets the stage for all that follows. Chapters 3, 4, and 5 scrutinize more closely the course of the first fifty years of neo-evangelical theology by introducing three contrasting pairs of thinkers. Chapter 3 sketches the shaping influence of two first-generation neo-evangelical theologians, Carl F. H. Henry and Bernard Ramm. By attempting to fulfill the neo-evangelical ideal of engaging constructively with the modern context, Henry and Ramm set the standard for their successors. Yet as their careers unfolded, their own theological programs diverged. Henry's goal was to set forth the foundations for an evangelical theology that could both win intellectual credibility in the modern context and counter the irrationality he sensed in much of modern theology. As a result, Henry set a basically rationalistic and culturally critical cast to neo-evangelical theology. Although Ramm was no less academically rigorous in his approach, he charted a journey that sought to move evangelical theology out of the self-assured rationalism he found in fundamentalism. Consequently, he became the standard-bearer for a more irenic and culturally engaging evangelicalism.

Chapter 4 portrays the manner in which the character of neo-evangelical theology shaped by Henry and Ramm came to fruition in the work of the second generation represented by Millard Erickson and Clark Pinnock. Erickson's great accomplishment was that of systematizing neo-evangelical theology, a task that placed him in the center of the emerging "establishment" evangelicalism. While Erickson set out to embody aspects of the inheritance from both Henry and Ramm, serving as establishment theologian led him increasingly to a posture more indicative of the former than the latter. Pinnock reflects a theological odyssey that moved in a quite different direction. He began his career as a proponent of a thoroughgoing rationalist apologetic that in many respects reflected Henry's sympathies. Yet Pinnock's desire to fulfill the evangelical apologetic ideal by engaging in mutually enriching dialogue with alternatives launched a pilgrimage that led him to rethink many of his earlier views. In his willingness to learn from a variety of thinkers and traditions, Pinnock carried forward the irenic posture inherited from Ramm.

The transitional fifth chapter brings to an end the opening historical-theological section, while setting the stage for what follows. The chapter begins by raising the question as to whether contemporary neo-evangelical theology is indeed facing a crisis. I engage with the possibility of a bipolar split in the movement's theological ranks by first looking at the third generation of neo-evangelical theologians, introducing Wayne Grudem and John Sanders as potential successors to Erickson and Pinnock, and then by wondering if we stand on the verge of evangelicalism's demise, as David Wells fears, or at the dawn of the post-evangelical era, after the manner of Dave Tomlinson's proposal. Opting for neither, the second half of the chapter suggests that the emerging task of evangelical theology is that of coming to grips with the postmodern condition. This situation, I argue, provides the occasion for evangelical theologians representing a variety of viewpoints to move beyond the typical theological categorizations and think together how best to engage in the quintessential evangelical task of cultivating an apologetic theology appropriate to the emerging postmodern (and perhaps post-theological) context.

Unfortunately, "postmodern" means different things to different people. In an attempt to avoid the confusion such multiple meanings can create, the chapter rejects the tendency so prevalent among evangelical critics to equate postmodernism with deconstruction. Instead of limiting the postmodern phenomenon to this particular aspect, I characterize it as the call for a chastened rationality. More particularly, the postmodern condition entails a transition from realism to social construction and from the metanarrative to local stories. My goal in the second half of the book is to outline the parameters of a critical appropriation of these postmodern sensitivities that can facilitate the development of an evangelical apologetic theology for the sake of the church's gospel mission in the contemporary context. In this sense, the current volume presupposes, builds from, and advances the discussion set forth in my earlier book, *Revisioning Evangelical Theology.*[17]

Chapters 6, 7, and 8 follow through a single line of thinking. The discussion of the sixth chapter is framed by the question of epistemology that the postmodern condition raises so forcefully. Conscious of the problem that emerges in the aftermath of the demise of foundationalism, this chapter suggests the contours of a theological method that can lead to a construction of a Christian belief-mosaic for our times. The methodology proposed here maintains the evangelical commitment to the primacy of Scripture as theology's norm, while finding a role in the theological conversation for both the theological heritage of the church and contemporary cultural sensitivities. Moreover, chapter 6 explores the manner in which the local nature of all theology, occasioned by the "incredulity toward metanarratives" that characterizes the postmodern condition, can nevertheless result in a theological presentation that is truly Christian.

17. Stanley J. Grenz, *Revisioning Evangelical Theology* (Downers Grove, Ill.: InterVarsity, 1993).

Here I argue that a local theology remains properly "Christian" to the extent that it is thoroughly trinitarian, finds its central motif in the biblical concept of community (i.e., persons-in-relationship), and takes as its orientation point God's eschatological goal for all creation.

Chapter 7 takes up the conversation between theology and science that has been a central interest of evangelicals throughout the history of the movement and remains a key concern of neo-evangelical theologians today. What occasions my engagement with this issue, however, is the shift from realism to social construction indicative of the postmodern situation, a decisive shift that raises the ontological question of the "objectivity" of the world. Therefore, in this chapter the focus of the discussion moves from epistemology to ontology (while not leaving the epistemological problem behind). By exploring three quintessential ways of understanding the connection between theology and science, I conclude that present talk about the givenness of the world is closely tied to the eschatological orientation of Christian theology. This leads to the introduction of the concept of "eschatological realism" as the appropriate way of combining the insights of social construction with the concerns of the critical realists. Eschatological realism, in turn, provides the vantage point from which to view the church's calling to be a people who inhabit in the present a linguistic world that is created by the Spirit, finds its center in Jesus Christ who is the logos, and comprises the foretaste of God's eschatological new creation.

The eighth chapter turns to the pressing issue of "truth" that flows out of the conclusions of chapter 7. But as the discussion in this chapter reveals, in a global context characterized by cultural pluralism, this question can no longer be posed merely in conversation with science. Instead, it necessarily leads to the realm of the religions. The postmodern situation, therefore, requires a revised way of framing the question of truth, for evangelicals now must indicate how, in a world of many religions, theology can continue to "privilege" the world-constructing language of the Christian community. This crucial challenge demands an evangelical apologetic theology of religions that is not satisfied with simply perpetuating the typical debate about personal participation in eternal salvation, as important as that matter is, but also engages with the question of the possibility of a providential role of the various religions in the divine program within history. I argue that by considering religions as community-building, identity-confirming traditions, evangelical theology can provide an intellectual apologetic for the truth of the centrality of Christ for human salvation without constructing a new foundationalism. Such a non-foundationalist apologetic theology boldly asserts the uniqueness and finality of Jesus Christ as the one who mediates fellowship with God who is not merely the Most High, but is none other than the triune God of the biblical narrative. Moreover, the salvation in Jesus Christ that the church proclaims is for all people (Luke 2:30–32), for it entails the divinely given goal of human existence.

Chapter 9 brings into explicit conversation the strong ecclesiological orientation underlying the proposal for a renewed evangelical apologetic theology charted in chapters 6, 7, and 8. The concern for ecclesiology voiced in the chapter is motivated in part by the realization that this aspect has become more acute in a postmodern context that looks to the faith community to be the practical demonstration of the gospel it announces and of the message it proclaims as *the* truth. With this in view, I engage critically with the operative ecclesiology evangelicalism has evidenced throughout much of its history. Because of the "parachurch" nature of the movement, this ecclesiology has emphasized the "invisible" church to the detriment of a theologically motivated concern for, and a well-rounded theological conception of, the "visible" church. In response, the chapter calls for a renewal of the Reformation focus on the community gathered around the gospel proclaimed in "Word and sacrament." A communitarian ecclesiology, I argue, can in turn open the way for a renewed missional evangelical ecumenism.

The shorter tenth chapter brings the entire discussion to a conclusion by calling for a renewal of an evangelical center to the church of Jesus Christ, a center characterized by a "generous orthodoxy." To this end, the chapter introduces the current discussion of the appropriateness in the present of the "two-party" paradigm, in terms of which evangelicals have described the theological landscape over the past century, and from which they have gained their sense of identity. I argue that the postmodern situation necessitates a move beyond this taxonomy, a shift that in turn can occasion a recapturing of an understanding that characterized classic evangelicalism at its genesis and comprised the vision of the architects of neo-evangelicalism, namely, the renewal of the center of the one church. The chapter characterizes this renewed center as focused on the gospel of convertive piety, oriented toward the doctrinal consensus of the church, and motivated by a vision that is truly catholic, that is, a vision encompassing the whole church—and, beyond the church, all creation.

In offering this book-length call for a critical appropriation of postmodern insights in the evangelical theological task, I readily acknowledge that many voices are advising a variety of other suggestions as to how best to respond to the postmodern situation. These proposals differ not only in substance but also in overarching intent from my own. Despite the seemingly bewildering plethora of options currently touted, the most widely heralded submissions boil down to a few simple alternatives. We are told that as evangelicals we should either batten down the hatches and wait for the storm to pass, ignore postmodernism as a passing fad that will soon give way to "post-postmodernism," launch a philosophical jihad with the goal of stamping out postmodernism and thereby make the world safe for Christian faith, or do an end run around both postmodernism and modernism by resurrecting some idyllic premodern era.

Each of these suggestions has certain merits. And taken together, they voice an important reminder. The call for "critical appropriation" can lead to an exuberance that overlooks the aspects of postmodernism that are incompatible with, or inimical to, the Christian faith. As Paul declared, the gospel is a stumbling block (1 Cor. 1:23). Clearly, the offence of the gospel does not evaporate in the postmodern context.[18] Nevertheless, evangelicals must guard against the temptation to conclude too quickly that they know exactly where this offence lies, and thereby too readily discount the postmodern critique. For this reason, I am convinced that the risks engendered by the various cautionary stances proposed today are greater than those occasioned by the call for critical appropriation. Taken to the extreme, each of these alternatives encourages a type of escapist mentality that lets Christians off the postmodern hook too easily. They all risk failing to appreciate the depth of the transition that is now occurring as well as the pervasive and far-reaching implications of the postmodern condition.

For the purposes of this volume, however, such proposals entail an even more potentially debilitating risk. These various alternatives fall short of the posture that the evangelical theological heritage directs us to adopt. Only by tackling the task of critical engagement that takes seriously the postmodern condition and draws creatively from postmodern sensitivities for the sake of the advancement of the gospel in the world can this generation of evangelical theologians truly claim to stand in the legacy of their forebears, whose theological program involved an apologetic appropriation of the philosophical sensitivities of their day.

In his posthumously published masterpiece, *A History of the Work of Redemption*, Jonathan Edwards placed the events transpiring in his own backyard within the glorious sweep of the divine work in history from its beginnings in the primordial past to its anticipated consummation. He believed that the revivals that were dawning in New England in the late 1730s marked the beginning of the final phase of God's work in the world. Like many of the leaders of the fledgling evangelical movement, Edwards was convinced that he was participating in the great process of reformation and renewal that would open the way for Christ to reign truly and completely within the church, and that this in turn would lead to the ad-

---

18. For a sketch of the author's own critical appraisal of postmodernism, see Stanley J. Grenz, *A Primer on Postmodernism* (Grand Rapids: Eerdmans, 1996), 162–67.

vance of the gospel in the world. Later, in the eighteenth century, his Baptist protégé, Isaac Backus, drew from Edwards's theology of history to challenge the church to complete the reformation that had begun in the sixteenth century, had been advanced by the English Puritans, and was now reaching its final stages in New England. Drawing from Paul's words to the Romans, Backus declared to his contemporaries living in the closing decade of the eighteenth century, "If the church had not been asleep, iniquity could not have prevailed as it hath done. But our apostle says, 'it is high time to awake out of sleep; for now is our salvation nearer than when we believed . . .' Rom. xiii, 11–14. If he were truly obeyed, glory would soon dwell in our land."[19]

Edwards and Backus may have been mistaken about the ins and outs of the divine timetable for history, and they may have been overly optimistic about their own role as heralds of the eschatological consummation. Nevertheless, these eighteenth-century pastors were surely correct in their estimation of the crucial importance of an evangelical awakening for the reformation of the church and, in turn, for the mission of the church in the world. Edwards and Backus perceptively saw within the momentous changes transpiring in their day the Holy Spirit at work bringing renewal to the church and the world. And they were convinced that the time had come for the church to awaken so that Christ's followers might fulfill their mission to the world.

Evangelicals today can do no better than be admonished by, draw inspiration from, and follow after the example of Edwards, Backus, and a host of other evangelical luminaries. Like our forebears, we do well to look for the renewing presence of the same divine Spirit, who was so mightily at work in the eighteenth century, within the far-reaching transitions that mark the postmodern context. As we perceive the renewing presence of the Spirit within our context and, in doing so, awaken to the challenge of being faithful to our calling—including the calling to engage in theological reflection and construction—we might discover that despite the dangers that threaten its demise and despite its own perennially "confused, bewildered, divided, and almost defeated" state, through the Spirit who constantly seeks to reform Christ's church, evangelicalism does indeed have a bright future, to the glory of God.

19. Isaac Backus, *The Nature and Necessity of an Internal Call to Preach the Everlasting Gospel,* 2d ed. (Boston, 1792), 43–44.

one

The Gospel
AND Awakening
Evangelicalism

◆

In the June 14, 1999, issue of *Christianity Today*, executive editor David Neff noted the flagship evangelical magazine's newly formulated intent "to focus some of its energies on fostering renewed interest in beliefs" and more particularly in "classic Christian doctrines." In pinpointing the logical inaugural topic of such an endeavor, Neff added matter-of-factly, "As *evangel*-icals, we begin this enterprise with the gospel itself."[1] This typically evangelical prioritizing of "the gospel itself," Neff then reported, led to the fashioning of what its architects view as an evangelical consensus statement on the nature of the gospel, bearing the title, "The Gospel of Jesus Christ: An Evangelical Celebration."

Neff's statement and the document that emerged after a one-year drafting process indicate the extent to which evangelicals claim that the central concern uniting them is the Christian gospel. The connection between evangelicals and the gospel can boast a linguistic foundation. The group's preferred designation, "evangelical," arises from the Greek term *euangelion*, rendered "gospel" in English. In keeping with this etymological link, the movement's apologists routinely begin their descriptions of evangelicalism with an appeal to this biblical word.[2]

1. David Neff, "Inside *CT*," *Christianity Today* 43, no. 7 (June 14, 1999): 5.
2. See, for example, Morris A. Inch, *The Evangelical Challenge* (Philadelphia: Westminster, 1978), 10; Donald G. Bloesch, *The Future of Evangelical Christianity* (Garden City, N.Y.: Doubleday, 1983), 15; Robert E. Webber, *Common Roots* (Grand Rapids: Zondervan, 1978), 25–27; Ronald H. Nash, *Evangelicals in America* (Nashville: Abingdon, 1987), 22. This point was also foundational to the section concerning evangelical identity set forth in the document that arose from the 1989 consultation on Evangelical Affirmations cosponsored by the National Association of Evangelicals and Trinity Evangelical Divinity School. See *Evangelical Affirmations*, ed. Kenneth S. Kantzer and Carl F. H. Henry (Grand Rapids: Zondervan, 1990), 37.

Of course, every Christian tradition might rightly point out that they are interested in the gospel. What sets evangelicals apart is the form their interest in the gospel takes. The specifically evangelical concern to uphold the one true gospel follows a particular historical trajectory that in turn links evangelicals to a particular theological problem, namely, the attempt to delineate a true understanding of the gospel.

The Reformation Heritage

Standing at the inception of the trajectory that gave birth to evangelicalism and hence set the agenda for evangelical theology is the Reformation. In fact, just as "evangelical" is connected etymologically to "gospel," so also as a designation of a particular party in the church the word is linked to the Reformation. Even before they began using the label "Protestant" as a contrast to "Roman Catholic," the sixteenth-century Reformers distanced themselves from their opponents by appropriating the term "evangelical."[3] That the term had become a commonplace self-designation among the various reformers is evident in Luther's critique of the antinomians within the reformation party who "boast of being evangelicals."[4] Furthermore, Erasmus spoke of "some who falsely boast they are Evangelicals."[5] In keeping with Luther's arrogation of the term, the Lutheran churches in Germany have always been known officially as *evangelisch* (evangelical). By extension, all the churches that emerged from the sixteenth-century Protestant movement have at least a historical claim to this designation.

Luther and the Gospel of Justification

Why did the Reformers choose the designation "evangelical"? The standard Protestant historiography asserts that the Reformation entailed a rediscovery of the biblical gospel, which had been lost in the Middle Ages. More specifically, the Reformers elevated anew the gospel as the good news of justification by grace through faith alone (*sola fide*). As Roger Olson notes, this doctrine became "the heart and essence of Luther's theological contribution."[6] Likewise, Paul Althaus asserts that "the justification

3. For this judgment, see Kenneth S. Kantzer, "The Future of the Church and Evangelicalism," in *Evangelicals Face the Future*, ed. Donald E. Hoke (Pasadena, Calif.: William Carey Library, 1978), 128.

4. See Martin Luther, *Luther's Works*, ed. Jaroslav Pelikan et al. (St. Louis: Concordia, 1955–1986), 27:48.

5. Erasmus, *Epistola contra quosdom, qui se falso iactant Evangelicos* (1529).

6. Roger E. Olson, *The Story of Christian Theology: Twenty Centuries of Tradition and Reform* (Downers Grove, Ill.: InterVarsity, 1999), 380.

of the sinner through the grace that is shown in Jesus Christ and received through faith alone" is "the heart and center" of Luther's theology.[7] Luther was convinced that the doctrine of justification stood at the center of soteriology and that soteriology in turn stood at the center of theology. According to Althaus, for Luther, "The doctrine of justification is not simply one doctrine among others . . . but the basic and chief article of faith with which the church stands or falls, and on which its entire doctrine depends."[8]

Luther's formulation entailed a radical rejection of the medieval understanding that connected justification with actual righteousness. According to this view, justification marks the end of a gradual process that begins in baptism, continues throughout life, and reaches its climax in the next life. By means of this process God's own righteousness is infused into a sinner, and this infused righteousness, in turn, makes the person righteous in fact.

Against this view, Luther asserted that justification occurs as God in Christ freely forgives sinners and imputes Christ's righteousness to them *as if* it were their own. Thus, justification is God's free gift, bestowed by God not only apart from human merit but also apart from humans becoming themselves actually righteous. Luther acknowledged that justifying grace would eventually bring about fruit in the believer's life. Yet he steadfastly refused to focus attention on the fruits of righteousness, lest such attention reinstate the doctrine of works righteousness that he believed had so wantonly undermined the gospel.[9] In short, Luther's concern was to restore the gospel to the Church believing that in so doing he would be reestablishing a gospel Church.

Contemporary evangelicals likewise claim that their movement rests on the gospel of justification by grace through faith. In keeping with this self-understanding, after asserting that the *Christianity Today* program would begin with the gospel, David Neff reports (albeit stating the doctrine incorrectly),

> Preliminary research showed that the gospel of justification by faith still has a high commitment among CT readers: 100 percent declared that it was "essential for an evangelical to believe" that "those whom God saves he justifies by faith through grace alone."[10]

7. Paul Althaus, *The Ethics of Martin Luther*, trans. Robert C. Schultz (Philadelphia: Fortress, 1972), 3.

8. Paul Althaus, *The Theology of Martin Luther*, trans. Robert C. Schultz (Philadelphia: Fortress, 1966), 224.

9. Olson, *Story of Christian Theology*, 391.

10. Neff, "Inside *CT*," 5.

Through their chosen name, therefore, contemporary evangelicals are staking claim to the heritage that traces its beginnings to Luther. They routinely see themselves as the most forthright and consistent upholders of the Protestant principle of *sola fide*. Hence, in his introduction to evangelical Christianity, William W. Wells declares, "First and foremost evangelicals are people who believe in and live by the gospel of Jesus Christ as defined and articulated by the Protestant Reformers."[11] Luther's concerns appear between the lines in the following words from the 1999 *Christianity Today* document:

> As our sins were reckoned to Christ, so Christ's righteousness is reckoned to us. This is justification by the imputation of Christ's righteousness. All we bring to the transaction is our need of it. Our faith in the God who bestows it . . . is itself the fruit of God's grace. Faith links us savingly to Jesus, but inasmuch as it involves an acknowledgment that we have no merit of our own, it is confessedly not a meritorious work.[12]

While claiming the heritage of Luther, evangelicals are not simply followers of the German Reformer. Their understanding of the gospel of justification by grace through faith is not "Luther pure and simple," but has been mediated to them by subsequent thinkers and movements. The Lutheran ecumenist Mark Ellingsen concurs with this judgment:

> Lutheranism differs from all other churches in regard to its systematic-programmatic focus on the doctrine of justification by grace through faith. Other churches, including Conservative Evangelical churches, attend to this theme, but none with the single-minded emphasis of Lutherans. For this reason, the other mainline churches share more in common with the Evangelical movement's concern with sanctification and regeneration (being "born again") than does Lutheranism.[13]

In this statement, Ellingsen anticipates two further formative influences upon evangelicalism, one of which arose during the Reformation era itself.

The Sanctified Life

Luther was thoroughgoing in his pessimism about human ability to please God and hence in his conviction about our utter dependency on

11. William W. Wells, *Welcome to the Family: An Introduction to Evangelical Christianity* (Downers Grove, Ill.: InterVarsity, 1979), 129.

12. "The Gospel of Jesus Christ: An Evangelical Celebration," *Christianity Today* 43, no. 7 (June 14, 1999): 53.

13. Mark Ellingsen, *The Evangelical Movement: Growth, Impact, Controversy, Dialog* (Minneapolis: Augsburg, 1988), 42.

God for our justification. According to the Reformer, all our actions are products of a fallen, depraved human nature, and therefore, our righteousness—i.e., every attempt to please God and live up to God's standards—is like filthy rags. Because of our depravity, we cannot hope to win moral uprightness through obedience to the law, for while the law can command us to do right, it cannot produce in us obedience to God. In Luther's estimation, we cannot do God's will by striving to keep the law (or by making pilgrimages to holy places or purchasing indulgences). Instead, God's will is that we humbly acknowledge our sinfulness and in faith accept God's gracious provision.

Justification and the Law

This did not mean that Luther had no place for the law. On the contrary, he acknowledged that the law had at least two crucial "uses."[14] The law fulfills a general use, as it acts as God's gracious restraint on sin. Hence, Luther taught that human government "bears the sword" so that the rule of law might prevent humans from becoming as sinful as they otherwise would be.[15] More significant for Luther, however, is the law's theological or salvific use. The law serves as the prelude to the gospel. Or, to use the Pauline language, it acts as a schoolmaster bringing us to Christ. By showing us how we ought to be disposed or how we ought to live, the law indicates how woefully short of God's glory we fall.

Luther viewed this dynamic of law and grace as operative not only in the matter of human salvation, but also in day-to-day Christian living. For him, the role of the law does not stop at some supposed crisis or conversion point in our personal narrative. Rather, it continues throughout life. By continually showing us our sinfulness, the law leads us to see our desperate need for God's gracious justification at every moment. It points out how our motives and actions are always tainted by sin, so that we can never justify ourselves by claiming that we acted purely or rightly. Instead, we can only cry out continuously for the divine grace freely available in Christ and cast ourselves on the justifying God. For this reason, believers know they are *simul iustus et peccator*, "always sinner,"

---

14. There is some discussion among historians as to whether or not Luther also added a third use of the law. For a characterization of the sense in which Luther divides the function of the law into three uses, see Paul M. Hoyer, "Law and Gospel: With Particular Attention to the Third Use of the Law," *Concordia Journal* 6, no. 5 (September 1980): 194–99. Long offers a mediating position: "Luther hinted at a triple use of the law when he noted that the pious man and the impious man read the civil prescriptions of law very differently, but he never developed the fullblown conception which in Calvin provided the way of making the law a source of welcome and positive moral guidance for the believer." Edward LeRoy Long, Jr., *A Survey of Christian Ethics* (New York: Oxford University Press, 1967), 85.

15. See, for example, Luther's poignant statement from 1523 in *Luther's Works*, 45:75–129.

yet "always justified" by God's grace.[16] This dictum carried far-reaching consequences for Luther's view of the Christian life. Knowing that our actions are always tainted by sin, we can never hope for perfection in this life. For this reason, we never "progress" beyond the need for repentance. Rather, the Christian
pilgrimage consists in the life of continual repentance together with the experience of God's justifying grace.

His focus on the reception of grace in each moment of life meant that
Luther eschewed the idea of living according to prescriptive norms determined through rational reflection and applied in advance to life situations.
Instead, he advised that at every step of our journey we should seek to listen carefully so as to discern the voice of God instructing us about what is
right and then diligently attempt to act accordingly. When we intently
seek to do God's will as those who know that even our best efforts are
tainted with sin, we can "sin boldly, but believe and rejoice in Christ even
more boldly."[17] And this trust in Christ is pleasing to God and makes our
actions good in God's sight.[18] Only when we lay hold of Christ in faith,
therefore, do we love God and do good works.[19]

Insofar as they continue to focus on *sola fide*, contemporary evangelicals
rightly claim to follow Luther's lead. In this sense they are truly "Luther-
ans." Nevertheless, the typical evangelical reading of the gospel of justification has a strong Reformed theological cast to it. The evangelical understanding of the nature of justification is mediated by Calvin's alteration of
Luther. The most significant modification had to do with the divine law
and its implications for Christian living.

Sanctification and the Law

Like Luther, Calvin had a deep respect for the law. And like his predecessor, Calvin acknowledged the general and theological uses of the law.[20]
But the Geneva Reformer, following Melanchthon and Martin Bucer,[21]
saw yet an additional purpose. The law, he asserted, also reveals God's will
to believers so as to instruct them in holy living.[22]

---

16. Martin Luther, "In epistolam S. Pauli ad Galatas Commentarius," in *D. Martin Luthers
Werke, kritische Gesammtausgabe*, ed. J. K. F. Knaake et al. (Weimar: Hermann Boehlau,
1988), 40.1:368. For the English translation, see Luther, *Luther's Works*, 26:232.

17. Luther, *Luther's Works*, 48:282.

18. Ibid., 44:23–24, 54, 97; Luther, *Luthers Werke*, 6:204–5, 229, 263.

19. Luther, *Luthers Werke*, 40.1:275. For the English translation, see Luther, *Luther's
Works*, 26:161.

20. John Calvin, *Institutes of the Christian Religion*, trans. Henry Beveridge (Grand Rapids:
Eerdmans, 1989), 2.7.6–11.

21. See Francois Wendel, *Calvin: The Origins and Development of His Religious Thought*, trans.
Philip Mairet (New York: Harper and Row, 1963), 200.

22. Calvin, *Institutes*, 2.7.12.

According to Calvin, Christians express their gratitude for God's gracious mercy through their voluntary (albeit always imperfect) obedience to the law.[23] The Christian life, then, is to be characterized by continual growth in obedience to divine precepts, especially as codified in the Ten Commandments,[24] that is, by increasing in holiness or sanctification. But how can this be reconciled with Luther's doctrine of justification *sola fide*, which Calvin also affirmed? In his *Treatise on the Christian Life* Calvin argues that justification by grace through faith does not mean that believers are content to remain in sin. Rather, justified Christians seek to show the fruits of their justification.[25] This is made possible because God's act of justification is also an act of regeneration. Through this regenerative work, God progressively recreates the divine image that sin had deformed, so that the believer abounds in good works. Calvin is careful to add, however, that such good works are not the basis for our justification, but its result and sign.[26]

In adding the third use of the law, Calvin transformed the relationship between law and gospel in the Christian life. According to Luther, the two retain a dialectical relationship; the believer stands continuously in need of being confronted by the demands of the law, which point out sin, and of hearing the gospel message of divine forgiveness in Christ, which evokes faith. In Calvin, in contrast, the relationship becomes doubly sequential. In its salvific use, the law paves the way for the hearing of the gospel, but the acceptance of the gospel, in turn, opens the door for the reintroduction of the law which now functions according to its third use. And in this third use, the law accompanies the believer throughout life.

In effect, Calvin's addition of the *tertium usus legis* introduced a new understanding of sanctification into the sixteenth-century discussion of soteriology. Medieval Roman Catholic theology had collapsed justification into sanctification, in that it viewed justification as the product of, or as emerging out of, the process of sanctification. In his attempt to correct this teaching, which he deemed to be a theological error that had undermined the gospel, Luther elevated justification to the point that sanctification disappeared from view. Calvin, however, orchestrated the return of sanctification, a feat he accomplished by separating justification and sanctifica-

23. William F. Keesecker, "The Law in John Calvin's Ethics," in *Calvin and Christian Ethics*, ed. Peter De Klerk (Grand Rapids: Calvin Studies Society, 1987), 25.

24. Gordon Clark, for example, declares that according to Calvinism, "the Christian is sanctified by an ever more complete obedience to the Ten Commandments." See Gordon H. Clark, "Calvinistic Ethics," in *Baker's Dictionary of Christian Ethics*, ed. Carl F. H. Henry (Grand Rapids: Baker, 1973), 81.

25. Calvin, *Institutes*, 3.6–10.

26. Ibid., 3.18.

tion so as to make them two distinct temporal moments in the believer's history.

Although in his *Institutes* Calvin offered no separate chapter devoted to sanctification per se, subsequent Reformed thinkers followed the direction in which he pointed. Reformed theological treatments of the Christian life routinely view justification as a completed reality that marks the beginning of the process of sanctification (the climax of which is marked by the believer's eschatological glorification). Louis Berkhof, for example, asserts,

> Justification takes place once for all. It is not repeated, neither is it a process; it is complete at once and for all time. There is no more or less in justification; man is either fully justified, or he is not justified at all. In distinction from it sanctification is a continuous process, which is never completed in this life.[27]

Lutheran theologian Gerhard Forde warns against what he sees as the danger inherent in this Reformed tendency:

> The separation of justification from sanctification in this manner thus leads only in one direction: The process of sanctification becomes the primary reality; justification fades into the background as something everyone presupposes or takes for granted, but which possesses no real dynamic. Justification becomes a kind of frozen idea.[28]

Despite such warnings, contemporary evangelicals have generally followed Calvin and the Reformed tradition, rather than maintaining the Lutheran view.[29] In describing the Christian life, evangelical theologians routinely speak about justification as a past event that sets the believer on the road to sanctification. And in their systematic theologies they regularly divide the discussion of justification and sanctification into separate chapters.[30] Thus, Millard Erickson deals with the former under a section labeled "The Beginning of Salvation," while treating the latter as part of "The Continuation of Salvation," with glorification coming in yet a third section entitled "The Completion of Salvation."[31]

27. Louis Berkhof, *Systematic Theology*, rev. ed. (Grand Rapids: Eerdmans, 1953), 513–14.

28. Gerhard O. Forde, "Christian Life," in *Christian Dogmatics*, ed. Carl E. Braaten and Robert W. Jenson (Philadelphia: Fortress, 1984), 2:429.

29. Even Wiley, who argues for a strong Wesleyan view on entire sanctification, separates justification from sanctification and speaks of the former as "an instantaneous, personal and comprehensive act." H. Orton Wiley, *Christian Theology* (Kansas City, Mo.: Beacon Hill, 1952), 2:393.

30. See, for example, Gordon R. Lewis and Bruce A. Demarest, *Integrative Theology* (Grand Rapids: Zondervan, 1994), 3:123–236.

31. Millard J. Erickson, *Christian Theology* (Grand Rapids: Baker, 1985), 3:954, 967, 997.

The pervasive influence of Calvin within contemporary evangelicalism comes to expression in the 1999 *Christianity Today* statement: "The moment we truly believe in Christ, the Father declares us righteous in him and begins conforming us to his likeness. Genuine faith acknowledges and depends upon Jesus as Lord and shows itself in growing obedience to the divine commands." The declaration then adds, "By his sanctifying grace, Christ works within us through faith, renewing our fallen nature and leading us to real maturity."[32]

Insofar as evangelicals adhere to Calvin's conception of sanctification as theologically distinct from and temporally subsequent to justification, they are not merely "Lutheran," but also "Reformed." Yet, not all Reformed Christians are evangelicals, as is evident, for example, in the hesitancy of many within the various Reformed denominations in North America (e.g., the Reformed Church in America, the Christian Reformed Church, and the Netherlands Reformed Church) to identify themselves as evangelicals. This ambivalence is understandable, in that evangelicalism is not simply the contemporary embodiment of the Reformation. Although the theological trajectory that gave it birth may have begun in the Reformation, it underwent twists and turns, permutations and augmentations, during its journey from the sixteenth century to the present.

The Legacy of Puritans and Pietists

The most significant post-Reformation developments for the formation of evangelicalism and hence for the concerns of evangelical theology were the Puritan and Pietist movements. The confluence of these, in turn, opened the way for the emergence of evangelicalism in eighteenth-century Britain and North America.

Visible Saints

The chief theological issue with which the Puritans struggled was not soteriology per se and hence not the nature of the gospel. In their estimation, these foundational issues had been settled by Luther and especially by Calvin. Rather, the theologians who sought to complete the reformation of the church in England (and Scotland) focused their attention on matters of ecclesiology.

The concern for ecclesiology did not first surface with the Puritans, of course, but dates to the beginnings of the Reformation itself. In his debate

---

32. "Gospel of Jesus Christ," 53.

with his Catholic opponents, Luther raised the question as to what constitutes a gospel church. And the magisterial Reformers gave a definitive answer to this question: The true church is constituted by Word and sacrament. The *Confessio Augustana* codified the Reformation understanding,
when it defined the church as "the assembly of all believers, in which
among whom the gospel is purely preached in its purity and the holy Sacraments rightly are administered according to the Gospel."[33] Yet, as this
Lutheran creedal formulation indicates, the Reformers' pronouncements
on the nature of the church did not arise out of an interest in matters pertaining to ecclesiology as such, but were precipitated by a more fundamental issue. The concern to delineate the marks of the true church
emerged by necessity from what they saw as the central controversy in
which they were embroiled, the debate about the true nature of the gospel. In the crucible of their struggle for the soul of Christianity, Luther and
others determined that the true church is the one that proclaims and cel-
ebrates the true biblical gospel as they had rediscovered it, namely, the
good news of justification by grace through faith alone.

The Duly Constituted Church

The Puritans, however, pushed the question of a duly constituted
church to the center. This concern arose out of the nature of struggle that
initially launched the Puritan movement itself, namely, the task of ridding
the church of what the Puritans perceived to be the residue of papistry
that had remained after the break with Rome. In this conflict, the Puritans
elevated to a place alongside of Word and sacrament a third mark that had
already been gaining attention not only in Britain but also in continental
Reformed circles: discipline. The true church, earlier leaders such as John
Knox and John Hooper[34] had declared, was also characterized by church
discipline, including the ability to excommunicate the wayward, with the
attendant idea that the church is "the congregation of the faithful."[35]

In advancing this proposal, the Puritans could claim the precedent of
Bucer and Beza.[36] Yet the germ for such a move could be found already
in Calvin. In his *Reply to Sadoleto*, the Geneva reformer identified "three

33. Augsburg Confession, in *The Creeds of Christendom*, ed. Philip Schaff (New York: Harper
Brothers, 1877), 3:11–12, article 7.
34. For a helpful sketch of Hooper's contribution to the nascent Puritan movement, see
F. Ernest Stoeffler, *The Rise of Evangelical Pietism* (Leiden: Brill, 1971), 30–41.
35. John Hooper, *The Later Writings of Bishop John Hooper*, ed. Charles Nevinson (Cambridge: Cambridge University Press, 1852), 120–21.
36. According to J. H. Hall, Beza followed Bucer in distinguishing three marks of the true
church. See J. H. Hall, "Beza, Theodore," in *Evangelical Dictionary of Theology*, ed. Walter A.
Elwell (Grand Rapids: Baker, 1984), 135.

things on which the safety of the church is founded, viz., doctrine, discipline, and the sacraments,"[37] but he stopped short of listing discipline as one of the identifying "notes" of the church in the *Institutes*.[38] Bucer, in contrast, was less reluctant. He placed the discipline of the church with Word and sacrament as a third requirement for the presence of a true church,[39] and he praised the Hungarian Reformed churches for having accepted the discipline of Christ in addition to Christ's pure doctrine.[40]

The widespread acceptance of the third mark is evidenced by the speed with which it found its way into Reformed confessions both on the Continent and in Britain. Hence, the *Confessio Belgica* of 1561 declares,

> The marks by which the true Church is known are these: If the pure doctrine of the gospel is preached therein; if she maintains the pure administration of the sacraments as instituted by Christ; if church discipline is exercised in punishing of sin; in short, if all things are managed according to the pure Word of God, all things contrary thereto rejected, and Jesus Christ acknowledged as the only Head of the Church.[41]

Similarly, the *Scots Confession*, which appeared a year earlier, reads,

> The notes of the true Kirk, therefore, we believe, confess, and avow to be: first, the true preaching of the Word of God, in which God has revealed Himself to us, as the writings of the prophets and apostles declare; secondly, the right administration of the sacraments of Christ Jesus, with which must be associated the Word and promise of God to seal and confirm them in our hearts; and lastly, ecclesiastical discipline uprightly ministered, as God's Word prescribes, whereby vice is repressed and virtue nourished.[42]

Viewed through Puritan eyes, one of the characteristics of the Church of England which indicated that it was not yet truly Reformed was its demonstrative lack of church discipline. It was, of course, a short step from this

37. John Calvin, *Reply by John Calvin to Letter by Cardinal Sadolet to the Senate and People of Geneva*, in *Selected Works of John Calvin: Tracts and Letters*, ed. Henry Beveridge and Jules Bonnet, trans. Henry Beveridge (Grand Rapids: Baker, 1983), 1:38.

38. Calvin, *Institutes*, 4.1.9.

39. Martin Bucer, *De Regno Christi* 1.8, in *Martini Buceri auspiciis opera ordinis theologorum Evangelicorum Argentinensis edita* (Strasbourg: Guetersloh and Leiden, 1955), 15:70.

40. Bucer, *De Regno Christi* 1.4, in *Martini Buceri opera*, 15:42.

41. "Of the Marks of the True Church," *Belgic Confession* (1561, rev. 1619), article 29, in *Creeds of Christendom*, 3:419–20.

42. "The Notes by which the True Kirk shall be Determined from the False," in *The Confession of the Faith and Doctrine Believed and Professed by the Protestants of Scotland* (1560), ch. 18 of *Reformed Confessions of the Sixteenth Century*, ed. Arthur C. Cochrane (Philadelphia: Westminster, 1966), 176–77.

evaluation to the conclusion that some Puritans drew, namely, that the English church was no true church at all, or even decidedly antichrist.[43]

In the 1570s, a second, but closely related, key item emerged on the Puritan ecclesiological agenda. The quest for a truly constituted church led many members of the Puritan party to adopt what has come to be known as the pure church ideal. So central was this principle in Puritan thought that Olson lists it as one of three "universal theological ideas that together compose the Puritan consensus."[44] The goal of the gospel, the Puritans concluded, is to gather out of the world "pure" churches, that is, congregations that contain only, or consist solely of, the elect of God. This ideal lay behind, for example, John Field's statement in 1572, which defined a church as "a company or congregatione of the faiythfull called and gathered out of the worlde by the preachinge of the Gospell."[45] The Puritans, then, desired a "gathered church" consisting of "visible saints," that is, believers whose response to the gospel had made visible their divine election as being among those predestined for salvation.

Their commitment to the pure church ideal motivated the Puritans' strident critique of the church in England. In their estimation, rather than striving to be a church of the regenerate, the English church was content to remain a "mixed assembly" that refused to distinguish between the saints of God and the unregenerate. The doors to full membership in this church were open to every person born in the country, baptized in infancy and later confirmed. The result, the Puritans concluded, was a church populated by persons—and even clergy—who showed no evidence of true Christian belief or devotion to Christ. According to the Puritan diagnosis, a church that would be truly Reformed must rid itself not only of popish errors but of the unregenerate within it. Rather than tolerating the presence of unbelievers in its midst, such a church would strive to maintain a "regenerate church membership."

The pure church ideal raised a thorny ecclesiological question with soteriological roots: Who in fact could be included within the congregations of visible saints? The Puritan formulation and response to this question lay important groundwork for the emergence of evangelicalism.

In dealing with this perplexing issue, the Puritans could once again draw insight from the Reformation heritage. In addition to speaking of the church by appeal to Word and sacrament, the Reformers had also resurrected the Augustinian idea of the invisible church. Luther's systematizer Philip Melanchthon, for example, contrasted the true church of the elect,

43. William Haller, *The Rise of Puritanism* (New York: Harper and Row, 1957), 176.
44. Olson, *Story of Christian Theology*, 498.
45. As cited in Albert Peel, *The Seconde Part of a Register* (London: Cambridge University Press, 1915), 1:86.

known only to God, with the body that bears the name church but in fact opposes, even persecutes, the elect.[46]

The initial impetus for the reappropriation of this concept likely lay in the Reformers' ecclesiological conflict with the Roman Church. Against the Roman Catholic focus on the institutional church, especially the tendency to endow the church hierarchy with ecclesiological status and thereby erect a mediatorial priesthood between the people and God, the Reformers spoke of the church as the spiritual body of Christ which is essentially invisible at present,[47] but is linked to the visible church through the gospel proclamation.[48] Louis Berkhof represents this Reformation understanding when he writes,

> This church is said to be invisible, because she is essentially spiritual and in her spiritual essence cannot be discerned by the physical eye; and because it is impossible to determine infallibly who do and who do not belong to her. The union of believers with Christ is a mystical union; the Spirit that unites them constitutes an invisible tie; and the blessings of salvation, such as regeneration, genuine conversion, true faith, and spiritual communion with Christ, are all invisible to the natural eye;—and yet these things constitute the real *forma* (ideal character) of the Church.[49]

The "invisible church" underwent a seemingly slight yet crucial change in meaning under the influence of Calvinism's focus on predestination. The focal point of the hidden nature of the true church shifted from the mystical union with Christ to another Augustinian idea, the identity of those elected and predestined by God for eternal salvation.[50] The designation "invisible church" came to refer to the full number of the elect known only to God but who are to be brought into the church. As the *Westminster Confession* asserts, equating the invisible church with the universal church, "The catholic or universal Church, which is invisible, consists of the whole number of the elect, that have been, are, or shall be gathered into one, under Christ the head thereof."[51]

---

46. Philip Melanchthon, *Commentarii in Epist. Pauli ad Romanos*, in *Corpus Reformatorum*, ed. Carolus Gottlieb Bretschneider (Halis, Saxony: C. A. Schwetschke and Son, 1848), 15:678.

47. Berkhof, *Systematic Theology*, 566.

48. Jaroslav Pelikan, *Reformation of Church and Dogma 1300–1700*, vol. 4 of *The Christian Tradition: A History of the Development of Doctrine* (Chicago: University of Chicago Press, 1984), 174.

49. Berkhof, *Systematic Theology*, 565–66.

50. Edmund S. Morgan, *Visible Saints: The History of a Puritan Idea* (New York: New York University Press, 1963), 3.

51. *The Westminster Confession* 25.1, in *Creeds of the Churches*, ed. John H. Leith, 3d ed. (Atlanta: John Knox, 1982), 222.

The Truly Elect

Under the impulse of this understanding of the invisible church, the identification of the elect took on additional gravity. This new sense of urgency moved the discussion away from ecclesiology and back into soteriology, more specifically, into the ticklish matter of "assurance." Of course, the issue of assurance of salvation was not new. In their conflict with Rome, the Reformers asserted that assurance is linked with faith[52] and grounded in Christ.[53] Against the Roman Catholic denial that Christians could be sure of their salvation, they argued that faith entails assured trust that all one's sins are pardoned for Christ's sake.

Within Puritanism the question of assurance was personalized and individualized, resulting in a distinctive piety. As Sydney Ahlstrom notes, this "new kind of Christian piety . . . grew out of the anxieties produced by the doctrine of election."[54] The older Reformation issue reemerged in the form of the quest for a method whereby persons could determine whether or not they were among those selected by God to be saved. That is, the Puritans struggled with the problem of assurance of elect status. William Perkins, who in historian William Haller's estimation was "[at] the turn of the [seventeenth] century by far the most important Puritan writer,"[55] led the way in the discussion of this weighty matter. Perkins "set forth the process by which, as anyone might observe, God converts the sinful soul into a state of grace" and thereby produced "what may best be called the descriptive psychology of sin and regeneration."[56] A series of steps was involved: knowledge of God's law, conviction of personal sin resulting in fear and sorrow, repentance understood as the resolve to live in newness of life,[57] faith in Christ's work, internal combat, and true but imperfect assurance. This experience would allow believers to rest in the realization that they are likely to be among God's elect. And a subsequent life of sanctification, that is, of continuing death to sin and growth in life to Christ, could potentially lead the believer to "full assurance" of salvation and eternal election.[58]

---

52. Calvin, *Institutes*, 3.2.7.

53. Ibid., 3.24.5.

54. Sydney E. Ahlstrom, "From Puritanism to Evangelicalism: A Critical Perspective," in *The Evangelicals: What They Believe, Who They Are, Where They are Changing*, ed. David F. Wells and John D. Woodbridge, rev. ed. (Grand Rapids: Baker, 1977), 292.

55. Haller, *Rise of Puritanism*, 91.

56. Ibid., 92.

57. See Stoeffler, *Rise of Evangelical Pietism*, 56.

58. Ted A. Campbell, *The Religion of the Heart: A Study of European Religious Life in the Seventeenth and Eighteenth Centuries* (Columbia: University of South Carolina Press, 1991), 47–48.

The quest for assurance of elect status led many Puritans to chart in their diaries the slow and perhaps even painful process through which God had brought them out of rebellion and into obedience. Such accounts often noted how this process had eventually led to a breakthrough toward assurance of election. Some Puritans concluded that the focus on personal testimonies to God's work of grace in believers' lives seemed to provide a key facilitating the task of gathering congregations consisting solely of the elect. Consequently, sometime prior to 1635 the non-separating Puritans who had landed on the shores of the Massachusetts Bay colony in New England took an innovative step. They demanded that all candidates for church membership give verbal evidence of a religious experience that had made them aware of their elect status.

For many Puritans, however, a particular religious experience could not bring the process of determining one's elect status to an end. They knew that it was possible for a non-elect person to possess faith for a time but then to slip away from the fold.[59] Consequently, Puritans from Perkins[60] to the Westminster divines[61] concluded that rather than belonging to the essence of faith, infallible assurance often comes only after a long wait characterized by a struggle and by many difficulties. This left believers with little alternative but to wonder continually whether or not their faith was permanent and to engage in self-examination and self-scrutiny, looking for the presence of "signs of grace." The list of the signs of grace that mark God's elect soon came to include a believer's "walk," that is, evidence of good works.[62] Hence, in response to the question, "Who are the elect?" the Puritans now responded, "Whoever is truly converted and thereby is demonstrating signs of grace in daily life, that is, is growing in sanctification." This view finds expression in the *Westminster Confession*, which states: "These good works . . . are the fruits and evidences of a true and lively faith; and by them believers . . . strengthen their assurance."[63] In this manner, the Puritans came to base one's personal sense of election on the believer's own piety.[64] Or, stated theologically, they grounded assurance in sanctification. And the desire

---

59. R. T. Kendall, *Calvin and English Calvinism to 1649* (Oxford: Oxford University Press, 1979), 67–68.

60. William Perkins, "The Foundation of Christian Religion Gathered into Six Principles," in *The Work of William Perkins* (Abingdon, Berkshire, England: The Sutton Courtenay Press, 1969), 3:158; Perkins, "A Golden Chain or The Description of Theology," in ibid., 3:231.

61. *Westminster Confession*, 18.3.

62. M. Charles Bell, *Calvin and Scottish Theology: The Doctrine of Assurance* (Edinburgh: Handsel, 1985), 82.

63. *Westminster Confession*, 16.2.

64. R. W. A. Letham, "Puritan Theology," in the *New Dictionary of Theology*, ed. Sinclair B. Ferguson, David F. Wright and J. I. Packer (Downers Grove, Ill.: InterVarsity, 1988), 51.

for churches of visible saints, in turn, eventually led to the quest for churches of the visibly saintly.

The Transformed Heart

Puritanism, or the Puritan "reading" of the Reformation, was without a doubt the single most powerful molder of the ethos and theology of the evangelical movement. Yet the evangelicalism of the awakenings drew from another, albeit closely related, tributary as well: German Lutheran Pietism.

Reform of Church and Life

In many respects the Puritan movement, viewed as a self-conscious extension of the Reformation under Calvinist presuppositions, found a kindred spirit on Lutheran soil in Pietism. Like the Puritans, the Pietists saw themselves as standing in the wake of the Reformers and completing their work. And for both, the task of ecclesiastical reformation came to be closely linked to issues of soteriology. More particularly, the quest for a personal experience of God leading to sanctified living that emerged among the Puritans[65] lay at the heart of the Pietists' concerns as well.

While its antecedents lie earlier, the genesis of Pietism per se is associated with the consternation Philipp Jakob Spener (1635–1705) sensed at what he saw as the deplorable state of the church in Germany in the aftermath of the Thirty Years War. In response, he outlined a proposal for reform, which he set forth in his *Pia Desideria* (1675). At the heart of this proposal was a call for a church that involved and ministered to the laity, whom he termed the spiritual or universal priesthood. Rather than supplanting the ordained ministry, Spener was convinced that the activity of lay people would actually enhance the work of the church. He declared,

> No damage will be done to the ministry by a proper use of this priesthood. In fact, one of the principal reasons why the ministry cannot accomplish all that it ought is that it is too weak without the help of the universal priesthood. One man is incapable of doing all that is necessary for the edification of the many persons who are generally entrusted to his pastoral care. However, if the priests do their duty, the minister, as director and oldest brother, has splendid assistance in the performance of his duties and his public and private acts, and thus his burden will not be too heavy.[66]

65. Stoeffler observes that within Puritanism emerged a group of "Pietistic Puritans," whom he characterizes as those "in whom the desire for personal piety outweigh[ed] the desire for institutional purity." Stoeffler, *Rise of Evangelical Pietism*, 44.

66. Philipp Jakob Spener, *Pia Desideria*, trans. and ed. Theodore G. Tappert (Philadelphia: Fortress, 1964), 94–95.

As a concrete embodiment of this focus, Spener was instrumental in establishing gatherings of lay people within the parish churches who met weekly—generally Sunday evenings—for worship, Bible reading, prayer, fellowship, discussion, and mutual edification. These gatherings came to be known as the *collegia pietatis*, from which the designation "Pietism" arose. The gatherings of the pious provided occasions for lay persons to discuss the Sunday morning sermon and sometimes even for the local pastor to defend, explain, and expand his ideas.[67]

Unlike the Puritans, in calling for church reform the early Pietists did not elevate to center stage the question of the status of the Lutheran church as a true church of Jesus Christ and hence the propriety of withdrawing from the larger, state church. Rather, their intent was to reform the church solely from within. To this end, they were content to form through the establishment of the *collegia pietatis* what came to be characterized as *ecclesiolae in ecclesia*. The goal of these churches within the church was not to separate "true" Christians from the unregenerate, but to be agencies for bringing the church to reflect once again the image of the early Christian community.[68]

For the Pietists, ecclesiological reform was closely linked to the question of authentic and inauthentic Christianity. Seventeenth-century Lutheran orthodoxy tended to view authentic Christianity as involving outward matters such as proper baptism and adherence to the Lutheran creeds. Ernest Stoeffler offers this characterization of the theologians of the day:

> When their rigidly objective interpretation of justification was joined to an equally objective doctrine of baptismal regeneration the centrality of the saving relationship was rather effectively eliminated from seventeenth-century Lutheran orthodoxy. The Christian was now thought to be a person who interprets the Bible in terms of the Lutheran symbols as the truth of these symbols is expressed in an orthodox system of theology. *Fiducia* had become *assensus*, the liberty of the Christian . . . had given way to the tyranny of scholastic theology, and the Bible had once again become an arsenal of proof texts.[69]

Moreover, according to Dale Brown, in Lutheran scholasticism, "justification by faith became one of the dogmas instead of the source of dogma."[70]

Spener and his followers, in contrast, were convinced that Christianity is more than mere head knowledge and adherence to outward forms, but

---

67. Donald G. Bloesch, *The Evangelical Renaissance* (Grand Rapids: Eerdmans, 1973), 118.

68. Stoeffler, *Rise of Evangelical Pietism*, 237. Stoeffler cites *Philipp Jakob Spener's deutsche und lateinische theologische Bedenken*, 1838 edition, 466–67.

69. Stoeffler, *Rise of Evangelical Pietism*, 183–84.

70. Dale W. Brown, *Understanding Pietism* (Grand Rapids: Eerdmans, 1978), 24.

entailed Christian practice as well. The Lutheran reformation, they argued, had only been partial.[71] Luther's reformation in doctrine must lead to reformation in life, for faith must become active in love. The essence of Christianity, Spener taught, is a personal relationship with God expressed in a life that reflects God's will.[72] And this idea, in turn, became the central hallmark of the Pietist movement.[73]

Regeneration/New Birth

Whereas the major issue of the Reformation had been the origin of faith, in Pietism the focus shifted to the outcome of faith, as the Pietists elevated the new birth to center stage.[74] The new birth, which formed the fountain of personal holiness, became the principle article of faith.[75] As Dale Brown notes, "Regeneration was for Spener what justification had been for Luther."[76]

Against the Lutheranism of the day, the Pietists argued that authentic Christianity entails a personal conversion that is accompanied by a transformed heart leading to right living. Hence, Spener asserted, "Our whole Christian religion consists of the inner man or the new man, whose soul is faith and whose expressions are the fruits of life."[77] Roger Olson notes that the Pietists' "main concern became the experience of being 'born again' by God's grace through conscious decisions of repentance and faith accompanied by clear feelings of sorrow, trust and joy resulting in a transformed lifestyle in imitation of Christ by the power of the Holy Spirit."[78]

Beneath the Pietists' elevation of the new birth lay a radical shift in soteriology. The older Protestant theology had generally spoken of salvation as an objective given. Salvation, theologians asserted, consists in what God has done *for* people, which was, of course, consistent with the Reformers' interest in the concept of justification, understood as God's declaration of believers' new status of righteousness in Christ. In Lutheran orthodoxy, baptism emerged as the event in which this declaration occurs, and Christian living, in turn, came to be seen as the daily renewal of baptismal faith. The Pietists, in contrast, highlighted the subjective, the inner

---

71. Stoeffler, *Rise of Evangelical Pietism*, 235. Stoeffler cites *Philipp Jakob Spener's deutsche und lateinische theologische Bedenken*, 1838 edition, 435.

72. Stoeffler, *Rise of Evangelical Pietism*, 235.

73. Ibid., 13.

74. C. John Weborg, "Pietism: Theology in Service of Living Toward God," in *Variety of American Evangelicalism*, ed. Donald W. Dayton and Robert K. Johnston (Downers Grove, Ill.: InterVarsity, 1991), 168.

75. Spener, *Pia Desideria*, 64-65.

76. Brown, *Understanding Pietism*, 99.

77. Spener, *Pia Desideria*, 116.

78. Olson, *Story of Christian Theology*, 487.

nature of salvation. Salvation is what God does *within* people.[79] As a consequence, the locus of true Christianity shifted from baptism to personal conversion.

With this change came another. Although a Lutheran, Spener was also influenced by Genevan Calvinism,[80] as well as by the English Puritans,[81] and consequently through him several Reformed soteriological themes entered the Pietist movement. Yet the Pietists' elevation of regeneration effectively shifted the focus away from justification as the foundational soteriological concept. In Reformed theology, justification, understood in the Reformation sense of God's declaration of forgiveness through the imputation of Christ's righteousness to the sinner, remained the basis for sanctification, which was seen as the outgrowth of God's declaration of the believer's new status. In Pietist theology, in contrast, regeneration functioned in this foundational manner. It was viewed as the beginning point for sanctification, and in a certain sense it came to be seen as even the condition for justification itself.

In this transition, the Pietists retained the central Reformation focus on the gospel and bequeathed it, in turn, to the evangelical movement. Indeed, the Pietists' concern for the presence of the fruit of faith in the lives of believers was in part motivated by a concern for the advance of the gospel in the world. As John Weborg characterizes the Pietist position,

> A fruitful Christian life is evidence of the power and therefore of the truthfulness of the gospel. Hence the call for holiness of life, both of persons and of congregations, is not to promote a negative separatism but to show forth faith, hope, and love as signs of the gospel's triumph over unbelief, hopelessness, hate, and indifference.[82]

Yet the foundational motif through which Pietist theologians viewed the essence of the gospel marked a subtle but unmistakable shift. The focus on the objectivity of justification that had consumed Luther and to a lesser extent Calvin was replaced by a concern for the work of regeneration, understood as the transformation of the heart, as the wellspring of a transformed life. The completion of this transition within the context of the budding revivals in Britain and New England marked the genesis of the evangelical movement with its focus on the gospel of the new birth.

---

79. For this contrast, see ibid., 486.

80. For this judgment, see "Spener, Philipp Jakob," in *Evangelical Dictionary of Theology*, 1039–40.

81. Brown, *Understanding Pietism*, 17–18; Stoeffler, *Rise of Evangelical Pietism*, 231–32.

82. Weborg, "Pietism," 164.

A Gospel People: The Advent of Evangelicalism

In the fourth decade of the eighteenth century, the cross-pollination between Pietism and Puritanism burst into full bloom on British soil, both on the island and in the North American colonies. The context for this development lay in a revival inspired to a large degree by a renewal in preaching of the doctrine of justification by faith, specifically in the form of the need for lost sinners to trust Christ for salvation.[83] According to David Bebbington, the result was an event of monumental significance:[84]

> The decade beginning in 1734 witnessed in the English-speaking world a more important development than any other, before or after, in the history of Protestant Christianity: the emergence of the movement that became Evangelicalism.[85]

Convertive Piety

At the heart of the new movement was a concern, inherited from Puritanism but especially from Pietism, for true, heartfelt religion, in contrast to what the early evangelicals viewed as the nominalism of the day, which looked to baptism and church membership as the hallmarks of the faith. This is exemplified in George Whitefield's sermon, "The Nature and Necessity of our New Birth in Christ Jesus":

> It [is] too plain, beyond all contradiction, that comparatively but few of those who are "born of water" are "born of the Spirit" likewise; or, to use another scriptural way of speaking, many are baptized with water which were never, effectually at least, baptized with the Holy Ghost.[86]

This vision of the faith that focuses on personal regeneration rather than on outward rituals as the key to a changed life has continued to dominate evangelical theology to the present. It is evident, for example, in the "integrative theology" of Gordon Lewis and Bruce Demarest. Over against "Roman Catholic, Lutheran, and Anglo-Catholic Sacramentalism," the evangelical coauthors underscore the need for regeneration, noting that "only the Spirit of God can renew the basic orientation of the morally de-

---

83. David Bebbington, *Evangelicalism in Modern Britain: A History from the 1730s to the 1980s* (Grand Rapids: Baker, 1992), 21.

84. Ibid., 1.

85. Ibid., 20.

86. George Whitefield, "The Nature and Necessity of Our Regeneration or New Birth in Christ Jesus," in Timothy L. Smith, *Whitefield and Wesley on the New Birth* (Grand Rapids: Zondervan, 1986), 67.

praved and relationally dead human spirit." This "regeneration by the Spirit of life," they add, "renews the *heart and life*."[87]

One petal on the new flower of Christian thinking that bloomed in the eighteenth century was the Methodist movement spawned by John Wesley. In a sense, we might suggest that Wesley epitomizes the point where Puritanism and Pietism met.[88]

Like the Pietists, Wesley's central soteriological emphasis rested with conversion or regeneration, which he understood as being born again by the Holy Spirit through conscious faith in Jesus Christ, an event that he believed included justification.[89] In fact, Wesley elevated these two doctrines, justification (the forgiving of our sins through the atoning death of Jesus Christ) and the new birth (the renewing of our fallen nature, which occurs at the time of conversion), placing them at the center of his theology.[90]

This focus on the new birth was not limited to Methodism but encompassed the entire evangelical movement. Building from the Puritan practice while altering the contents, it gave rise to a parade of vivid accounts of conversion, each of which included elements such as agony, guilt, and finally relief. This pattern is evidenced by Isaac Backus's description of his spiritual awakening, which combined Puritan themes with the emerging evangelical ethos of the Great Awakening era:

> As I was mowing alone in the field, August 24th, 1741, all my past life was opened plainly before me, and I saw clearly that it had been filled up with sin. I went and sat down in the shade of a tree, where my prayers and tears, my hearing of the Word of God and striving for a better heart, with all my other doings, were set before me in such a light that I perceived I could never make myself better, should I live ever so long. Divine justice appeared clear in my condemnation, and I saw that God had a right to do with me as he would. My soul yielded all into his hands, fell at his feet, and was silent and calm before Him. And while I sat there, I was enabled by divine light to see the perfect righteousness of Christ and the freeness and riches of His grace, with such clearness, that my soul was drawn forth to trust him for salvation. And I wondered that others did not also come to Him who had enough for all. The Word of God and the promise of His grace appeared

---

87. Lewis and Demarest, *Integrative Theology*, 105.

88. For a helpful sketch of the background influences on Wesley, see Bebbington, *Evangelicalism in Modern Britain*, 34–42. For Wesley as the intersection between Puritanism and Pietism, see Scott Kisker, "John Wesley's Puritan and Pietist Heritage Reexamined," *Wesleyan Theological Journal* 34, no. 2 (Fall 1999): 266–80.

89. Kenneth J. Collins, *The Scripture Way of Salvation: The Heart of John Wesley's Theology* (Nashville: Abingdon, 1997), 101–30.

90. John Wesley, "The New Birth," in *The Works of John Wesley*, ed. Albert C. Outler et al. (Nashville: Abingdon, 1984), 2:187.

firmer than a rock, and I was astonished at my previous unbelief. My heavy burden was done, tormenting fears were fled, and my joy was unspeakable.[91]

Soon after his experience of "divine light," Backus, the quintessential "evangelical Puritan," received the "inner witness" which assured him that he was indeed a true saint predestined for salvation.

In a similar manner, Sampson Staniforth, who was converted while a soldier and later became an early Methodist preacher, offered what Matthew Arnold sets forth as a classic conversion narrative. Although written by a Methodist, Staniforth's experience follows many of the same lines evident in the testimony of the Calvinist Puritan, Isaac Backus:

> As soon as I was alone, I kneeled down, and determined not to rise, but to continue crying and wrestling with God, till He had mercy on me. How long I was in that agony I cannot tell; but as I looked up to heaven I saw the clouds open exceeding bright, and I saw Jesus hanging on the cross. At the same moment these words were applied to my heart, "Thy sins are forgiven thee." My chains fell off; my heart was free. All guilt was gone, and my soul was filled with unutterable peace.[92]

The similarities in language between this testimony and the penultimate stanza of Charles Wesley's hymn "And Can It Be" are unmistakable. But in addition to offering a musical version of the typical evangelical conversion experience, the famous hymn reflects the budding evangelical focus, inherited from Pietism, on the primacy of conversion and regeneration to justification. Hence, after speaking about the Savior's death for "Adam's helpless race," the hymnwriter narrates the conversion experience—"My chains fell off, my heart was free"—before announcing that the regenerated believer is now "clothed in righteousness divine" so as to approach "th'eternal throne" and to claim "the crown through Christ alone."

As these testimonies indicate, its roots in Puritanism and Pietism mediated to eighteenth-century evangelicalism a concern for, and emphasis on, a conscious experience of the grace of God in conversion.[93] Thus, at the heart of the evangelical movement has always been what Donald Dayton calls "convertive piety"[94] or what Roger Olson terms "conversional pi-

---

91. Isaac Backus, *Isaac Backus's Life: An Account of the Life of Isaac Backus* (unpublished manuscript), 16–18. See also Isaac Backus, *Isaac Backus, his writing containing Some Particular account of my Conversion* (unpublished manuscript), 5–6.

92. *Wesley's Veterans*, ed. J. Telford (London: Robert Culley, n.d.), 1:74–75.

93. Wells, *Welcome to the Family*, 119.

94. Donald W. Dayton, "The Limits of Evangelicalism," in *The Variety of American Evangelicalism*, ed. Donald W. Dayton and Robert K. Johnston (Downers Grove, Ill.: InterVarsity, 1991), 48.

ety," i.e., the vision of the faith that proclaims that "true Christian piety—devotion, discipleship, sanctification—begins with a distinct conversion experience not identical with [infant] baptism."[95]

The focus on convertive piety marked the climax of the shift away from the interest in what constitutes a gospel church that had initially spawned the Puritan movement. With the advent of evangelicalism, the quest for the truly Reformed church in which the gospel is truly preached gave way to the interest in the proclamation of the gospel of conversion and new birth, whether inside ecclesiastical structures or beyond them.

Convertive piety as the central hallmark of evangelicalism has, in turn, given shape to evangelical theology. The theological task as understood by generations of evangelical theologians since the early eighteenth century has focused not only on holding forth the heritage of Reformation doctrine, as was the case in Protestant scholasticism, but more importantly on reflecting on and delineating the nature of the conversion experience, which evangelicals all share. As a result, evangelical theologians routinely concern themselves with issues such as the interplay of the divine and the human in conversion, the marks of salvation, the relationship of conversion to sanctification, and the certainty of a believer's saved status. Questions such as these often overshadow the crucial issues of ecclesiology that played such an important role in the early years of the Puritan movement.

The reason for this evident fixation with the personal aspects of the *ordo salutis* and the devaluing of ecclesiology is quite simple. For evangelicals, the conversion experience that unites them takes precedence over the various particularities of doctrine, polity, and ecclesiastical practice that since the seventeenth century have increasingly divided the church into competing denominations. This evangelical ethos is reflected in the attitude of the mid-nineteenth-century London Baptist pastor G. W. McCree, who held that "conversion was far above, and of greater importance than, any denominational differences of whatever kind."[96]

Experimental Piety

The advent of evangelicalism was also marked by a new emphasis on assurance of salvation. This shift was mediated in part by certain Moravian leaders who held that assurance was integral to faith, i.e., that believers cannot have peace with God without knowing that they have it. In this manner, assurance was catapulted to the "normal experience" of the converted believer. Bebbington offers this succinct summary of the transition: "Whereas the Puritans had held that assurance is rare, late and the fruit of

95. Olson, *Story of Christian Theology*, 486, 593.
96. C. W. McCree, *George Wilson McCree* (London: James Clarke and Co., 1893), 20.

struggle in the experience of believers, the Evangelicals believed it to be general, normally given at conversion and the result of simple acceptance of the gift of God."[97]

The topic of assurance was of special interest to Wesley and his followers. In fact, in the estimation of Kenneth Collins, the doctrine of assurance comprised "one of the principal contributions of Methodism to the broader Christian community during the eighteenth century."[98]

In Wesley's recounting of his Aldersgate experience (May 24, 1738), the founder of Methodism noted, "An assurance was given me that he had taken away *my* sins, even *mine*, and saved *me* from the law of sin and death."[99] This statement indicates that for Wesley assurance entails both a sense of forgiveness and of deliverance, that is, a confirmation of both justification and the new birth. This assurance, in turn, comes through both the witness of our spirit and the witness of the Holy Spirit. The witness of our spirit, Wesley maintains, is indirect, arising as an inference from evidences such as the marks of the new birth (e.g., faith, hope, and love), obedience to God's commandments, and a good conscience. The witness of the Spirit, in contrast, is direct and is the cause of the indirect evidences. Nevertheless, both testimonies are connected and present together. For Wesley, "there cannot be any real testimony of the Spirit without the fruit of the Spirit just as there cannot be any fruit of the Spirit without the testimony of the Spirit."[100]

Wesley's interest in the believer's assurance was closely connected with his concern for sanctification, in that justifying faith is to some extent associated with sanctification understood as holy living. For him, "if sanctification does not follow justification, justification has not occurred."[101] Justification, understood as imputed righteousness, is the basis for the believer's acceptance with God. Sanctification, which emerges from inherent righteousness or regeneration, is the fruit of such acceptance.[102]

The interest in assurance was not limited to the Wesleyans, however. In the wake of the evangelical revivals even certain Puritan Calvinists came to accept the new evangelical understanding. Hence, in his *Journals* Whitefield reported, "O! with what joy—joy unspeakable—even joy that was full of, and big with glory, was my soul filled, when the weight of sin went off, and an abiding sense of the pardoning love of God, and a full as-

97. Bebbington, *Evangelicalism in Modern Britain*, 43.

98. Collins, *Scripture Way of Salvation*, 131.

99. John Wesley, *Journals and Diaries*, ed. W. Reginald Ward and Richard P. Heitzenrater, vols. 18–24 of *The Works of John Wesley* (Nashville: Abingdon, 1984), 18:250.

100. Collins, *Scripture Way of Salvation*, 134.

101. Ibid., 75.

102. Ibid., 94.

surance of faith broke in upon my disconsolate soul!"[103] Based on his research into the conversions occurring in New England, the great Puritan theologian Jonathan Edwards suggested that converts seeing the glory of Christian truths could no more doubt them than doubt the existence of a blazing sun in a clear sky.[104]

The idea of assurance of salvation has remained with evangelical theologians to the present. Wayne Grudem, to cite one example, gives expression to the classic evangelical approach in suggesting that genuine assurance arises from such evidences as the believer's perseverance in faith, evidence of the work of the Spirit in the believer's heart, and a long-term pattern of growth in the believer's life.[105] The abiding influence of this basically eighteenth-century evangelical understanding of assurance is likewise evident in the 1999 *Christianity Today* statement on the gospel: "The Gospel assures us that all who have entrusted their lives to Jesus Christ are born-again children of God . . . indwelt, empowered, and assured of their status and hope by the Holy Spirit."[106]

The shift from the Puritan quest for assurance of elect status to evangelicalism's understanding of assurance as the believer's normal experience is a dimension of the focus on personal, experiential piety that has characterized the movement from its inception. In recent years, historians of evangelicalism have increasingly concluded that at least in this aspect, the movement is a child of early modernity.[107] In fact, Bebbington goes so far as to claim that the Enlightenment provided the "essential novel ingredient" that ignited the evangelical fire in the 1730s.[108] More particularly, the evangelicals drew from the empiricist, inductive, scientific method that included the elevation of experimentation, mediated to them largely through John Locke. In keeping with this newfound ethos, eighteenth-century evangelicals repeatedly referred to their approach as "experimental religion." By this designation, they meant a religion that had been tried and proved by experience. In their view, to be Christian requires that re-

103. Whitefield's journals, as quoted in Rev. L. Tyerman, *The Life of the Rev. George Whitefield* (1876; reprint, Azle, Tex.: Need of the Times Publishers, 1995), 1:25, n. 3. Tyerman suggests that because Whitefield's first account of his conversion was "tinged with fanaticism," the revivalist revised it in the subsequent edition of his journals.

104. Jonathan Edwards, "A Narrative of Surprising Conversions" [1737], in *The Select Works*, (London: Banner of Truth Trust, 1961), 1:95.

105. Wayne Grudem, *Systematic Theology: An Introduction to Biblical Doctrine* (Grand Rapids: Zondervan, 1994), 803–6.

106. "Gospel of Jesus Christ," 53.

107. George M. Marsden, "Evangelicals, History, and Modernity," in *Evangelicalism and Modern America*, ed. George M. Marsden (Grand Rapids: Eerdmans, 1984), 98.

108. Bebbington, *Evangelicalism in Modern Britain*, 53.

ligious affiliation be experienced in life, and its truth confirmed through personal experience, through "experiment."

One theologian who typified the evangelical use of the Enlightenment in an attempt to forge an empirical religion was Jonathan Edwards. As an Enlightenment thinker, Edwards was more confident than his Puritan forebears about the powers of human knowledge. Assured knowledge of God is possible, he argued, because at conversion the Holy Spirit authors "a new inward perception or sensation" in the believer's mind.[109] In making this claim, Edwards was applying to the realm of religion the emerging Enlightenment epistemology with its focus on experience or experimentation as the source of all knowledge. Locke had argued that all knowledge is derived from the senses and that such knowledge is certain. So also Edwards maintained that the experiential knowledge of God mediated by the Holy Spirit was indubitable. This greater confidence in the possibility of human knowledge led the New England theologian to reject the older Puritan practice of protracted waiting for assurance in favor of the newer evangelical linking of assurance with the experience of faith that occurs in conversion. And on this basis, he set forth a framework for the evangelical approach to Christian experience.[110]

Equally significant as an appropriator of the Enlightenment is John Wesley.[111] He too followed Locke in rejecting innate ideas in favor of an empiricist epistemology. And like Edwards, Wesley drew a correlation between a person's natural senses and the believer's spiritual senses. In his view, faith is a "spiritual" sense that is able to discern a spiritual object, just as the natural senses (sight, hearing, taste, touch, and smell) can discern natural objects.[112]

The Enlightenment scientific method that informed Edwards and Wesley is evident as well in contemporary evangelicals such as Lewis and Demarest:

> Assurance of salvation varies with the degree of mental assent to converging lines of evidence supporting the truth of the Gospel. These lines of evidence strongly support one's intellectual perception of the probability that the Gospel is true, leading one on to *psychological certitude*. That settled conviction of resting on the sufficiency of the evidence brings *moral responsibility* for life in accord with belief. By the illumination and conviction of the Holy Spirit Christians rest their hearts on the sufficiency of the evidence.[113]

---

109. Jonathan Edwards, *Religious Affections* [1746], vol. 2 of *The Works of Jonathan Edwards*, ed. J. E. Smith (New Haven: Yale University Press, 1959), 205.

110. See, for example, Jonathan Edwards, *The Distinguishing Marks of a Work of the Spirit of God* [1741], in *Works*, 4:226–88.

111. Campbell, *Religion of the Heart*, 175–76.

112. Collins, *Scripture Way of Salvation*, 78.

113. Lewis and Demarest, *Integrative Theology*, 3:107.

"Classical" Evangelicalism

The convergence of Puritan and Pietist elements in the early eighteenth century led to the rise of what Dayton calls "classical evangelicalism."[114] The evangelical movement began in Britain and the colonies simultaneously. Yet this new vision of the Christian faith characterized by convertive-experimental piety found its most fertile soil in the United States. The beginnings of American evangelicalism lie in the Great Awakening of the colonial era, a revival of such significance that it has been termed a "national conversion," the event that served as the womb in which American evangelicalism was formed.

Although formed in the eighteenth century, the actual heyday of the evangelical movement in both Britain and America came in the next century. During that era, the fledgling coalition took on institutional expression through the formation in Britain and Europe of the Evangelical Alliance in 1846, which in turn served as the predecessor of the World Evangelical Fellowship.[115] Meanwhile in the United States, evangelicals came to constitute the dominant religious force. Mark Shibley observes, "Throughout most of the nineteenth century, the term *evangelical* was more or less synonymous with *Protestant*."[116] Evangelicals exercised a formative influence on the emerging national ethos. Historian William McLoughlin observes, "The story of American Evangelicalism is the story of America itself in the years 1800 to 1900."[117] Mark Noll elaborates as to what it means to connect evangelicalism so closely with nineteenth-century America:

> Antebellum America was "evangelical" not because every feature of life in every region in the United States was thoroughly dominated by evangelical Protestants but because so much of the visible public activity, so great a proportion of the learned culture, and so many dynamic organizations were products of evangelical conviction.

Noll underscores the success of evangelicalism at this stage of American history: "This achievement of the evangelicals was remarkable: they managed to forge a relatively cohesive religious culture out of disparate elements and make it effective throughout a sprawling, expanding land."[118]

---

114. Dayton, "Limits of Evangelicalism," 48.

115. For a helpful sketch of this, see Ellingsen, *Evangelical Movement*, 116–22.

116. Mark A. Shibley, *Resurgent Evangelicalism in the United States: Mapping Cultural Change since 1970* (Columbia: University of South Carolina Press, 1996), 16.

117. William G. McLoughlin, "Introduction," in *The American Evangelicals, 1800–1900*, ed. William G. McLoughlin (New York: Harper and Row, 1968), 1.

118. Mark Noll, *A History of Christianity in the United States and Canada* (Grand Rapids: Eerdmans, 1992), 243.

As the dominant religious force in the nation, evangelicals set out in their own way to fulfill the dream of the Puritan colonists and transform the United States into the kind of nation they believed God desired it to become. And armed with an understanding of the gospel that drew not only from the Reformation but also from the Puritan and Pietist movements, evangelicals in both Europe and America preached the new birth and sought to convert the world.

two

Scripture

AND THE Genesis

OF THE New Evangelicalism

Like their predecessors, contemporary evangelicals view themselves as a gospel people. They see their task, in the words of Kenneth Kantzer, as "addressing the lost, confused, and desperately needy world . . . with the gospel of God's redeeming love and the sure biblical chart for sailing on life's uncharted seas."[1] For this reason, theologians such as Kantzer routinely claim that the "material principle" of evangelicalism is "the gospel of Christ."[2]

Eighteenth-century evangelicalism expressed its commitment to this material principle through an understanding of the gospel characterized by "convertive piety" and "experimental religion." By the mid-twentieth century, however, many evangelical theologians had begun to define the nature of the movement by augmenting the traditional interest in gospel proclamation with another, decidedly cognitive concern, namely, the desire to maintain correct doctrine. They located the genius of evangelicalism in the combination of a material and a formal principle.[3]

1. Kenneth S. Kantzer, "Unity and Diversity in Evangelical Faith," in *The Evangelicals: What They Believe, Who They Are, Where They are Changing*, ed. David F. Wells and John D. Woodbridge, rev. ed. (Grand Rapids: Baker, 1977), 81.

2. Ibid., 73.

3. See, for example, the statement produced by the 1989 consultation on Evangelical Affirmations cosponsored by the National Association of Evangelicals and Trinity Evangelical Divinity School as published in *Evangelical Affirmations*, ed. Kenneth S. Kantzer and Carl F. H. Henry (Grand Rapids: Zondervan, 1990), 37–38.

These thinkers described evangelicalism's formal principle in terms of loyalty to the Bible as the completely true and trustworthy, final and authoritative source of all doctrine. This formal or formative principle, Kantzer claimed, "represents a basic unifying factor throughout the whole of contemporary evangelicalism."[4] Unswerving loyalty to this principle, he added, carries grave implications for theology, for rather than looking to reason, experience, or tradition, "the evangelical . . . seeks to construct his theology on the teaching of the Bible, the whole Bible, and nothing but the Bible."[5]

Under the influence of this understanding of the movement's formal principle, its material principle became not so much the gospel itself but what mid-century evangelical theologians saw as the basic doctrines of the Bible. More particularly, thinkers such as Kantzer equated the core doctrinal truths of the Bible with the "so-called fundamentals" that in his estimation had "served to unify fundamentalism in its battle against liberal theology." These great fundamental doctrines, he added, "continue to unite the evangelical movement."[6]

Kantzer's connection of the doctrinal core of evangelicalism with the "fundamentals" indicates that the evangelical movement of which he is a self-conscious participant lies at the end of a historical trajectory that encompasses more than the awakening evangelicalism of the eighteenth and early nineteenth centuries. Rather, Kantzer is a spokesperson for what in the 1940s came to be known as neo-evangelicalism. Proponents of this development were committed to maintaining orthodox doctrines, but one doctrine in particular emerged as of central importance, as Kantzer's delineation of its formal principle reveals: the doctrine of Scripture.

Scripture and the Classical Evangelical Heritage

Christians have always been to some degree a "people of the book." All Christian traditions value the Bible as Scripture. But the Reformation elevated Scripture as its special concern, and consequently Protestants, especially conservative Protestants, are cognizant of the foundational role of the Bible. As those who see themselves as the true heirs of the Reformation, evangelicals quite naturally uphold the Scriptures. This elevation of Scripture in personal and community life is evident in the typical evangelical equation of the Bible with "God's Word." Mark Noll points out,

4. Kantzer, "Unity and Diversity in Evangelical Faith," 72.
5. Ibid.
6. Ibid., 73.

> When examining the evangelical study of Scripture, everything hinges upon a recognition that the evangelical community considers the Bible the very Word of God. . . . Whatever else one may say about the Word of God (and many evangelicals are willing to recognize the supremacy of Christ as Word or to organize community life around the Word of proclamation), the Word of God always involves the Bible. Although evangelicals typically give some attention to the human character of the Bible, they believe that Scripture itself teaches that where the Bible speaks, God speaks.[7]

In elevating the Bible to the very foundation and center of theology, contemporary evangelical thinkers see themselves as maintaining the gains of the Reformation.

The Bible and the Reformation

Luther's rediscovery of the gospel of justification by faith gave rise to a second theological focus that has formed the evangelical movement, namely, *sola scriptura*, or commitment to the Bible as the sole authority for Christian teaching and living. Like the question of the true nature of the gospel, the Reformation position on Scripture arose in the midst of theological conflict with the Roman Catholic Church.

The explosive issue of final authority had already charted a two-hundred-year history by the time it came to a head in the sixteenth century. From the late patristic era through the Middle Ages, theologians had acknowledged the primacy of Scripture, while granting authority to tradition as well. Theologians sensed no contradiction between the two; nor could they envision a possible conflict between the conclusions of biblical exegesis and the pronouncements of the church's teaching office. Beginning in the fourteenth century, however, the renewed focus on the literal meaning of the texts led certain late medieval thinkers to assert that the exegesis of Scripture carries primacy over the teaching authority of the papal office.[8] Luther entered this fray, raising the flag of the primacy of Scripture against the official Roman Catholic position that ascribed authority to Scripture, as interpreted by the magisterium, plus tradition.

Luther and Sola Scriptura

Luther did not join the controversy over the locus of authority through the academic doorway. Rather, he was catapulted into affirming *sola scrip-*

---

7. Mark Noll, *Between Faith and Criticism: Evangelicals, Scholarship and the Bible in America* (San Francisco: Harper and Row, 1986), 6.

8. Wolfhart Pannenberg, "The Crisis of the Scripture Principle," *Basic Questions in Theology*, trans. George H. Kehm (Philadelphia: Fortress, 1970), 1:4–5.

tura by his disagreements with Rome on other issues. The parting of ways was initiated by his search for a gracious God. This quest led Luther to the Bible, in the pages of which he discovered the God who through Jesus Christ justifies the unrighteous. The Reformer's pitting of Bible against Church soon moved into other areas of official teaching and practice.

Luther's public struggle with the Roman Church began in 1517, when he posted the Ninety-five Theses on the door of the castle church in Wittenberg. The monk questioned, among other things, the practice of granting indulgences. But by extension, he was implicitly challenging the power of the papacy. Two years later (1519), at his Leipzig debate with Johann Eck, Luther enunciated his idea of the centrality of Scripture:

> It is not in the power of the Roman pontiff or of the Inquisition to construct new articles of faith. No believing Christian can be coerced beyond holy writ. By divine law we are forbidden to believe anything which is not established by divine Scripture or manifest revelation.[9]

Then, in his appearance before the Imperial Diet at Worms (1521), in response to the order of the Pope's representative that he repudiate his writings and thereby recant his "heretical" views, Luther reiterated his Scripture principle in words memorialized in the title of Roland Bainton's classic biography of the Reformer:

> Unless I am convinced by Scripture and plain reason—I do not accept the authority of popes and councils, for they have contradicted each other—my conscience is captive to the Word of God. . . . Here I stand. I cannot do otherwise.[10]

In both of these circumstances, Luther indicated the theological context for his affirmation of *sola scriptura*. The Reformer's intent was not to devise a theology of the Bible. Rather, his purpose was to undercut the Roman Catholic position which endowed the Pope and Church councils with ultimate authority, and thereby effectively set the Church above the Bible. Luther, in contrast, claimed that Scripture must take priority over the Church. Reversing the order articulated by the Church of his day, Luther declared, "The Scripture is the womb from which are born theological

---

9. As translated in Roland H. Bainton, *Here I Stand: A Life of Martin Luther* (Nashville: Abingdon, 1978), 89.

10. As translated ibid., 144. There is some question as to whether the final sentence is genuine. After citing Luther's declaration, "My conscience is captive to the Word of God," Bainton begins a new paragraph and explains, "The earliest printed version added the words: 'Here I stand.' The words, though not recorded on the spot, may nevertheless be genuine, because the listeners at the moment may have been too moved to write."

truth and the Church."[11] In keeping with his focus on the priority of Scripture, Luther acknowledged the creeds of the ancient church only because he saw in them the saving message of the Bible, and not because they had been drafted and ratified by church councils.[12]

Luther's position in the question of authority was closely connected to his understanding of the gospel. In his estimation, justification by faith meant that humans are completely dependent on God's mercy, which we cannot earn and for which we can do nothing. For Luther, this dependency is not only operative in salvation, but affects the realm of knowing God as well. Luther attacked the reigning theology of the day for its denial of this gospel principle. In his estimation, Roman Catholic theologians suggested that one could discover God through human ability unaided by supernatural grace and the gift of faith.[13] Luther, in contrast, was convinced that true knowledge of God does not come through human striving, such as through the use of natural reason alone, but arises only out of God's self-disclosure in God's own Word and through God's own Spirit. Luther likewise attacked the Roman Catholic claim that tradition ought to be placed alongside of Scripture and that only the Church's teaching office can interpret Scripture properly. In response to what he saw as the erroneous foundation upon which Roman Catholic theology was constructed, Luther introduced the principle of *sola scriptura*, i.e., the claim that Scripture alone is the ultimate authority for Christian faith and practice.

Luther's response before the Diet of Worms indicates that his elevation of *sola scriptura* was closely connected with his understanding of the nature of God's Word. Jaroslav Pelikan goes so far as to assert categorically, "The theology of Martin Luther was a theology of the word of God."[14] Despite this focus, the great Reformer developed no thoroughgoing doctrine of Scripture. As Pelikan notes, "He and his immediate followers seemed to manifest a striking lack of specificity, or even of interest, in some of the most crucial questions involved in the doctrine of the authority of the word."[15] Actually Luther's goal was not to contend for the primacy of Scripture in the strict sense, but for the primacy of the gospel to which

11. Martin Luther, *First Lectures on the Psalms I*, in *Luther's Works*, ed. Jaroslav Pelikan et al. (St. Louis: Concordia, 1955–1986), 10:397.

12. Jack B. Rogers and Donald K. McKim, *The Authority and Interpretation of the Bible: An Historical Approach* (San Francisco: Harper and Row, 1980), 77.

13. See, for example, Martin Luther, "The Heidelberg Disputation," in *Martin Luther's Basic Theological Writings*, ed. Timothy Lull (Minneapolis: Fortress, 1989), 30–33.

14. Jaroslav Pelikan, *Reformation of Church and Dogma 1300–1700*, vol. 4 of *The Christian Tradition: A History of the Development of Doctrine* (Chicago: University of Chicago Press, 1984), 183. See also Geoffrey W. Bromiley, *Historical Theology: An Introduction* (Grand Rapids: Eerdmans, 1978), 210.

15. Ibid., 183.

Scripture attests[16] and hence for the primacy of Scripture as the attestation to the gospel. Understood strictly, the Word of God is the gospel, the good news about Jesus Christ and the justification available through Christ. For Luther, the Bible is valuable, in turn, because it is God's chosen instrument for bringing the gospel to sinful humans. As Pelikan observes, "The Scriptures were the 'Word of God' in a derivative sense for Luther—derivative from the historical sense of Word as deed and from the basic sense of the Word as proclamation."[17]

Luther valued the Bible, therefore, because it is the cradle that holds Christ. For this reason, the gospel of justification by grace through faith served as Luther's hermeneutical key to Scripture: "The Scriptures must be understood in favor of Christ, not against him. For that reason they must either refer to him or must not be held to be true Scriptures."[18] This understanding of the gospel, which Luther discovered in the Bible, became the basis for determining the relative authority of the various canonical writings, and on this basis he offered his famous assessment of the Book of James as "an epistle of straw."[19]

Calvin and the Self-Authenticating Word

Whereas Calvin pushed the Reformation discussion of the gospel beyond Luther into the realm of sanctification, the Geneva Reformer's understanding of the primacy of Scripture was in most respects quite similar to that of Luther. Like both Luther and Zwingli, Calvin hammered out his position in opposition to that of the Roman Catholic Church (as well as the radical "Anabaptists"). And in this context he, like his predecessors,[20] elevated the Scripture principle to the center of theological inquiry.

Calvin's papist opponents maintained that divine truth is guaranteed by the consensus of the catholic church as governed by the Holy Spirit. Similar to other Reformers, Calvin responded to this position by forging a close link between the Spirit and the Word. He pointed out uncompro-

16. Justo L. Gonzalez, *A History of Christian Thought* (Nashville: Abingdon, 1975), 3:42–43.

17. Jaroslav Pelikan, *Luther the Expositor,* companion volume to *Luther's Works* (St. Louis: Concordia, 1959), 67.

18. Martin Luther, *Theses Concerning Faith and Law,* trans. Lewis W. Spitz, in *Luther's Works* (Philadelphia: Muhlenberg, 1960), 34:112.

19. Martin Luther, "Prefaces to the New Testament," in *Martin Luther's Basic Theological Writings,* ed. Timothy Lull (Philadelphia: Fortress, 1989), 117.

20. One such predecessor was Zwingli. In the first article of his "Sixty-Seven Articles" of 1523, Zwingli declared, "Everyone who says that the Gospel is nothing without the sanction of the Church, errs and blasphemes God." For Zwingli, gospel is interchangeable with the Word of God and Scripture. Huldrych Zwingli, *The Defense of the Reformed Faith,* trans. E. J. Furcha, vol. 1 in *Huldrych Zwingli's Writings* (Allison Park, Pa.: Pickwick, 1984), 7.

misingly that the Spirit who governs the church had "bound it to the word."[21]

Ultimately for Calvin of course, Christ is the Word of God.[22] Yet Calvin also spoke of the Bible as the Word,[23] in that it is God's testament, or witness, to us[24] and the content of divine revelation is Christ himself.[25] As the Word of God, Scripture does not derive its authority from the church.[26] Rather, the church is built on the foundation of the prophets and apostles, and this foundation is now found in Scripture.[27] Consequently, Calvin marked out clearly the chief point of disagreement between the Reformers' position and that of their opponents. Alluding to the characterization of the church in 1 Timothy 3:15, he declared,

> The difference between us and the papists is that they do not think that the church can be "the pillar of the truth" unless she presides over the word of God. We, on the other hand, assert that it is because she reverently subjects herself to the word of God that the truth is preserved by her and passed on to others by her hands.[28]

Calvin was uncompromising in his elevation of biblical authority. Yet for him the authority of the Bible does not emerge sui generis, but arises from God, or more specifically, from the fact that God in person speaks in it. Hence, rather than depending on philosophical argumentation to support this claim, Calvin viewed the authority of the Bible as in a certain sense self-authenticating.[29] That is, the believers' assurance of the authority of the Scriptures is connected to the internal testimony of the Spirit within their hearts.

Luther, of course, had already pointed the Reformation in this direction. Drawing an analogy to the incarnation, the German Reformer had declared, "It is only the internal working of the Holy Spirit that causes us

---

21. John Calvin, *Reply by John Calvin to Cardinal Sadolet's Letter* in *Selected Works of John Calvin: Tracts and Letters*, ed. Henry Beveridge and Jules Bonnet, trans. Henry Beveridge (Grand Rapids: Baker, 1983), 1:35.

22. John Calvin, *Institutes of the Christian Religion*, trans. Henry Beveridge (Grand Rapids: Eerdmans, 1989), 1.13.8.

23. Ibid., 1.7.

24. John Calvin, *Sermons Sur Le Deuteronome*, in *Corpus Reformatorum*, ed. Carolus Gottlieb Bretscheider (Halis, Saxony: C. A. Schwetschke and Son, 1848), 56:617.

25. Calvin, *Institutes*, 4.8.5; John Calvin, *Commentary on the Gospel According to John*, trans. William Pringle, in *Calvin's Commentaries* (Grand Rapids: Baker, 1981), 17:218.

26. Calvin, *Institutes*, 1.7.1.

27. Ibid., 1.7.2.

28. Calvin, *De Scandalis*, in *Joannis Calvini opera selecta*, ed. Peter Barth (Monachii: C. Kaiser, 1926), 2:234–35.

29. Calvin, *Institutes*, 1.7.5.

to place our trust in this Word of God, which is without form or comeliness."[30] Calvin, in turn, expanded on Luther's idea:

> The testimony of the Spirit is superior to reason. . . . The same Spirit, therefore, who spoke by the mouth of the prophets, must penetrate our hearts, in order to convince us that they faithfully delivered the miracles with which they were divinely intrusted. . . . Let it therefore be held as fixed that those who are inwardly taught by the Holy Spirit, acquiesce implicitly in Scripture; and that Scripture, carrying its own evidence along with it, deigns not to submit to proofs and arguments; but owes the full conviction with which we ought to receive it to the testimony of the Spirit.[31]

For Calvin, then, the recognition of the Bible as our authority is closely connected with God's gracious salvific work. As Gonzalez declares, "The reason that Scripture is authoritative for him is the experience of grace."[32] As a result, Calvin did not begin his theological construction with an exposition of the doctrine of Scripture. His starting point was not Scripture per se, but the providence and love of God.[33]

The Legacy of Puritanism and Pietism

The insights of Reformers such as Luther and Calvin formed the cradle for the understanding of Scripture in evangelicalism. Although a line can readily be traced from the sixteenth century to the eighteenth, this line does not run directly from the Reformers to the evangelicals but through territory marked out by Puritans and Pietists.

The Puritans and the Regenerate Mind

Calvin's approach, including his emphasis on the self-authenticating nature of Scripture through the internal testimony of the Spirit, lived on in the Puritan movement. While the scholastic theologians on the Continent were busying themselves with the task of solidifying the gains made by Luther and charting the boundaries between the Lutheran and Roman Catholic Churches, the English Calvinists were seeking to form a scriptural church. This quest, in turn, eventually led to the very practical concern as to how the insights of the Bible might be applied not only to church order but also to the daily life of the saints.[34]

---

30. Luther, *Weimarer Ausgabe*, 16.82. Cited in Willem Jan Kooiman, *Luther and the Bible*, trans. John Schmidt (Philadelphia: Muhlenberg, 1961), 238.

31. Calvin, *Institutes*, 1.7.4–5.

32. Gonzalez, *History of Christian Thought*, 3:160.

33. Ibid.

34. F. Ernest Stoeffler, *The Rise of Evangelical Pietism* (Leiden: Brill, 1971), 20.

The Puritan understanding of biblical authority that undergirded their program of church and personal reform came to expression in the *Westminster Confession of Faith*.[35] Because this statement was written in the context of controversy reminiscent of that experienced by the Reformers, it not surprisingly called for a link between Word and Spirit.

In their ongoing battle with the Protestants, the Roman Catholic theologians acknowledged Scripture to be a rule of faith. But they quickly added that the church served as the judge which applied the scriptural rule. To counter their Roman Catholic opponents, the authors of the *Westminster Confession* appealed to the Spirit as the one who guides the reader in understanding Scripture. In fact, the Puritans went so far as to claim that the Spirit continually leads God's people into ever clearer understandings of Scripture.[36] Further, the Roman Catholics and High Church Anglicans attributed authority to creeds, councils, and the opinions of the patristic writers. In their response, the Puritans acknowledged the importance of such considerations but, in a manner akin to their forebears in the Reformation, quickly added that human opinion was valid only insofar as it agreed with Scripture.

While following the basic Reformation line of *sola scriptura*, at one point the Westminster divines seemed to take the teaching of their mentors a step farther. The Puritans placed themselves squarely against the widespread teaching of their day that argued from the clarity of the Bible to the conclusion that even unregenerate persons could understand Scripture correctly. In contrast to this apparent epistemological Pelagianism, the Puritans were convinced that the true significance of Scripture could be understood only by those whose minds were enlightened by the Spirit. In the words of the *Westminster Confession*, "we acknowledge the inward illumination of the Spirit of God to be necessary for the saving understanding of such things as are revealed in the Word."[37] In this manner, the link between Word and Spirit that the Reformers had forged came to include the regenerate mind as the location of the Spirit's operation through the Word.

Maintaining this position, however, required that the Puritans differentiate between two levels of meaning in the text: the grammatical and the spiritual. Thus the Puritan Edward Reynolds asserted that their opponents were guilty of "foolishly confounding and impiously deriding the spiritual and divine sense of holy Scriptures, with the grammatical construction."[38]

35. For a helpful summary, see Rogers and McKim, *Authority and Interpretation of the Bible*, 200–218.

36. Jack B. Rogers, *Scripture in the Westminster Confession* (Grand Rapids: Eerdmans, 1967), 425–26.

37. *The Westminster Confession*, 1.6, in *Creeds of the Churches*, ed. John H. Leith, 3d ed. (Atlanta: John Knox, 1982), 195.

38. Edward Reynolds, "The Sinfulness of Sin," in *The Whole Works of the Right Rev. Edward Reynolds, D.D. Lord Bishop of Norwich*, ed. J. R. Pitman (London: S. and R. Bentley, 1826), 1:103.

The Pietists and the "Born-Again" Reader

As noted in chapter 1, the early Pietists sought to bring the Reformation to completion in response to what they considered to be the deadness of Lutheran orthodoxy. Nowhere was this conflict with the reigning seventeenth-century Lutheran theology more evident than in the question of the purpose of Scripture.[39]

Reminiscent of the Reformers, the Pietists sought to reaffirm the authority of the Bible in an age in which Scripture had been set aside in favor of churchly authorities. The target of their critique, however, was not the Roman Catholic but the Lutheran Church itself. The Pietists were convinced that their own church had elevated the Lutheran confessions to where they, not Scripture, determined what constituted orthodox belief. Spener feared that by according such authority to humanly devised documents such as the Formula of Concord, the Lutheran divines had undermined the exegesis of Scripture, for the growing creedalism in the church led readers of the Bible to find in the text only what was sanctioned by the Lutheran standards.

In contrast to the orthodox theologians, Spener claimed that a believer studies the Scriptures "to discover the will of God in the Bible rather than to prove the authority of a confession of faith."[40] Hence, the Pietists believed that Scripture was not so much a source of doctrine as a devotional resource and a guide to life. According to Spener, the goal of exegesis was practical, namely, "to bring abundantly the Word of God among us."[41]

Also reminiscent of the Reformers, the Pietists were concerned that Word and Spirit be linked together in a living relationship. They feared that Lutheran orthodoxy had elevated the written Word to the neglect of the Spirit and in so doing had transformed the life of faith into a cold, dead religion. Echoing his predecessors, including some of the theologians of Lutheran orthodoxy,[42] Spener asserted that the Holy Spirit does not work without the Bible or outside the Bible, but always in and through the Bible,[43] for the Scriptures are the means through which the Spirit operates.

---

39. For a helpful summary of the Pietist view of Scripture, see Dale W. Brown, *Understanding Pietism* (Grand Rapids: Eerdmans, 1978), 64–82.

40. Philipp Jakob Spener, *Consilia Theologia Latina* (Francofurti ad Moenum: D. Zunneri, 1709), 3:144, as cited in Brown, *Understanding Pietism*, 66.

41. Tadakazu Uwoke, "The Significance of Philipp Jakob Spener in the Development of Protestant Thought" (unpublished S.T.M. thesis, Union Theological Seminary, 1924), 15, as cited in Brown, *Understanding Pietism*, 68.

42. Quenstedt, for example, declared, "God does not work separately without the Word nor the Word separately without God but God works with the Word and through the Word." Johann Andreas Quenstedt, *Theologia Didactico-Polemica sive Systema Theologicum* 2.704, as cited in Geoffrey W. Bromiley, *Historical Theology: An Introduction* (Grand Rapids: Eerdmans, 1978), 323.

43. Philipp Jakob Spener, *Erste Geistliche Schrifften* (Frankfurt am Main: Zunner, 1699), 2:122, as cited in Brown, *Understanding Pietism*, 71.

In their attempt to maintain the link between Word and Spirit, the Pietists followed Calvin in appealing to the internal testimony of the Spirit. But here they, like the Puritans, took a step beyond the Reformers. By the *testimonium spiritus internum*, Spener meant the enlightening work of the Spirit within believers that leads them to understand the Scriptures. According to the Pietist leader, the presence of the Holy Spirit within the believer enables the dead letter of the sacred writings to become a living power. In Spener's words, true faith "is awakened through the Word of God by the illumination, witness, and sealing of the Holy Spirit."[44] Thus, although he acknowledged that Scripture is objectively true, Spener asserted that it is transformative only in the life of the reader who allows the Spirit to work through Scripture. And this cooperation includes bathing biblical exegesis with prayer, meditating on the truth the Bible reveals, and attempting to lead a holy life as delineated in the Bible.

In his understanding of the working of the Bible, Spener reacted against the tendency of the theologians of his day to view this phenomenon in a mechanistic, almost *ex opera operato*, manner. Against his opponents who claimed that the Bible's divine origin guaranteed its efficacy and intrinsic power, Spener insisted that the Word must be brought to life in the human soul by the Holy Spirit. Consequently, for Spener it is not possible to grasp the spiritual significance of the Bible unless the reader is illumined by the Spirit, that is, unless the reader is born again. In short, like the Puritans, the Pietists concluded that only the regenerate can understand the deep, internal meaning of the Scriptures.[45]

Spener paralleled the Puritans in another manner as well. Somewhat similar to Reynolds, who distinguished between the spiritual sense and the grammatical construction, Spener differentiated sharply between mere theological knowledge, which anyone can attain, and true saving knowledge, which only the Spirit can give. The theologians of Lutheran orthodoxy suggested that the content of saving faith consisted largely in propositions rationally derived from the Bible or in the saving acts of God disclosed in the Bible. Consequently, they viewed the Spirit's illumination as influencing the human understanding in a largely cognitive manner. The Pietists, in contrast, moved the locus of illumination beyond the intellect to the will.[46] The Spirit's activity, they maintained, not only informed the mind, it came with convincing power, and working through the Bible in the human heart, the Spirit imparted true saving knowledge.

---

44. Spener, *Pia Desideria*, trans. and ed. Theodore G. Tappert (Philadelphia: Fortress, 1964), 46.

45. August Francke, *A Guide to the Reading and Study of the Holy Scriptures*, trans. William Jacques (London: D. Jacques, 1813), 67–68, 88.

46. Stoeffler, *Rise of Evangelical Pietism*, 241.

Thus, Francke's assistant, Johann Anastasius Freylinghausen, offered this definition of illumination:

> Illumination itself consists in this, that, in his light the Holy Spirit mediates the heavenly truth of the Word of God to the human understanding, introducing it and giving it to be recognized so clearly, so powerfully, and so convincingly that from this the human person recognizes it as truth, believes it with divine certainty, and thereby knows what has been sent to them by God's grace, and that spiritual things are to be spiritually judged.[47]

F. Ernest Stoeffler provides this summary of Francke's approach:

> In opposition to Orthodoxy Francke deliberately emphasized the psychological as over against the objective efficacy of Scripture and preaching. In reading Scripture or hearing a sermon the worshiping believer is brought face to face with the revelatory activity of the divine Spirit, for the Word is God's means to communicate to a receptive human being his Law and Gospel.[48]

One long-term result of the Pietists' reformulation of biblical authority was the renewal of devotion to Scripture: "Pietism represented a revival of the reading and study of the Bible for all and a new impetus to biblical theology among the more scholarly."[49] True to Luther's legacy, the Pietists sought to place the Bible in the hands of the laity. Francke and his associates put wings on their theological convictions by establishing a publishing venture for the purpose of producing inexpensive editions of the Bible for mass consumption. Consequently, Stoeffler concludes, "It was Francke who, above all others in the history of later Protestantism, supplied the initial inspiration to make the Bible really a book of the people." Stoeffler then notes that "Francke and his followers not only supplied the funds for this publishing venture, but they were to a substantial degree responsible for creating the market for it."[50]

The Evangelical Reverence for Scripture

As Puritan concerns and Pietist renewal converged in the eighteenth century, they gave birth to an evangelicalism that looked to Scripture as the vehicle through which the Spirit worked the miracles of salvation and sanctification. Sparked by their experience of the nurturing work of the

---

47. Johann Anastasius Freylinghausen, *Grundlegung der Theologie, darinn dir Glaubenslehren aus göttlichem Wort deutlich fürgetragen*, 1712 edition, 166. Translation mine.
48. F. Ernest Stoeffler, *German Pietism during the Eighteenth Century* (Leiden: Brill, 1973), 22. Stoeffler cites August Hermann Francke, *Catechismuspredigten*, 1729 edition, 93–94.
49. Brown, *Understanding Pietism*, 73.
50. Stoeffler, *German Pietism*, 36.

Spirit through the pages of the Bible, evangelicals' overriding aim was to allow the message of the Bible to penetrate into human hearts and to encourage the devotional use of the Bible.

Evangelicals were generally in agreement that the Bible is inspired by God. Nevertheless, like their Pietist forebears,[51] they were not particularly concerned to devise theories to explain the dynamics of inspiration. Further, evangelicals displayed a remarkable fluidity of opinion about the ins and outs of inspiration. Some British evangelicals, including John Wesley,[52] spoke of the Bible as an infallible book. Hence, in 1763 Henry Venn linked the Bible to "the infallible decisions of the word of God."[53] Many, however, were quite unexacting in their statements about Scripture. Charles Simeon, for example, declared, "No error in doctrine or other important matter is allowed; yet there are inexactnesses in reference to philosophical and scientific matters, because of its popular style."[54] In fact, Henry Martyn, who served as a missionary to Persia, did not hold to verbal inspiration in any form.[55] In any case, the evangelicals who emerged from the awakenings exhibited little interest prior to the 1820s in elaborating precise theories about biblical infallibility or inerrancy.[56]

Rather than constructing theories about the Bible, awakening evangelicals were content simply to cherish the Scriptures. This evangelical devotion to the Bible is exemplified in John Wesley's classic statement found in the preface to a collection of his sermons: "Let me be *homo unius libri* [a person of one book]."[57] The early evangelicals were immersed in Scripture, giving them a wealth of biblical images from which to draw. One observer claims to have discovered in a Charles Wesley hymn no less than twenty-six biblical allusions crowded into sixty-four lines.[58] Evangelicals often expressed their devotion to Scripture in symbolic acts of reverence for the actual physical copies of the Bible they possessed. Hence the biographer of nineteenth-century evangelist Henry Moorhouse claimed, "He would not suffer anything, not even a sheet of paper, to be laid upon his

51. Mark Ellingsen, *The Evangelical Movement: Growth, Impact, Controversy, Dialog* (Minneapolis: Augsburg, 1988), 113.

52. John Wesley, *The Journal of the Rev. John Wesley, A.M.*, ed. Nehemiah Curnock (London: Kelly, n.d.), 6:117. The journal entry date is August 24, 1776.

53. Henry Venn, *The Complete Duty of Man* (London: Religious Tract Society, n.d.), 51.

54. As cited in Robert S. Dell, "Simeon and the Bible," in *Charles Simeon (1759–1836)*, ed. Michael Hennel and Arthur Pollard (London: SPCK, 1959), 44.

55. For this judgment, as well as other early-nineteenth-century examples, see David Bebbington, *Evangelicalism in Modern Britain: A History from the 1730s to the 1980s* (Grand Rapids: Baker, 1992), 86–87.

56. Ibid., 13.

57. R. P. Heitzenrater, *John Wesley His Own Biographer*, vol. 1 of *The Elusive Wesley* (Nashville: Abingdon, 1984), 149.

58. J. Dale, "The Theological and Literary Qualities of the Poetry of Charles Wesley in Relation to the Standards of His Age" (Ph.D. thesis, Cambridge University, 1961), 145.

Bible. There alone, apart, it must lie, unique, matchless, wonderful, the very mind and presence of the infinite and eternal God."[59]

The Rise of the Scripture Focus

Beginning in the 1820s, the reticence to theologize about the Bible began to wane. Some evangelical theologians came to insist that the truly evangelical approach to Scripture includes the affirmation of verbal inspiration and biblical inerrancy, together with a literalist hermeneutic. The result was a growing division within the movement. Bebbington reports that "attitudes toward the Bible grew apart until, in the wake of the First World War, the Evangelical world divided into conservatives and liberals primarily on the issue."[60]

Beginnings in Protestant Scholasticism

Robert Haldane of Scotland may have been responsible for introducing into British evangelicalism a stricter doctrine of biblical inspiration.[61] In his book *The Evidence and Authority of Divine Revelation* (1816), Haldane asserted that the Scriptures themselves speak of the extent of their inspiration, making "a claim of infallibility and of perfection."[62] But the focus on theories of biblical authority that emerged among evangelicals in the nineteenth century was no new phenomenon in Protestant circles. Its roots lay in the post-Reformation era, in what is often known as "Protestant scholasticism."

The Bible in Lutheran Orthodoxy

Luther and his associates had elevated the Bible as the sole authority for faith and practice, but they had not concerned themselves with developing a particular doctrine of Scripture. This task fell to the seventeenth-century Lutheran theologians, whose loyalty to Luther's principle of *sola scriptura* in an age of ongoing controversy with the Roman Catholic Church led them to seek out a clearer Protestant understanding of biblical authority, by concerning themselves with questions regarding the origin, inspiration, and authority of Scripture. To this end, they borrowed from

---

59. J. Macpherson, *Henry Moorhouse: The English Evangelist* (London: Morgan and Scott, n.d.), 94.

60. Bebbington, *Evangelicalism in Modern Britain*, 14.

61. Ibid., 87.

62. Robert Haldane, *The Evidence and Authority of Divine Revelation* (London: Hamilton, Adams and Co., 1834), 158.

various sources, including the Aristotelian philosophy that had typified medieval theological discourse.

Aristotle's distinction between matter and form gave the Lutheran scholastics the tool necessary to differentiate between the biblical text itself and the Word of God, understood as the message that God wishes to communicate through the text, while maintaining that the two are so bound together as to be inseparable in actual practice.[63] However, in their attempts to contend for the faith of the Reformation the Lutheran scholastics increasingly elevated the divine origin of Scripture above its human authorship. Many came to treat Scripture as precisely accurate in every detail, a storehouse of revealed propositions. Johann Andreas Quenstedt, for example, reasoned that if the biblical authors were moved by the Spirit of truth, then "it follows that they could under no condition make mistakes in their writing, and no falsification, no error, no danger of error, no untruth existed or could exist in their preaching or writing."[64] Quenstedt was convinced that to attribute to the biblical writers "fault or untruth . . . error or lapse of memory" is tantamount to "blaspheming the Holy Spirit who spoke and wrote through them."[65] Not only did seventeenth-century Lutheran theologians believe that the Bible had been verbally inspired, some went so far as to assert that even the vowel points in the Masoretic text were as inspired as the consonants.[66] In so doing, these Lutheran thinkers transformed the doctrine of Scripture from an article of faith into the foundation of the entire systematic-theological program.[67]

The Bible and "Reformed Scholasticism"

This development within Lutheranism was paralleled by a similar move within the Reformed tradition. Stoeffler observes that the Reformation churches in seventeenth-century Europe, both Calvinist and Lutheran, sported "an ecclesiastical atmosphere in which a premium was placed on intellectualism" and "a heavy scholasticism prevailed." He adds, "Feeling was almost entirely discounted while reason was exalted. The emphasis was upon right belief, upon religious truth set forth in carefully reasoned propositions." Reformed theologians in particular, he notes, had "succeeded in refashioning Calvinism into a scholastic system of thought which

63. Gonzalez, *History of Christian Thought*, 3:238–39.

64. Quenstedt, *Theologia Didactico-Polemica*, 1.79, as cited in Bromiley, *Historical Theology*, 321.

65. Quenstedt, *Theologia Didactico-Polemica*, 1.80, as cited in Bromiley, *Historical Theology*, 321.

66. Gonzalez, *History of Christian Thought*, 3:240.

67. Gary Dorrien, *The Remaking of Evangelical Theology* (Louisville: Westminster John Knox, 1998), 21–22.

served admirably as a theological structure but could do little for the sinner in need of God, or for the Church which stands in perpetual need of reforming its life."[68]

While Stoeffler's statement may be overly harsh, the development he decries is evident as early as the *Second Helvetic Confession* (1566), insofar as it marks "the beginning of a tendency to set up the Bible as the book of the divine decrees from whose text theology is then drawn out as a series of propositions."[69] Perhaps the theologian most closely connected with the genesis of the so-called "Reformed scholasticism" is Francis Turretin (1623–1687), whom Gonzalez calls "the most important systematic theologian of Calvinist orthodoxy on the Continent."[70] Turretin's theological approach was an outworking of the desire to forge a theological orthodoxy, a system of "right-doctrine."[71] According to Turretin, the purpose of theology is to teach savingly of God.[72] Because theology's object is God as he has revealed himself in his Word,[73] theology fulfills its purpose primarily as it systematizes the teachings of Scripture.[74]

Turretin's theological method required an error-free Bible as its foundation, and he argued for the same. "The prophets did not fall into mistakes in those things which they wrote as inspired men and as prophets, not even in the smallest particulars," he assured his readers, for "otherwise faith in the whole of Scripture would be rendered doubtful."[75] But Turretin was also convinced that the text of Scripture had been miraculously preserved in its pristine purity. In fact, to suggest that God allowed corruption to occur by the hands of copyists would be to deny divine providence in the preservation of the divine Word which God gave through inspiration, and it would impinge on the deity of Christ, in that our Lord could not "bear to use corrupted books."[76]

Like the theologians of Lutheran orthodoxy, Turretin's thoroughgoing commitment to the full inspiration of the biblical documents led to the claim of the Helvetic Consensus Formula (1675), composed under his influence, that the divine inspiration of the Old Testament extended beyond the consonants of the Hebrew words to encompass "either the vowel

68. Stoeffler, *Rise of Evangelical Pietism*, 115.

69. Gonzalez, *History of Christian Thought*, 3:250.

70. Ibid., 3:251.

71. Richard A. Muller, "Scholasticism Protestant and Catholic: Francis Turretin on the Object and Principles of Theology," *Church History* 55, no. 2 (June 1986): 205.

72. Muller, "Scholasticism Protestant and Catholic," 204.

73. Francis Turretin, *Institutes of Elenctic Theology*, trans. George Musgrave Giger, ed. James T. Dennison, Jr. (1679; reprint, Phillipsburg, N.J.: Presbyterian and Reformed, 1992), 1:16.

74. Ibid., 1:5.

75. Ibid., 1:55–56, 62–63.

76. Ibid., 1:107.

points themselves, or at least the power of the points."[77] This position was not unique to theologians on the Continent, but found its way among the Puritans as well. Over a decade prior to the Swiss consensus statement, John Owen, whose work Rogers and McKim see as marking a transition to Protestant scholasticism,[78] concluded that "whoever weighs up the matter seriously and without bias will find the pointing to be perfect, divine, and absolutely complete, like all the other works of God, from which nothing may be taken away, and to which nothing may be added."[79]

The Nineteenth Century: The Bible and the Scientific Method

In the opening decades of the nineteenth century, the interest in defending the Bible as an inerrant source of theological truths that had played such an important role in the older Protestant orthodoxy entered the evangelical mainstream. But the approach that emerged in the 1800s was generated by a quite different theological problem. The early Protestant theologians viewed their work as that of solidifying the gains of the Reformation, especially in the wake of the Roman Catholic Counter-Reformation. However, as the seventeenth century gave way to the eighteenth, theologians found the Christian faith challenged from another quarter, the rising influence of the scientific method. And this called for a related but altered response.

With the ascendancy of the empirical scientific method came an increasing interest in "natural religion"—those beliefs that were seemingly demonstrable by reason—in contrast to "revealed religion"—the more particular doctrines taught by specific religious communities. The theologians of Protestant orthodoxy realized that the growing interest in natural theology required the establishment of a rational foundation for Christian theology, if it was to maintain its intellectual integrity and appeal. They believed that God was the author of all truth, whether it be philosophical or theological, and consequently that no proposition could be true theologically if it were false philosophically. Armed with this assumption, these theologians freely made use of reason and philosophy in their theological endeavors.[80] In the task of making Christian theology compatible with the new empirical science, John Locke became a powerful ally, for

---

77. John H. Leith, *Creeds of the Churches*, 3d ed. (Atlanta: John Knox, 1982), 310.

78. Rogers and McKim, *Authority and Inspiration of the Bible*, 218–23.

79. John Owen, *Biblical Theology, or, The Nature, Origin, Development, and Study of Theological Truth, In Six Books* (1661), trans. Stephen P. Westcott (Pittsburgh: Soli Deo Gloria Publications, 1994), 501.

80. Gillian R. Evans, Alister E. McGrath, and Allan D. Galloway, *The Science of Theology* (Grand Rapids: Eerdmans, 1986), 161.

he argued that when divested of its dogmatic baggage, Christianity was the most reasonable form of religion.[81]

The Princeton Theology

As the eighteenth century drew to a close, many intellectuals had abandoned even the religion of reason for either skepticism[82] or religious relativism.[83] This provided theologians with an opportunity to elevate the other side of the natural/supernatural divide and reassert the significance of "revealed religion." These thinkers, however, had drunk deeply at the well of Enlightenment foundationalist rationalism. For this reason, they sought an intellectually unassailable bedrock upon which to construct their theological house.

The quest for a firm foundation for theology led some theologians to religious experience. In a sense, the focus on experience marked an extension of the interest in experimental religion that had characterized eighteenth-century evangelicalism, and it lives on in certain streams within the contemporary evangelical movement. At the same time, the focus on religious experience put some thinkers on the road to what emerged as the most serious theological alternative to the conservative orthodoxy of the forebears of contemporary evangelicalism, classical Protestant liberalism.

While not ignoring the experiential dimension of the faith, the neo-evangelicalism that emerged in the mid-twentieth century was far more indebted to the attempts of those theologians who sought to follow the lead of their scholastic forebears and set forth an invulnerable foundation for theology in an error-free Bible, viewed as the storehouse for divine revelation.[84] Above all, this agenda, characteristic of the theology inaugurated by Archibald Alexander, dominated Princeton Seminary throughout the nineteenth and early twentieth centuries. It occupied the energies of a string of Princeton theologians that included Charles Hodge, Archibald Alexander Hodge, Benjamin Breckinridge Warfield, and J. Gresham Machen.

---

81. Hence, Locke sought to demonstrate the existence of God in such a manner that this postulate carried mathematical certainty. See Evans, *Science of Theology*, 191.

82. David Hume was the exemplar of enlightened skepticism. See Arthur Cushman McGiffert, *Protestant Thought Before Kant* (London: Duckworth, 1911), 230–51.

83. Paradigmatic was the position of Gotthold Lessing. For a summary of Lessing's views, see William C. Platcher, *A History of Christian Theology* (Philadelphia: Westminster, 1983), 249–50.

84. Hodge, for example, asserted that the Bible is "free from all error, whether of doctrine, fact, or precept." Charles Hodge, *Systematic Theology* (New York: Scribner, Armstrong, and Co., 1872), 1:152.

Lying behind the Princeton theology was the Scottish common sense realism devised by Thomas Reid and imported to Princeton by John Witherspoon. The latter assumed the presidency of the College of New Jersey, later Princeton College, in 1768. According to Reid, our psychological constitution draws us irresistibly to accept certain first principles as self-evident. Because we have no reason to suspect that these psychological processes are misleading we are epistemically entitled to accept and employ these first principles.[85] On American soil this view entailed the principle that knowledge requires the assumption of the basic reliability of the human senses to perceive objects as they actually exist, together with the ability of the mind to classify the evidence so gleaned and carefully organize it into facts about the world.[86]

Charles Hodge accepted common sense realism, albeit not uncritically.[87] In his theology, this variety of Enlightenment epistemology worked hand in hand with the empirical scientific method with its focus on induction.

The die for the nineteenth-century Princeton theology was clearly cast by the reigning scientific method of the day. Hodge and his followers viewed the theological discipline as a science, understood in the empiricist sense of the study of "the ordered phenomena which we recognize through the senses."[88] Convinced that theology and science shared a common empirical and inductive method,[89] Hodge patterned his work after that of the scientist. Just as the natural scientist uncovers the facts pertaining to the natural world, he asserted, so the theologian brings to light the theological facts found within the Bible.[90] And these facts are uncovered through the application of the inductive method to the Scriptures.

Hodge's appropriation of the reigning scientific model also affected how he viewed the products of his labors. He assumed that the theological propositions they drew from the Bible stated universal, even eternal, facts.

85. W. Jay Wood, *Epistemology: Becoming Intellectually Virtuous* (Downers Grove, Ill.: Inter-Varsity, 1998), 100.

86. See, for example, James H. Smylie, "Defining Orthodoxy: Charles Hodge (1797–1878)," in *Makers of Christian Theology in America*, ed. Mark G. Toulouse and James O. Duke (Nashville: Abingdon, 1997), 154.

87. For a summary statement of Hodge's critical appropriation of common sense realism, see John D. Woodbridge, *Biblical Authority: A Critique of the Rogers/McKim Proposal* (Grand Rapids: Zondervan, 1982), 136–37.

88. For a discussion of this definition, formulated by Charles Hodge but indicative of other nineteenth-century conservatives, see George Marsden, "The Collapse of American Evangelical Academia," in *Faith and Rationality: Faith and Belief in God*, ed. Alvin Plantinga and Nicholas Wolterstorff (Notre Dame, Ind.: University of Notre Dame Press, 1983), 245–47.

89. John W. Stewart, "Mediating the Center: Charles Hodge on American Science, Language, Literature, and Politics," *Studies in Reformed Theology and History* 3, no. 1 (Winter 1995): 26.

90. Hodge, *Systematic Theology*, 1:18.

The chief goal of theology as an intellectual, scientific discipline was to compile these various facts. Hodge's theology contained a pietistic strand,[91] evident in his alleged warning to his students to "beware of a strong head and a cold heart."[92] Nevertheless, his focus on propositions led him to view the Bible as above all the source for religious teachings, with faith being primarily assent to truth or "the persuasion of the mind that a thing is true."[93] These teachings may include precepts for living, but the central, foundational, and most significant dimension of biblical truth lay in the area of doctrine.[94] In Hodge's words,

> Revelation is the communication of truth by God to the understandings of men. It makes known doctrines. For example, it makes known that God is . . . that Christ is the Son of God; that he assumed our nature; that he died for our sins, etc. These are logical propositions.[95]

The quest for scientific theology required an unassailable foundation, one that could endow the theological construction with epistemological certitude when subjected to the canons of empirical science. The Princeton theologians believed that this sure foundation lay in an error-free Bible. Although Hodge grounded the error-free nature of Scripture in its divinely inspired character, he and his followers also looked to rational evidences. They boldly asserted that the Bible's special status could be justified by appeal to scientific arguments,[96] such as empirical evidence that the Bible contains prophecies that were subsequently fulfilled, or that the various facts the biblical writers present are completely accurate. Hodge's successors at Princeton, his son A. A. Hodge and B. B. Warfield, viewed

91. This is evident, for example, in his declaration, "It would be safe for a man to resolve to admit into his theology nothing which is not sustained by the devotional writings of true Christians of every denomination." Ibid., 1:16–17. Hodge also wrote a devotional book entitled, *The Way of Life* (1842), reprinted in *Charles Hodge: The Way of Life*, ed. Mark A. Noll (New York: Paulist, 1987), 45–233. For a recent treatment of the piety of the Princeton theologians, see Andrew Hoffecker, *Piety and the Princeton Theologians: Archibald Alexander, Charles Hodge, and Benjamin Warfield* (Grand Rapids: Baker, 1981).

92. "Charles Hodge," in *Princeton Sermons* (London: The Banner of Truth Trust, 1958), xvi. For this and other similar anecdotes, see David O. Beale, *In Pursuit of Purity: American Fundamentalism since 1850* (Greenville, S.C.: Unusual Publications, 1986), 136–37.

93. Hodge, *Systematic Theology*, 3:42.

94. Richard J. Mouw, "The Bible in Twentieth-Century Protestantism: A Preliminary Taxonomy," in *The Bible in America: Essays in Cultural History*, ed. Nathan O. Hatch and Mark A. Noll (New York: Oxford, 1982), 143.

95. Charles Hodge, "The Theology of the Intellect and That of Feelings, Article II," *Essays and Reviews* (New York: Robert Carter and Bros., 1857), 609–10.

96. This was especially the case with Warfield, who viewed apologetics as the foundation for theology. For a helpful delineation of his position, see Rogers and McKim, *Authority and Interpretation of the Bible*, 328–30, 333–34, 337–39.

themselves as the true heirs not merely of the Reformation but also of the entire Christian tradition on this point. They affirmed what they called "the great Catholic doctrine of Biblical Inspiration," namely, "that the Scriptures not only contain, but ARE THE WORD OF GOD, and hence that all their elements and all their affirmations are absolutely errorless, and binding the faith and obedience of men."[97]

Warfield and Inerrancy

The emphasis on the cognitive, doctrinal dimension of faith that lay at the heart of the nineteenth-century Princeton theology not only resurrected, but also brought to center stage the concept of inerrancy that had been present within seventeenth-century Protestant orthodoxy. Hodge and his successors saw themselves as merely reaffirming the Reformed tradition, especially as it had been articulated by Francis Turretin, and the *Westminster Confession*. Turretin's three-volume *Institutio theologia elenchticae* was standard reading at Princeton throughout most of the nineteenth century. The *Westminster Confession* was thought to represent as closely as is humanly possible the Bible's own doctrinal system.[98]

Despite their claims to stand squarely in the Reformed tradition, the Princeton dogmatists' elevation of inerrancy to the centerpiece of their apologetic for biblical authority was motivated by a task unlike that which had consumed the thinkers of the seventeenth century. In contrast to their forebears who appealed to the inerrancy of Scripture against Rome's claim to be the repository of certain truth, the Princeton theologians needed an error-free Bible to respond to the challenges of an increasingly secular culture, on the one hand, and a rising liberal Christianity, on the other.

B. B. Warfield was perhaps the most influential of the Princeton theologians in giving shape to inerrancy as it came to be accepted by neo-evangelicals in the mid-twentieth century. Whereas Charles Hodge drew from the scientific method to defend Reformed orthodoxy in the face of the embryonic form of liberalism he saw in Friedrich Schleiermacher, his son A. A. Hodge and Warfield encountered seemingly more insidious challenges to biblical Christianity. Foremost among these challenges were an increasingly secular scientific view of the universe and German higher criticism, which had been on the rise throughout the century but hit America with full force only after the Civil War.

---

97. A. A. Hodge and B. B. Warfield, "Inspiration," *Presbyterian Review* 2 (April 1881): 237. For a similar claim to be representing the teaching of the whole church, see Charles Hodge, *Systematic Theology*, 1:154.

98. For this judgment, see George Marsden, *Fundamentalism and American Culture* (New York/Oxford: Oxford University Press, 1980), 110.

Actually, the roots of the challenge from higher criticism lay in the Reformation itself. In addition to the principle of *sola scriptura*, the Reformers asserted that every text of scripture has but one meaning and that this one meaning could be determined, at least in theory, by application of proper exegetical methods. As a result, Protestant exegetes set out, confident that they would eventually reach agreement as to the one correct understanding of Scriptures. Unanimity, however, proved to be an illusive goal. When in the wake of the Enlightenment scholars began applying scientific methodological principles to the study of history and of historical documents, biblical scholars welcomed the new historical-critical approach as offering a promising means of resolving hitherto perplexing exegetical difficulties. But as biblical criticism netted conclusions that questioned traditional views as to the authorship, date, and composition of biblical documents, it set off what Wolfhart Pannenberg has termed a "crisis of the Scripture principle."[99]

A. A. Hodge and B. B. Warfield set themselves to combat what they saw as the dangerous erosion of biblical authority that came in the wake of these developments. Warfield believed that the only effective response to this modernist challenge to Reformed theology lay in a reaffirmation of the scholastic teaching about the inspiration of the Bible. For Warfield, the very authority of the Bible was at stake in the battle over "inerrancy" that was raging in the Presbyterian Church of his day. Hence, he declared,

> The present controversy concerns something much more vital than the bare "inerrancy" of the Scripture, whether in the copies or in the "autographs." It concerns the trustworthiness of the Bible in its express declarations, and in the fundamental conceptions of its writers as to the course of the history of God's dealings with his people. It concerns, in a word, the authority of the Biblical representations concerning the nature of revealed religion, and the mode and course of its revelation.[100]

In his understanding of systematic theology, Warfield followed the basically inductive approach inspired by empirical science and pioneered by Charles Hodge.[101] In keeping with this method, Warfield sought to build his doctrine of Scripture from the teachings about biblical authority he

---

99. Wolfhart Pannenberg, *Basic Questions in Theology* (Philadelphia: Fortress, 1970), 1–14; see also Henning Graf Reventlow, *The Authority of the Bible and the Rise of the Modern World* (Philadelphia: Fortress, 1985).

100. B. B. Warfield, "The Inerrancy of the Original Autographs," *The Independent* (March 23, 1893), as reprinted in *The Princeton Theology: 1812–1921*, ed. Mark Noll (Grand Rapids: Baker, 1983), 270.

101. See, for example, B. B. Warfield, "The Idea of Systematic Theology," *Presbyterian and Reformed Review* 7 (April 1896): 262.

found in the various texts. At the same time, however, Warfield's method in constructing his doctrine of Scripture was in a sense also highly deductive.[102] The Princeton theologian reasoned from the divine, "God-breathed" nature of Scripture as attested by the biblical authors to the entire trustworthiness of the Bible and hence to the fidelity of each biblical text. Hence, Warfield declared,

> This much we can at least say without straining, that the designation of Scripture as "scripture" and its citation by the formula, "It is written," attest primarily its indefectible authority; the designation of it as "oracles" and the adduction of it by the formula, "It says," attest primarily its immediate divinity. Its authority rests on its divinity and its divinity expresses itself in its trustworthiness; and the New Testament writers in all their use of it treat it as what they declare it to be— a God-breathed document, which, because God-breathed, as through and through trustworthy in all its assertions, authoritative in all its declarations, and down to its last particular, the very word of God, His "oracles."[103]

While acknowledging that the Bible was written through the instrumentality of human agents, Warfield's central concern was the divine nature of Scripture. This emphasis led him to elevate the concept of biblical inerrancy. He asserted that in the view of the biblical authors, as well as Christ himself, "the whole of Scripture in all its parts and in all its elements, down to the least minutiae, in form of expression as well as in substance of teaching, is from God."[104]

In holding to their understanding of the nature of inspiration and biblical authority, the Princeton theologians claimed the legacy of Reformation theology. Nevertheless, their articulation of the doctrine marked a significant innovation from that of many of the seventeenth-century scholastics. The Lutheran theologian J. A. Quenstedt had taken the position that not only the original autographs of Scripture but also the copies are divinely inspired, in that they preserve the words as well as the content of the autographs. Quenstedt applied this principle primarily to the copies of the Old Testament, for these alone were available to the New Testament writers, and consequently it is to these that the term *theopneustos* (2 Tim. 3:16) applies.[105] But the Re-

---

102. See B. B. Warfield, "The Present Problem of Inspiration," *Homiletic Review* 21 (May 1891): 416. For a discussion of the inductive versus deductive method in Warfield, see Donald Westblade, "Benjamin B. Warfield on Inspiration and Inerrancy," *Studia Biblica et Theologica* 10, no. 1 (April 1980): 27–43.

103. B. B. Warfield, *The Inspiration and Authority of the Bible*, ed. Samuel G. Craig (Philadelphia: Presbyterian and Reformed, 1948), 150.

104. Ibid.

105. Quenstedt, *Theologia Didactico-Polemica* 1.206, as cited in Bromiley, *Historical Theology*, 321.

formed theologians such as Turretin and his followers were not so cautious. They held to the inerrancy not only of the original autographs of Scripture but also to the documents, on the basis of the belief that in his providence God had preserved them from corruption at the hands of copyists.

On this point, the Princeton theologians reversed the direction charted by Turretin. Their work in textual criticism made them well aware of the presence of textual variations among the existing manuscripts. Consequently, A. A. Hodge and B. B. Warfield were content to argue only for the inerrancy of the original autographs.[106] In his bid to deny any originality for his position, A. A. Hodge claimed, not without cause,[107] that this was the position of the church throughout its history: "The church has never held the verbal infallibility of our translations, nor the perfect accuracy of the copies of the original Hebrew and Greek Scriptures now possessed by us." Rather, "the Church has asserted absolute infallibility only of the original autograph copies of the Scriptures as they came from the hands of their inspired writers."[108]

The Princeton dogmatists went beyond Turretin in another significant manner as well. As noted already, seventeenth-century Reformed theologians were convinced that to admit that the biblical writers made even a minute mistake was to "render doubtful the whole of Scripture."[109] Charles Hodge, in contrast, acknowledged the presence of apparent discrepancies and factual problems in Scripture, declaring "we are perfectly willing to let these difficulties remain."[110] Rather than concluding that such problems disprove the Bible, he dismissed them as irrelevant to the question of biblical authority, saying, "No sane man would deny that the Parthenon was built of marble, even if here and there a speck of sandstone should be detected in its structure."[111] A. A. Hodge and B. B. Warfield were equally undaunted by the difficulties they discovered in the Bible. They advised that problems and internal discrepancies that could be neither dismissed as errors in the transcription process nor harmonized with each other simply be left as difficul-

106. Rogers and McKim observe that A. A. Hodge moved to this position sometime between 1860 and 1879; *Authority and Interpretation of the Bible*, 304.

107. In defending Hodge, Woodbridge points out that according to "Augustine, Erasmus, Richard Baxter, the English apologist Whitaker, and the Roman Catholic critic Richard Simon . . . copies in fact do have errors." Woodbridge, *Biblical Authority*, 134.

108. A. A. Hodge, *Outlines of Theology*, rewritten and enlarged ed. (London: The Banner of Truth Trust, 1879), 75. See also page 66.

109. Turretin, *Institutes of Elenctic Theology*, 1:55–56, 62–63.

110. Charles Hodge, "Inspiration," *Biblical Repertory and Princeton Review* 29 (October 1857), as reprinted in Noll, *Princeton Theology*, 140–41.

111. Charles Hodge, *Systematic Theology*, 1:170. For a summary of the debate about the meaning of Hodge's statement, see Woodbridge, *Biblical Authority*, 130–31.

ties.[112] Warfield expressed confidence that future "earnest study of the Word" could remove all such apparent discrepancies.[113]

In this manner, the Princeton theologians put into practice the inductive-to-deductive approach to the doctrine of inerrancy they had developed over the course of the nineteenth century.[114] The conclusion that the Bible is inerrant, which Warfield had derived from the Bible's own teaching about its authority, meant a priori that every text in Scripture was completely free from error of any kind.

Scripture as the Central "Fundamental"

The Princeton theology provides the model for much of neo-evangelical theology in the second half of the twentieth century. Neo-evangelicals routinely assume that the task of the theologian is to apply the scientific method, assisted by the canons of logic, to the deposit of revelation found in Scripture in the quest to compile the one, complete, timeless body of right doctrines.[115] Also commonplace among neo-evangelicals is the view that the Bible is a compendium of truths unlocked through "scientific" induction.[116] And in the opinion of many neo-evangelical theologians inerrancy is not only a hallmark of evangelicalism but also a safeguard against the slide into heterodoxy[117] and therefore a test for full participation in the evangelical movement. In the words of Harold Lindsell, "It is my conviction that a host of those evangelicals who no longer hold to inerrancy are still relatively evangelical. I do not for one moment concede, however, that in a technical sense anyone can claim the evangelical badge once he has abandoned inerrancy."[118]

112. Hodge and Warfield, "Inspiration," 238–41. See also Hodge, *Outlines of Theology*, 75.

113. B. B. Warfield, *The Bible Doctrine of Inspiration Not Invalidated* (New York: Ketcham, 1893), 180.

114. Although Charles Hodge seemed to be initially drawn to induction by his adherence to the method of empirical science, he apparently came to see the usefulness of the deductive approach. For an example of his elevation of deduction as a general methodological principle, see Charles Hodge, "The Unity of Mankind," *Princeton Review* 31 (January 1859): 104–5. For a helpful sketch of this development in Charles Hodge, see Rogers and McKim, *Authority and Interpretation of the Bible*, 296–97. For the apex of this development in Warfield, see Rogers and McKim, 347–48.

115. See, for example, Gordon R. Lewis and Bruce A. Demarest, *Integrative Theology* (Grand Rapids: Zondervan, 1987), 1:25–27.

116. Hence, Wayne Grudem, *Systematic Theology: An Introduction to Biblical Doctrine* (Grand Rapids: Zondervan, 1994), 21.

117. See, for example, the cautious statement to this effect by R. C. Sproul, "*Sola Scriptura*: Crucial to Evangelicalism," in *The Foundation of Biblical Authority*, ed. James Montgomery Boice (Grand Rapids: Zondervan, 1978), 116.

118. Harold Lindsell, *The Battle for the Bible* (Grand Rapids: Zondervan, 1976), 210. See also Francis A. Schaeffer, *The Great Evangelical Disaster* (Westchester, Ill.: Crossway, 1984), 57, 64.

Yet, the new evangelicalism that was launched in the 1940s did not inherit its theological ethos directly from the Princeton dogmatists. Rather, the temporal gap between the two was spanned by fundamentalism, a phenomenon that roughly paralleled the lifespan of the last of the Princeton theologians, J. Gresham Machen (1881–1937).[119]

The fundamentalist coalition comprised an impressive array of diverse groups: revivalists such as D. L. Moody; dispensationalists, including Lewis Sperry Chafer; holiness and victorious life (e.g., Keswick) advocates of the likes of Charles G. Trumbull;[120] prophecy conference organizers such as A. C. Gaebelein; leaders of more traditional churches, especially Presbyterians (William G. Moorehead) and Baptists (A. C. Dixon); and even erudite academics such as James M. Gray. What brought this variety of turn-of-the-century religionists together was their shared militant opposition to theological liberalism. The early fundamentalists were all convinced that liberalism marked a radical departure from classic Christianity. Machen spoke for many when in the opening pages to his *Christianity and Liberalism*, he declared, "Despite the liberal use of traditional phraseology, modern liberalism not only is a different religion from Christianity but belongs in a totally different class of religions."[121] Machen asserted, "The chief modern rival of Christianity is 'liberalism.' An examination of the teachings of liberalism in comparison with those of Christianity will show that at every point the two movements are in direct opposition."[122]

Fundamentalists likewise were united in their elevation of doctrine as the mark of authentic Christianity. In fact, the movement itself took its name from the publication of a series of tracts, *The Fundamentals: A Testimony to the Truth*, published by its leaders beginning in 1910 with the purpose of defending certain classical Christian doctrines. The focus on doctrine, rather than experience as had been the case in awakening evangelicalism as well as in the revivalism that had in part spawned the fundamentalist movement, was also connected to the perceived liberal threat. Roger Olson offers an explanation:

> Early fundamentalists did not deny that personal experience of repentance and conversion is important. But because of the threat they saw in liberal theology, they tended to emphasize assent to unrevisable doctrinal propositions as the es-

119. For a contemporary fundamentalist telling of the history of the movement to the 1980s, see David O. Beale, *In Pursuit of Purity: American Fundamentalism since 1850* (Greenville, S.C.: Unusual Publications, 1986).

120. For a critical treatment of the victorious life phenomenon at the turn of the century, see Douglas W. Frank, *Less Than Conquerors: How Evangelicals Entered the Twentieth Century* (Grand Rapids: Eerdmans, 1986), 103–66.

121. J. Gresham Machen, *Christianity and Liberalism* (New York: Macmillan, 1923), 7.

122. Ibid., 53.

sential and timeless core of Christianity. Whereas the motto of many pietists had become "If your heart is warm, give me your hand," fundamentalists would say, "If your beliefs are correct, give me your hand." They distrusted religious experience and affections because liberals could claim to have them.[123]

Finally, fundamentalism was characterized by a belief that the only sure antidote for the ills of liberalism lay in an uncompromising loyalty to Scripture arising out of a high view of biblical authority. Liberalism, with its attack on the Bible, the fundamentalists believed, could only be combated through a vigorous defense that included a clear statement of the divine inspiration of the Bible.

It was at this point that the Princeton theology initially sparked the interest of the early fundamentalists. Despite their differences on other matters, the fundamentalists shared with each other and with the Princeton theologians a fierce loyalty to the Bible in the face of the challenge to biblical authority they perceived both in "modernism" and in its theological expression, liberalism. Consequently, even though Reformed thinkers such as Warfield were somewhat ambivalent toward the movement[124] and hence not fundamentalists in the strict sense, the fundamentalists themselves welcomed the Princetonians into the fold because these theologians provided an intellectual framework for elaborating fundamentalism's felt loyalty to the Bible and their commitment to the Bible's complete trustworthiness.[125] For this reason, it was almost inevitable that fundamentalism would come to be characterized by an unswerving adherence to a Warfield style understanding of inerrancy, even though many of the currents that fed into fundamentalism had not previously used the term to articulate their view of biblical inspiration.[126]

Warfield's was by no means the only view of inerrancy found among the early fundamentalists.[127] In fact, the Scottish theologian James Orr, who wrote one of the initial volumes of *The Fundamentals*, was an outspoken critic of this approach to maintaining biblical authority in the face of the liberal challenge. Based on an inductive study of the phenomena of

123. Roger Olson, *The Story of Christian Theology* (Downers Grove, Ill.: InterVarsity, 1999), 567.

124. Beale, *In Pursuit of Purity*, 138–39.

125. For a helpful summary of the connections between the Princeton theologians and the Fundamentalists, see Ellingsen, *Evangelical Movement*, 77–80.

126. Ellingsen cites the 1878 Niagara Creed as an example of a statement that does not include the term inerrancy; *Evangelical Movement*, 53.

127. Marsden cites A. H. Strong, Robert Stuart MacArthur, and Curtus Lee Laws as leading Baptist conservatives or fundamentalists who did not subscribe to inerrancy; Marsden, *Fundamentalism and American Culture*, 107.

the biblical documents, which he believed attested to their status as the carriers of divine revelation, Orr concluded that "a just view of the actual historical genesis of the Bible" simply does not support the claim "that 'inerrancy' in every minute particular is involved *in the very idea* of a book given by inspiration by God."[128] He therefore rejected as "a most suicidal position for any defender of revelation" the claim that "unless we can demonstrate what is called the 'inerrancy' of the Biblical record, down even to its minutest details, the whole edifice of belief in revealed religion falls to the ground."[129] Instead of attempting to establish the authority of the Bible by demonstrating the facticity of the biblical records, a demonstration that essentially looks to human reason, Orr appealed to the effect of the Bible in human hearts. He concluded his *Revelation and Inspiration* by declaring,

> In the last resort, the proof of the inspiration of the Bible—not in every particular, but in its essential message—is to be found in the life-giving effects which that message has produced, wherever its word of truth has gone. . . . The Bible has the qualities claimed for it as an inspired book. . . . It leads to God and to Christ; it gives light on the deepest problems of life, death, and eternity; it discovers the way of deliverance from sin; it makes men new creatures; it furnishes the man of God completely for every good work. . . . The Bible that embodies this word will retain its distinction as *the Book of Inspiration* till the end of time![130]

Despite its rejection by leaders such as Orr, the Princeton viewpoint prevailed among American fundamentalists. At the height of the modernist-fundamentalist controversy in the 1920s, fundamentalists rallied around modified versions of the Warfield-influenced five-point declaration of "essential" doctrines adopted by the Presbyterian General Council in 1910,[131] which likely formed the foundation for the various formulations[132] of the so-called "five fundamentals." The first of the five assertions in the Presbyterian document was an affirmation of biblical inerrancy. From then on, adherence to this doctrine became a central feature of the entire fundamentalist coalition. Fundamentalism, in turn, bequeathed the doctrine of inerrancy and the defense of the Bible to its neo-evangelical offspring.

128. James Orr, *Revelation and Inspiration* (London: Duckworth, 1910), 213.
129. Ibid., 197–98.
130. Ibid., 217–18.
131. Marsden, *Fundamentalism and American Culture*, 117.
132. For an early historical discussion of the five fundamentals, see Stewart Grant Cole, *The History of Fundamentalism* (New York: R. R. Smith, 1931), 34.

Fundamentalism and the New Evangelicalism

When the controversies subsided, the fundamentalists found themselves divested of control of most major Protestant denominations, which had defected to "modernism." In response, many of the remnants of the older fundamentalist coalition retreated from theological engagement with the mainline churches—choosing to practice "second-order separation"—and retreated from engagement with the wider culture as well.

In the 1940s, however, a new coalition coalesced out of fundamentalism, which, thanks to one of its guiding lights, Harold Ockenga, came to be known as "the new evangelicalism"[133] or neo-evangelicalism, a designation that was then simplified to "evangelicalism." The new evangelicalism began as a protest by several younger fundamentalists against the internal division, anti-intellectualism, departmentalization of life, and social irrelevance that had come to characterize the older movement.[134] In opposition to the stance that in their estimation many fundamentalists had adopted, the neo-evangelicals believed that their task was, in Ockenga's words, to display a "spirit of cooperation, of mutual faith, of progressive action, and of ethical responsibility."[135] The architects of the new coalition saw their role as that of standing between liberalism and fundamentalism. They desired to remain true to the basic doctrines of Christian orthodoxy in the face of the accommodationist tendencies of theological liberalism. Hence, Ockenga declared, "Doctrinally, the fundamentalists are right, and I wish to be always classified as one."[136] But to a greater extent than their

133. George Marsden, *Reforming Fundamentalism: Fuller Seminary and the New Evangelicalism* (Grand Rapids: Eerdmans, 1987), 3, 146. Ockenga later claimed that he coined the term in 1947. See Harold J. Ockenga, "From Fundamentalism, through New Evangelicalism, to Evangelicalism," in *Evangelical Roots*, ed. Kenneth Kantzer (New York: Thomas Nelson, 1978), 38. Millard Erickson, in contrast, attributes the first public use of the term to Carl F. H. Henry; Millard J. Erickson, *The Evangelical Left: Encountering Postconservative Evangelical Theology* (Grand Rapids: Baker, 1997), 23 n. 22.

134. Daniel B. Stevick, *Beyond Fundamentalism* (Richmond, Va.: John Knox, 1964), 28. One significant early expression of that protest was Harold John Ockenga's "Can Fundamentalism Win America?" *Christian Life and Times* (June 1947). The author's answer to the query in the title of the article was a resounding no. Fundamentalism was hampered by its divisive spirit, aloofness from social problems, and unethical practices, he asserted. Ockenga's short piece was echoed in a book-length critique, Carl F. H. Henry's *The Uneasy Conscience of Modern Fundamentalism* (Grand Rapids: Eerdmans, 1947). Like Ockenga, Henry chastised his fellow fundamentalists for their aloofness from society and their lack of a social vision.

135. Ockenga, "Can Fundamentalism Win America?" 13–15. See also Ockenga, "From Fundamentalism, through New Evangelicalism, to Evangelicalism," 44.

136. Ockenga, "From Fundamentalism, through New Evangelicalism, to Evangelicalism," 40.

fundamentalist co-religionists, the new evangelicals desired to be open to engagement with the world and to dialogue with other viewpoints.

The new evangelicals focused their attention on several crucial areas: the development of a new social ethic, the setting forth of an intellectually credible Christian apologetic, a bold thrust in evangelism, the founding of institutions promoting education and scholarship, and transdenominational cooperation based on a sensed underlying spiritual unity.[137] To bring together a greater cooperation among less separatistically inclined fundamentalists, these leaders founded a new organization, the National Association of Evangelicals (NAE),[138] designed to assist in the revitalization of conservative Christianity in America and to provide an alternative to both the liberal-influenced National Council of Churches and the newly formed, separatist American Council of Christian Churches.

The appropriation of the label "evangelical" by the post-fundamentalist conservative Protestants, or what George Marsden calls the "card-carrying evangelicals,"[139] was a masterful move. In so doing, they claimed for themselves the heritage of evangelicalism that emerged over two hundred years earlier, as well as the claim of the Reformation churches to be the carriers of the true "evangel." This tactic was an overwhelming success. According to the Lutheran ecumenist Mark Ellingsen,

> The way in which this group of theological conservatives has so thoroughly succeeded in appropriating the title "Evangelical" for themselves, so that at least in North America it is only they and not the mainline Protestant churches who are regarded as "evangelical" in the mind of the public, indicates the profound impact of this new coalition.[140]

The connection in nomenclature to the earlier evangelical movement is, of course, not totally specious, for the "card-carrying evangelicals" shared much with their eighteenth-century forebears. The most significant connection was the continuing heritage of convertive piety that stands at the heart of evangelicalism in all its forms and permutations. But the new evangelicalism was not merely an extension or replication of its eighteenth-century predecessor. Rather, neo-evangelicalism was deeply

137. For a discussion of these, see Millard Erickson, *The New Evangelical Theology* (Westwood, N.J.: Revell, 1968), 31–44.

138. For the genesis of the NAE, see Joel A. Carpenter, *Revive Us Again: The Reawakening of American Fundamentalism* (New York: Oxford, 1997), 141–60.

139. George M. Marsden, "Contemporary American Evangelicalism," in *Southern Baptists and American Evangelicals*, ed. David S. Dockery (Nashville: Broadman and Holman, 1993), 30; George M. Marsden, "Introduction," in *Evangelicalism and Modern America*, ed. George M. Marsden (Grand Rapids: Eerdmans, 1984), xv.

140. Ellingsen, *Evangelical Movement*, 101.

affected by the fundamentalist experience which to a great degree had formed it. While claiming the mantle of the earlier evangelical movement, the new evangelicals drew their identity more immediately from fundamentalism—or, perhaps more accurately stated, from the fundamentalist struggle with liberalism. Sociologist Christian Smith notes this connection in characterizing the contribution of the new evangelicalism as providing what might be called a "third way" for Christianity in America:

> What the evangelical movement *did* accomplish was to open up a "space" between fundamentalism and liberalism in the field of religious collective identity; give that space a name; articulate and promote a resonant vision of faith and practice that players in the religious field came to associate with that name and identity-space; and invite a variety of religious players to move into that space to participate in the "identity-work" and mission being accomplished there.[141]

Further, the new evangelicalism drew from and extended the broad-based coalition forged by fundamentalism, a coalition that not only crossed denominational lines, but also attracted or influenced traditions that did not belong to its natural constituency. As Joel Carpenter notes,

> Many holiness Wesleyans came to accept the doctrine of biblical inerrancy even though that belief is not a Wesleyan way of understanding the Bible's inspiration and authority. Enough Dutch Calvinists, German-speaking Mennonites and Scandinavian Lutherans were attracted to the fundamentalists' Bible institutes, radio programs, and gospel tabernacles to raise sharp concern among these traditions' leaders.

Carpenter then concludes that throughout much of the twentieth century the fundamentalist ethos has determined the shape of "the American evangelical impulse," marking this century as the "fundamentalist era" of American evangelicalism.[142]

Nowhere is neo-evangelicalism's genesis in fundamentalism more evident than in its theology. The fundamentalist acceptance of the Princeton understanding of inspiration, especially Warfield's formulation of inerrancy, gave a particular nineteenth-century cast to neo-evangelicalism's emphasis on biblical authority.

Equally significant for the fledgling new evangelicalism was their acceptance of fundamentalism's tendency to reduce essential Christianity to adherence to basic doctrines. This elevation of particular doctrines that

141. Christian Smith, *American Evangelicalism: Embattled and Thriving* (Chicago: University of Chicago Press, 1998), 14–15.

142. Carpenter, *Revive Us Again*, 237–38.

fundamentalists were intent on defending moved the focus of theological engagement away from the question of the nature of salvation, that had been so central to the *solas* of the Reformation response to medieval Roman Catholicism. In its place fundamentalism substituted the more cognitively oriented discussion of naturalism versus supernaturalism. This debate lay at the heart of the struggle with liberalism and determined the shape of the core beliefs that fundamentalists viewed as constituting true Christian orthodoxy. By perpetuating the fundamentalist struggle against liberalism as waged on the terms set out by the Princeton theology, the new evangelical theology oriented itself to questions of propositional truth, in contrast to the issue of one's relationship with God characteristic of classical evangelicalism.

In short, the trajectory through fundamentalism had the effect of transforming the ethos of the theological tradition of the purveyors of convertive piety from that of a gospel-focused endeavor that viewed the Bible as the vehicle of the Spirit's working to that of a Bible-focused task intent on maintaining the gospel of biblical orthodoxy. While the new evangelical theology never lost the concern to facilitate the evangelical church in its mission to convert the world, the impulse it assimilated from fundamentalism's attachment to the Princeton theology marked at least a partial victory of Protestant scholasticism over the Puritan-Pietist legacy. As a result, from the 1940s onward the theology of the new evangelicalism was marked by the interplay of two motifs—the cognitive-doctrinal and the practical-experiential—both of which belong to its heritage.

three

The Shaping of Neo-Evangelical Apologetic Theology

The perceived "ghettoizing" of fundamentalism in the aftermath of the infamous Scopes "monkey" trial in 1925 led to the formation of a new coalition in the 1940s known as the neo-evangelical movement, or simply evangelicalism. By reviving this designation, the movement claimed for itself the mantle of the entire evangelical tradition. Since its advent in the 1940s, the new evangelicalism has served as the cradle for vigorous theological work. Many capable thinkers have contributed to the evangelical theological conversation. But perhaps none of the early theologians of the movement had more impact upon the theology of "card-carrying evangelicals" than Carl F. H. Henry and Bernard Ramm.

Henry and Ramm happen to be Baptists, but both came to find their Christian identity more through participation in the evangelical movement than in their denominational affiliation. Their understanding of the essence of the Christian faith was likewise shaped more by their self-consciousness as evangelicals than through loyalty to a particular denomination. Consequently, both Henry and Ramm became representative evangelicals and quintessential evangelical theologians.

In prolific writing careers that spanned the first forty years of the new evangelical movement, Henry and Ramm demonstrated the kind of intellectual engagement that Harold Ockenga had in mind when he voiced his desire for a coalition of conservative Protestants who would "infiltrate rather than separate." These two thinkers epitomized the new evangelicalism in its best attempt to be obedient to Ockenga's call to engage in, rather than withdraw from, the theological discussions underway in the mainline seminaries as well as to tackle the challenges posed by changes transpiring in the wider culture. By their example, Henry and Ramm provided not only precedence but also inspiration for a host of evangelical scholars who have benefited from, built upon, and emulated their pioneering work.

Henry and Ramm were motivated by a similar goal, namely, to move beyond fundamentalism while remaining true to orthodox belief. They likewise shared a common starting point, a commitment to Scripture as the unquestioned authority for theological reflection. Nevertheless, as the decades unfolded, the two evangelical thinkers followed trajectories that took them in increasingly divergent directions. These differing paths, in turn, both typified and fostered what developed into a growing divergence within neo-evangelical theology.

Carl F. H. Henry (1913-): The (Rational) Foundations for an Apologetic Theology

The most prominent theologian of the neo-evangelical movement is without a doubt Carl Henry. In 1983, Bob Patterson hailed Henry as "the prime interpreter of evangelical theology, one of its leading theoreticians, and . . . the unofficial theologian for the entire tradition."[1] Five years earlier, *Time* magazine named Henry evangelicalism's "leading spokesman."[2] And in 1990, R. Albert Mohler went so far as to rank Henry as "one of the theological luminaries of the twentieth century."[3]

Apologist to Modern Culture

In a sense, Henry was a member of the neo-evangelical movement from "day one." In fact, the stance he took against fundamentalism was one of the important intellectual impulses that helped launch the new evangelicalism. During the formative years of the mid-1940s, his short diatribe, *The Uneasy Conscience of Modern Fundamentalism*,[4] exploded like a

1. Bob E. Patterson, "Carl F. H. Henry," in *Makers of the Modern Theological Mind*, ed. Bob E. Patterson (Waco: Word, 1983), 9.
2. "Theology for the Tent Meeting," *Time* 109, no. 7 (Feb. 14, 1977), 52.
3. R. Albert Mohler, "Carl Ferdinand Howard Henry," in *Baptist Thinkers*, ed. Timothy George and David S. Dockery (Nashville: Broadman, 1990), 518.
4. Carl F. H. Henry, *The Uneasy Conscience of Modern Fundamentalism* (Grand Rapids: Eerdmans, 1947). For his later reflections on the problematic areas of fundamentalism and the need for evangelicals to move beyond them, see Carl F. H. Henry, *Evangelical Responsibility in Contemporary Theology*, Pathway Books (Grand Rapids: Eerdmans, 1957).

bombshell in the corner of the American religious landscape where the fundamentalists had circled the wagons.

Evangelical Engagement versus Fundamentalist Separation

Doctrinally, Henry remained a fundamentalist. In fact, a decade after publishing his critique of the movement, he affirmed once again his adherence to the "fundamentals."[5] Rather than reforming fundamentalism doctrinally, Henry sought to rid it of the "harsh temperament," the "spirit of lovelessness and strife"[6] he saw displayed by many of its mid-century leaders.

In addition to its unhelpful argumentativeness, Henry discerned in 1940s-style fundamentalism several intellectual problems. The most notable of these were in the realm of ethics. In his estimation the fundamentalism of the day lacked a social program, for the humanitarianism or benevolent regard for the interests of humankind that it once possessed had evaporated.[7] As a result, the movement had abrogated its task to be a truly gospel people. By refusing to acknowledge the present reality of the kingdom of God and divorcing the Christian faith from the great social reform movements, fundamentalism failed to apply the gospel to world political and economic conditions.

To remedy the malaise Henry envisioned a revitalization of fundamentalism that would involve practical engagement with the world. This concern led him to move beyond personal ethics[8] (which had become a favorite topic among fundamentalists) to address the vexing issue of social ethics.[9] He was convinced that biblical Christianity ought to foster not only personal salvation but social transformation as well. In his estimation, truly biblical Christians are concerned about both individual conversion and social justice,[10] which Henry understood not only as involving ministry to the victims of injustice but also remedying and eliminating the causes of that injustice.[11] Henry went so far as to call upon evangelicals to

---

5. Henry, *Evangelical Responsibility*, 66.

6. Ibid., 43.

7. Henry, *Uneasy Conscience*, 16.

8. Carl F. H. Henry, *Christian Personal Ethics* (Grand Rapids: Eerdmans, 1957).

9. In addition to scattered discussions in *God, Revelation and Authority*, 6 vols. (Waco: Word, 1976–1983), Henry's most important statements concerning social ethics are in his book *Aspects of Christian Social Ethics* (Grand Rapids: Eerdmans, 1964), and certain essays in *A Plea for Evangelical Demonstration* (Grand Rapids: Baker, 1971), *The Christian Mindset in a Secular Society* (Portland: Multnomah, 1984), and *The God Who Shows Himself* (Waco: Word, 1966).

10. Henry, *A Plea for Evangelical Demonstration*, 107; Henry, *The God Who Shows Himself*, 31. For an extended discussion of justice, see Henry, *God, Revelation and Authority*, 6:402–54.

11. Henry, *A Plea for Evangelical Demonstration*, 115.

voice an "authentic challenge to the status quo" in the name of the social and political implications of the biblical message.[12]

This stance, of course, put him at odds with mid-century fundamentalism as well as with certain participants in the new evangelical coalition. But it did not lead him to embrace the alternative widely touted by theological liberals. Henry maintained the classic evangelical position that social change must begin with the individual, rather than on the societal level. The church, he declared, "must rely on spiritual regeneration for the transformation of society."[13] In his estimation, this principle requires the church to avoid wielding direct pressure on government or public agencies to adopt specifically church-approved programs; instead, the church must look to its members "to fulfil their duties as citizens of two worlds."[14]

In addition to chiding fundamentalism for its loss of a social conscience, Henry concluded that the movement had abandoned its intellectual task, which he saw as that of shaping the mindset of society. He feared that unless fundamentalism changed its course, it would soon be reduced to an insignificant sect having no impact on the wider culture. Therefore, he boldly challenged his colleagues to seize the hour, convinced that the time was ripe "for a rediscovery of the Scriptures and of the meaning of the Incarnation for the human race."[15] As an evangelical "restorationist," he envisioned nothing less than the reemergence of "historic Christianity" as a vital "world ideology," because "the redemptive message has implications for all of life."[16] The task of setting forth the intellectual foundations for such a revitalizing of historic Christianity formed Henry's passion and consumed his career.

Evangelical Spokesperson

Henry's challenge to the fundamentalism of the 1940s catapulted him into the limelight as arguably the most widely acknowledged intellectual voice for the new evangelical movement, an informal position he held until his retirement elevated him to a type of "elder statesman" role. Henry was well situated theologically to serve as the intellectual spokesperson for the new evangelicalism. Writing in 1996, Millard Erickson offered this apt characterization: "He is Calvinistic, but moderately so. He is noncharismatic, but not militantly so. He is nondispensational but not antidispensational. He is a Baptist, but not polemical toward non-Baptists. His

12. See, for example, Henry, *God, Revelation and Authority*, 4:573–77.

13. Henry, *Aspects of Christian Social Ethics*, 16.

14. Henry, *A Plea for Evangelical Demonstration*, 46–47. For an extended discussion of Christian political duty, see Henry, *God, Revelation and Authority*, 6:436–54.

15. Henry, *Uneasy Conscience*, 9.

16. Ibid., 68.

stance on doctrinal issues is firm, but not rancorous."[17] Yet Henry's credentials for appointment as "Mr. Evangelical Theology" extended beyond these characteristics to encompass his entire spiritual pilgrimage,[18] at the heart of which is what has been the hallmark of evangelicalism since its birth in the womb of Pietism, namely, a personal experience of the new birth.

Henry's childhood religious exposure was minimal, even though his father was Lutheran and his mother Roman Catholic. Conversion, therefore, came to the twenty-year-old Henry (1933) through Christian influences from outside his parental home.[19] His conversion was typically evangelical. It included prayer for forgiveness and for the presence of God in his life; a sense of inner assurance of forgiveness and Jesus as his personal Savior; a committing of his entire life into God's hands that included a willingness to follow wherever God would lead; and a zeal to tell others of his new-found relationship with God. His conversion was likewise typically evangelical in that it transcended any specifically denominational orientation or loyalty. Henry had become a believer, not a participant in any particular denomination. And influences from persons representing a variety of denominations had been instrumental in this event, including, as he later enumerated them,

a pilfered Bible, fragmentary memories of the Episcopal prayer book, a Methodist friend's insistence on the new birth, an Oxford Grouper's daring call for changed lives, all coalescing around my need for vocational direction and crowned by the Holy Spirit's work of grace and inner assurance.[20]

In the months that followed, Henry discovered that his commitment would mean a change in career plans, as he sensed God steering him away from his chosen vocation in newspaper journalism and into theological studies. In fall, 1935, Henry enrolled in Wheaton College, a choice precipitated in part by his positive impression of a lecture delivered by its president, J. Oliver Buswell, in which he set forth the importance of reason to faith (a theme that would loom central in Henry's own theological work), and the resurrection as a historical event.[21] The interdenominational environment at Wheaton provided a basis for Henry's future relationship to the new evangelicalism. During this time, he established friendships with

17. Millard J. Erickson, "Carl F. H. Henry," in *A New Handbook of Christian Theologians*, ed. Donald W. Musser and Joseph L. Price (Nashville: Abingdon, 1996), 215.
18. For his own recounting of his pilgrimage, see Carl F. H. Henry, *Confessions of a Theologian* (Waco: Word, 1986), 210–11.
19. Ibid., 44.
20. Ibid., 47.
21. Ibid., 55.

future neo-evangelical leaders, including Billy Graham and Harold Lindsell. More significant theologically, his basically rationalist-oriented
worldview was strengthened by Wheaton's premier philosophy professor,
Gordon H. Clark, perhaps the single most important intellectual influence
on Henry's thought. At the same time, the Wheaton experience led him
to embrace what he found to be the distinctives of the Baptists, including
believer's baptism by immersion and the primacy of Scripture.

Henry launched his academic career armed with academic credentials
from both Wheaton (M.A. 1941) and Northern Baptist Theological Seminary (B.D. 1941, Th.D. 1942), a school founded in the height of the modernist-fundamentalist controversy by conservatives within the Northern
Baptist Convention as an alternative to the liberal course set by the University of Chicago Divinity School. Although his first teaching post was at
Northern, his commitment to the evangelical movement soon led to an
invitation for him to join the faculty of Fuller Theological Seminary, the
fledgling school inaugurated with the purpose of convening America's
best evangelical theological scholars and thereby sparking a renaissance in
evangelical scholarship.[22]

Although Henry wrote nine books while at Fuller, the context for his ongoing contribution to evangelical theology was not to be the seminary classroom. Rather, religious journalism loomed on the horizon as he was named
the founding editor of a new evangelical effort, *Christianity Today*, which was
being launched in response to the dream of several evangelical leaders (including Billy Graham and Harold Ockenga) for a conservative alternative to
The Christian Century. Henry held the post for twelve stormy years (1956–
1967). Despite the internal controversies that dogged his tenure,[23] during
these years Henry's prominence grew and his influence spread. After being
divested of the helm of the magazine (1967), Henry devoted himself more
fully to research and writing, climaxing in the publication of his magnum
opus, the monumental six-volume *God, Revelation and Authority*.[24]

Theological Commentator

Carl Henry has been an articulate shaper and articulator of evangelical
theology; yet he did so without being a systematic theologian per se or
producing a full delineation of Christian doctrine. Rather than a system-
atician, Henry is perhaps better characterized as a commentator on the

---

22. For this characterization of the inaugural purposes of Fuller Theological Seminary,
see Joel A. Carpenter, *Revive Us Again: The Reawakening of American Fundamentalism* (New
York: Oxford, 1997), 194.

23. For Henry's perspective on developments at *Christianity Today* as well as his departure
from the scene, see Henry, *Confessions of a Theologian*, 264–301.

24. Carl F. H. Henry, *God, Revelation and Authority*, 6 vols. (Waco: Word, 1976–1983).

fortunes of theology, as well as of evangelicalism, in the twentieth century.[25] This role provided the chief motivation for many of his articles[26] and books.[27] Even in his most systematic theological work, *God, Revelation and Authority*, Henry repeatedly immerses the reader in analyses of contemporary theological currents.

Henry's vision of an engaged and engaging evangelicalism was sounded already in his editorial in the inaugural issue of *Christianity Today*. He declared that the new magazine "has its origin in a deep-felt desire to express historical Christianity to the present generation." He was convinced that "evangelical Christianity needs a clear voice to speak with conviction and love, and to state its true position and its relevance to the world crisis." This was necessary because "a generation has grown up unaware of the basic truths of the Christian faith taught in the Scriptures and expressed in the creeds of the historic evangelical churches." In short, Henry's vision for the fledgling magazine was that it be "*salt* and *light* in a decaying and darkening world."[28]

Throughout his career Henry was appalled by what he perceived to be the malaise of evangelicalism. Writing in 1964 he bemoaned its tendency "to neglect the frontiers of formative discussion in contemporary theology." Through this neglect, he added, evangelicals "forfeit the debate at these points to proponents of subevangelical points of view, or to those who assert evangelical positions in only a fragmentary way." He likewise chastised evangelical theological writing for its lack of "an air of exciting relevance." Henry placed the blame squarely on the shoulders of his co-religionists: "The problem is not that biblical theology is outdated; it is rather that some of its expositors seem out of touch with the frontiers of doubt in our day."[29] Henry's mission was to alter this deplorable situation.

As disturbing as the problems of evangelicalism were, Henry was even more upset by the tragic situation he perceived in mainline Protestantism. To its own peril modern theology had forsaken its roots by giving up belief in divine revelation as an objective given, a betrayal that carried disastrous consequences for Western society as a whole. Already in the 1940s he pinpointed the years 1914–1946 as marking "the midnight of modern cul-

25. E.g., Carl F. H. Henry, *Evangelicals in Search of Identity* (Waco: Word, 1976). Even his autobiography concludes with a presentation of his perspective on "The Evangelical Prospect in America"; Henry, *Confessions of a Theologian*, 381–407.

26. E.g., Carl F. H. Henry, "Crosscurrents in Contemporary Theology," in *Jesus of Nazareth: Saviour and Lord*, ed. Carl Henry (Grand Rapids: Eerdmans, 1966), 3–22.

27. E.g., Carl F. H. Henry, *Frontiers in Modern Theology: A Critique of Current Theological Trends* (Chicago: Moody, 1964).

28. "Why Christianity Today?" *Christianity Today* 1 (October 15, 1956): 20–21.

29. Henry, *Frontiers in Modern Theology*, 140–41.

ture."[30] During this period, he explained, the tragedy of two world wars had led to widespread questioning of the assumptions of modernity: the inevitability of human progress, the inherent goodness of humankind, the ultimate status of nature, and the basic animality of humanity.[31]

By 1986, Henry was growing increasingly fearful that evangelicalism would not fulfill what he saw as its divinely given cultural mission. He wrote, "I remain profoundly convinced that evangelicals are now facing their biggest opportunity since the Reformation, and yet are forfeiting it."[32] For him, the options were quite simple. Reminiscent of Ockenga's earlier call to engage society, Henry voiced the need for the kind of "creative interaction and dialogue that advanced evangelical penetration" into what in his estimation was becoming an increasingly decadent society.[33] The only alternative was to be defeated by that decadence. According to Henry, penetrating society required the kind of intellectual engagement that provided a rational apologetic for Christian orthodoxy.

Rationalist Apologist

Henry staked his entire career on his belief that the demise of modern theology afforded a great opportunity for the Protestant orthodoxy of which evangelicalism had become the contemporary carrier. But for evangelicals to avail themselves of this opportunity, it was imperative that they set forth the evangelical case in a manner that could win intellectual respectability. That is, the theologians in the movement must offer an intellectually credible apologetic for the evangelical worldview. In 1964, Henry charted an agenda that proved to be an apt summary of his entire theological program:

> If Christianity is to win intellectual respectability in the modern world, the reality of the transcendent God must indeed be proclaimed by the theologians—and proclaimed on the basis of man's rational competence to know the transempirical realm. Apart from recognition of the rational Creator of men made in his image and of the self-revealed Redeemer of a fallen hu-

30. Carl F. H. Henry, *The Protestant Dilemma* (Grand Rapids: Eerdmans, 1949), 18. See also Carl F. H. Henry, *Remaking the Modern Mind* (Grand Rapids: Eerdmans, 1946), 26. He delineated the misfortunes of liberalism from a mid-century vantage point in Henry, *Fifty Years of Protestant Theology* (Boston: Wilde, 1950).

31. Henry, *Remaking the Modern Mind*, 26, 265. For an alternate list, see Henry, *The Protestant Dilemma*, 18–21.

32. Henry, *Confessions of a Theologian*, 402. See also his elaboration of this theme in Henry, *Christian Mindset in a Secular Society*, 9–25.

33. Henry, *Confessions of a Theologian*, 283. Henry, *Christian Mindset in a Secular Society*, 23. See also pp. 383, 388.

manity, who vouchsafes valid knowledge of the transempirical world, the modern Athenians are left to munch the husks of the religious vagabonds.[34]

His concern for the credibility of the evangelical witness in the modern world led Henry to the task of establishing the foundations of a truly apologetic theology in the modern context. His efforts to fulfill this calling were crowned by his *God, Revelation and Authority*, in which Henry lays out the methodological groundwork for evangelical theology. After setting forth the nature of theology in the opening volume, he turns his attention in volumes 2, 3, and 4 to a delineation of fifteen foundational theses about the divine revelation. These are followed in volumes 5 and 6 by a development of a largely classical orthodox approach to the doctrine of God. By placing revelation prior to the doctrine of God, Henry intended to make clear that whatever may be said about the being and attributes of God arises solely out of God's own self-disclosure as found in the Scriptures. In short, God is who God shows himself to be in the Bible.

His magnum opus marks a continuation of the concern that Henry displayed throughout all his writings, namely, to provide the foundations for an apologetic theology, one that shows the reasonableness of the Christian position in the midst of an increasingly irrational intellectual climate. He was convinced that only by returning to the classical emphasis on the reasonableness of the faith could we hope to experience a revitalization of theology in our day. This program marked Henry as a rationalist, of course, but he wore the label with pride. In fact, he told his co-religionists, "Evangelicals need not tremble and take to the hills whenever others charge us with rationalism."[35]

Revelation and Rationality

Henry's attempt to lay out the foundations for a truly valid apologetic theology found its genesis in the concept of revelation. He was convinced that the foundation for theology can only be the divine revelation of God as deposited in the Scriptures.[36]

Revelation was no stranger to the theological realm, of course, for it had become a focal point of nearly all theology in the twentieth century. What set Henry's approach apart was his understanding of the nature of revelation. For him, the reality of revelation means that God has both acted in history and spoken to humankind. However, God's speaking takes precedence over God's acting, for the divine word provides the rationale and meaning of the divine historical acts.[37] Moreover, in contrast to what he saw as a fallacy in

34. Henry, *Frontiers in Modern Theology*, 154–55.

35. Henry, *God, Revelation and Authority*, 3:480.

36. For an early statement of this theme, see Henry, *The Protestant Dilemma*, 225. See also Henry, *God, Revelation and Authority*, 1:222–23.

37. Henry, *The Protestant Dilemma*, 95–96, 217.

neo-orthodoxy, Henry asserted that this revelation is objective and hence available to human reason. Thus, Henry defined revelation as

> that activity of the supernatural God whereby he communicates informa-
> tion essential for man's present and future destiny. In revelation God, whose
> thoughts are not our thoughts, shares his mind; he communicates not only
> the truth about himself and his intentions, but also that concerning man's
> present plight and future prospects.[38]

As a good Calvinist, Henry accepted the Reformation doctrine of total depravity. But he denied that this meant that human reason was totally corrupted. On the contrary, reason is a divine gift possessed by Christians and non-Christians alike, and consequently the truth claims of Christianity are open to rational inquiry in much the same way as the claims of the natural or social sciences.[39]

Henry's goal in articulating a high view of reason and the rationality of revelation was to combat the irrationality and subjectivity he saw in much of modern theology. Thus, he asserted, "If a person must first be a Christian believer in order to grasp the truth of revelation, then meaning is subjective and incommunicable."[40] But Henry's position also aligned him with the scholastic tradition and set him at odds with the Pietist strand within the evangelical heritage. Undaunted, Henry announced in no uncertain terms that "the new birth is not prerequisite to a knowledge of the truth of God."[41]

Henry took the fall seriously, of course. But he averred that the will, and not reason, is the dimension of the human constitution most greatly affected by original sin. He offered this explanation: "Man wills not to know God in truth, and makes religious reflection serviceable to moral revolt. But he is still capable of intellectually analyzing rational evidence for the truth-value of assertions about God."[42] Whereas Christians quite rightly differentiate between a regenerate and an unregenerate will, the only appropriate parallel distinction in the realm of reason is that of valid and invalid thinking.

If revelation consists primarily of communicating information, then in Henry's estimation it is objective and propositional. In his magnum opus he went to great lengths to develop the thesis that "God's revelation is rational communication conveyed in intelligible ideas and meaningful

---

38. Henry, *God, Revelation and Authority*, 3:457.
39. Ibid., 1:233.
40. Ibid., 1:229.
41. Ibid.
42. Ibid., 1:226–27.

words, that is, in conceptual-verbal form."[43] He agreed with the modern emphasis on the functional, dynamic, and teleological dimensions of revelation, but argued that these cannot be separated from the propositional. For him, the reality that God has spoken means that the intellect plays an integral role in the revelatory process.[44] Revelation, in other words, is objective,[45] conceptual,[46] intelligible, and coherent.[47] Rather than being an escape from rationality, Christianity is oriented toward the intellect.[48]

The Divine Foundation for Rational Revelation

Henry's far-reaching thesis did not emerge in a theological vacuum. Behind the rational character of the Christian faith he found "the rational living God"[49] who "addresses man in his Word."[50] Hence, revelation is "rationally consistent and compelling," because "rationality has its very basis in the nature of the Living God."[51] Henry chided those theologians who omit the rational dimension, claiming that doing so leaves theology with "a stuttering deity, a transcendental self who roams about in a super-rational sphere not fully subject to the categories of thought."[52]

For Henry, the concept of the logos, understood as the mediating agent of the divine self-disclosure, forges the link between revelation and God.[53] This logos, the Word of God, comes from beyond the world, for it is "transcendentally given, and not immanent in man as a conception or abstraction achieved by human imagination or reflection."[54] Further, the God who approaches creatures through the logos, does so as the transcendent one. Reminiscent of Barth, Henry bemoaned the unfortunate loss of the focus on transcendence he saw in modern thought,[55] and he argued that the future fortunes of humankind were dependent on the regaining of a proper sense of the transcendence of God. But above all, the divine tran-

---

43. Ibid., 3:248–487.

44. Henry, *The Protestant Dilemma*, 97.

45. Henry, *God, Revelation and Authority*, 4:426.

46. Ibid., 3:173.

47. Henry, *The Protestant Dilemma*, 99.

48. Henry, *Remaking the Modern Mind*, 213.

49. Henry, *God, Revelation and Authority*, 1:244.

50. Ibid., 1:199.

51. Carl F. H. Henry, "The Fortunes of Theology," *Christianity Today* 6, no. 18 (June 9, 1972): 30.

52. Henry, *The Protestant Dilemma*, 115.

53. This theme forms thesis nine in Henry's magnum opus; Henry, *God, Revelation and Authority*, 3:164–247.

54. Ibid., 3:174.

55. E.g., Henry, *Remaking the Modern Mind*, 209–10; Henry, *The God Who Shows Himself*, 4.

scendence was vital for Henry because he was convinced that it is out of God's transcendence that God speaks to humankind.

The emphasis on the propositional dimension of revelation as arising out of the rational God who communicates rationally finds its counterpoint in Henry's anthropology. In keeping with the rationalist orientation of scholastic theology, Henry saw reason as the foundational dimension of the human person, a view, he claimed, that was universally held prior to the modern era.[56] Moreover, he found in the biblical concept of the image of God the anthropological linchpin for the phenomenon of divine revelation.[57] Henry argued that the *imago dei* includes not only a certain knowledge of God and ethical accountability, but also rational competence. Furthermore, this divine image remains present in some measure in every human being, despite the fall.[58] The rational God can communicate in a rational manner with humans because humans share the divine rationality.

Although Henry acknowledged the presence of the divine image in everyone, as well as the doctrinal importance of general revelation,[59] he rejected any attempt to construct a natural theology.[60] For him, true theology could be based only on the self-disclosure of God found in the Bible, for here alone can true knowledge of God be found. In this way, he set himself apart not only from the Thomist tradition, but also from the evangelical "evidentialists" who sought to ground Christian faith on arguments from reason and empirical evidence. Insofar as he based all theology solely on the presupposition of the truthfulness of the Bible,[61] Henry followed a "presuppositionalist" approach,[62] although neither slavishly nor without tipping his hat to the positive contribution evidentialists had made.

Henry's presuppositionalist leanings as an evangelical rationalist and biblicist led him to elevate the propositional character of Scripture. Following his mentor Gordon Clark, Henry held that the Bible is almost exclusively propositional in content.[63] That is, as the revelation of the God who communicates, the primary purpose of Scripture is to convey understandable truth, which means that biblical truth can be put in the form of propositional sentences. The purpose of theology, in turn, is to explicate

56. Henry, *Remaking the Modern Mind*, 247.

57. Henry, *God, Revelation and Authority*, 1:394.

58. Ibid., 1:405; 2:136.

59. Ibid., 2:83–85.

60. Ibid., 2:123.

61. Henry lays down the thesis that the Bible is the sole foundation for theology in Henry, *God, Revelation and Authority*, 1:181–409.

62. For a lengthier discussion of this label and its significance in Henry's thought, see Patterson, "Carl F. H. Henry," 58–83.

63. Henry, *God, Revelation and Authority*, 3:468.

in the form of axioms and theorems (i.e., propositions) the Bible's revelational content.[64] Henry brought revelation, reason, and Scripture together in what he set forth as his basic epistemological axiom:

> Divine revelation is the source of all truth, the truth of Christianity included; reason is the instrument for recognizing it; Scripture is its verifying principle; logical consistency is a negative test for truth and coherence a subordinate test. The task of Christian theology is to exhibit the content of biblical revelation as an orderly whole.[65]

Biblical Authority

If theology is the explication of revelation as disclosed in the Bible, then in Henry's estimation, the Bible is the central authority for theology. His emphasis on biblical authority placed him squarely in the center of the neo-evangelical movement. Like many of his colleagues, Henry decried "the compromise of the authority of the Bible" he discerned in mainline Protestantism. He was convinced that modern theology had surrendered "scriptural perspectives to modern critical speculations" and in so doing had called into question long cherished Christian commitments, including "historical and propositional revelation, plenary inspiration, and verbal inerrancy."[66] Henry's self-appointed task included setting forth a credible defense of these elements of the classical view of Scripture.

Henry focused attention on Scripture because he believed that it provided the foundation for the entire Christian worldview. He declared forthrightly, "The doctrine of the Bible controls all other doctrines of the Christian faith."[67] He feared that any diluting of the emphasis on biblical authority would remove the Bible as the authoritative voice in theology and endanger central Christian commitments, such as salvation by grace and even the authority of Jesus Christ, and it would lead to the undoing of crucial aspects of Christian anthropology and Christology.[68]

At the heart of Henry's delineation of biblical authority is the doctrine of inspiration. But the foundation for affirming that the Bible is inspired and authoritative lies in Henry's view of God. In his estimation, the Bible is the message of God, and the authoritative source of the biblical message "was, is and forever remains the transcendent God."[69] Henry even went

---

64. Ibid., 1:240–41.
65. Ibid., 1:215.
66. Henry, *Frontiers in Modern Theology*, 134–35.
67. Ibid., 138.
68. Ibid., 138–39. See also Henry, *The Protestant Dilemma*, 221–24.
69. Henry, *God, Revelation and Authority*, 6:51.

so far as to assert that the question about biblical authority is, in the final analysis, not about the Bible at all but about God. In his mind, the conclusion is inescapable: "If one believes in a sovereign divine mind and will, in God who personally speaks and conveys information and instruction, then the presuppositions of scriptural inspiration lie near at hand."[70]

According to Henry, biblical authority means that the Bible is divinely inspired, and this in turn leads inevitably to the conclusion that Scripture is inerrant.[71] Hence, he saw these two crucial dimensions of the fundamentalist doctrine of Scripture—inspiration and inerrancy—as intimately related. For Henry, the genesis of inspiration is the superintending work of the Holy Spirit on the authors of Scripture, which results in an inspired text. Thus, he declares that inspiration is "a supernatural influence upon divinely chosen prophets and apostles whereby the Spirit of God assures the truth and trustworthiness of their oral and written proclamation."[72] As this statement indicates, Henry saw the doctrine of inspiration as asserting that God is the ultimate author of Scripture, with the result that the Bible is God's revelation. Further, the divine truth inheres "in the propositions or sentences of the Bible, and not merely in the concepts and thoughts of the writers," for the Bible "inscripturates divinely revealed truth in verbal form."[73] As a result, although inspiration begins with the Spirit's work upon the authors of Scripture, for Henry it in fact becomes "primarily a statement about God's relationship to the Scripture, and only secondarily about the relationship of God to the writers."[74]

Henry was convinced that the divine authorship of the Bible leads logically to inerrancy. Because God is the author of Scripture, the divine revelation in the Bible is free from error. In Henry's terse words, "the Holy Spirit superintended the scriptural writers in communicating the biblical message . . . safeguarding them from error."[75] In offering this thoroughly deductive argument for inerrancy, Henry was merely traveling more consistently the direction Warfield had charted over a half century earlier.

Although Henry affirmed the standard Warfield-inspired inerrancy position that the earlier fundamentalists appropriated, he distanced himself from intellectually suspect positions that some in the movement were taking. Hence, he was quick to reject any suggestion that the Bible was the

70. Ibid., 3:428.
71. Henry set forth his understanding of inspiration, inerrancy, and infallibility in ibid., 4:103–219.
72. Ibid., 4:129.
73. Ibid.
74. Ibid., 4:143.
75. Ibid., 4:166–67.

product of divine dictation.[76] Nor did inerrancy imply modern technical precision or exactitude in New Testament quotations from the Old.[77]

The most controversial divergence[78] came in his refusal, shared by some neo-evangelicals including Kenneth Kantzer,[79] to go along with those of his colleagues (especially Harold Lindsell[80]) who sought to make adherence to inerrancy a test of evangelical authenticity.[81] Henry's reluctance was due in part to his fear that doing so would sidetrack evangelicals from their true calling. In the midst of the often heated debate of the 1970s, he declared in his usual forthright tone,

> The somewhat reactionary elevation of inerrancy as the superbadge of evangelical orthodoxy deploys energies to this controversy that evangelicals might better apply to producing comprehensive theological and philosophical works so desperately needed in a time of national and civilizational crisis.[82]

For Henry, issues such as revelation and culture, hermeneutics, and propositional revelation were at least as important as inerrancy.

In addition to this pragmatic reason, Henry's reticence arose from theological grounds. He criticized his opponents for making inerrancy the first claim to be made for the Bible, thereby effectively elevating it above the more foundational concepts of authority and inspiration,[83] in contrast to the nineteenth-century Princeton theologians who began with biblical authority, moved to biblical inspiration, and then deduced inerrancy from the Bible's testimony to its inspiration. Taking his cue from the Princetonians, Henry denied that the Bible directly teaches its own inerrancy, arguing instead that inerrancy is a logical implication of the divine inspi-

---

76. Ibid., 4:138.

77. For Henry's discussion of what inerrancy does and does not imply, see ibid., 4:201–10.

78. For an illuminating summary of the issues involved in this controversy, see Gary Dorrien, *The Remaking of Evangelical Theology* (Louisville: Westminster John Knox, 1998), 118–23.

79. Kantzer declared, "Inerrancy, the most sensitive of all issues to be dealt with in the years immediately ahead, should not be made a test for Christian fellowship in the body of Christ." Kenneth S. Kantzer, "Evangelicals and the Inerrancy Question," in *Evangelical Roots: A Tribute to Wilbur Smith*, ed. Kenneth S. Kantzer (New York: Thomas Nelson, 1978), 89.

80. See especially, Harold Lindsell, *The Battle for the Bible* (Grand Rapids: Zondervan, 1976); *The Bible in the Balance* (Grand Rapids: Zondervan, 1979).

81. This point is noted by Mohler, "Carl Ferdinand Howard Henry," 528, who cites Henry's discussion of the issues in Carl F. H. Henry, *Conversations with Carl Henry: Christianity for Today* (Lewiston, N.Y.: Edwin Mellon, 1986), 23–30.

82. Carl F. H. Henry, "Reaction and Realignment," *Christianity Today* 20, no. 20 (July 2, 1976): 30.

83. See, for example, the interview with Carl Henry, "The Concerns and Considerations of Carl F. H. Henry," *Christianity Today* 25, no. 5 (March 13, 1981): 19.

ration of Scripture.[84] This suggests that those who wished to make inerrancy a test for evangelical orthodoxy were elevating to creedal status a doctrinal statement that the Bible itself does not explicitly affirm.

Henry and the Shaping of Evangelical Theology

Henry's work on behalf of the neo-evangelical movement arose from his conviction that theology had taken a wrong turn at an earlier fork in the road. He believed that only by returning to that point and once again reaffirming the older, orthodox conception of the transcendent God who discloses himself in the Bible can the crisis in modern theology be overcome. Henry was likewise convinced that divine revelation is primarily the communication of information. Because its primary author is God, this communication is coherent, entirely true, and within the grasp of humans, who are made in the divine image.

While the scope and interconnectedness of Henry's program is breathtaking, in a sense, Henry's goal was actually quite modest. His task was not to set forth a complete apologetical theology. He merely desired to lay down the epistemological and methodological foundation upon which other evangelicals could construct a solid theological system. Because the divine communication is ultimately rational, being the disclosing of knowledge from a rational God to rational humans, this foundation and the theological edifice it facilitated needed to be intellectually credible.

Henry scholar and devotee, R. Albert Mohler, concedes the existence of a "great divide between those who define evangelicalism primarily by a set of theological commitments and those who point instead to an evangelical faith experience and concern for personal holiness." Mohler sees Henry standing squarely on one side of this divide. He offers his evaluation cautiously but starkly: "Henry has evidenced a concern for both dimensions, but has given the cognitive dimension primary attention in his writings."[85]

In this observation Mohler is surely correct. Henry never lost sight of his own conversion experience. And he truly desired that evangelicals would be a gospel people, that is a people who both articulate and live the good news of God's power to transform individuals and society. Yet he was convinced that the evangelical message would never gain a hearing in the modern world unless it could stand the test of intellectual scrutiny and therefore that the key to making the evangelical message credible in the modern world lay in the ability of evangelicals to engage intellectually with the modern worldview. In the process of carving out the space in which his co-religionists could do their work, Henry gave wings to the

84. For this point, Lindsell, *Bible in the Balance*, 35.
85. Mohler, "Carl F. H. Henry," 538 n. 47.

scholastic impulse and the focus on right doctrine as the defining mark of essential Christianity, emphases that post-fundamentalist evangelicals inherited from seventeenth-century Protestant orthodoxy via the nineteenth-century Princetonians and the fundamentalist movement. In this sense, Henry was instrumental in the triumph of the formal principle of evangelicalism over the material, leading to a transformation of the latter from its original focus on the gospel message itself to a particular understanding of the essential doctrines of the Bible.

Moreover, Henry accomplished this transformation in a particular manner. In his fervor to set out the foundations for a credible apologetic theology, he introduced into the still fluid goo of the emerging neo-evangelical theology a thoroughgoing rationalism together with a thoroughgoing propositionalism. Henry's theological method would be emulated and the theological project he envisioned continued by others who possessed greater or lesser measures of the spirit of charity that characterized the founding lights of the neo-evangelical movement, and which they hoped would characterize their followers.

Henry's contribution to the shape of neo-evangelical theology came in another form as well. His writings reveal a gifted thinker who embodied the post-fundamentalist neo-evangelical concern for a bold engagement with modern culture as well as with the theological innovations of the twentieth century. Yet in his encounter with the wider context, Henry was a cautious discussion partner. Throughout his career he was consistently critical of impulses from beyond the evangelical tradition and retained a reticence to incorporate them into his articulation of evangelical theology. He was especially suspicious of any potential contribution that modern theology might make, voicing sharp criticism of various attempts, from Karl Barth[86] to narrative theology,[87] to reformulate the Christian faith in the context of the contemporary situation. In this manner, Henry illustrated the tendency among many neo-evangelicals to see the new evangelical movement as merely a replication in the modern context of the grand tradition of Protestant orthodoxy and to see themselves primarily as guardians of the tradition and apologists for the faith as they had

---

86. His criticisms of Barth were set forth in a series of articles published in *Christianity Today*: Carl F. H. Henry, "Between Barth and Bultmann," *Christianity Today* 5, no. 6 (May 8, 1961): 24–26; "The Deterioration of Barth's Defenses," *Christianity Today* 9, no. 1 (October 9, 1964): 16–19; "The Pale Ghost of Barth," *Christianity Today* 15, no. 10 (February 12, 1971): 40–43; "Wintertime in European Theology," *Christianity Today* 5, no. 5 (December 5, 1960): 12–14. Henry described an encounter with Barth at George Washington University in Henry, *Confessions of a Theologian*, 210–11. An appraisal of Henry's rejection of Barth is presented in R. Albert Mohler, "Evangelical Theology and Karl Barth: Representative Models of Response" (Ph.D. diss., Southern Baptist Theological Seminary, 1989), 107–34.

87. E.g., Carl F. H. Henry, "Narrative Theology: An Evangelical Appraisal," *Trinity Journal* 8 (1987): 3–19.

received it. Convinced that evangelicals are the contemporary trustees of the "faith once delivered," they, following in Henry's footsteps, willingly enter into dialogue with their context not so much to learn from it, as much as to point out the shortcomings of all other options and the superiority of their own supposedly orthodox convictions.

Bernard Ramm (1916-1992): Apologetic Theology in Dialogue with Modern Culture

Like Carl Henry, Bernard Ramm took up Ockenga's challenge to "infiltrate, not separate," which he, like Henry, interpreted as calling for engagement with the intellectual dimensions of modern culture. Whereas Henry envisioned the development of an apologetic theology that could provide an alternative to the modern worldview, Ramm saw his role as bringing a biblical, and hence evangelical, theology into conversation with human knowledge, which in the modern intellectual context meant the realm of science.

Ramm's pilgrimage was sparked by what he perceived as the inability of his fundamentalist roots to bear the insights that he discovered through his engagement with science and the scientific method. Consequently, his interaction with modern learning eventually led him away from what he came to see as the overly cautious stance—"obscuranticism," to use his word—that characterized fundamentalism.[88] And it suggested to him the way in which an apologetic post-fundamentalist evangelical theology might engage in constructive dialogue with modern culture.

Evidentialist Apologist to Modern Scientific Culture

The juxtaposing of science and conversion that occurred during Ramm's young adulthood placed him in an appropriate position to take up the challenge of relating theology to scientific knowledge. Raised in a small mining and college city in Montana, Ramm was interested in science from early youth and assumed that he would grow up to become a scientist. But his vocational goals changed during the summer prior to entering university, in that "the gospel came to him,"[89] resulting in an instantaneous, life-transforming conversion experience.[90]

88. See Bernard L. Ramm, "Are We Obscurantists?" *Christianity Today* 1, no. 10 (February 18, 1957): 14.

89. Bernard L. Ramm, *The God Who Makes a Difference: A Christian Appeal to Reason* (Waco: Word, 1972), 16.

90. Bernard L. Ramm, *Protestant Christian Evidences: A Textbook of the Evidences of the Truthfulness of the Christian Faith for Conservative Protestants* (Chicago: Moody, 1953), 220–21.

After completing university studies (1938), Ramm entered the B.D. program at Eastern Baptist Theological Seminary, a school initially founded to carry the conservative banner among the academic institutions sponsored by the Northern Baptist Convention. After two short pastorates on the West Coast (1942–1944)[91] and a one-year teaching appointment at the Los Angeles Baptist Theological Seminary (1943–1944), he took a post as head of the Department of Philosophy and Apologetics at the fundamentalist-oriented Bible Institute of Los Angeles (Biola). During his tenure at Biola, he completed his formal education in philosophy of science at the University of Southern California (M.A. 1947, Ph.D. 1950). The bent toward apologetics that typified the new evangelical movement and that would initially determine his scholarly contribution emerged in his doctoral dissertation, "An Investigation of Some Recent Efforts to Justify Metaphysical Statements from Science with Special Reference to Physics."[92]

Degree in hand, Ramm left Biola and returned to the Baptists for the educational contexts in which he carried out his teaching vocation: Bethel College and Seminary (1951–1954), Baylor University (1954–1959), the American Baptist Seminary of the West (formerly the California Baptist Theological Seminary, 1959–1974), Eastern Baptist Seminary (1974–1977), and ABSW once again (1978–1986). This institutional trajectory was symbolic of his own theological pilgrimage from the fundamentalism that typified Biola in the 1940s to the open posture of ABSW (which participates in the Graduate Theological Union at Berkeley).

Evidentialist Apologetics

Early in his career, Ramm's interest in reconciling Christian faith with human knowledge, especially science, followed a typically neo-evangelical path, namely, the apologetical trail. Rather than affirming the presuppositionalism espoused by Van Til and Henry, however, Ramm pursued evidentialism, the other major approach that neo-evangelicals were exploring. This strategy looked for observable or verifiable data (Ramm called them "facts") that offered evidences for the truth of the Christian faith. Ramm tackled the topic in his initial three writing ventures.[93]

In the first two volumes, *Problems in Christian Apologetics* and *Types of Apologetic Systems*, Ramm surveyed the major methodological options found in the Christian tradition. This sketch leads to the conclusion that a

91. See Wilbur M. Smith, "Preface," in *Protestant Biblical Interpretation: A Textbook for Conservative Protestants*, by Bernard L. Ramm (Boston: Wilde, 1950), xvi–xvii.

92. See Bernard L. Ramm, *The Christian View of Science and Scripture* (Grand Rapids: Eerdmans, 1954), 8.

93. Bernard L. Ramm, *Problems in Christian Apologetics* (Portland, Ore.: Western Baptist Theological Seminary, 1949); Bernard L. Ramm, *Types of Apologetic Systems: An Introductory*

proper apologetic must be based on revelation, that is, on the divine self-disclosure "in creation, in the nature of man, in the history of Israel and the Church, in the pages of Holy Scripture, in the incarnation of God in Christ, and in the heart of the believer by the gospel."[94] Only this approach, Ramm claimed, constitutes historic Christianity, in contrast to modernism or Protestant liberalism, and leads to a defensible statement of the faith.

In the third installment, *Protestant Christian Evidences*, Ramm delineated his own proposal for such an apologetic, which he directed toward critically thinking Christians and persons outside the faith "who still have enough flexibility in their mentality to hear a case on its own merit."[95] In this volume he distinguished between "apologetics" and "evidences." "Apologetics" consists of the verification of the Christian system of belief, i.e., "the strategy of setting forth the truthfulness of the Christian faith and its right to the claim of the knowledge of God."[96] "Evidences" constitutes the subdivision of this discipline that has as its goal "the demonstration of the *factuality* of the Christian religion."[97] Believing that this factuality, this relationship between Christianity and reality, could in fact be demonstrated, Ramm harnessed such traditional evidences as fulfilled biblical prophecy and biblical miracles, Jesus' character and resurrection, and Christian experience. These, he argued, together with the Bible's perennial ability "to grip profoundly the human soul,"[98] work together to witness to the divine inspiration of the Bible, so that the supernatural character of the Bible forms the final verification of Christianity.[99]

Scripture and Science

Ramm's evidentialism, coupled with his longstanding interest in science, brought him to focus on one particular dimension of the apologetic task, the exploration of the interface of the Bible and modern scientific knowledge. His proposal, embodied in *The Christian View of Science and Scripture*, catapulted him into the evangelical limelight.

Study to the Christian Philosophy of Religion (Wheaton: Van Kampen, 1953), subsequently revised as *Varieties of Christian Apologetics* (Grand Rapids: Baker, 1961); Bernard L. Ramm, *Protestant Christian Evidences: A Textbook of the Evidences of the Truthfulness of the Christian Faith for Conservative Protestants* (Chicago: Moody, 1953).

94. Ramm, *Protestant Christian Evidences*, 33.
95. Ibid., 7.
96. Ramm, *Varieties of Christian Apologetics*, 13.
97. Ramm, *Protestant Christian Evidences*, 13.
98. Ibid., 224.
99. Ibid., 249.

In this work, Ramm offered a critique of the fundamentalist approach, which in his estimation pitted Christianity against scientific findings. This "ignoble tradition," he remarked, "has taken a most unwholesome attitude toward science, and has used arguments and procedures not in the better traditions of established scholarship."[100] Ramm's goal was "to call evangelicalism back to the noble tradition,"[101] which views God as the author of both creation and redemption, and therefore engages in dialogue under the assumption that true science and the Bible were in agreement.[102] Ramm claimed that this tradition had enjoyed ascendancy in the closing years of the nineteenth century, but had been buried by "a narrow bibliolatry" that had arisen as "the product not of faith but of fear."[103]

While finding apologetical value in such attempts at demonstrating the harmony between Scripture and science, he viewed them as only a precursor to faith. In the book's concluding comments he characterized the apologetical value of his labors:

> We have tried to show that no man of science has a proper reason for not becoming a Christian on the grounds of his science. We have tried to show the inoffensive character of the Biblical statements about Nature; the relevance of so much of Biblical truth to fact; and the credibility of the miraculous. We have not tried to force a man to Christ by these chapters, but if a man is a Christian, a scientist cannot question on scientific grounds the respectability of that man's faith.[104]

Hence, by showing "the correlation of Christianity with *material fact*,"[105] *The Christian View of Science and the Bible* provided an interaction with one of the three types of facts pursued by Christian evidentialists[106] that Ramm had set forth in his earlier textbook on apologetics.

Already in 1950, in *Protestant Biblical Interpretation*,[107] Ramm had spelled out the hermeneutic that in turn yielded his conclusions in *The Christian View of Science and Scripture*. In the earlier work he had called for "a full-fledged, intelligent Biblicism," claiming that it alone "is adequate to

100. Ramm, *Christian View of Science and Scripture*, 8.
101. Ibid., 9.
102. See, for example, ibid., 25–29.
103. Ibid., 9.
104. Ibid., 245.
105. Ibid., 29–30. See also 43, 169, 238, 244.
106. Ramm, *Protestant Christian Evidences*, 17–25.
107. Bernard L. Ramm, *Protestant Biblical Interpretation: A Textbook for Conservative Protestants* (Boston: Wilde, 1950). This book went through two revisions, the third edition being published by Baker in 1972. See also Bernard L. Ramm, "Biblical Interpretation," in *Hermeneutics* (Grand Rapids: Baker, 1971), 5–28.

the present day situation in science, philosophy, psychology, and religion."[108] Yet, the "biblicism" Ramm had in mind did not involve only traditional Protestant hermeneutical assumptions such as the clarity of Scripture, but also the principle that revelation is accommodated, i.e., that Scripture has an "anthropomorphic character" that the exegete must acknowledge.[109]

Despite the wide reception of Ramm's text on hermeneutics, *The Christian View of Science and Scripture* unleashed a firestorm.[110] Convinced that the langauge of the Bible was popular and phenomenal rather than scientific (in the strict sense), Ramm went beyond simply harmonizing Scripture with science to assert that the Bible contained culturally conditioned statements and that the biblical writers were not teachers of science in the modern sense. On this basis, Ramm allowed for such possibilities as a local flood, a figurative "long day of Joshua," an ancient earth, and even theistic evolution (although he preferred the term "progressive creation").[111] Fundamentalists accused Ramm of having gone too far down the accommodationist road, while liberals chided him for failing to follow his accommodationist instincts to their logical conclusions.[112]

The Turn to Theology

The ruckus that greeted *The Christian View of Science and Scripture* foreshadowed things to come. Ramm's passion for engagement as a Christian apologist with modern scientifically oriented knowledge would lead him toward new vistas, but his proposals would be controversial, especially within some sectors of his neo-evangelical constituency. More importantly, at this stage of his career Ramm began a long process through which he came to look upon theology itself, rather than the search for evidences, as the vehicle for engagement with modern scientific culture.

---

108. Bernard L. Ramm, *Protestant Biblical Interpretation*, 3d ed. (Grand Rapids: Baker, 1972), 95.

109. Ibid., 99–101. See also Bernard L. Ramm, *Special Revelation and the Word of God* (Grand Rapids: Eerdmans, 1961), 33, 36–40, 74.

110. The controversial nature of the book was noted already in 1957. See E. C. Rust's review in *Review and Expositor* 54 (January 1957): 130.

111. Ramm, *The Christian View of Science and Scripture*, 76–78.

112. See, for example, the review by Francis I. Andersen in *Reformed Theological Review* 14 (1955): 92–93. Even some evangelicals did not think Ramm had provided a sufficiently innovative proposal, as is evident in the review by D. R. Denman in *Evangelical Quarterly* 27 (Oct.–Dec. 1955): 225–26. For later reflections on the controversy, see George Marsden, *Reforming Fundamentalism: Fuller Seminary and the New Evangelicalism* (Grand Rapids: Eerdmans, 1987), 158; James Barr, *Fundamentalism* (Philadelphia: Westminster, 1977), 94–98, 244–47.

Biblical Authority

As the 1950s were drawing to a close, Ramm turned his attention to questions surrounding Scripture and authority.[113] Rather than marking a shift away from apologetics, however, his pursuit of these questions was motivated by his overarching apologetical concern for the demonstration of the truth of the Christian faith.[114]

Ramm's intent was to chart a middle course[115] between the subjectivism he saw in liberalism's emphasis on religious experience as the final authority[116] and the authoritarianism that characterized fundamentalism. To facilitate this, he located ultimate authority in divine revelation, which, he declared, in the final analysis is Christ. He also sought to maintain a balance between the inspired Scripture and the illumined reader, that is, between the outer and the inner, the objective and the subjective dimensions.[117] In this, Ramm claimed the mantle of the Reformation[118] and the Protestant principle of authority that emerged in the sixteenth century, which he defined as "the Holy Spirit speaking in the Scriptures which are the product of the Spirit's revelatory and inspiring action."[119]

According to Ramm, the primary principle of authority—God in his own self-disclosure—produces the immediate principle of authority—the Spirit speaking in the Scriptures.[120] As a result, final authority lies neither in the book itself, nor in the Spirit, but in the revelation (Jesus Christ) to which the Bible witnesses as the Spirit effects illumination.[121] This means that the New Testament is authoritative because it is the apostolic witness to the revelation of God in Christ.[122]

---

113. This interest is evident in a series of three volumes published in rapid succession: Bernard L. Ramm, *The Pattern of Authority* (Grand Rapids: Eerdmans, 1957), reprinted as *The Pattern of Religious Authority* (Grand Rapids: Eerdmans, 1959); Bernard L. Ramm, *The Witness of the Spirit: An Essay in the Contemporary Relevance of the Internal Witness of the Holy Spirit* (Grand Rapids: Eerdmans, 1959); and Bernard L. Ramm, *Special Revelation and the Word of God* (Grand Rapids: Eerdmans, 1961).

114. In his final treatment of apologetics, Ramm cites the three volumes devoted to the doctrine of revelation as also related to this topic; *The God Who Makes a Difference*, 11.

115. Ramm, *The Pattern of Religious Authority*, 18.

116. Ibid., 73–84.

117. E.g., Ramm, *Witness of the Spirit*, 33.

118. For Ramm's fullest treatment of the Reformation heritage on the nature of authority, see ibid., 11–27.

119. Ramm, *Pattern of Religious Authority*, 28.

120. Ibid., 38.

121. Ibid., 36; Ramm, *Witness of the Spirit*, 62–65. In fact, the internal witness of the Spirit can be operative in situations where there is no written word, such as through sermon, song, or Christian literature. Ramm, *Witness of the Spirit*, 98–99.

122. Ramm, *Pattern of Religious Authority*, 54.

Ramm did not deny the doctrine of inspiration, but rather made it subservient to revelation. In his understanding, the function of inspiration is to preserve revelation in a trustworthy and sufficient form.[123] For Ramm, however, the inspired product is not simply the actual words of the Bible; inspiration relates to units of meaning, not isolated words (contra Henry).[124] Hence, Ramm distinguished between the external form (the words of the original documents in their original languages) and the internal form (the inspired meaning of the text, which is in the final analysis the Word of God).[125]

His interpretation of the Reformation understanding led Ramm to reject both liberalism and fundamentalism,[126] but the latter was the special target of his critique. In his estimation, fundamentalists had become so concerned to defend the inspiration of Scripture that they had lost track of the more comprehensive Reformation doctrine of revelation and thereby failed to understand that "inspiration lives on revelation and not vice versa."[127] Similarly, the fundamentalists had neglected the instrumental character of Scripture, that is, its role as the document the Spirit uses in enlightening the believing reader.[128] They had equated "the Word" with the Bible, thereby giving Scripture a life of its own independent of the Spirit.[129]

Above all, despite their stated abhorrence for accommodation in any form, the fundamentalists had sought to enlist "the mighty voice of science" on behalf of orthodoxy and in the process had "let the spirit of science permeate their apologetic." Hence, they sought to defend Christianity through scientifically verifiable proofs, proofs for God's existence, for Jesus' resurrection, but above all for the Bible's inspiration.[130] The result, in Ramm's estimation, was theologically disastrous, for it destroyed the Reformation doctrine of Scripture. No longer was Scripture seen as self-authenticating.[131] And no longer was the *testimonium spiritus* necessary.

During the 1970s debate over inerrancy, Ramm's approach to the question of authority resulted in his taking a position that was quite different from Lindsell's. Ramm affirmed "inerrancy,"[132] but he viewed it as a broad, nonrestrictive category and felt that debates about it "pay no

123. Ramm, *Special Revelation and the Word of God*, 176.
124. Ibid., 177.
125. Ibid., 196.
126. Ramm, *Witness of the Spirit*, 124–27.
127. Ibid., 124.
128. Ramm, *Special Revelation and the Word of God*, 120.
129. Ramm, *Witness of the Spirit*, 125.
130. Ibid., 126.
131. Ibid., 107.
132. See Ramm, *Protestant Biblical Interpretation*, 3d ed., 201–14.

great dividends."[133] And he differed categorically with those neo-evangelicals who claimed that their understanding of the doctrine of Scripture was integral to the essence of Christianity.[134] For him, the "first line of defense" was neither a particular doctrine of inspiration nor even Scripture itself, but the content of Scripture, Jesus Christ.[135] Already in 1961 he cautioned: "The temptation of biblicism is that it can speak of the inspiration of the Scriptures *apart from* the Lord they enshrine. . . . There can be no formal doctrine of inspiration; there can be only a Christ-centered doctrine of inspiration."[136]

Beyond Evidentialism

Ramm's reflections on the issue of authority led him to rethink his approach to apologetics. As early as 1958 he appeared to be moving toward a course correction. In an essay entitled "The Evidence of Prophecy and Miracle," he sought to combat the mistaken suggestion that evidences alone are able to stir the heart.[137] Appropriating the differentiation between "the inner and outer witness" that dates to Augustine and Calvin, Ramm argued that the inner work of the Spirit and evidences such as fulfilled prophecy and miracles work together to assure the Christian of the validity of belief. He explained,

> The fulfilled promise of a prophetic word, the miraculous act of an apostle, are part of the divine *indicia* which inform the believing heart that the religion he holds within his heart by reason of the witness of the Spirit in the Word exists also in the world (prior to his personal experience) by the supernatural acts of the Living God.[138]

Ramm's journey beyond evidentialism reached its climax in *The God Who Makes a Difference*, written nineteen years after his trilogy on apologetics. Ramm had come to realize that "individual facts, no matter how many of them, do not constitute effective knowledge."[139] As a result, he

133. Bernard L. Ramm, "Welcome Green-Grass Evangelicals," *Eternity* 25 (March 1974): 13. See also "Is 'Scripture Alone' the Essence of Christianity?" in *Biblical Authority*, ed. Jack Rogers (Waco: Word, 1977), 107–23.

134. See "Is 'Scripture Alone' the Essence of Christianity?" in *Biblical Authority*, 122–23.

135. See Bernard L. Ramm, *An Evangelical Christology: Ecumenic and Historic* (Nashville: Thomas Nelson, 1985), 202.

136. Ramm, *Special Revelation and the Word of God*, 117.

137. Ramm soon revised his appeal to prophecy and miracles; Bernard L. Ramm, "The Evidence of Prophecy and Miracles," in *Revelation and the Bible*, ed. Carl F. H. Henry (Grand Rapids: Eerdmans, 1958), 253–63.

138. Ibid., 263.

139. Ramm, *God Who Makes a Difference*, 32.

now spoke of Christianity (specifically the Reformed faith as its best expression) as a postulate or hypothesis. And he recast the evidences he had compiled in his earlier works around three concentric circles: the persuasion of the Holy Spirit, God's action in creation and history, and a "synoptic vision" of humankind, the world, and God.

Again building from the differentiation between the inner and outer witness, Ramm differentiated between "certitude" and "certainty." He acknowledged that Scripture and the internal witness of the Spirit may give a believer "full spiritual certitude" about the great truths of personal salvation.[140] But Ramm quickly added that the historical dimension of the Christian faith can never be known with certainty, only with a high degree of probability. He wrote, "The Christian apologist then says that spiritually, inwardly, convictionally he rests his faith in full certitude; in reference to the objective historical, factual, etc., basis of the Christian revelation, he believes with a high degree of probability."[141] In Ramm's estimation, the error of the fundamentalists came at precisely this point; they erroneously sought rational religious certainty for the history narrated by the Bible.[142]

Acknowledging Barth

This conclusion indicates how far Ramm had moved away from evidentialism, a shift precipitated by his encounter with Augustine, the Reformers, and finally Karl Barth. Ramm had come to agree with Barth's dictum (which he claimed Barth drew from Luther and Calvin) that "if something external to the Word of God is necessary to establish the Word of God as true, then it is greater than the Word of God."[143] But Ramm's move beyond evidentialism also marked the climax of a shift in his evaluation of Barth, which was perhaps the greatest development in Ramm's thinking.[144]

At the beginning of his career, Ramm joined the neo-evangelical chorus that dismissed the Swiss theologian. In 1953, for example, he declared in no uncertain terms, "The Christ of atheism, of liberalism, and of Barthianism is not the Christ of the historical documents."[145] However, a time

---

140. Ibid., 73. For the background of this certainty as inherent in the concept of the *testimonium,* see Ramm, *Witness of the Spirit,* 1959, 84–87.

141. Ramm, *God Who Makes a Difference,* 73.

142. Ramm, *Special Revelation and the Word of God,* 99.

143. Bernard L. Ramm, *After Fundamentalism* (San Francisco: Harper and Row, 1983), 61.

144. For a summary of Ramm's encounter with Barth, see R. Albert Mohler, "Bernard Ramm: Karl Barth and the Future of American Evangelicalism," in *Perspectives on Theology in the Contemporary World: Essays in Honor of Bernard L. Ramm,* ed. Stanley J. Grenz (Macon, Ga.: Mercer University Press, 1990), 29–37.

145. Ramm, *Protestant Christian Evidences,* 180.

of study in Basel during the academic year 1957–1958 inaugurated a slow mellowing in Ramm's stance.[146] In 1971 he concluded his article on "Biblical Interpretation" with a mixed review of Barth, declaring that his "particular exegesis" may be questioned, "but his notion of exegesis" is sound.[147] One year later, he could acknowledge Barth's influence on his own thinking in the area of apologetics.[148] Then in his highly controversial book *After Fundamentalism* (1983),[149] Ramm expressed appreciation for Barth's theological method as well, an influence evident already in Ramm's trilogy on authority published in the late 1950s and early 1960s.

In an essay published three years later, Ramm outlined in more concrete terms the particular insights he had gleaned from Barth. First, Barth had shown him "the futility and intellectual bankruptcy" of the defensive and suspicious posture he had inherited from fundamentalism, and had demonstrated how "[I] could be just as free a person in theology as I would be if I were an experimental scientist."[150] In addition, Barth had given him a sense of the importance of historical theology for contemporary theological work.[151]

Above all, however, in "the manner in which he correlated the critical study of Scripture with the inspiration and authority of Scripture,"[152] Barth had helped Ramm overcome his earlier bias against critical studies. Barth had convinced him that "the way a portion of Holy Scripture came to be written or composed does not invalidate it as the Word of God."[153] The basis for this lay in Barth's insight that there is a disjuncture, "indirect identity" or *distasis* between the Word and the words of Scripture. Following Barth, Ramm argued that because of the accommodation of the Word to the languages and cultures in which it was given, "there is not a one-to-one corre-

---

146. For Ramm's own account of the influence of Barth on his thinking, see Bernard Ramm, "Helps from Karl Barth," in *How Karl Barth Changed My Mind*, ed. Donald K. McKim (Grand Rapids: Eerdmans, 1986), 121–25.

147. Bernard Ramm, "Biblical Interpretation," in *Hermeneutics*, 28.

148. Ramm, *The God Who Makes a Difference*, 12.

149. Ramm's book, which was both lauded and lambasted, triggered a vigorous debate among evangelicals. The importance of this debate is evident in that *Christianity Today* published parallel (albeit somewhat bland) reviews of the book by Robert K. Johnston and Donald Bloesch under the heading "After Fundamentalism: The Future of Evangelical Theology," *Christianity Today* 27 (December 16, 1983): 54–56.

Significant reviews of the book included those by Donald T. Williams, *Journal of the Evangelical Theological Society* 26 (June 1983): 201–4; James Daane, *Reformed Journal* 33, no. 5 (May 1983): 26–27; Gordon H. Clark, *Fundamentalist Journal* 2 (June 1983): 52–53. Important as well were review essays including Fred Klooster, "Barth and the Future of Evangelical Theology," *Westminster Theological Journal* 47, no. 2 (Fall 1985): 301–17; Ed L. Miller, "Is Barth the Future of Evangelical Theology? *Christian Scholars' Review* 14, no. 1 (1985): 46–51.

150. Ramm, "Helps from Karl Barth," 121.

151. Ibid., 122–23.

152. Ibid., 123.

153. Ibid., 125.

lation between the Word of God as it originates in the mind of God and the expression of that Word in the Old and New Testaments."[154]

In *After Fundamentalism* Ramm drew from this third Barthian insight to challenge both fundamentalism and many of his colleagues in the neo-evangelical movement. By acknowledging no *distasis* between the Word and Scripture, Ramm declared, post-fundamentalist evangelicals committed themselves to propositionalism, and thereby unwittingly fell prey to the modern philosophical dream of discovering a pure conceptual language that could serve as the perfect language of truth. Ramm chided his colleagues pointedly and forcefully: "It is amazing how the current evangelical stress on propositional revelation is but an alternate version of this Hegelian theory of a pure conceptual language."[155] Further, by denying the *distasis*, Ramm's colleagues were by necessity committing themselves to a thoroughgoing, strict, and ultimately indefensible view of inerrancy. "If there is no interval between the Word of God and the words of Scripture," Ramm quipped, "then not one trace of an old world view can be allowed to stand in the text, for that would be approving an error." He was convinced that their basically fundamentalist doctrine of Scripture meant that "the accuracy of every biblical statement must be defended down to the last decimal point."[156]

The three material influences Ramm outlined in his essay on Barth do not yet indicate the central reason that Ramm felt himself drawn to the Swiss theologian. The ultimate reason lies simply in Ramm's growing sense that in Barth he had discovered a kindred spirit. Barth was doing exactly what Ramm had himself set out to do. And Barth provided a model or method for accomplishing the task Ramm had inherited as a neo-evangelical.

Ramm's life's passion was the pursuit of Christian theology in the aftermath of the Enlightenment. He sought to take seriously the radical changes this era of human intellectual history had produced. In fact, he believed that the dividing line between evangelicalism and fundamentalism ran through the Enlightenment. "Fundamentalism," he asserted, "attempts to shield itself from the Enlightenment," whereas "the evangelical believes that the Enlightenment cannot be undone."[157] At the same time, Ramm found in classical Christianity the fundamental truth for life. Consequently, the challenge he had accepted was that of demonstrating how Christians can be intellectually responsible in the face of the Enlightenment without making the concessions characteristic of liberalism nor resorting to the hyperrationalism prevalent in fundamentalism.

154. Ibid., 124.
155. Ramm, *After Fundamentalism*, 90.
156. Ibid., 91.
157. Bernard L. Ramm, *The Evangelical Heritage* (Waco: Word, 1973), 70.

Finding no satisfactory answers in the fundamentalism of his earlier years, Ramm's concern to set forth credible theology in the wake of the Enlightenment eventually led him to look for help in other theological circles. Indeed, on one occasion, he cautioned his colleagues to avoid accepting "trashy theology, substandard by all academic criteria, as evangelical, and to brand as nonevangelical some great biblical theology."[158] Ramm found the help he was seeking in Karl Barth, whose theology offered him a model of theological engagement with modern culture. As Ramm put it, *"Barth's theology is a restatement of Reformed theology written in the aftermath of the Enlightenment but not capitulating to it."*[159]

Constructive Theology

Once Ramm "went public" with his long-standing indebtedness to Barth, he turned his sights toward constructive theology. As a result, his final two volumes deal with two core Christian doctrines, sin and Christ, which he addressed through the use of a basically Barthian mode of thinking, albeit one that was already anticipated in his widely read volume, *Special Revelation and the Word of God*. In that book, Ramm declared that the theological task must be pursued with a view toward both its possibilities and its limits.

Theology is possible, Ramm declared optimistically, because it is related to the knowledge of God that arises out of God's self-disclosure. As a result, he drew a crucial connection between theology and divine revelation. Although admitting that "the theologian does not treat God *in himself*, but God *in his revelation*,"[160] Ramm nevertheless asserted that theology leads to a certain knowledge of God. The task of the theologian, he declared, is to set out the genesis and structure of God's ectypical revelation which God has given humankind in special revelation.[161] God's ectypical revelation is "that segment of the archetypal knowledge of God [i.e., God's self-knowledge] which God wishes man to know."[162]

At the same time, however, Ramm knew the limits of theology. Theology's limits arise from both divine incomprehensibility and human sinfulness. Because God is incomprehensible, he declared, humans simply cannot adequately conceive of God or properly describe God.[163] If humans are to know God, God must condescend to them. This is precisely what God does in revelation, choosing thereby to impart to humans partial knowledge of God's own reality.

---

158. Ramm, "Is 'Scripture Alone' the Essence of Christianity?" 115.
159. Ramm, *After Fundamentalism*, 14; emphasis his.
160. Ramm, *Special Revelation and the Word of God*, 14.
161. Ibid., 17.
162. Ibid., 141, 145.
163. Ibid., 21.

According to Ramm, human sinfulness likewise places limits on theological engagement. Cognizant of this, he spoke of the necessity for a degree of pessimism in evangelicalism, that ought to arise out of its "inherent serious doctrine of sin." This doctrine, he added, means that "the evangelical believes in amelioration (things may be made better) but not in utopia (things may be made perfect)."[164] Yet, given the choice of elevating sin or human possibility, Ramm preferred the latter. In this sense, he reflects the Calvinist emphasis on the doctrine of creation as mediated to him by Abraham Kuyper, who asserted that the entrance of sin did not negate completely God's original purpose for humankind.[165]

Although Ramm turned away from apologetics as such in 1972, he never left behind his interest in the apologetic task, but retained that dimension even when writing constructive theology. In fact, he had come to see that constructive theology was in a sense apologetic by its very nature. Hence, in *Offense to Reason* (1985) Ramm presents his theology of sin in dialogue with modern understandings of the human phenomenon. Despite its offensive nature or apparent unreasonableness, the doctrine of sin is not a parochial Christian teaching, Ramm maintains, but a human reality with which many scholarly disciplines wrestle. For this reason, he adds, this doctrine is necessary for a true and complete understanding of human existence in the world.

In his constructive writings, Ramm likewise continues the dialogue with science that occupied his attention throughout his career. For example, in *Offense to Reason* he takes up the question of human origins that he handled earlier in *The Christian View of Science and Scripture*. And although his conclusions are somewhat different, he still advocates the mediating position he charted in the 1950s, albeit one that emphasizes more strongly the *theological*, rather than the purely *historical*, character of the biblical narrative. Hence, he refers to Genesis 1–3 as "divinely inspired reconstruction" and "theology by narration,"[166] that is, Hebrew reflection on creation and on the nature and origin of sin expressed through the telling of a story.[167] In short, Ramm remained convinced that the Bible and science are both correct, when each is viewed in its proper perspective.

Ramm and the Development of Evangelical Theology

Ramm and Carl Henry shared many characteristics. Above all, they agreed on the apologetical task of evangelical theology. And both were

---

164. Ramm, *The Evangelical Heritage*, 135.

165. Bernard Ramm, *The Christian College in the Twentieth Century* (Grand Rapids: Eerdmans, 1963), 78.

166. Bernard L. Ramm, *Offense to Reason* (San Francisco: Harper and Row, 1985), 68–69.

167. Ibid., 72.

convinced that this task demanded that evangelical theologians move out of the intellectual ghetto fundamentalism had created so as to engage the modern world with a credible presentation of the truth of the Christian faith. Nevertheless, Ramm and Henry soon diverged.

This divergence began in their approaches to the apologetic task. Henry was basically a presuppositionalist who concluded that evidentialism provided a means to avoid the subjectivism to which pure presuppositionalism readily led. Ramm, in contrast, began as an evidentialist, but later concluded in a manner somewhat akin to presuppositionalism that the divine Word is self-authenticating.

This development in Ramm's thinking carried far-reaching theological implications. His discovery of the self-authenticating character of the Word opened Ramm's eyes to see that the great error of fundamentalism lay in its self-assured rationalism, which blinded its practitioners to the limits of theology. According to Ramm, rationalistic fundamentalism "reads the revelation of God as a transcript without mystery."[168] Ramm, in contrast, sought to move evangelical theology beyond rationalism, which he feared held it captive, and restore to it a profound sense of the mystery of revelation. In his words, "The mystery and wonder of grace is that the transcendent God has willed to reveal himself. The incomprehensible God has spoken and in this speaking we understand that he is incomprehensible."[169]

Ramm shared with Henry the typical evangelical methodological assumption that theology is built from the self-disclosure of God to sinful creatures. Yet Ramm differed with many neo-evangelicals in that he believed that the divine revelation was not in competition with the best of modern learning but that the two coalesced. For this reason, he was able to gain an appreciation for the positive contributions of the Enlightenment and thereby to move beyond the cautious stance of Henry (whom Ramm eventually viewed as a type of throwback to an earlier, even pre-Enlightenment era in theological history).[170] By turning his face toward modern thinking, in particular toward contemporary scientific advances and non-evangelical theologies, Ramm laid the foundation for younger evangelical thinkers to engage in positive dialogue with modern culture. Ramm modeled an evangelicalism that could remain convinced that the hallmarks of the evangelical movement from the Reformation through fundamentalism capture the core of the faith while engaging with the modern context, not only to bear witness to the truth but also to learn from other traditions and viewpoints.

168. Ramm, *Special Revelation and the Word of God*, 23–24.
169. Ibid., 24.
170. Ramm, *After Fundamentalism*, 26–27.

R. Albert Mohler once described Ramm's life as one of the "paradig-matic models of evangelical development."[171] That is, Ramm epitomizes a journey charted by many neo-evangelicals who have moved out of a nar-row and defensive type of fundamentalism into what has been termed "a learned and thoughtful evangelicalism." Wesley Brown, former president of the American Baptist Seminary of the West, offered his appraisal of Ramm's influence in this regard:

> Part of Bernard Ramm's great appeal has been his ability to express the Chris-tian faith and relate to contemporary issues with theological competence and intellectual integrity. Far too often evangelicals have been viewed as anti-intellectual, as lacking historical perspective, or as failing to understand the struggles of the scientific community when talking of matters of faith. Bernard Ramm dispelled those stereotypes for many young Christians, who found in his writing and speaking that they did not need to close their minds nor sac-rifice their integrity when thinking and talking about their faith.[172]

In short, more than the actual theological positions he advocated, Ramm's contribution to evangelical theology resided in the spirit he evi-denced. Perhaps more than any other of the original card-carrying evan-gelical theologians, Ramm epitomized the irenic side of evangelicalism.[173]

171. Mohler, "Bernard Ramm," 26.

172. Wesley H. Brown, "Bernard Ramm: An Appreciation," in *Perspectives on Theology in the Contemporary World*, 6.

173. Ramm's irenic tone is exemplified in *The Devil, Seven Wormwoods and God* (Waco: Word, 1977), in which he points out what evangelicals can learn from seven modern think-ers who are generally "bad-mouthed" as the devil's "hacks."

four

The Expansion
OF Neo-Evangelical
Theology

In many respects, Carl Henry and Bernard Ramm epitomize the first generation of "card-carrying" evangelical theologians. Moreover, they passed to their theological heirs a legacy of intellectual engagement worthy of emulation. Both sought to move beyond fundamentalism while retaining orthodox belief, and thereby to rejuvenate the evangelical tradition. Although Henry and Ramm shared a common starting point, they trod different paths to this common goal. In so doing, they set the stage for the development of a divergence within neo-evangelical theology that became starkly evident among the second generation theologians.

The growing theological divergence that emerged in neo-evangelical theology during the final third of the twentieth century is exemplified in the careers of two thinkers who were a mere fifteen and ten years old respectively when Carl Henry published *The Uneasy Conscious of Modern Fundamentalism*: Millard Erickson and Clark Pinnock. Yet these two later emerged as arguably the most influential theologians of the second generation.[1] Indeed, of the "next generation" of neo-evangelical theologians

---

1. It might be argued that insofar as Pinnock has to date not set forth a systematic theology, another thinker might better serve as counterpoint to Erickson. On the strength of his seven-volume *Theology of Word and Spirit*, Donald Bloesch looms as a likely candidate. However, in contrast to Bloesch, Pinnock grew up within the neo-evangelical coalition, while Bloesch came to it from a Reformed perspective.

none has been greeted with more widespread acceptance than Erickson, and none has stirred up more controversy than Pinnock.

It has grown customary to invoke the proverbial idea of midgets standing upon the shoulders of giants when speaking about the second generation. In the case of neo-evangelical theology, however, the proverb is of only limited validity. As epitomized by Erickson and Pinnock, the second generation has had the distinct advantage of building upon the foundational work of the pioneers, who by necessity devoted their major energies to the task of getting the movement off the ground. Being the beneficiaries of the labors of their forebears, Erickson and Pinnock were able to expand upon the neo-evangelical theological deposit they received from thinkers like Henry and Ramm through a literary output that exceeded that of the first generation in depth as well as quantity.

Millard Erickson (1932–): From Ramm's Student to Henry's Successor

Perhaps the clearest statement of theology that follows Henry's basically rationalist program came from neither Erickson nor Pinnock but from veteran Denver Seminary theologian Gordon Lewis, together with his younger colleague Bruce Demarest. Their efforts were crystalized in the massive and impressive three-volume *Integrative Theology* (1987–1994),[2] which is noted for a rationalist, scientifically oriented theological method that tests theological hypotheses to determine which explain the greatest amount of relevant biblical data.

Although *Integrative Theology* may in fact exemplify more faithfully Henry's own theological method, the mantle of theological leadership and influence that Henry wore so competently appears to have fallen on another member of the second generation of neo-evangelicals, Millard Erickson. Erickson's three-volume *Christian Theology* (1983–1985, revised 1998), which has served as the textbook of choice for an impressive number of evangelical seminaries, catapulted its author into the theological limelight and won him a large following among evangelicals, especially in North America but also worldwide. The stature that *Christian Theology* has afforded Erickson is evident in David Dockery's 1990 citation of him as "the most outstanding writing theologian in the evangelical world."[3]

2. Gordon R. Lewis and Bruce A. Demarest, *Integrative Theology*, 3 vols. (Grand Rapids: Zondervan, 1987–1994).
3. David S. Dockery, "Millard J. Erickson," in *Baptist Theologians*, ed. Timothy George and David S. Dockery (Nashville: Broadman, 1990), 640.

The Making of a Neo-Evangelical Theologian

Millard Erickson was raised in a pious Swedish Baptist family on a Minnesota farm. He was converted as a youth through "an unemotional experience"[4] in the country church that had been organized in the family house and where his grandfather had served as lay pastor for five years. Following what for him was an especially significant chapel message at Bethel College where he was a first-year student, Erickson concluded that God was calling him to preach. In order to gain exposure to secular thought, particularly philosophy, psychology, and sociology, Erickson transferred to the University of Minnesota after his second year at Bethel, graduating in 1953. He then returned to Bethel Seminary, where he encountered Bernard Ramm and, through him, the work of other prominent neo-evangelicals. But rather than staying at his denomination's school, Erickson transferred to Northern Baptist Theological Seminary in Chicago (where Carl Henry had been a student and had briefly taught a decade earlier), completing the B.D. in 1956. A pastorate and a master's degree in philosophy at the University of Chicago (1958) followed. Then Erickson moved on to Ph.D. work at Garrett Theological Seminary and Northwestern University. There he studied under the supervision of the Lutheran neo-orthodox theologian, William Hordern, completing the work while serving as the pastor of a church in Minneapolis.

Erickson's academic career began in 1964. His credentials as a neo-evangelical landed him an appointment at Wheaton College as professor of Bible and apologetics. Five years later he returned to his denominational roots, taking a teaching post in theology at Bethel Seminary, where he eventually became academic dean. Since leaving Bethel in February 1992, Erickson has taught at several Baptist seminaries, including Southwestern (Ft. Worth), Western (Portland), and Truett (Waco). Throughout his teaching career, Erickson has remained active in church leadership, including several interim pastor positions in a variety of congregations. His commitment to his own denomination, which has been more evident than in many other neo-evangelical leaders,[5] has been expressed through his work over the years in the Baptist World Alliance.

The Promise of the New Evangelical Theology

The theological program that Erickson set forth early in his career was typically neo-evangelical, in that it was deeply apologetic in orientation. In fact,

---

4. Ibid., 642.
5. See Warren C. Young, "Review of *The New Evangelicals,*" *Foundations* 12 (January 1969): 95–96.

throughout his life, his goal has been to relate Christian belief to contemporary thinking and thereby carve out a theology that is both biblical and relevant.

Erickson's concern for the relevancy of theology arose initially out of his early experiences in the pastorate in Chicago and Minneapolis, where he was, in the words of David Dockery, "challenged to relate the Christian message to both the urban intellectual and the blue-collar worker."[6] At this formative stage in his theological development, Erickson derived assistance from Paul Tillich's method of correlation.[7] But above all, sitting under Ramm at Bethel Seminary had deeply affected the young Swedish Baptist. Through Ramm, Erickson had come under the tutelage of the theological leaders of the neo-evangelical movement, including Carl Henry and Edward J. Carnell. They, in turn, became the topic of his doctoral dissertation at Northwestern. And his first book, *The New Evangelical Theology*,[8] was an exposition of, and to a large degree an apologetic for, neo-evangelicalism. Although not the first exemplar of the new genre of evangelical theological literature,[9] it was widely and positively received.

The Gains of the New Evangelical Theology

In 1968, Erickson saw great promise in the new evangelical theology. In keeping with the goals of the founders of the movement, he asserted that neo-evangelical theology "has sought to state the Christian faith in an intellectually respectable fashion. It has endeavored to heal the schism between the theological right and left, at least to the point where meaningful theological dialogue could be pursued."[10] As his first literary endeavor indicates, Erickson saw his life's mission as participating in this apologetic task.[11]

Erickson began his study with the typical neo-evangelical rendition of the rise of the movement. The story begins with the degeneration of fundamentalism: "Because fundamentalism found itself under attack, it developed a defensive mentality. A harsh and uncharitable spirit came to predominate. . . . Within its own ranks, internal suspicion and bickering over minor points of doctrine increased." The result was disastrous: "From

6. David S. Dockery, "Millard J. Erickson: Theologian for the Church," in *New Dimensions in Evangelical Thought: Essays in Honor of Millard J. Erickson*, ed. David S. Dockery (Downers Grove, Ill.: InterVarsity, 1998), 19.

7. Dockery, "Erickson: Theologian for the Church," 19.

8. Erickson completed his dissertation in 1963. His first published book was a revision of his doctoral thesis. See Millard J. Erickson, *The New Evangelical Theology* (Westwood, N.J.: Revell, 1968).

9. Erickson's book was preceded five years earlier by a quite similar treatment. See Ronald H. Nash, *The New Evangelicalism* (Grand Rapids: Zondervan, 1963).

10. Erickson, *New Evangelical Theology*, 218.

11. See S. Heavenor, "Review of *The New Evangelical Theology*," *Scottish Journal of Theology* 24 (August 1971): 355–57.

a movement of genuine scholarship, positive statement, and a certain latitude of evangelical position, fundamentalism came to be increasingly a negative, defensive, and reactionary movement with a narrowing of its theological options."[12] Out of this malaise the new evangelicalism was born. This rebirth came through the efforts of a group of "well-trained young scholars" who were "determined to state the evangelical position competently, avoiding the errors into which fundamentalism had fallen."[13] The advent of the neo-evangelical movement, Erickson adds, marked "a new development in the history of American Christianity."[14]

After recounting its genesis in the degeneration of fundamentalism, Erickson describes the chief characteristics of the new evangelical theology. He notes that it is based on the fundamental conviction that "God Himself is the authority in belief and conduct." More particularly, evangelical theology arises out of the self-manifestation of God, in general revelation but also and primarily in special revelation,[15] which leads to a "genuine knowledge of God" that includes information about God.[16]

According to Erickson, the new evangelicals agree that because human sin distorts the revelation of God in nature, the primary datum for knowledge of God is biblical revelation, not philosophical evidences which can only be secondary and supportive.[17] Although God's special revelation is a past occurrence, this revelation has been preserved through inspiration, which Erickson describes as the supernatural influence of the Spirit in the writing of Scripture that renders the writings "an accurate record of the revelation" so that what the biblical writers composed "was actually the Word of God."[18] Erickson notes that the new evangelicals appeal to both the Bible's teaching about its own inspiration and to evidences that its claim about itself is true. But then, citing Ramm as the chief example, he adds that rather than looking to such evidences, the neo-evangelical conviction that the Bible is the Word of God stems from the internal testimony of the Spirit. Inspiration by an omniscient, omnipotent, and truthful God, in turn, guarantees an inerrant Bible. In Erickson's words, "while the Bible does not itself explicitly claim freedom from error, this is a corollary, or an implication, of its view of inspiration."[19]

---

12. Erickson, *New Evangelical Theology,* 29.

13. Ibid., 45.

14. Ibid., 31.

15. Ibid., 48.

16. Ibid., 56.

17. Ibid., 88–89.

18. Ibid., 57.

19. Ibid., 74. Erickson's characterization of the new evangelical theology on this important point is in keeping with Nash's similar description; Nash, *New Evangelicalism,* 76.

The theory of inspiration Erickson saw in the new evangelicalism in 1968 acknowledged the role of culture and accommodation, and, by extension, the metaphorical nature of theology. He asserts, "When God describes Himself in His revelation, He speaks of himself not as He is in Himself, but as we conceive of Him." Consequently, revelation comes through ordinary human language, and therefore it "actually takes place *through* the culture" connected to the languages of the original autographs of Scripture.[20] Hence the new evangelicals are convinced that "the Bible bears the impress of its culture upon it. Revealed truth came through the culture of its day and must be interpreted within that context."[21] As a result, revelation is analogical: "God selects those elements, or factors, from our realm of experience which bear a resemblance to the truth about Himself. While they are not perfect replicas of God, they are nonetheless adequate reproductions."[22] This leads the new evangelicals to a functional view of Scripture. Erickson writes, "The Bible is not an end in itself. Its value is instrumental: It is intended to bring the reader into a certain relationship with the God who stands behind it."[23]

In *The New Evangelical Theology*, Erickson notes the apologetic orientation of his mentors. He suggests that their approach is largely presuppositionalist in orientation; that is, it builds from the assumption of "the existence of a God who has revealed Himself, particularly in the Scriptures."[24] But the neo-evangelicals also acknowledge that a case can be made for the truth of Christianity:

> The evangelical theologians say that, since man must have an understanding of the universe about him in order to live meaningfully, Christianity can be shown to be true if it can be demonstrated that it gives a more complete and consistent explanation of our universe than any other competitive system, and if it satisfies the need of the human heart.[25]

This outlook leads the new evangelicals to a positive outlook toward modern knowledge, especially the findings of science. In summarizing the general characteristics of the new theology, Erickson notes, "There can never be any conflict between the Bible, properly interpreted, and natural knowledge, correctly construed."[26] The neo-evangelical conception of general revelation, Erickson adds, "produces a positive attitude toward culture." It is here, Erickson concludes, that his mentors diverge significantly from their fundamentalist co-religionists: "Whereas fundamental-

20. Erickson, *New Evangelical Theology*, 52.
21. Ibid., 201.
22. Ibid., 52.
23. Ibid., 82.
24. Ibid., 131.
25. Ibid., 136.
26. Ibid., 200.

ism had been rather culture-rejecting, the new evangelicalism is culture-affirming. Although the truth and its expression may be distorted as a result of sin, it is nonetheless to be found in various places."[27]

Going beyond the Fathers

In 1968, Erickson was clearly enamored with his neo-evangelical mentors and saw great promise in the movement. Nevertheless, he concluded that the new evangelical theology had its weaknesses. The drawbacks he perceived had less to do with glaring errors in the theological program itself than with the failure of his mentors to take their insights far enough.

For example, Erickson voiced the opinion that neo-evangelical theologians had not as of yet "completely solved the issue of inerrancy." What above all drew his ire was their "tendency toward elasticity of the word." Carnell came under special censure. Erickson chided the neo-evangelical leader in no uncertain terms:

> One sometimes gets the impression, in reading Carnell's *Case* book, for instance, that he has sought at all lengths to preserve the word "inerrancy," but has so redefined it as almost to have lost the original meaning. The possible usage which he suggests seems particularly weak and subject to criticism. If inspiration simply guarantees an inerrant copying of what may be an erroneous source, inerrancy would be refuted only if the original source were available and discrepancy of the Biblical record from it could be established. The practical significance of the doctrine seems to have been lost.[28]

Erickson also complained that the neo-evangelical thinkers had failed to keep up-to-date with recent scientific research. He cites as one example their inability to take seriously new findings in psychology and sociology. Erickson writes, "The sovereignty of God and the freedom of man ought to be related to recent research in the behavioral sciences." He then underscores the importance of keeping up with the times: "While the doctrines of the new evangelicals are not basically different from those held by the early fundamentalists, the intellectual milieu is quite different. Relating the timeless truths to yesterday's problems will not be adequate."[29]

The most glaring weakness Erickson noted in 1968, however, was the lack of a systematic presentation of orthodox doctrine. In this aspect, the young critic gave his mentors the benefit of the doubt. He excused their "sin of omission" because he realized that to date neo-evangelical thinkers had "primarily

---

27. Ibid.
28. Ibid., 223. For Carnell's discussion, see Edward John Carnell, *The Case for Orthodox Theology* (Philadelphia: Westminster, 1959), 99–111.
29. Erickson, *New Evangelical Theology*, 224.

dealt with certain problem areas, rather than constituting a complete systematic theology." Nevertheless, he called for action on this front, claiming that "there is a pressing need for an up-to-date conservative systematic theology text."[30] Apparently the recently published treatise, *A Systematic Theology of the Christian Religion* (1962) written by former Wheaton College president J. Oliver Buswell, was not what the young professor had in mind. In any case, fourteen years later Erickson set out to correct this perceived oversight.

Erickson's initial literary production suggests that at this stage in his career he was truly the student of Bernard Ramm. Like his mentor, he was eager to push the neo-evangelical theological agenda forward. Like Ramm, Erickson seemed to favor a positive engagement with modern knowledge in a manner that would not only offer critique but also gain insight from contemporary impulses beyond the pale of evangelicalism. Like Ramm he also seemed to favor ongoing reflection on the doctrine of inspiration that could result in the delineation of a more intellectually credible understanding of biblical inerrancy.

Solidifying the New Evangelical Theology

In the 1970s, Erickson contributed to the neo-evangelical cause in several ways, the most significant of which was perhaps the trilogy of primary sources in doctrine he edited, *Readings in Christian Theology*.[31] But his lasting contribution was not to lie in his work as a collector of the writings of others but in his own constructive theological proposal. His three-volume *Christian Theology* would expand the work of his forebears and serve to solidify the shape of the emerging neo-evangelical theology.

Erickson began the monumental project in June 1982 and composed it at a phenomenal speed. Drafting a chapter per week, he completed the initial volume by the end of November. The manuscript of volume two followed during the ten-week winter quarter at Bethel. A sabbatical leave occasioned the writing of the third volume, and the next year was devoted to revising volumes two and three. In the meantime, the first installment appeared, and its initial reception boded well for the success of the entire project, upon which Erickson had expended four thousand hours of diligent effort.[32]

The Content of a Neo-Evangelical Theology

In the opening chapter of *Christian Theology*, Erickson engages with the question of the nature of theology. He relates the discipline to the dimen-

30. Ibid., 85.

31. Millard J. Erickson, ed., *Readings in Christian Theology*, 3 vols. (Grand Rapids: Baker, 1973–1979). The volumes are entitled: *The Living God* (1973), *Man's Need and God's Gift* (1976), and *The New Life* (1979).

32. Dockery, "Erickson: Theologian for the Church," 20.

sion of discipleship that involves "holding the beliefs that Jesus held and taught." The particular concern of Christian theology is "the study of these beliefs," so that its central task becomes "examining, interpreting, and organizing the teachings of the one from whom this religion takes its name."[33] Because theology involves reflection on the practice of the Christian religion, "theology is a second-level activity."[34] On this basis, Erickson offers a composite definition. Theology, he writes, is "that discipline which strives to give a coherent statement of the doctrines of the Christian faith, based primarily upon the Scriptures, placed in the context of culture in general, worded in a contemporary idiom, and related to issues of life."[35] What follows is some twelve hundred pages delineating Erickson's understanding of this coherent statement.

In many respects, Erickson's theology is a systematic statement of the beliefs and emphases that had characterized the neo-evangelical movement from its beginnings in fundamentalism. He restates what he calls "classical orthodoxy"[36] in dialogue with modern currents in theology, philosophy, and science, as well as challenges from those on his theological right. For example, Erickson offers what is a largely traditional understanding of the divine "constancy" in the context of what he sees as the errors of process theology.[37] Then in the anthropology section, conservative "young earth" proponents become his target, as Erickson follows Ramm in arguing for progressive creationism.[38] Likewise, the early post-fundamentalist concern for a social ethic finds its theological foundation in Erickson's articulation of the universality of humankind, and emerges in his discussion of the social dimensions of sin.[39] Although not specifically developed in the three-volume work,[40] Erickson's anthropology results in an egalitarianism on issues of gender and church leadership that has allowed him to serve on the board of reference for Christians for Biblical Equality.

Christian Theology also displays Erickson's generally irenic, "generic" neo-evangelicalism. The moderate Calvinism that typified the original card-carrying evangelicals is evident throughout the three volumes. This mild Calvinism allows Erickson to take Arminianism seriously, and even to break ranks with his co-religionists by suggesting that in the *ordo salutis* conversion occurs before regeneration.[41] Likewise, Erickson shows himself to be a true

33. Millard J. Erickson, *Christian Theology* (Grand Rapids: Baker, 1983), 1:20.
34. Ibid., 1:21.
35. Ibid.
36. Ibid., 1:13.
37. Ibid., 1:278–81.
38. Ibid., 1:380–82.
39. Ibid., 2:641–58.
40. Erickson does offer an indication of where his sympathies lie; see ibid., 2:548–49.
41. Ibid., 3:932.

neo-evangelical when dealing with the thorny issues surrounding ecclesiology. Despite his clear preference for congregational polity, he refuses to throw stones at other traditions, insofar as "the evidence from the New Testament is inconclusive."[42] As a neo-evangelical, one of Erickson's ecclesiological interests is the promotion of a true evangelical church unity in the face of the ecumenical movement, on the one hand, and the separatism that characterizes fundamentalism and leads to schism, on the other.[43]

The Method of a Neo-Evangelical Theology

In David Dockery's estimation, Erickson's major contributions lie in "the creative construction of his theological method and his doctrine of revelation."[44] In fact, these matters comprise a lengthy two hundred fifty-nine-page prolegomenon to the original edition of the work (expanded to two hundred eighty-five pages in the revised edition).

In response to the question of the beginning point for a systematic theology, Erickson opts for a basically presuppositionalist approach. However, following the legacy of his theological mentors, especially Ramm, his approach presupposes "the self-revealing God," whose revelation is found above all in Scripture. Erickson then concludes, "From this basic postulate we may proceed to elaborate an entire theological system by unfolding the contents of the Scriptures."[45] In this statement, Erickson sets the basically propositionalist tone that characterizes the entire work. He further suggests that Scripture itself, as the focus of the divine self-disclosure, will be the unifying theme of his systematic theology, though he later identifies "the magnificence of God" as his integrative motif.[46]

Erickson offers a nine-step process for charting a systematic theology. At the heart of this process is the task of distinguishing "the permanent, unvarying content of the doctrine from the cultural vehicle in which it is expressed," so that the "abiding truth" can then be clothed in a form appropriate to the contemporary context. This procedure involves a method of correlation that Erickson acknowledges is deeply indebted to Paul Tillich.[47]

His acceptance of Ramm's starting point leads Erickson immediately to the concept of revelation, out of which in turn will emerge the doctrine of God,

---

42. Ibid., 3:1084.

43. Ibid., 3:1129–46. See also Millard J. Erickson, "Separation," in *Evangelical Dictionary of Theology*, ed. Walter A. Elwell (Grand Rapids: Baker, 1984), 1002–3.

44. Dockery, "Erickson: Theologian for the Church," 31.

45. Erickson, *Christian Theology*, 1:33.

46. Ibid., 1:78. See also his disclaimer in Erickson, *Christian Theology*, revised edition, 82 n. 24. Although Erickson claims that God's magnificence functions as the "'soft' integrative motif" of this theology, the index of the revised edition contains only one reference to the term.

47. Erickson, *Christian Theology*, 1:71, 73, 74–75.

in a manner reminiscent of Henry's program in *God, Revelation and Authority*. Deepening several themes he saw in the new evangelical theology in 1968, Erickson divides God's self-disclosure into two aspects, general revelation and special revelation, which, he adds, can ultimately never be in conflict. This presumed harmony lies behind Erickson's stated positive outlook toward culture. In fact, he goes so far as to assert that general revelation makes possible some knowledge of divine truth beyond the realm of special revelation.[48]

While not denying that special revelation is also personal, Erickson focuses on its propositional dimension,[49] which leads to the Bible as the locus of inscripturated revelation and more importantly to the discussion of inspiration. Following Henry, Erickson accepts the Warfield-inspired approach that looks to the Bible's teaching about itself as the basis for the doctrine, but he nevertheless believes the phenomena of Scripture provide a secondary consideration.[50] Basically, divine inspiration involved God directing the thoughts of the writers of Scripture so that they were precisely the thoughts God wanted expressed. The Spirit's activity extended even to the exact choice of words, a process that Erickson suggests was "not greatly unlike mental telepathy."[51] This divine action assures that the Bible is truthful, trustworthy, and accurate. And in creating this book, Erickson adds, God has delegated his authority to the Bible, which is the Word of God,[52] so that "the Bible carries the same weight God himself would command if he were speaking to us personally."[53]

The theological term for the Bible's truthfulness is inerrancy. Flowing out of his 1968 characterization of the new evangelical theology and in keeping with Henry's position, Erickson contends that inerrancy is not directly taught in Scripture, but that it nevertheless arises out of the Bible's teaching about itself. He offers this definition of the term: "The Bible, when correctly interpreted in the light of the level to which culture and the means of communication had developed at the time it was written and in view of the purposes for which it was given, is fully truthful in all that it affirms."[54]

Although in typical neo-evangelical fashion Erickson argues for inerrancy in a basically deductive manner, he still desires to take the phenomena of Scripture seriously. Doing so, however, leads him into a minefield that Carnell and other neo-evangelical pioneers had likewise encountered. Erickson protects the concept of inerrancy by limiting its extent to

48. Ibid., 1:173.
49. Ibid., 1:196.
50. Ibid., 1:208–9.
51. Ibid., 1:218.
52. Ibid., 1:199.
53. Ibid., 1:246.
54. Ibid., 1:233–34.

what the Bible actually affirms or asserts in contrast to what it merely reports. And he extends this principle, which he finds articulated (albeit not directly affirmed) in Carnell, to encompass even "certain statements of godly men who were not speaking under the inspiration of the Holy Spirit."[55]

As an example of this principle, Erickson accounts for the inaccuracy of the chronological statement Stephen made before the Jewish officials (Acts 7:6) by suggesting that the early martyr "may not have been inspired, although he was filled with the Holy Spirit."[56] In other words, all that the doctrine of inerrancy guarantees in this case is that Luke gave an inerrant report of the content of Stephen's apparently errant speech. Erickson then suggests that the same principle can be applied to Jude's use of the apocryphal books Enoch and Assumption of Moses.

Erickson's delineation of inerrancy is perhaps the finest expression of the Warfield/post-fundamentalist understanding of the doctrine found anywhere. Yet these examples suggest that in 1983 Erickson was not able to rectify fully the problem in the neo-evangelical concept of inerrancy that he had so insightfully flagged in 1968. Now cast in the role of the systematizer and solidifier of neo-evangelical theology, Erickson ends up not only appropriating but also expanding the very principle that he had fifteen years earlier chided Carnell for invoking, when the young professor had accused that neo-evangelical pioneer of straining to preserve the word "inerrancy" but losing the practical significance of the doctrine.[57]

Henry's Successor

With his major theological project completed, Erickson was able to devote his energies to exploring in greater detail several theological topics that he had always wanted to tackle.[58] This interest resulted in a series of works devoted to such theological topics as Christology,[59] the Trinity,[60] and the doctrine of God.[61] The positive reception evangelicals gave to these books, together with *Christian Theology*'s widening reception, propelled Erickson into the theological leadership of the movement. As a result, he increasingly found himself cast in the role of "elder statesman" and defender of neo-evangelical theological orthodoxy, or

55. Ibid., 1:234.
56. Ibid.
57. Erickson, *New Evangelical Theology*, 223.
58. See, for example, his statement to this effect in Millard J. Erickson, *God the Father Almighty: A Contemporary Exploration of the Divine Attributes* (Grand Rapids: Baker, 1998), 9–10.
59. Millard J. Erickson, *The Word Became Flesh* (Grand Rapids: Baker, 1991).
60. Millard J. Erickson, *God in Three Persons: A Contemporary Interpretation of the Trinity* (Grand Rapids: Baker, 1995).
61. Erickson, *God the Father Almighty*.

orthodoxy as he had come to understand it. In assuming this role, he completed his journey from Ramm's student to Henry's successor.

A Change in Loyalty

Erickson's positive relationship to Ramm reached its zenith with the publication in 1983 of the initial installment of *Christian Theology*. Erickson dedicated the book to Ramm, singling Ramm out as "my first theology professor." In the subsequent two volumes Erickson paid his respects to his doctoral mentor William Hordern and his postdoctoral mentor Wolfhart Pannenberg.[62] Soon, however, Ramm began to fall into disfavor. By 1997 Erickson cast his former professor with those thinkers who comprised a new and, in his estimation, theologically dangerous development within evangelicalism, the so-called postconservative movement. Erickson characterized this movement somewhat erroneously and in an oversimplified manner as "the evangelical left."

In *The Evangelical Left*, Ramm comes under Erickson's scrutiny. Erickson notes that his mentor was at one time "a staunch defender of the received or traditional conservative doctrines"[63] as well as a proponent of "a propositional view of revelation as the communication of divine truth."[64] Erickson then summarizes Ramm's conversion to Barth's theological method as recounted in *After Fundamentalism*. This conversion led to what Erickson describes as Ramm's "rather remarkable recommendation"[65] that evangelicals consider Barth's potential contribution to a constructive theology in the wake of the Enlightenment, a development that Erickson had flagged already in 1993.[66]

And yet, Erickson does not directly dismiss his old teacher. Rather, he concludes his treatment of Ramm by criticizing him for only one fault, namely, for not being sufficiently explicit:

> What is amazing about Ramm's adoption and defense of Barth's methodology is that he never, in this reader's judgment, tells us just what that method is. . . . Thus, one is left wondering, at the end, how to apply Barth's method, rather than simply accepting the results of that method.[67]

62. Actually, in the first edition the dedication to Pannenberg in volume three does not explicitly mention this connection but reads, "whose theological scholarship has been an inspiration to me." In the revised edition (1998), Erickson changed the reference, in part perhaps to keep the symmetry with the other two characterizations in the composite dedication.

63. Millard J. Erickson, *The Evangelical Left: Encountering Postconservative Evangelical Theology* (Grand Rapids: Baker, 1997), 33.

64. Ibid., 34.

65. Ibid., 35.

66. Millard J. Erickson, *The Evangelical Mind and Heart: Perspectives on Theological and Practical Issues* (Grand Rapids: Baker, 1993), 35.

67. Erickson, *Evangelical Left*, 38.

Lying within Erickson's presentation, however, is the strong suggestion that in Erickson's eyes Ramm had shipwrecked his theological legacy as a neo-evangelical pioneer on the shoals of neo-orthodoxy.[68]

As Ramm's star diminished, Henry's seemed to rise. In the 1990s, the evangelical luminary appeared to have taken on new importance to Erickson. Hence, in his 1993 book *How Shall They Be Saved?* Erickson lauds Henry as "perhaps the premier theologian within evangelicalism."[69] Five years later, Erickson dedicated his treatise on the doctrine of God, *God the Father Almighty* (1998), to Henry. In the dedication Erickson elevates him to the status of "dean of twentieth-century American evangelical theologians."[70]

A Concern for the Future

As he donned Henry's mantle, Erickson not only bemoaned the theological drift he had seen in his first theology professor, but expressed increasing concern about trends occurring around him. Like Henry, he was especially apprehensive about what he perceived as a degeneration within evangelicalism. In *The Evangelical Mind and Heart* Erickson concluded that "in certain respects, it appears that modern evangelicalism has retained some of the less desirable features of the old fundamentalism, and adopted some of the poorer qualities of the modernism which fundamentalism opposed."[71] But of the two debilitating trends, over the last decade Erickson has consistently voiced greater concern for what he perceives as a shift to the left.

What apparently triggered his expression of consternation were recent studies that suggested to Erickson that younger evangelicals were being conformed to society rather than transforming it. On the basis of these reports, Erickson expressed fear that "the strength of evangelicalism was being sapped."[72] One such study, Richard Quebedeaux's *The Worldly Evangelicals*, had in Erickson's estimation given ample indication that evangelicalism was being pulled closer to liberalism. Unlike Quebedeaux, who concluded the book on an optimistic note, intimating that "the radical evangelicals may be pointing the church as a whole in the right direction,"[73] Erickson greeted these developments with alarm. Even more disturbing in his estimation, however, were sociologist James Davison

68. Hence, his comments about Ramm and Barth in ibid., 78, 82.

69. Millard J. Erickson, *How Shall They Be Saved? The Destiny of Those Who Do Not Hear of Jesus* (Grand Rapids: Baker, 1996), 59–60.

70. Erickson, *God the Father Almighty*, 5.

71. Erickson, *Evangelical Mind and Heart*, 206.

72. Ibid., 32–39.

73. Richard Quebedeaux, *The Worldly Evangelicals* (San Francisco: Harper and Row, 1978), 168.

Hunter's findings, published in *Evangelicalism: The Coming Generation*[74] documenting a noticeable shift in the beliefs and lifestyles of evangelical young people.[75] As he developed in his 1994 work, *Where Is Theology Going?* Erickson believed that such sociological findings did not bode well for the future of evangelical theology, for "the views of young people . . . will become the views of the church."[76]

Erickson was likewise apprehensive about developments in the surrounding culture, especially in the philosophical milieu. As early as 1993, the rise of postmodernism caught his attention, as is evident in his little book, *Evangelical Interpretation*.[77] Like other evangelicals, Erickson has repeatedly expressed deep reservations about what he sees as the detrimental implications of this philosophical and cultural trend. However, he initially saw a certain degree of promise in some postmodern insights, at least as far as they might foster a rethinking of biblical hermeneutics.[78] True to his neo-evangelical moorings, Erickson viewed his task as entering into constructive engagement with the postmodern phenomenon.

Yet Erickson at best cautiously embraced postmodernism. He grew increasingly leery of the way certain younger evangelicals were seeking to draw insights for their own work from the postmodern context. Thus, in his *Postmodernizing the Faith*[79] Erickson on the one hand chides evangelicals David Wells, Thomas Oden, and Francis Schaeffer for responding negatively to postmodernism, but on the other hand he levels a cursory attack on a group of younger thinkers who were attempting a positive engagement with it. In what is even more incomprehensible than Erickson's inclusion of Schaeffer in the volume, the neo-evangelical standard-bearer placed within the latter company a largely unpublished young philosopher of religion at Southwestern Baptist Theological Seminary, B. Keith Putt. The sharp critique, coming from the well-respected guardian of evangelical orthodoxy, helped eventually to force Putt's departure from the Southwestern faculty.

The Evangelical Left and *Postmodernizing the Faith* suggest the seriousness with which Erickson approached the role that came with the stature he had been afforded within the movement. This role included warning of the potentially erroneous ideas of younger theologians with whom he dif-

74. James Davison Hunter, *Evangelicalism: The Coming Generation* (Chicago: University of Chicago Press, 1987).

75. See Millard J. Erickson, *Where Is Theology Going? Issues and Perspectives on the Future of Theology* (Grand Rapids: Baker, 1994), 81.

76. Ibid., 24.

77. Millard J. Erickson, *Evangelical Interpretation: Perspectives on Hermeneutical Issues* (Grand Rapids: Baker, 1993).

78. Ibid., 114–25.

79. Millard J. Erickson, *Postmodernizing the Faith: Evangelical Responses to the Challenge of Postmodernism* (Grand Rapids: Baker, 1998).

fered. Yet more important for Erickson were the dangers to the future of evangelical theology posed by senior evangelical scholars who were propounding what he saw as significant departures from tenets of evangelical orthodoxy lying at the very heart of evangelicalism, namely, issues about salvation and the destiny of the lost. This concern is evident in the discussions of these matters found within many of his books published in the 1990s, as well as in his book-length treatment of the problem, *How Shall They Be Saved?* [80]

As is readily evident in *How Shall They Be Saved?* and *The Evangelical Left*, the special target of Erickson's consternation increasingly became Clark Pinnock. In the early 1980s the two viewed each other with mutual admiration. In 1983, Erickson acknowledged a personal indebtedness to Pinnock in the preface to *Christian Theology* volume 1.[81] Pinnock returned the compliment one year later by including Erickson with Donald Bloesch and Gabriel Fackre in the dedication of *The Scripture Principle*, citing them as "friends and colleagues" and as representing "the growing company of good evangelical scholars, valiant for truth and creative in expression, currently at work in the service of Christ and his church."[82] Soon, however, Pinnock's star followed the same downward trajectory as Ramm's had. Erickson came to fear that the unorthodox ideas of his former friend might have a detrimental influence, especially over younger thinkers.

Erickson sounded the alarm in 1993 with regard to Pinnock's annihilationism. Erickson feared Pinnock's position on this question could lead to universalism among evangelicals. He confessed that he did not suppose that Pinnock himself was in any immediate danger: "given the force of his apparent conviction, a future move toward universalism seems relatively unlikely." But he feared for younger evangelicals who would be tempted to take Pinnock's thinking a step further. He asked, "But what about the next generation of believers, pastors, and theologians? They may enter the intellectual arena less certain of Christ's exclusiveness than are present-day evangelicals. They may extend the logic Pinnock has used in arguing for annihilationism."[83] Later, Erickson expanded this concern to encompass the potentially disastrous influence of the entire "evangelical left."[84]

---

80. Millard J. Erickson, *How Shall They Be Saved? The Destiny of Those Who Do Not Hear of Jesus* (Grand Rapids: Baker, 1996).

81. Erickson, *Christian Theology*, 1:14.

82. Clark H. Pinnock, *The Scripture Principle* (San Francisco: Harper and Row, 1984), iv.

83. Erickson, *Evangelical Mind and Heart*, 151.

84. Erickson, *Evangelical Left*, 133.

Erickson and Establishment Evangelicalism

As seen in his concern about the "wider hope" theologians, Erickson never lost sight of the gospel-centered and Pietist-influenced nature of evangelicalism. In *The Evangelical Mind and Heart* he declared, "Evangelicalism is, at its core, a view of the nature of salvation. According to evangelicalism, salvation involves regeneration, a supernatural transformation based upon Jesus Christ's atoning death and received by an exercise of faith in him."[85] Erickson opened the volume with a definition of evangelicalism that he thought drew a net wide enough to encompass "the evangelical denominations as well as evangelicals in independent, mainline Protestant, and Roman Catholic churches" together with "the large number of Pentecostals":[86]

> We are here referring to as evangelicals those who believe that all humans are in need of salvation and that this salvation involves regeneration by a supernatural work of God. Based upon his grace, this divine act is received solely by repentance and faith in the atoning work of Jesus Christ. Further, evangelicals urgently and actively seek the conversion of all persons worldwide to this faith. They regard the canonical Scriptures as the supreme authority in matters of faith and practice.[87]

Erickson likewise retained enough of the Pietist heritage of the Swedish Baptists to maintain the practical aspect of theology. Hence, in *God the Father Almighty* he notes that "the goal of theology is not merely knowledge but life."[88]

Yet in the waning years of the twentieth century, as Erickson picked up the mantle of Henry, he seemed to be drifting to the right. This was noticed by no less an astute observer than the veteran Baptist theologian and one-time colleague of Erickson, James Leo Garrett. In his review of *The Evangelical Left*, Garrett contrasts certain convictions Erickson expresses in the latter volume with those propounded in *Christian Theology*. For example, in 1983, Erickson favored the use of sources, in addition to the Bible, in theological construction,[89] whereas in 1997 he criticized those theologians who use such sources, claiming against them that true evangelicalism has only one source.[90] Garrett notes as well that Erickson, having declared in 1983 that special revelation is both propositional and personal,[91] had shifted in 1997 to a rejection of personal or relational revelation in

---

85. Erickson, *Evangelical Mind and Heart*, 86.
86. Ibid., 14.
87. Ibid., 13.
88. Erickson, *God the Father Almighty*, 281.
89. Garrett cites Erickson, *Christian Theology*, 1:256–58; James Leo Garrett, Jr., "Review of *The Evangelical Left*," *Southwestern Journal of Theology* 42, no. 1 (Fall 1999): 91.
90. Garrett cites Erickson, *Evangelical Left*, 29, 47, 53; Garrett, "Review," 91.
91. Garrett points to Erickson, *Christian Theology*, 1:196; Garrett, "Review," 91.

favor of propositional revelation alone.[92] Such changes in Erickson's views lead Garrett to conclude, "while deploring a leftward drift among Evangelicals, Erickson himself evidences a shift from Evangelicalism toward Fundamentalism."[93]

In a volume that helped to prompt Erickson to take up the mantle of defender of orthodoxy, Richard Quebedeaux offered the following characterization of "the evangelical establishment":

> Largely Baptists and Presbyterians, they were rational Calvinist scholastics, committed to the total inerrancy of Scripture and the propositional revelation contained therein. The Bible is completely free from error because it is God's inspired word, and God cannot lie or contradict himself. Biblical revelation is propositional in that God has expressed himself objectively and clearly in words, in language that must be believed as true, usually in its literal sense. This position is most at home in post-Reformation scholastic orthodoxy as mediated to modern evangelicalism by the nineteenth-century Old Princeton theology.[94]

While Erickson never became a biblical literalist, his theological journey moved him into the forefront of the evangelical establishment as Quebedeaux describes it. In becoming the defender of this version of evangelical orthodoxy, Erickson increasingly shuffled his feet toward one particular side—the fundamentalist side—of the growing divide that became evident in the post-fundamentalist neo-evangelical theology that took shape in the last third of the twentieth century.

Clark Pinnock (1937-): From Henry Protégé to Theological Pilgrim

In 1998, Clark Pinnock offered this glimpse into his attitude toward theological work: "I approach theology in a spirit of adventure, being always curious about what I may find. For me, theology is like a rich feast, with many dishes to enjoy and delicacies to taste. It is like a centuries-old conversation that I am privileged to take part in, a conversation replete with innumerable voices to listen to." He then painted a portrait of his theological career: "More like a pilgrim than a settler, I tread the path of discovery and do my theology en route."[95] Seventeen years earlier, in the

---

92. Garret finds this in Erickson, *Evangelical Left*, 55, 77, 85; Garrett, "Review," 91.

93. Garrett, "Review," 91.

94. Quebedeaux, *Worldly Evangelicals*, 22–23.

95. Clark H. Pinnock, "A Pilgrim on the Way," *Christianity Today* 42, no. 2 (February 9, 1998), 43.

midst of the storm of protest that greeted his rethinking of inerrancy, Pinnock provided insight into what it means to be a theological pilgrim: It involves listening ever "more carefully to what the Scriptures actually say and teach" and making appropriate "course corrections" in response.[96]

Pinnock's willingness to be a theological pilgrim, constantly on a journey, has engendered a faithful following of thinkers who view him as a theological scout canvassing future terrain. In their estimation, he stands "in the forefront of positioning evangelical Christianity for the rigors of what lies ahead," to cite the words of Barry Callen.[97] Yet as Randy Maddox notes, "One person's 'scout' is another person's 'drifter.'" Pinnock's detractors interpret his pilgrim approach as a sign of the directionless wanderings or theological instability[98] of a thinker who lacks a proper grounding. Hence the prominent Southern Baptist, Adrian Rogers, referred to his former teacher as a brilliant theologian on a "curious theological odyssey" that so far has yielded "ephemeral theological oddities."[99]

Whatever may be the final verdict of his peers, throughout his life Pinnock has remained a quintessential neo-evangelical theologian in at least one respect. Through its many twists, turns, and permutations his theological orientation has never lost the apologetic character that has typified the new evangelical theology from the beginning. At a midpoint in his journey, Pinnock gave evidence to this abiding apologetical orientation. In a letter to a seminary student he indicated what had always been, and still remained, his central ministry concerns: "To blend my writing, speaking, teaching, witnessing, relating into an effective and relevant witness to Jesus Christ. To respond to those points where the witness is under a threat, and to give some helpful direction beyond current impasses."[100]

Neo-Evangelical Apologist

Pinnock was reared in a liberal Baptist church in Toronto. Through the influence of his godly paternal grandmother and a pious Sunday school teacher, he was converted in 1950. Being a young "born again" Christian in a liberal congregation left an indelible mark, for it made him aware of "the

96. Clark H. Pinnock, "Response to Rex A. Koivisto," *Journal of the Evangelical Theological Society* 24 (June 1981), 155.

97. Barry L. Callen, *Clark H. Pinnock: Journey Toward Renewal* (Nappanee, Ind.: Evangel, 2000), 5.

98. See, for example, Roger Nicole, "The Scripture Principle: Clark Pinnock's Precarious Balance between Openmindedness and Doctrinal Instability," *Christianity Today* 29, no. 2 (February 1, 1985): 71.

99. Adrian Rogers, "Response to 'Parameters of Biblical Inerrancy,'" in *The Proceedings of the Conference on Biblical Inerrancy, 1987* (Nashville: Broadman, 1987), 106.

100. As cited in Callen, *Clark H. Pinnock*, 37.

need to be alert to defections from the true faith and to maintain a theologically sound testimony."[101] Even in the 1980s Pinnock had occasion to refer to the deep impression this experience had made: "It has been about thirty years since I was saved, and I have never been able to shake off the feeling of outrage at the arrogance of the liberal decision to revise the New Testament message to make it acceptable to modern men. I suppose my deepest concern as a theologian today is to expose and refute this deadly error."[102]

Although retaining his Baptist affiliation, during the years following his conversion Pinnock was quickly inaugurated into the neo-evangelical movement. This sociological and theological baptism came through his attraction to such parachurch ministries as *The Hour of Decision,* Youth for Christ, the Canadian Keswick Bible Conference, InterVarsity Christian Fellowship, and Wycliffe Bible Translators.

In 1956, Pinnock entered the Ancient Near Eastern Studies Program at the University of Toronto. His vocational goal was to follow in the footsteps of his paternal grandfather, who had served as a missionary in Nigeria, and pursue some type of Bible translation ministry. What followed university graduation, however, were doctoral studies in New Testament with F. F. Bruce (completing his work in 1963), plus two additional years in Manchester as a lecturer, during which time Pinnock enjoyed ongoing contact with the apologist Francis Schaeffer at L'Abri Fellowship.

These experiences equipped Pinnock to launch his missionary career. But rather than doing Bible translation, he would serve as a missionary to academia in North America. Apparently at Carl Henry's recommendation,[103] Pinnock was invited to join the faculty at the New Orleans Baptist Theological Seminary. He became professor of New Testament, but switched to theology two years later.

The preoccupation with "apologetic certainty" that characterized this stage of his career[104] led Pinnock on a foray into apologetics that resulted in his first major literary ventures, *A Defense of Biblical Infallibility*[105] and *Set Forth Your Case*.[106] The latter work was a Schaeffer-style defense of the Christian faith in the modern context. In this book, Pinnock set forth the

101. Clark H. Pinnock, "Baptists and Biblical Authority," *Journal of the Evangelical Theological Society* 17 (Fall 1974): 193.

102. Clark H. Pinnock, *Three Keys to Spiritual Renewal* (Minneapolis: Bethany, 1985), 18. See also Pinnock, "I Was a Teenage Fundamentalist," *Wittenberg Door* 70 (December 1982–January 1983): 18.

103. Callen, *Clark H. Pinnock,* 36.

104. Pinnock, "Response to Rex Koivisto," 154.

105. Clark H. Pinnock, *A Defense of Biblical Infallibility* (Philadelphia: Presbyterian and Reformed, 1967).

106. Clark H. Pinnock, *Set Forth Your Case: Studies in Christian Apologetics* (1968; reprint, Chicago: Moody, 1971).

case for Christianity on the basis of rational proofs. Above all, he looked
to confirmations of the accuracy of the New Testament documents and
the historicity of the resurrection of Christ to provide the foundational evidence for the truth of Christianity. In Pinnock's estimation "the beauty of
the gospel in the avalanche of competing religious claims is precisely the
possibility we have of checking it out historically and factually."[107]

Pinnock's deep consternation over the inroads of neo-orthodoxy in
Southern Baptist circles crystalized in his book-length appeal to the denomination, *A New Reformation*.[108] Pinnock called on Southern Baptists to return
to a high view of Scripture and to purge their educational institutions of
professors who had forsaken it. At the same time, Pinnock gave apologetic
expression to his neo-evangelical Calvinism in a little book entitled *Evangelism and Truth*,[109] in which he argued not only that biblical authority but
also a Calvinist foundation was crucial to biblical evangelism.

A move to Trinity Evangelical Divinity School in 1969 resulted in another apologetic text, carrying forward the argument announced in *A Defense of Biblical Infallibility*. Pinnock's goal was to shore up the foundations
of the neo-evangelical doctrine of Scripture. Hence the work defended not
only what he saw as the orthodox doctrine of revelation but also the bedrock neo-evangelical tenet, inerrancy. Pinnock's impression as to the fundamental importance of this concept was indicated in the title itself, *Biblical Revelation: The Foundation of Christian Theology*.[110]

In keeping with the approach of Warfield that neo-evangelicals had
gained via their fundamentalist forebears, Pinnock asserted that "inerrancy is to be regarded as an essential concomitant of the doctrine of inspiration, a necessary inference drawn from the fact that Scripture is *God's*
Word."[111] Following the deductive pathway others before him had trod,
he asserted, "Inerrancy . . . is the conclusion reached by inductive examination of the doctrine of Scripture taught by Christ and the biblical writers."[112] And marching lockstep with the typical neo-evangelical reasoning
pattern, he then added, "If the biblical writers erred in one particular, we
have no assurance they did not err in many more."[113]

At this stage, apparent difficulties within the Bible were not a worry.
On the contrary, in a manner even more vigorous than the nineteenth-

107. Ibid., 67.
108. Clark H. Pinnock, *A New Reformation: A Challenge to Southern Baptists* (Tigerville, S.C.:
Jewel, 1968).
109. Clark H. Pinnock, *Evangelism and Truth* (Tigerville, S.C.: Jewel, 1969).
110. Clark H. Pinnock, *Biblical Revelation: The Foundation of Christian Theology* (Chicago:
Moody, 1971).
111. Ibid., 73.
112. Ibid., 74.
113. Ibid., 73.

century Princeton theologians, Pinnock had already insisted in 1967 that "inductive difficulties encountered in the text cannot change the fact that the Bible claims not to err."[114] Now he repeated the claim, asserting that the Bible's teaching about itself, "and not an assortment of problem passages, is the truly relevant data for our knowledge of what Scripture is."[115] The propositionalist view of theology followed almost automatically. Pinnock defined this discipline as "the art of articulating the cognitive substance of divine revelation of which Scripture is the medium."[116]

In the 1960s, Pinnock was convinced that the very lifeblood of evangelicalism as a gospel-proclaiming movement was at stake in the question of biblical authority. In *Evangelism and Truth*, he declared,

> Evangelism is the declaration of a specific *message*. It is not holding meetings, or getting results. It is communication of the good news. Therefore, *evangelism and truth are inseparable*. Biblical evangelism requires divine truth; divine truth requires revelation in language; revelation in language requires the deposit of infallible Scripture. As soon as confidence is weakened in the integrity of our source material, evangelism is weakened to a corresponding degree.[117]

With *Biblical Revelation* on the bookshelves, Pinnock could breathe a sigh of relief. He had provided the underpinnings for the neo-evangelical theological commitment to an inerrant Bible.

Biblical Revelation was an instant success in neo-evangelical circles. Gordon R. Lewis, for example, praised the book as "the most vigorous scholarly statement of verbal, plenary inspiration since Warfield."[118] The notice and accolades that Pinnock's work had generated catapulted him into the limelight. Reflecting later on the host of evangelical theological luminaries of the day, David Scaer placed Pinnock at the top of the list, asserting that his defense of inerrancy marked him the "class valedictorian."[119] Or as Gary Dorrien notes, "No evangelical theologian appeared more determined or equipped than Pinnock to press the case for a credible fundamentalist alternative."[120] It seemed that Pinnock was the young, promising, neo-evangelical theologian upon whom the mantle of Carl Henry would eventually fall.

---

114. Pinnock, *Defense of Biblical Infallibility*, 18.

115. Pinnock, *Biblical Revelation*, 74–75.

116. Ibid., 107.

117. Pinnock, *Evangelism and Truth*, 18–19.

118. Gordon R. Lewis, "Review of *Biblical Revelation*," *Eternity* 23, no. 1 (January 1972): 50.

119. David Scaer, "The Rise and Fall of Clark H. Pinnock," *Concordia Theological Quarterly* 46 (January 1982): 40.

120. Gary Dorrien, *The Remaking of Evangelical Theology* (Louisville: Westminster John Knox, 1998), 131.

Rethinking the Neo-Evangelical Paradigm

But changes were in the wind.[121] Together with another up-and-coming neo-evangelical theologian, David F. Wells, Pinnock edited a collection of essays, *Toward a Theology for the Future*.[122] The goal of this volume was to chart the frontiers of a constructive, evangelical proposal in various fields of theological study. In his contribution to the work, "Prospects for Systematic Theology," Pinnock called for a fresh evangelical theology that takes seriously opposing viewpoints.[123] His own subsequent writings would be the response to this call, albeit in ways that Pinnock could not have anticipated in 1971.

Rethinking Calvinism

One immediate change proved later to be foundational for Pinnock's entire theological pilgrimage. Influenced in part by a study of the Book of Hebrews and such writings as I. Howard Marshall's *Kept by the Power of God*,[124] Pinnock came to the conclusion that the Calvinism in which he had been nurtured was flawed.[125] More specifically, Pinnock questioned the validity of the Calvinist doctrine of perseverance in the light of the biblical admonitions to Christians to persevere and not fall away.

Pinnock came to reject the Calvinist idea of the "terrible decree" (i.e., that God has destined some to eternal damnation) and to accept such classic Arminian teachings as the corporate view of election and human free will. By taking a few short steps, Pinnock had walked away from the Calvinism that for many leading neo-evangelical theologians was unquestioned theological orthodoxy, and had become instead a full-fledged Arminian. This shift found an initial literary expression in a collection of essays entitled *Grace Unlimited*[126] that Pinnock edited. Fourteen years later a second collection of essays appeared, *The Grace of God, the Will of Man: The Case for Arminianism*.[127]

121. Price suggests that 1971 marks the first major transition point in Pinnock's theological odyssey; Robert M. Price, "Clark H. Pinnock: Conservative and Contemporary," *Evangelical Quarterly* 60 (April 1988): 173.

122. Clark H. Pinnock and David F. Wells, eds., *Toward a Theology for the Future* (Carol Stream, Ill.: Creation House, 1971).

123. Clark H. Pinnock, "Prospects for Systematic Theology," in *Toward a Theology for the Future*, 96.

124. I. Howard Marshall, *Kept by the Power of God: A Study in Perseverance and Falling Away* (London: Epworth, 1969).

125. Clark H. Pinnock, "From Augustine to Arminius: A Pilgrimage in Theology," in *The Grace of God, the Will of Man: A Case for Arminianism*, ed. Clark H. Pinnock (Grand Rapids: Zondervan, 1989), 17.

126. Clark H. Pinnock, ed., *Grace Unlimited* (Minneapolis: Bethany, 1975).

127. Clark H. Pinnock, ed. *The Grace of God, the Will of Man: A Case for Arminianism* (Grand Rapids: Zondervan, 1989).

Through the influence of Jim Wallis and several other Trinity students, Pinnock also forsook the political conservatism of the neo-evangelical context in which he had been nurtured. His newly radical political stance led him in 1974 to vote for a communist candidate in a civic election. Pinnock did not remain a leftist, however. Around 1978 he underwent a "return to the center" that included an embrace of democratic capitalism together with a sympathy for the "neo-Puritan vision" that he saw embedded in the Christian reconstructionist movement.[128] In keeping with this vision, Pinnock now asserted that "the Bible also promises long-term blessings of both worldwide peace and economic abundance to those who heed God's law."[129]

Rethinking Apologetics

In 1974 Pinnock left Trinity for Regent College in Vancouver, British Columbia. However, his longest tenure was not to be in a parachurch educational institution, but at the theological school of the denomination of his upbringing, McMaster Divinity College in Hamilton, Ontario. After three years at Regent, Pinnock returned to the Toronto area hopeful that he could help spark an evangelical renewal both at McMaster, which had hitherto been a liberal stronghold, and in the churches of the Baptist Convention.

In Hamilton, Pinnock continued the process begun in Chicago and continued in Vancouver, of rethinking the standard neo-evangelical theological paradigm. One aspect of his former outlook that came under scrutiny was his approach to apologetics. In 1980, Pinnock published a new statement of the Christian apologetical task, *Reason Enough: A Case for the Christian Faith*.[130] The use of the indefinite article in the subtitle may have been a subtle indication of Pinnock's more humble stance toward the ability of reason to act as the arbiter of truth.

In *Reason Enough*, Pinnock called for an exercise of "critical judgment." He was confident that, while not proving the faith, critical judgment would show that faith is reasonable, that is, that "the Christian world view is adequate intellectually, factually and morally."[131] He broadened the base of evidence to include other circles of credibility, or categories of complementary evidence, that support the Christian understanding of reality: the pragmatic, the experiential, the cosmic or metaphysical, the historical, and the community bases of faith.[132] In Pinnock's estimation, these confirm that there is "reason enough" to believe that the gospel is "the true end to our quest for meaning

128. Clark H. Pinnock, "A Pilgrimage in Political Theology: A Personal Witness," in *Liberation Theology*, ed. Ronald Nash (Milford, Mich.: Mott Media, 1984), 111–19.

129. See Pinnock, *Three Keys to Spiritual Renewal*, 76.

130. Clark H. Pinnock, *Reason Enough: A Case for the Christian Faith* (Downers Grove, Ill.: InterVarsity, 1980).

131. Ibid., 10.

132. Ibid., 13–16.

and our quest for the intelligibility of the world, true to the religious longings of our heart, true to the biblical record, and true to the moral intuition that we need a new kind of human community on this groaning planet."[133]

Reason Enough marked Pinnock's shift away from the pure evidentialism that characterized his earlier apologetic endeavors. And it illustrated his newfound willingness to adopt more from the presuppositionalism he once opposed. In a 1979 lecture at New College, Berkeley, Pinnock acknowledged this shift in perspective. "Now I'm halfway between where I used to be and the Reformed fideists,"[134] he admitted, referring to Van Til and his followers.

Rethinking Inerrancy

As significant as these shifts were, perhaps no change caused a greater stir within the neo-evangelical movement than Pinnock's rethinking of inerrancy, a process that began during his three-year tenure in Vancouver.[135] His reflections led him to reject the typical approach of neo-evangelical theology, which he had earlier so forcefully championed.[136] Pinnock later offered this reflection on his earlier position: "The deep reason I defended the strict view of inerrancy in my earlier years was because I desperately wanted it to be true. I wanted it to be true so badly that I passed over its obvious problems."[137]

Several factors worked together to trigger Pinnock's change of mind. One crucial provocation was the influence of a number of scholars who were challenging many of the assumptions that lay behind the classic neo-evangelical position on inerrancy. The most important of these was likely Stephen Davis's *Debate about the Bible*,[138] for which Pinnock wrote a foreword. Pinnock himself suggested a second impetus. Reflecting back on the process, Pinnock reported that he had come to realize that he had earlier "inflated the biblical claims for inspiration in the interests of a rationalist paradigm." He then admitted, "I had been engaged in making the Bible say more than it wanted to in the interests of my system."[139] Another significant catalyst was undoubtedly Pinnock's growing appreciation for the

133. Ibid., 15.

134. Price, "Clark H. Pinnock," 181.

135. See, for example, Clark H. Pinnock, "Three Views of the Bible in Contemporary Theology," in *Biblical Authority*, ed. Jack Rogers (Waco: Word, 1977), 47–73; Clark H. Pinnock, "Evangelicals and Inerrancy: The Current Debate," *Theology Today* 35 (April 1978): 65–69.

136. For a helpful summary of Pinnock's new understanding of inerrancy that emerged in the 1970s, see Dorrien, *Remaking of Evangelical Theology*, 133–38.

137. Clark H. Pinnock, "Parameters of Biblical Inerrancy," in *The Proceedings of the Conference on Biblical Inerrancy, 1987* (Nashville: Broadman, 1987), 96.

138. Stephen T. Davis, *The Debate about the Bible: Inerrancy versus Infallibility* (Philadelphia: Westminster, 1977). For this judgment, see Callen, *Clark H. Pinnock*, 56.

139. Clark H. Pinnock, "Foreword," in Ray C. W. Roennfeldt, *Clark H. Pinnock on Biblical Authority: An Evolving Position* (Berrien Springs, Mich.: Andrews University Press, 1993), xix.

dynamic of the Spirit not only in the writing of Scripture but also in illuminating the reader. As Robert K. Johnston notes in his treatment of Pinnock's shift, "The perfect errorlessness of non-extant autographs . . . failed
to prove the dynamic authority of the present text."[140]

Ultimately, however, Pinnock's rethinking of inerrancy was triggered by
the deeper theological shift that had been smoldering beneath the surface of
all this theological thinking since the days in Chicago, namely, his embracing
of Arminianism. Ray Roennfeldt offered this perceptive observation:

> In the formulation of his early view of Scripture, Pinnock used the presup-
> positions of Reformed theism, whereas the later Pinnock consciously works
> from a more Arminian model without rejecting all aspects of Calvinism. He
> now considers that Scripture should be understood as the result of both di-
> vine initiative and human response. It is his contention that a strict belief in
> biblical inerrancy is incompatible with anything less than belief in Calvinis-
> tic determinism. The Arminian paradigm, which took about ten years to af-
> fect Pinnock's doctrine of Scripture, has been gradually filtering down into
> all of his theological reflections.[141]

This gradual "filtering down" would soon lead Pinnock to rethink other
cherished neo-evangelical theological positions.

Whatever the reasons, Pinnock could no longer endorse the attempt of
many neo-evangelicals not only to defend a strict biblical inerrancy but also
to claim that it is the essential foundation for true Christianity. At the same
time, he was not prepared to go all the way with those who rejected the
concept outright. He therefore committed himself to the task of carving out
a third option between the two, one that retained a commitment to inerrancy, but understood it in functional, even metaphorical, terms, namely,
as "a metaphor for the determination to trust God's Word completely."[142]

Pinnock was aware of the crossfire this nuanced position would attract.
Those to his right would surely suspect that he was guilty of "watering down
the inerrancy conviction close to meaninglessness," whereas those on his left
would "ridicule the effort to be critically honest and still retain biblical inerrancy
in any form."[143] Pinnock correctly predicted that a storm would break loose
among his colleagues. Occurring as it did in the height of the "battle for the Bible," many of his former allies reacted with disappointment or even anger.[144]

140. Robert K. Johnston, "Clark H. Pinnock," in *Handbook of Evangelical Theologians*, ed.
Walter A. Elwell (Grand Rapids: Baker, 1993), 434.

141. Roennfeldt, *Pinnock on Biblical Authority*, 364.

142. Clark H. Pinnock, *The Scripture Principle* (San Francisco: Harper and Row, 1984), 225.

143. Pinnock, "Evangelicals and Inerrancy," 66–67.

144. See, for example, Harold Lindsell, *The Bible in the Balance* (Grand Rapids: Zondervan,
1996), 36–43; Rex A. Koivisto, "Clark Pinnock and Inerrancy: A Change in Truth Theory?"
Journal of the Evangelical Theological Society 24 (June 1981): 139–51.

Undaunted, Pinnock moved forward. At McMaster he found himself in a context in which he could articulate the middle position he was advocating. The result was *The Scripture Principle* (1984). In this book, Pinnock seeks to develop a holistic doctrine of Scripture that balances three dimensions: the divine authorship and authority of Scripture, the Bible's human character and frailty, and the spiritual dynamic at work in the process of understanding the text.

In *The Scripture Principle*, Pinnock once again defended the neo-evangelical commitment to the Bible as the written Word of God. He even went so far as to maintain that as the divine Word, Scripture is "a contentful language deposit"[145] that includes "propositional communication."[146] But in elevating the divine dimension of the Bible, Pinnock now shows that his chief interest is in the function of Scripture. In commenting on 2 Timothy 3:15–17, he asserts, "In this wonderful text Paul places his emphasis on the plenary profitability of the Scriptures in the matter of conveying a saving and an equipping knowledge of God." Pointing at the neo-evangelical position he once advocated, he then adds, Paul "does not present a theory about a perfect Bible given long ago but now lost, but declares the Bible in Timothy's possession to be alive with the breath of God and full of the transforming information the young disciple would need in the life of faith and obedience."[147]

Even more radical, however, was Pinnock's about-face regarding the human dimension of the Bible. Pinnock argues that in the Bible divine revelation comes in human form. God accommodates his Word to human modes of thought and expression as well as to human modes of literary and historical composition. On this basis, Pinnock, walking the same pathway that Ramm had charted earlier, suggests the possibility that Scripture may include such features as sagalike story, legend, and hero narrative. Ironically, Pinnock found this suggestion preposterous, if not potentially blasphemous, in the 1960s.

This divine-human document, Pinnock concludes, is the authoritative message of God for people today. As such, it speaks truth, whether doctrinal, ethical, or spiritual.[148] Pinnock brought the two together in what he termed "the Scripture principle." This principle, he explained,

> means that there is a locus of the Word of God in a humanly accessible form available to us. It means that the Bible is regarded as a creaturely text that is at the same time God's own written Word, and that we can consult his Word, which reveals his mind, and seek to know his will in it. It means that God has communicated authoritatively to us on those subjects about which Scripture teaches, whether doctrinal, ethical, or spiritual, and that we believers willingly subject ourselves to this rule of faith.[149]

145. Pinnock, *Scripture Principle*, 62.
146. Ibid., 27.
147. Ibid., xviii.
148. Ibid., 62.
149. Ibid.

As his articulation of the Scripture principle indicates, Pinnock had not given up the basically apologetic stance that had always characterized his approach to theology. Christianity, he continued to believe, requires a deposit of truth. But what is quite new in *The Scripture Principle* is Pinnock's elevation of the illuminating work of the Spirit in interpretation. Pinnock complained that in their zeal to defend inerrancy, evangelicals had given little attention to what he saw as "the equally important matter of its interpretation."[150] While voicing caution and critique, in 1997 Millard Erickson drew this conclusion about Pinnock's doctrine of Scripture: "It is apparent that his aim is not to propound a Barthian view of revelation but to revitalize the evangelical doctrine of illumination of Scripture by the Holy Spirit."[151]

Rethinking Traditional Doctrines

Had Pinnock stopped here, the storm within neo-evangelical circles might have subsided. But his pilgrimage was not yet over. Pinnock's Arminianism continued to seep through his theology, albeit taking him in directions that even many classical Arminians would not affirm.[152] Increasingly Pinnock's apologetic concern drew his attention toward beliefs about the final destiny of non-Christians and even about the nature of the biblical God.

As a people of the evangel, evangelicals have always been interested in the gospel and its proclamation to those who have not yet heard or responded positively to it. Likewise, as a people characterized by "convertive piety," evangelicals have always been concerned about missions, as well as the eternal destiny of the unconverted. It was therefore almost inevitable that Pinnock's theological odyssey would lead him to reconsider the traditional positions in these areas. His conclusions resulted in *A Wideness in God's Mercy*.[153] In this work, Pinnock carves out what is often referred to as an "inclusivist" position[154] that lies between the pluralism of much contemporary liberal thought and the classic exclusivism retained by many neo-evangelicals. Pinnock argues that while salvation is found only through Christ, the possibility of salvation extends even to persons who in this life on earth have not heard the gospel and hence have not come into conscious

150. Clark H. Pinnock, "Catholic, Protestant, and Anabaptist: Principles of Biblical Interpretation in Selected Communities," *Brethren in Christ History and Life* (Dec. 1986): 268, 275, as cited in Callen, *Clark H. Pinnock*, 68.

151. Erickson, *Evangelical Left*, 79.

152. The Arminian theologian Robert Rakestraw parts company with Pinnock at precisely these points; see Robert V. Rakestraw, "Clark H. Pinnock," in *Baptist Theologians*, ed. Timothy George and David S. Dockery (Nashville: Broadman, 1990), 672–73.

153. Clark H. Pinnock, *A Wideness in God's Mercy: The Finality of Jesus Christ in a World of Religions* (Grand Rapids: Zondervan, 1992).

154. This is the term he uses in Clark H. Pinnock, "An Inclusivist View," in *More Than One Way?* ed. Dennis Okholm and Timothy Phillips (Grand Rapids: Zondervan, 1995), 93–148.

relationship with Christ. This controversial position was related to a second one that he had embraced as early as 1987, a position that was equally troubling to his critics.[155] Pinnock had joined a small but significant group of largely British evangelical theologians who rejected the traditional view of hell as eternal conscious punishment in favor of "conditional immortality," that is, the belief that after the judgment the lost simply cease to exist.[156]

Yet, perhaps the most far-reaching and controversial rethinking occurred in Pinnock's conception of God. Already at a meeting of the Evangelical Theological Society in 1977, Pinnock signaled that he was reevaluating the traditional understanding. In an essay addressing the "classical synthesis" of revelation and rationalism, Pinnock insisted that classical theism, infused as it was with Greek philosophical ideas, ought not to be equated with biblical theism. Biblical theism is characterized by a dynamic ontology, he asserted, which invariably clashes with the static ontology of Greek thinkers. For this reason, Pinnock declared, problems arise whenever theologians attempt to interpret the biblical message "which is historical and personal at its core" by means of Greek metaphysical categories that at their core are "ahistorical and impersonal."[157]

In the 1980s and 1990s, Pinnock devoted his energies to the task of laying the foundation for what in his estimation would be a truly biblical theism. He wished to overcome the problems inherent in the classical view, wedded as it is in the synthesis of the Bible with Hellenism. The result of his efforts was a new model of God, sometimes termed "creative-love theism"[158] or, more commonly, either free-will theism or the "openness of God."[159] These came to be set forth in two coauthored works that appeared in 1994, *Unbounded Love* and *The Openness of God*.

In the mid-1980s, this reconstructive task focused on the divine sovereignty. Driven in part by the perennial question of evil, as well as his desire to maintain human freedom, Pinnock argued that the Calvinist idea of a God who exercises control over creation like a "puppet master who pulls all

155. Clark H. Pinnock, "Fire, Then Nothing," *Christianity Today* 31, no. 5 (March 20, 1987). See also Clark H. Pinnock, "The Destruction of the Finally Impenitent," *Criswell Theological Review* 4 (1990): 243–59.

156. See also Clark H. Pinnock, "The Conditional View," in *Four Views on Hell*, ed. William Crockett (Grand Rapids: Zondervan, 1996), 135–66.

157. Clark H. Pinnock, "The Need for a Scriptural, and Therefore a Neo–Classical Theism," in *Perspectives on Evangelical Theology*, ed. Kenneth Kantzer and Stanley Gundry (Grand Rapids: Baker, 1979), 41.

158. This is actually Robert Brow's designation; see Clark H. Pinnock and Robert C. Brow, *Unbounded Love: A Good News for the Twenty-first Century* (Downers Grove, Ill.: InterVarsity, 1994), 8.

159. See Clark H. Pinnock et al., *The Openness of God: A Biblical Challenge to the Traditional Understanding of God* (Downers Grove, Ill.: InterVarsity, 1994), 7.

the strings" must be replaced. His proposal was the model of a God who gives creation a degree of autonomy. "To say that God is the sovereign Creator," Pinnock wrote in 1986, "means that God is the ground of the world's existence and the source of all its possibilities." Pinnock then suggests that the divine sovereignty is not about God's determining control, but his omnicompetence. It means that "God is . . . able to deal with any circumstances which might arise, and nothing can possibly defeat or destroy God."[160]

Pinnock took his rethinking of the divine sovereignty a step farther, however. Agreeing with certain Calvinists that foreknowledge necessarily entails foreordination, Pinnock concluded that human freedom meant that God's knowledge of the future is limited. Hence, in contrast to the classical Calvinist view, Pinnock concluded that the future is "really open and not available to exhaustive foreknowledge even on the part of God."[161] This does not entail a diminishing of God's omniscience, however, Pinnock adds. Rather, because free actions do not yet exist, they cannot be known ahead of time, not even by God.[162]

Pinnock's understanding of the divine sovereignty is an important dimension of a larger rethinking of God's nature. Through this rethinking, Pinnock has come to a greater awareness of what he sees as the biblical picture of a triune, and therefore eternally relational, God who in turn enters into relationship with creation. This God is "pure relationality." This relationality "seeks to draw all things into the symphony of love that is played eternally within the divine life," to cite Frank Macchia's helpful summary of Pinnock's position.[163]

Pinnock's "openness of God" view has brought him into dialogue with leading North American process theologians, including Delwin Brown[164] and John Cobb.[165] While acknowledging many points of agreement between the two models, Pinnock is adamant that there are likewise significant differences. Against the collapsing of God into the world he sees in process thinking, Pinnock wants above all to hold on to God's objectivity and ontological transcendence.[166]

160. Clark H. Pinnock, "God Limits His Knowledge," in *Predestination and Free Will: Four Views of Divine Sovereignty and Human Freedom*, ed. David Basinger and Randall Basinger (Downers Grove, Ill.: InterVarsity, 1986), 146.

161. Ibid., 145.

162. Ibid., 157.

163. Frank Macchia, "Tradition and the *Novum* of the Spirit: A Review of Clark Pinnock's *Flame of Love*," *Journal of Pentecostal Theology* 13 (1998): 34.

164. See Clark H. Pinnock and Delwin Brown, *Theological Crossfire* (Grand Rapids: Zondervan, 1990).

165. See Clark H. Pinnock and John B. Cobb, Jr., eds., *Searching for an Adequate God* (Grand Rapids: Eerdmans, 2000).

166. See, for example, Clark H. Pinnock, "Between Classical and Process Theism," in *Process Theology*, ed. Ronald Nash (Grand Rapids: Baker, 1987), 321; Pinnock and Brown, *Theological Crossfire*, 67–68.

Anticipating a Postmodern Paradigm: Pinnock and the Future of Evangelical Theology

Observers of Pinnock's theological odyssey have repeatedly commented on his role as a type of theological gadfly who challenges widely accepted beliefs and assumptions. Randy Maddox, for example, writes,

> [Pinnock] has been ever ready to engage contested theological issues within evangelicalism and has proven open to revising his views on these issues when he found the evidence for change compelling. In the creative and sometimes turbulent process, he has helped to clarify what is at stake in the debates and has scouted a way forward for others who share his evangelical background and his questions about certain reigning assumptions within this large and diverse Christian movement known as evangelicalism.[167]

In keeping with this observation, Robert Rakestraw predicts that Pinnock's influence on evangelical theology "will be more in forging new patterns of thought than in honing or defending established evangelical doctrines."[168] If Rakestraw's assessment is correct, then Pinnock's abiding significance as a second-generation neo-evangelical theologian lies more in the mood or method his journey has modeled than in the particular theological conclusions he has drawn, especially his hotly contested and at times seemingly overdrawn views on salvation and God. This mood is evident in several aspects of his mature thought.

Turn toward an Experience-Chastened Reason

The "Pinnock mood" includes a tempering of the reliance on reason that typified the neo-evangelical theology he inherited from his forebears, such as Carl Henry, and therefore which characterized his own approach early in his career. Pinnock spelled out this shift in the more methodological sections of *Tracking the Maze*.[169]

In this volume, he admitted that reason is always embedded in history and culture, and consequently that it is not an omnicompetent judge of truth.[170] Having embraced the Wesleyan quadrilateral, Pinnock indicated the extent to which experience as well as intuition were playing an important role in his theologizing. As sympathetic critic Robert Rakestraw noted already in 1990, "His heart often leads his head, both regarding his personal longing for a cer-

---

167. Randy Maddox, "Foreword," in Callen, *Clark H. Pinnock*, ix.

168. Rakestraw, "Clark H. Pinnock," 675.

169. Clark H. Pinnock, *Tracking the Maze: Finding Our Way through Modern Theology from an Evangelical Perspective* (San Francisco: Harper and Row, 1990).

170. Ibid., 179.

tain matter to be true, but also with regard to his desire to make the gospel appealing to outsiders or to Christians who are considering defection."[171]

Turn toward Narrative

In *Tracking the Maze*, Pinnock indicated another aspect of the new mood of his theology. In this book, he expressed openness to the idea of narrative that had been gaining center stage in contemporary theology.

Drawing from this impulse, Pinnock announced, "In my judgment the central message of Christianity and therefore its essence is the epic story of redemption, enshrined in its sacred texts and liturgies, that announces the salvation and God's liberation of the human race." The plot of this narrative is the great "eucatastrophe," "the intervention of God in history for human salvation" that is simultaneously history and myth.[172] Pinnock's newfound appreciation for narrative drew him to subordinate the role of propositions in theological reflection. "Truth and meaning for Christianity lie with the narrative before it is expressed in the doctrinal form,"[173] he noted. And this, in turn, led him to criticize the reigning neo-evangelical propositionalism: "Christian theology, then, should not be primarily rational-propositional in form, even though it usually is, especially among evangelicals. Its primary task ought to be to explore and proclaim the Christian story, which is what gives meaning to doctrines in the first place."[174] In short, "Theology exists to serve the story and not the other way around."[175]

Subsequent to 1990, Pinnock seems to have retreated somewhat from his bold move toward narrative. He did not invest his energies in delineating further the contours of a narrative theology, but moved on to explore what for him were more pressing interests. Nevertheless, he had opened the door for others to engage in what some have hailed as a fruitful avenue of postmodern theological engagement.

Turn toward the Spirit

Pinnock's writings have likewise anticipated a postmodern paradigm through the "turn toward the Spirit" they reflect. Pinnock's interest in pneumatology dates to his doctoral dissertation, which addressed the concept of the Spirit in Paul's epistles. During his tenure in New Orleans, Pinnock came to a point of profound dissatisfaction with his spiritual life. In the midst of this spiritual crisis, he asked some friends to lay hands on him

---

171. Rakestraw, "Clark H. Pinnock," 671.
172. Pinnock, *Tracking the Maze*, 153.
173. Ibid., 182.
174. Ibid., 183.
175. Ibid., 182.

and pray that he might receive the Spirit in power, which resulted in what he termed "the infilling of the Spirit." Since then Pinnock has repeatedly called for a more favorable attitude among neo-evangelicals for Pentecostal practices,[176] while remaining open to charismatic-style workings of the Spirit, including even the Toronto Blessing.[177]

Already in 1972 Pinnock gave literary expression to his interest in the Spirit. In his little book on Galatians, *Truth On Fire*, he declared that only through "a Spirit-filled life," that is, only by lining up behind the Spirit and being led by the Spirit, can a Christian "find victory and bear fruit to God."[178] He took an additional step in *The Scripture Principle* by calling neo-evangelicals to rediscover the importance of the Spirit's illuminating work. But the high point of his pneumatological reflections came in *Flame of Love*,[179] which its publishers have dubbed Pinnock's magnum opus. Later Pinnock noted that this book "puts on display before the reader my restlessness: in experience to know the living God and in theology to grow as a hearer of God's Word."[180] In *Flame of Love*, Pinnock invites his readers into a widely inclusive understanding of the Spirit's person and role:

> I invite us to view Spirit as the bond of love in the triune relationality, as the ecstasy of sheer life overflowing into a significant creation, as the power of creation and new creation, as the power of incarnation and atonement, as the power of new community and union with God, and as the power drawing the whole world into the truth of Jesus.[181]

Pinnock's turn toward the Spirit translated into a greater realization of the important connection between theology and the renewing of the Spirit. He expressed the importance of spiritual renewal even for the theologically minded in 1985, when he declared, "It is not enough to be bibli-

176. See, for example, Clark H. Pinnock and Grant R. Osborne, "A Truce Proposal for the Tongues Controversy," *Christianity Today* 16, no. 1 (October 8, 1971); "The New Pentecostalism: Reflections by a Well-Wisher," *Christianity Today* 17, no. 24 (September 14, 1973); "Charismatic Renewal for the Radical Church," *Post American* 4, no. 2 (February 1975); "Opening the Church to the Charismatic Dimension," *Christianity Today* 25, no. 11 (June 12, 1981).

177. See, for example, Clark H. Pinnock, "Should Baptists Catch the Fire?" *Canadian Baptist* 141, no. 3 (March 1995): 8–10.

178. Clark H. Pinnock, *Truth On Fire: The Message of Galatians* (Grand Rapids: Baker, 1972), 8.

179. Clark H. Pinnock, *Flame of Love: A Theology of the Holy Spirit* (Downers Grove, Ill.: InterVarsity, 1996).

180. Clark H. Pinnock, "A Bridge and Some Points of Growth: A Reply to Cross and Macchia," *Journal of Pentecostal Theology* 13 (October 1998): 49.

181. Pinnock, *Flame of Love*, 247.

cally sound if we are not spiritually alive at the same time."[182] And he was keenly aware that as a theologian he was dependent on the Spirit's renewing work: "Surely a Spirit-led orientation in theology will not produce theological tedium or a stuck-in-the-mud kind of work. There is so much to be done—may the Spirit make us thirsty to see that it is done."[183] By sounding this note, Pinnock was anticipating yet another aspect of a postmodern evangelical theological paradigm.

Turn toward Pietism

Throughout his life, Pinnock has been on a pilgrimage of renewal. In 1998, he characterized his journey as that of finding his way "from the scholastic to the pietistic approach" to Christian believing and living. His rediscovery of the Pietist impulse, in turn, allowed him to greet the postmodern emphasis on the particular and the experiential, for he saw these developments as boding well for an "evangelical pietism."[184]

According to Robert Price this is no new dimension in Pinnock's theology. On the contrary, in 1988 Price asserted—perhaps with slight exaggeration[185]—that Pinnock's "whole theological and apologetical structure is built on the foundation of piety."[186] In any case, there is an unmistakable connection between Pinnock's underlying orientation toward Pietism and his positive view of the emerging postmodern context. And it is here above all that his contribution as a catalyst for a rebirth of a centrist evangelical theology may be found. Gary Dorrien stated it well when he concluded, "As a respected figure in a movement of mostly young theologians, he supported the 'postmodern' evangelical claim that it was time for evangelicals to move beyond the categories and defensive positions established by the modernist-fundamentalist conflict."[187] Pinnock may have been too controversial, and ultimately perhaps too tied to the categories of modernity, to be able to move through that door himself. But by raising questions about the reigning neo-evangelical theological paradigm, he opened the door at least part way for the next generation of evangelical thinkers.

---

182. Pinnock, *Three Keys to Spiritual Renewal*, 10.
183. Clark H. Pinnock, "Divine Relationality: A Pentecostal Contribution to the Doctrine of God," *Journal of Pentecostal Theology* 16 (April 2000): 5.
184. Clark H. Pinnock, "Evangelical Theologians Facing the Future: Ancient and Future Paradigms," *Wesleyan Theological Journal* 33, no. 2 (Fall 1998): 11.
185. For what is perhaps a more balanced appraisal, see Callen, *Clark H. Pinnock*, 80–85.
186. Price, "Clark H. Pinnock," 164.
187. Dorrien, *Remaking of Evangelical Theology*, 145.

five

Evangelical Theology IN Transition

As the careers of Carl Henry and Bernard Ramm indicate, seeds of divergence lie deep within the heart of neo-evangelical theology. In the second generation, these seeds sprouted, coming to bloom in the differing directions that the successors of the pioneers have trod. This is exemplified by Millard Erickson's move from young innovator to establishment statesman and by Clark Pinnock's odyssey from young establishment apologist to theological pilgrim. The parting of ways visible in the work of Erickson and Pinnock leads almost inevitably to the question of the outworking of this apparent fissure among the next generation of evangelical theologians and consequently to the deeper question of the future of evangelical theology itself.

In recent years, an increasing number of commentators have expressed fears that the theological division they see within the movement portends a pending disaster. In their estimation, the evangelical theological coalition is dangerously close to breaking apart.

Perhaps the most provocative and controversial taxonomy of the growing fissure came in a 1998 *Christianity Today* essay by Roger Olson. Although the article carried the somewhat bland title, "The Future of Evangelical Theology," the byline was more penetrating: "Roger Olson argues that a division between traditionalists and reformists threatens to end our theological consensus."[1] By "traditionalists," Olson means those theologians who view their main task as upholding "traditional interpretations and formulations as binding and normative," and who as a result tend "to look with suspicion upon

1. Roger E. Olson, "The Future of Evangelical Theology," *Christianity Today* 42, no. 2 (February 9, 1998): 40.

any doctrinal revisions and new proposals arising out of theological reflection." "Reformists," in contrast, value "the continuing process of constructive theology seeking new light breaking forth from God's word."[2]

Olson's appraisal was met with cries of protest from many quarters. Even his call for a "truce" between the warring parties, because it was itself a "dividing," was labeled "divisive" by one commentator.[3] Yet many of Olson's critics found themselves agreeing that some type of divergence is clearly evident among evangelical theologians.[4] As the discussion that ensued from Olson's essay has indicated, there are several possible ways of viewing the current situation in evangelical theology. The goal of this chapter is to chart briefly one perspective, then to draw attention to a wider development that has appeared on the radar screen and indicate its implications for the future of evangelical theology.

Neo-Evangelical Theological Ferment

The closing two decades of the twentieth century have been marked by spirited theological engagement among evangelical thinkers. One sign of this theological revival is the number of systematic theologies that have emerged from the pens of evangelical theologians since the publication of Millard Erickson's three-volume *Christian Theology* in the mid-1980s. In the late 1980s and 1990s several self-consciously evangelical thinkers hovering on either side of retirement set themselves to the task of crystalizing their systematic theological reflections. Among them were James William McClendon,[5] Thomas Oden,[6] Gordon Lewis,[7] James Leo Garrett,[8] Paul Jewett,[9] and Donald Bloesch.[10] Perhaps more significant, however,

2. Ibid., 41.

3. John G. Stackhouse, Jr., "The Perils of Left and Right," *Christianity Today* 42, no. 9 (August 10, 1998): 59.

4. See, for example, the responses to Olson's essay published in the same issue; Clark H. Pinnock, "A Pilgrim on the Way," *Christianity Today* 42, no. 2 (February 9, 1998): 43; Thomas C. Oden, "The Real Reformers are Traditionalists," ibid., 45–46; Timothy George, "A Theology to Die For," ibid., 49–50.

5. James William McClendon, Jr., *Systematic Theology*, 3 vols. (Nashville: Abingdon, 1986–).

6. Thomas C. Oden, *Systematic Theology*, 3 vols. (San Francisco: Harper and Row, 1987–1992).

7. Gordon R. Lewis and Bruce A. Demarest, *Integrative Theology*, 3 vols. (Grand Rapids: Zondervan, 1987–1994).

8. James Leo Garrett, *Systematic Theology: Biblical, Historical, and Evangelical*, 2 vols. (Grand Rapids: Eerdmans, 1990–1995).

9. Paul K. Jewett, *God, Creation, and Revelation: A Neo-Evangelical Theology* (Grand Rapids: Eerdmans, 1991).

10. Donald G. Bloesch, *A Theology of Word and Spirit*, 7 vols. (Downers Grove, Ill.: InterVarsity, 1992–).

was the fact that a number of the next generation of evangelicals, theologians in their forties, also took up the task.

In 1996, the prodigious output of evangelical systematic theology caught the attention of Lutheran theologian Carl Braaten, who reviewed six of the recent volumes[11] in an essay entitled, "A Harvest of Evangelical Theology."[12] Seeing them as indicative of "the creative flux within American evangelicalism,"[13] Braaten praised the evangelical theological efforts under discussion for their focus "on what is of first importance," namely, "the revelation of God in Christ." In contrast to liberal theology, he noted, "These theologians know that the gospel can only be given *to* experience, and can never arise *out of* experience. God, and not religious experience, is the *fons et origo.*"[14] Although he went on record as being a sympathetic observer of the current renaissance of interest in systematic theology among evangelicals, Braaten came away from his study expressing weariness at the sheer number of offerings. Drawing the review to a close, Braaten's final words were, "I think I've read enough evangelical dogmatics to last for a while."[15]

Signs of lively activity at the close of the millennium were not limited to such lengthier treatises. In addition to systematic theologies, during these years younger evangelical theologians composed shorter introductory works exploring the nature of theology. And they devoted their energies to investigating a variety of theological doctrines and issues. The "third generation" heirs of the legacy of pioneers such as Henry and Ramm, and of shapers like Erickson and Pinnock, indicated that they were eager to tackle the questions passed on to them by their forebears.

Picking Up the Mantle

The immensity of the theological output of evangelicals during the past several years leads naturally to questions about the direction being charted by the generation of neo-evangelical theologians who follow in the wake of Erickson and Pinnock. More specifically, to what extent are younger thinkers carrying on the formative work of these two second-generation path-

11. These six are: Donald G. Bloesch, *Holy Scripture: Revelation, Inspiration and Interpretation* (Downers Grove, Ill.: InterVarsity, 1994); Stanley J. Grenz, *Theology for the Community of God* (Nashville: Broadman and Holman, 1994); Wayne Grudem, *Systematic Theology: An Introduction to Biblical Doctrine* (Grand Rapids: Zondervan, 1994); James William McClendon, *Systematic Theology*, vol. 2 (Nashville: Abingdon, 1994); Alister E. McGrath, *Christian Theology: An Introduction* (Cambridge, Mass.: Blackwell, 1994); and Christopher Morse, *Not Every Spirit: A Dogmatics of Christian Disbelief* (Valley Forge, Pa.: Trinity, 1994).

12. Carl E. Braaten, "A Harvest of Evangelical Theology," *First Things* 63 (May 1996): 45–48.

13. Ibid., 48.

14. Ibid., 45.

15. Ibid., 48.

finders? Who appears on the horizon as the likely heir of Erickson's mantle? And who is developing further the work begun by Pinnock?

Claiming the Traditionalist Legacy

One potential successor to Erickson is Wayne Grudem. Since its appearance in 1996, Grudem's massive *Systematic Theology: An Introduction to Biblical Doctrine* has been challenging Erickson's *Christian Theology* as the textbook of choice in many evangelical schools. Armed with degrees from Harvard (B.A.), Westminster Seminary (M.Div.), and Cambridge (D.Phil.), and as professor of systematic theology at Trinity Evangelical Divinity School, Grudem is strategically placed to carry on the Henry-Erickson legacy within the neo-evangelical movement.

There are, of course, marked theological differences between the third-generation neo-evangelical Grudem and the second-generation theologian Erickson. For example, Grudem seems to be less "classical" than Erickson in his treatment of the issue of the divine impassibility, which has become increasingly a topic of debate in recent years. In contrast to Erickson's cautiously articulated mediating position,[16] Grudem states categorically, "I have not affirmed God's impassibility in this book. Instead, quite the opposite is true, for God . . . certainly does feel emotions."[17] At first glance, this statement would suggest more affinities with Pinnock than Erickson.

Perhaps a more discernable and significant difference lies in the views Erickson and Grudem espouse on the ticklish issue of the gifts of the Spirit. Erickson had maintained the traditional neo-evangelical caution toward the successive waves of the Pentecostal movement,[18] including the so-called "third wave" epitomized in the Vineyard fellowship and its founder John Wimber.[19] On this issue, Grudem's affinities with Pinnock over against Erickson are even more pronounced. Like Pinnock, and unlike Erickson, Grudem has been deeply influenced by both the charismatic renewal and the Vineyard fellowship. During his college days Grudem served one summer as an assistant to a prominent spokesman for the charismatic renewal movement. However, Grudem shares with Wimber[20] the traditional neo-evangelical po-

---

16. Millard J. Erickson, *God the Father Almighty: A Contemporary Exploration of the Divine Attributes* (Grand Rapids: Baker, 1998), 160–64.

17. Grudem, *Systematic Theology*, 166.

18. See Millard J. Erickson, *Christian Theology* (Grand Rapids: Baker, 1985), 3:880–82.

19. Millard J. Erickson, *The Evangelical Mind and Heart: Perspectives on Theological and Practical Issues* (Grand Rapids: Baker, 1993), 153–72. In the 1998 revision of his systematic theology, Erickson adds a paragraph mentioning the Vineyard movement. Millard J. Erickson, *Christian Theology*, 2d ed. (Grand Rapids: Baker, 1998), 872–73.

20. Grudem draws his position on this issue partly from Wimber; see Grudem, *Systematic Theology*, 763 n. 2, 783 n. 33.

sition which sees the baptism of the Spirit as an alternative term for conversion itself.[21] Later Grudem came to view John Wimber as a mentor, and during the early 1990s he helped launch a Vineyard church before joining a Baptist congregation closer to his home.[22] Since then, Grudem's writings have shown him to be an avid supporter of the Vineyard teaching that miraculous gifts such as healing remain valid for today.[23]

A third point of difference between Erickson and Grudem can be found in the two theologians' stance toward women in ministry. Like several other prominent first- and second-generation neo-evangelicals (most notably Roger Nicole), Erickson is an egalitarian. He has lent his name to the board of reference of Christians for Biblical Equality, and he offers a veiled expression of support for women in church leadership in the anthropology section of his *Christian Theology*.[24] Grudem, in contrast, is an outspoken "complementarian."[25] In fact, he has given institutional form to his theological position by functioning as founding president of the Council on Biblical Manhood and Womanhood. In this role, Grudem became a vocal critic of the proposed inclusive language version of the New International Version of the Bible, which stance gained him an invitation to appear on James Dobson's *Focus on the Family* radio program.

Despite these important differences, in many ways Grudem stands at the head of those third-generation theologians who continue the legacy of Henry and Erickson. For Grudem, one aspect of this lies in his own theological posture, for he clearly sees himself as standing at the center of neo-evangelical orthodoxy. This is evident in the theological self-portrait Grudem offers to readers of his *Systematic Theology*. He describes himself by setting forth a succinct statement of his stance on the doctrinal issues "disputed within evangelical Christianity," namely, inerrancy, divine sovereignty and human responsibility, predestination and eternal security, women in ministry, church government, baptism, spiritual gifts, and the eschatological constellation of rapture, tribulation, and millennium.[26] To summarize: Grudem is an inerrantist, Calvinist, complementarian, elder-oriented congregational baptist, third-wave charismatic, post-tribulation premillennialist. At the same time, Grudem stands within the irenic tradition of neo-evangelical theology insofar as he expresses a

21. Ibid., 766–75.

22. Wayne A. Grudem, "Preface," in *Are Miraculous Gifts for Today? Four Views*, ed. Wayne Grudem (Grand Rapids: Zondervan, 1996), 15.

23. Grudem, *Systematic Theology*, 1043–46, 1063–69.

24. Erickson, *Christian Theology*, 2:548–49.

25. For an explication and defense of the complementarian position as Grudem understands it, see John Piper and Wayne Grudem, eds., *Recovering Biblical Manhood and Womanhood: A Response to Evangelical Feminism* (Wheaton: Crossway, 1991). See also Grudem, *Systematic Theology*, 937–45.

26. Grudem, *Systematic Theology*, 16.

willingness to engage in dialogue with, and affirm as "evangelical," a cross section of systematic theologies that hold to inerrancy while differing with him on some of these doctrinal issues.[27] By tackling these particular issues under the implicit and unquestioned assumption that they constitute the crucial questions of the day, Grudem sets himself in the role of torchbearer of the neo-evangelical theological tradition.

Grudem continues the neo-evangelical theological legacy in another manner as well, namely, in his understanding of the task of theology. In his monumental one-volume treatise, Grudem defines systematic theology as "any study that answers the question, 'What does the whole Bible teach us today?' about any given topic."[28] He then adds, "Systematic theology involves collecting and understanding all the relevant passages in the Bible on various topics and then summarizing their teachings clearly so that we know what to believe about each topic."[29] In distinguishing his approach from related disciplines such as philosophical theology or apologetics, Grudem reiterates that his work "interacts directly with the biblical text in order to understand what the Bible itself says to us about various theological subjects."[30] To this end, Grudem advises a three-stage process in dealing theologically with any topic: find all the relevant Bible verses, note the points made by these verses, and finally summarize in a few conclusions what the Bible affirms about the topic.[31]

In this manner, Grudem continues the propositionalist approach to systematic theology which has as its goal the summarization of correct doctrine. This information is assumed to be given in a less systematic manner in the Bible. Further, following the style of argument early neo-evangelicals appropriated from Warfield, he claims to build his systematic statement of biblical teachings from a Bible that is inerrant.

At first glance, Grudem's *Systematic Theology* appears to be a restatement and continuation of the Henry-Erickson theological legacy, albeit written in the light of "third generation" neo-evangelical sensitivities, such as an openness to impulses from the Vineyard movement. Yet even in certain methodological respects Grudem's project departs significantly from that set forth by his predecessors.

One intriguing difference lies in their respective starting places. The older works generally begin with the concept of revelation, which can be general or special. The Bible, in turn, is elevated as the inscripturation of special rev-

---

27. See, for example, ibid., 17. The irenic dimension has been noted as well by Roy Kearsley, "Review of *Systematic Theology: An Introduction to Biblical Doctrine,*" *Themelios* 22 (1996): 66.
28. Grudem, *Systematic Theology,* 21.
29. Ibid.
30. Ibid., 22.
31. Ibid., 36.

elation. Because both types of revelation come from the same God, the classic neo-evangelical argument asserts, there can be no ultimate contradiction between what is given in Scripture and the findings of science.

Grudem, in contrast, does not begin with revelation, but with the concept of the Word of God, then quickly moves to the Bible as the Word of God written. Not until two hundred seventy-five pages into his treatise does he engage in the question of science and the Bible. Grudem agrees that there can be no final conflict between Scripture and science. Yet, the only theological basis he offers for this belief comes in one brief, philosophically flimsy assertion of the omniscience of God: "God, who speaks in Scripture, knows all facts, and he has not spoken in a way that would contradict any true fact in the universe."[32]

This example indicates a deeper methodological difference between Grudem and his neo-evangelical forebears. Grudem's project, at least as it is outlined in his *Systematic Theology*, simply does not provide the depth of engagement that the neo-evangelical pioneers set before themselves. Thus, his approach to the systematic-theological task does not differ significantly from that of second-generation thinkers like Gordon Lewis. But Grudem's work lacks the elaborated philosophical foundation for testing doctrinal hypotheses that characterizes Lewis and Demarest's three-volume *Integrative Theology*.

More significantly, Grudem's project falls short of his predecessors' in that it does not advance their clear apologetic purpose. At its beginning, the new evangelical program was fundamentally apologetic. Despite their differences, Henry and Ramm were in agreement that the goal of their work was to foster theological engagement with the wider cultural and theological world. Erickson and Pinnock, in turn, have carried on this enterprise.

In contrast to this crucial aspect of the neo-evangelical legacy, Grudem has set before himself only the task of engaging in the intramural evangelical conversation. His stated purpose is to construct a "true system of theology," and he is convinced that this endeavor makes interaction with the broader theological world superfluous. In a move that reviewers of the work[33] have repeatedly flagged as "arbitrary and reductionist,"[34] "myopic,"[35] or "provincial,"[36] Grudem lumps this wider world together super-

32. Ibid., 275.

33. See, for example, Tim Bradshaw, "Review of *Systematic Theology: An Introduction to Biblical Doctrine*," *Anvil* 14, no. 1 (1997): 65; I. Howard Marshall, "A Biblical Systematic Theology," *Expository Times* 106 (May 1995): 243.

34. David Parker, "Review of *Systematic Theology: An Introduction to Biblical Doctrine*," *Evangelical Review of Theology* 20 (April 1996): 190.

35. Kearsley, "Review of *Systematic Theology*," 65.

36. Randall E. Otto, "Review of *Systematic Theology: An Introduction to Biblical Doctrine*," *Journal of Psychology and Theology* 24 (Winter 1996): 339.

ficially and unhelpfully under the label "liberal," his blanket term for all "who deny the absolute truthfulness of the Bible, or who do not think the words of the Bible to be God's very words." Although he expresses gratitude for "evangelical friends who write extensive critiques of liberal theology," Grudem is not convinced that "an extensive analysis of liberal views is the most helpful way to build a positive system of theology." In fact, he voices the outlandish opinion, "I think someone needs to say that it is doubtful that liberal theologians have given us any significant insights into the doctrinal teachings of Scripture that are not already to be found in evangelical writers."[37]

Grudem's approach falls short of the vision of his predecessors in another way as well. He seems to equate his theological system with that of the Bible itself in a completely naive manner. Not only does he believe that he has captured "what the Bible itself says" about the topics he has chosen for inclusion in his work, he also intimates that the topics themselves are simply those that the Bible intends to address. He writes, "The adjective *systematic* in systematic theology should be understood to mean something like 'carefully organized by topics,' with the understanding that the topics studied . . . will include all the major doctrinal topics of the Bible."[38] In short, Grudem is of the opinion that he has accomplished the task of moving directly from the Bible to systematic theology without any "alien" presuppositions clouding his vision or even determining his categories. In so doing he has simply explicated what is taught in the Bible itself. As David Parker, writing in the *Evangelical Review of Theology*, points out,

> Defining systematic theology in this way makes for a mechanistic approach to the discipline, which does little to provide the broader understanding of the relation of theological ideas to each other and to other areas of life that is so necessary for a mature approach to Christian thinking and living in today's complex world.[39]

In his sampling of the current crop of evangelical systematic theologies, Carl Braaten takes the kind of critique Parker offers a step further. Pinpointing the difficulty with Grudem's assumption, Braaten declares, "A purely biblical dogmatics that claims to go straight to Scripture . . . is surely self-deluded." He then remarks, "Yet this seems to be what is going on in Wayne Grudem's *Systematic Theology: An Introduction to Biblical Doctrine*."[40] On this basis, Braaten characterizes Grudem as an "evangelical

---

37. Grudem, *Systematic Theology*, 17.
38. Ibid., 24.
39. Parker, "Review of *Systematic Theology*," 190.
40. Braaten, "Harvest of Evangelical Theology," 47.

fundamentalist,"[41] a description echoed in I. Howard Marshall's appraisal of Grudem as "a 'fundamentalist' in the current (but not the classical) sense of that term."[42]

In 1993, Erickson voiced a grave fear that history was repeating itself through what he perceived as a leftward drift among younger evangelical thinkers.[43] In the years since he voiced this consternation, the neo-evangelical movement appears to have witnessed a repetition of history in the form of a pronounced shift to the "right." As was indicated in the previous chapter, Erickson's own theological pilgrimage illustrates this move, at least in the estimation of commentators such as James Leo Garrett. If Braaten and Marshall are correct in their characterization of Grudem, the shift to the right that Erickson prefigured is in certain respects even more pronounced among certain third-generation thinkers who draw inspiration from Henry and Erickson. The seemingly irenic and charitable Grudem stands as a case in point, in that he appears to have narrowed his forebears' grand vision of a new evangelical engagement with the world to the fundamentalist quest for the delineation of the one, timeless, systemization of the doctrine that supposedly lies waiting to be discovered in the pages of the Bible.

Continuing the Reform

While Wayne Grudem was busily writing his massive *Systematic Theology*, calling for an openness among evangelicals to "signs and wonders," and solidifying the opposition to evangelical feminism, other third-generation evangelicals were setting themselves to the task of carrying forward Clark Pinnock's rethinking of neo-evangelical theology. Bethel College theologian Greg Boyd has in some respects become the new target of Pinnock's detractors, at least in certain circles. But another theologian, John Sanders, has to date fleshed out more extensively Pinnock's more explicitly theological themes. In this sense, Pinnock's mantle appears to rest on Sanders, at least for now.

Sanders reached many of his views apart from Pinnock's direct influence, particularly those on the destiny of the unevangelized and the "openness of God." Like Pinnock, Sanders began his pilgrimage attracted to a rationalist approach to apologetics. But during his undergraduate philosophical studies, and subsequently at Trinity Evangelical Divinity School, he began to see problems with the Enlightenment criteria for rationality and, in turn, with the evangelical hermeneutics he was receiving. The formative influence that Sanders does attribute to Pinnock is the en-

41. Ibid., 48.
42. Marshall, "Biblical Systematic Theology," 243.
43. Erickson, *Evangelical Mind and Heart*, 38.

couragement to pursue these ideas through writing. In fact, Sanders originated the concept of a book on "free-will theism," and he did the initial leg work for Pinnock, such as lining up potential contributors. Sanders himself wrote the chapter on "Historical Considerations," leaving to Pinnock the task of developing the "Systematic Theology" section.

The connection between Sanders and Pinnock is incontestable. *No Other Name*,[44] Sanders's first major literary contribution, explored an increasingly significant theological issue that Pinnock had flagged as early as 1988.[45] Sanders jumped on the same question, producing what Pinnock lauded as the "fine explanation and defense" that the inclusivist position deserved but "has not received before."[46] Sanders, in turn, offered a seven-page analysis of Pinnock's position, in which he highlights Pinnock as "one of the stronger evangelical proponents"[47] of the view Sanders himself affirms. Sanders and Pinnock were working on their respective treatments of the topic simultaneously, so Sanders had Pinnock's statement—*A Wideness in God's Mercy*—in manuscript form prior to the completion of his own work, and Pinnock, in turn, wrote the foreword for *No Other Name*. In *A Wideness in God's Mercy*, he also lists Sanders among the several evangelicals who were rethinking the issue, and notes Sanders's "soon-to-appear manuscript" on the topic.[48]

Yet it was Sanders's 1998 publication *The God Who Risks*[49] that offered him the best occasion to date to delineate the theological perspective he shares with Pinnock. The stage for this volume was set already in Sanders's contribution to *The Openness of God* project. The stated goal of his historical chapter was to indicate how the Hellenization of Christian theology, i.e., the inroads of Greek philosophy, is a root cause of the loss of the biblical conception of God as the one who "responds to us and may change his mind."[50] Sanders concluded his historical sketch by calling for Christian theology "to reevaluate classical theism in light of a more relational metaphysic . . . so that the living, personal, responsive and loving God of the Bible may be spoken of more con-

44. John Sanders, *No Other Name: An Investigation into the Destiny of the Unevangelized* (Grand Rapids: Eerdmans, 1992).

45. Clark H. Pinnock, "The Finality of Jesus Christ in a World of Religions," in *Christian Faith and Practice in the Modern World: Theology from an Evangelical Point of View*, ed. Mark A. Noll and David F. Wells (Grand Rapids: Eerdmans, 1988), 152–68.

46. Clark H. Pinnock, "Foreword," in Sanders, *No Other Name*, xv.

47. Sanders, *No Other Name*, 257.

48. Clark H. Pinnock, *A Wideness in God's Mercy: The Finality of Jesus Christ in a World of Religions* (Grand Rapids: Zondervan, 1992), 12, 186 n. 12.

49. John Sanders, *The God Who Risks: A Theology of Providence* (Downers Grove, Ill.: InterVarsity, 1998).

50. John Sanders, "Historical Considerations," in *The Openness of God*, ed. Clark H. Pinnock et al. (Downers Grove, Ill.: InterVarsity, 1994), 59.

sistently in our theological reflection and not merely in our devotional practice."[51] *The God Who Risks*, which is a revision of his doctoral thesis under Adrio Konig, delineates Sanders's attempt to respond to the challenge he articulated in his contribution to *The Openness of God*.

The intent of this sketch is not to engage critically with the particular theological position Sanders espouses. For the purposes of the discussion here, *The God Who Risks* is significant because of the theological method it embodies. Sanders spells out this method in the second chapter of the book. He notes that theology deals with metaphors or models that describe God in relationship to the world, certain of which function as "key models" or "root metaphors" because they control or orient our thought and life.[52] Sanders then proposes three criteria for evaluating any particular Christian theological model: consonance with tradition, conceptual intelligibility, and adequacy for the demands of life.[53] His task in the volume is to evaluate the model of "divine providence as risk taking" in accordance with the three criteria he has established. By delineating a sophisticated theological method by which he confirms and fleshes out the relational model of God, Sanders marks a continuation as well as an advancement of the theological orientation Pinnock has spearheaded.

Despite his claim that biblical theological language is metaphorical, Sanders still maintains that such language says something about how God really is. He writes, "Metaphors (even those about God) are reality depicting in that they tell us of a real relationship between God and the world."[54] Consequently, Sanders is convinced that to say that God is a "personal agent" is to speak in "a literal sense" about God, or at least about God in relationship to the world.[55] In this manner, Sanders avoids the rationalist propositionalism that characterizes much of neo-evangelical theology from Henry to Grudem, while retaining—albeit not completely convincingly—the classic neo-evangelical commitment to the objectivity of theological language. Further, Sanders stands in the legacy of neo-evangelical theology in that, insofar as it arises out of the problem of evil, his work reflects the apologetic orientation that characterized the first- and second-generation neo-evangelicals. Yet, Sanders is a typical "third-generation" evangelical in that his work seems to be more oriented toward a practical, as opposed to an apologetic, goal than is the case with either Pinnock or Erickson.[56]

51. Ibid., 100.
52. Sanders, *God Who Risks*, 16.
53. Ibid., 16–18.
54. Ibid., 16.
55. Ibid., 26, 38.
56. Hence, Sanders begins the book with a narrative of a crisis of faith that was triggered by a traffic accident involving his brother, and he concludes it with practical applications to Christian life. See Sanders, *God Who Risks*, 9–14, 237–79.

At the heart of *The God Who Risks* Sanders presents a highly controversial perspective on the divine nature. Apart from whatever difficulties may beset the content of his theological proposal, Sanders's perspective is problematic in the particular manner in which it arises. He asserts that Christian theology must first clear away the residue of Greek philosophy that has captivated it over the centuries before the true biblical picture of God can emerge. Sanders is, of course, correct in pointing out that philosophical assumptions color our reading of the text and distort what we claim to find there. Yet his thesis shares with the "openness of God" in general a typical yet overdrawn claim of disjuncture between Hebrew and Greek thought.

What is perhaps even more disquieting about Sanders's proposal is that it seems to require the rejection of such a broad swath of the Christian theological tradition. He intimates that on something as fundamental as our basic conception of God nearly everyone from the fifth century to the present has deviated far from the true understanding of biblical texts. Proponents of the "openness of God" rightly critique the neo-evangelical Calvinist "establishment" for reading the Bible solely through Reformed eyes, and thereby effectively sidelining other aspects of the broader evangelical tradition. But by rejecting categorically Christian theology's long tradition of appropriating Greek philosophy, Sanders's work risks replacing one neo-evangelical sectarianism with another. And it comes dangerously close to the typical evangelical temptation to claim to be able to jump directly from the text to the contemporary situation.

In short, in different yet parallel ways, both Grudem's project, with its claim to be able to read the text without reference to the interpretive tradition and its superficial dividing of theology into "liberal" and "evangelical," and Sanders's pitting of the text against one major line of the tradition suggest that neo-evangelical theology has not yet devised a way to foster a truly catholic reading of Scripture. Further, the work of both scholars indicates that while third-generation evangelical theologians are seeking to continue the work of their second-generation benefactors, in many ways they are also charting their own course. This may entail both promise and pitfalls for the future of evangelical theology.

The Demise of Evangelicalism

The word *ferment*, found in the title of this section, is laced with double meaning. On the one hand, its synonyms include terms like *upheaval, tumult, turmoil,* and even *excitement*. But it also can refer to a substance, such as yeast, that causes the decomposition of organic compounds. Taken as a whole, contemporary evangelical theology is indeed characterized by ferment. Yet there are today differing opinions as to whether this ferment is leading to a new and exciting rebirth of theological engagement or is symptomatic of the decomposition of the entire movement.

The Great Evangelical Disaster

Since the publication of Francis Schaeffer's parting shot to the movement in 1984,[57] a variety of evangelical thinkers have bemoaned what they see as the disastrous state of evangelicalism. These concerned observers are convinced that the current ferment in evangelical theology is not only a symptom of decomposition but a warning signal. Some prophetic voices go so far as to foretell the impending demise of the evangelical movement itself.

Perhaps no purportedly theological jeremiad has been better received than David Wells's full-length assessment of the crisis entitled *No Place for Truth, or Whatever Happened to Evangelical Theology?*[58] In this book, Wells claims that evangelicalism has capitulated to the spirit of modernity, a capitulation evident in "the disappearance of theology from the life of the Church"[59] and the "antitheological mood that now grips the evangelical world."[60] The theology whose loss Wells bemoans consists of three constellations: confession, understood as "what the Church believes"; reflection, or "the intellectual struggle to understand what it means to be the recipient of God's Word in this present world," which process looks to the whole of Scripture, to God's past working in the Church, and to what the contemporary society views as normative; and finally, "the cultivation of those virtues that constitute a wisdom for life."[61]

Wells is convinced that this kind of theology, which, he adds, is driven by a "passion for truth"[62] and which characterized the church in Puritan New England, is disappearing. This disappearance has occurred as the three dimensions of theology separate from one another and "are now each attracting different constituencies." But perhaps more importantly, passionate theology has been banished from the church, Wells argues, in that the classical doctrines, while still professed by evangelicals, "are no longer defining what it means to be an evangelical or how evangelicalism should be practiced."[63]

Wells's solution to this debilitating situation is quite simple. Basically, he calls evangelicals to rediscover the traditional doctrine of God's holiness. In fact, in Wells's estimation, the loss of a sense of the holiness of God constitutes the ultimate disaster of contemporary evangelicalism: "It is this God, majestic and holy in his being, this God whose love knows no

---

57. Francis A. Schaeffer, *The Great Evangelical Disaster* (Westchester, Ill.: Crossway, 1984).
58. David F. Wells, *No Place for Truth, or Whatever Happened to Evangelical Theology?* (Grand Rapids: Eerdmans, 1993).
59. Ibid., 95.
60. Ibid., 96.
61. Ibid., 99–100.
62. Ibid., 12.
63. Ibid., 109.

bounds because his holiness knows no limits, who has disappeared from the modern evangelical world."[64]

Although it walked away with *Christianity Today* "book of the year" honors, *No Place for Truth* was not greeted with universal applause.[65] One point of controversy is the extent to which Wells's basic thesis is accurate. A cursory look at the paltry offerings on the "theology" shelf of most evangelical bookstores confirms that on one level Wells has correctly depicted the current reality in evangelicalism. He is likewise right in bemoaning that many evangelical church leaders do not consciously look to the doctrines they claim to affirm for the foundation for the practice of ministry in which they engage. In the face of these trends, Wells has sounded a much needed admonition.

Yet, this is not the entire story. The situation may not be as dire as Wells suggests. Many evangelical congregations do give the kind of central place to theology that Wells envisions, although—and that may be where the real conflict lies—not necessarily to the particular theology he prefers. Willow Creek Community Church, to cite an obvious example, has from the beginning had a theologian, Gilbert Bilezikian, as part of the leadership team, and its leaders seek to build the congregation's ministry upon the theological base he represents. Equally significant are the many newer so-called GenX churches, such as Seattle's Mars Hill Fellowship, which are led by pastors who are keenly interested in intellectual trends in general and theology in particular, and who desire to shape congregational life on the basis of solid theology. However, the theological emphases driving these ministries do not necessarily line up with Wells's view of evangelical theology. This suggests that ultimately a difference in fundamental theological commitment, rather than the supposed banishment of theology from the center of congregational life, is at least in part what triggered Wells's censure. When viewed from this perspective, the answer to the question as to whether the evangelical movement has ejected theology from its center depends to a great degree on what particular "theology" is meant.

This observation, in turn, leads to the central doctrinal question *No Place for Truth* poses: Is Wells correct in his elevation of holiness as the fundamental divine attribute? Posed in this manner, the answer is clearly no. In contrast to Wells's stated position, many evangelical theologians argue (correctly) that the God of the Bible is marked ultimately by love, with holiness deriving its significance from divine love, and not vice versa.[66] If this

---

64. Ibid., 300.

65. Even as sympathetic a theologian as Erickson found much about the book to criticize; see Millard J. Erickson, *Postmodernizing the Faith: Evangelical Responses to the Challenge of Postmodernism* (Grand Rapids: Baker, 1998), 39–41.

66. For the author's discussion of this point, see Grenz, *Theology for the Community of God*, 92–95, 121–22.

is the case, evangelicals who have rediscovered divine love (which is of course holy) and who seek to minister out of a profound understanding of God as the loving one have not abandoned orthodox theological moorings, contra Wells.

This question must be taken a step further, however. In an essay that appeared five years before *No Place for Truth*, Wells indicated that he reads the evangelical movement through the lense of the mid-twentieth-century post-fundamentalist neo-evangelical coalition. Writing as a participant in an evangelical-Jewish dialogue, Wells bemoans the loss of cohesion in the evangelicalism of the 1980s, in contrast to its united front in the 1950s. But the united front Wells glorifies in the essay was simply that of the neo-evangelical coalition, which according to Wells centered on the Billy Graham Crusades, the National Association of Evangelicals, and Carl Henry, who supposedly "gave intellectual thrust and coherence to the movement."[67]

A similar reading emerges in an essay published a decade later in a volume edited by John Armstrong, *The Compromised Church: The Present Evangelical Crisis*. In this mini-jeremiad, Wells alludes to the typical neo-evangelical historiography that views the movement as arising directly out of fundamentalism.[68] Following the received neo-evangelical history, Wells notes that early twentieth-century fundamentalism took the path of "cognitive dissonance" and chose to reject the reigning intellectual paradigm of modernity. When this choice led to anti-intellectualism, neo-evangelicalism emerged with the express goal of avoiding the mistakes of the fundamentalists. Thus, the new evangelicalism "would not be anti-intellectual, separatistic, legalistic, or culturally withdrawn."[69]

In his 1998 essay, however, Wells finds it necessary to call evangelicals back to their fundamentalist roots, a call he issued implicitly in *No Place for Truth*.[70] More particularly, he lauds fundamentalism for its strong Christ-against-culture stance and accuses contemporary evangelicalism of gross cultural accommodation. Evangelicalism is guilty of displaying "a disposition to adapt to [contemporary] culture rather than to sustain a moral and spiritual antagonism to it."[71] In contrast, the fundamentalists, who took a stand against the culture, succeeded in "preserving the Word of God and the Gospel." Wells concludes that recent years have witnessed a transition from "too much" to "too little" strife with

---

67. David F. Wells, " 'No Offense: I Am an Evangelical': A Search for Self-Definition," in *A Time to Speak: The Evangelical-Jewish Encounter*, ed. A. James Rudin and Marvin R. Wilson (Grand Rapids: Eerdmans, 1987), 36.

68. David F. Wells, "Introduction: The Word in the World," in *The Compromised Church: The Present Evangelical Crisis*, ed. John H. Armstrong (Wheaton: Crossway, 1998), 26–27.

69. Ibid., 26.

70. Wells, *No Place for Truth*, 128–29.

71. Wells, "Introduction: The Word in the World," 24.

culture. And he worries that in the end neo-evangelicals will "fail where the fundamentalists had succeeded."[72]

Throughout his diagnosis, Wells makes the typical neo-evangelical move of espousing a truncated understanding of the evangelical movement's genesis, character, and composition. Commenting on Wells's 1988 offering, Thomas Askew insightfully observes that Wells equates evangelicalism with Calvinist fundamentalism. Askew, in contrast, writes: "I see the evangelical faith and motif as a much broader tradition or current in American church history, one with a dozen substreams and marked by great diversity. Fundamentalism is merely one exclusivistic subculture within that stream."[73] Wells's narrowing the boundaries of evangelicalism goes hand in hand with his revisionist historiography. He erroneously claims that commitment to right doctrine is what gave birth to the evangelical movement. As noted in chapter 1, the sine qua non of evangelicalism from the beginning has not been doctrine but convertive piety. Doctrine plays an important role, to be sure, but its role is that of servant to the church in its mission to live and witness as a gospel people.

The Dawn of the "Post-Evangelical" Era

Wells represents the various thinkers who interpret the current ferment in evangelical theology largely as "decomposition." These theologians see convincing signs that evangelicalism has fallen from the sound theological moorings that guided it in the past. Other evangelicals, in contrast, welcome the ferment as an exciting sign of vitality. Some even intentionally stir up the evangelical theological pot, hoping to coax it even further along the pathway of reform. One such "stirring," Dave Tomlinson's *The Post-Evangelical*,[74] went so far as to celebrate the "demise" of evangelicalism. Although written from a British perspective, the book has direct application to the North American context as well.

Tomlinson's thesis is quite simple. He calls his co-religionists to become "post-evangelical," and he offers a terse definition as to what this entails: "To be post-evangelical is to take as given many of the assumptions of evangelical faith, while at the same time moving beyond its perceived limitations."[75] As this statement indicates, viewed from one perspective Tomlinson is no wild-eyed radical. He does not want to undo what he sees as the great gains of the evangelical movement. On the contrary, he believes that this tradition has made a significant contribution to the church and

---

72. Ibid., 27.
73. Thomas A. Askew, "A Response to David F. Wells," in *A Time to Speak*, 43.
74. Dave Tomlinson, *The Post-Evangelical* (London: Triangle, 1995).
75. Ibid., 7.

cites two aspects of the evangelical ethos that are especially worthy of continuation. One contribution is the love for Scripture that characterizes evangelicals. In Tomlinson's estimation, "evangelicalism brings an acute expectation that God will speak through [the Scriptures]—they are the word of God. They do not exist primarily to be dissected and analysed; they exist as a sacrament, or a means of God communicating himself to us."[76] In addition, evangelicalism is characterized by a crucial gospel focus. He lauds the evangelical tradition for its "robust emphasis on the gospel as something that can be expressed in a simple form, and which challenges each and every one of us on a personal level."[77]

At the same time, Tomlinson calls for major rethinking of several key points of evangelical theology, including its doctrine of Scripture for which, in a manner reminiscent of Bernard Ramm, he offers a basically Barthian alternative. But more important than his own highly controversial and often overdrawn proposals[78] is the rationale that motivates Tomlinson's call. He is convinced that far-reaching cultural transitions require a corresponding shift in religious ethos. Tomlinson asserts that present-day evangelicalism was shaped by the modern context; it was in this context that evangelicals needed to experience and express their faith. But the context has shifted. Modernity is giving place to postmodernity. And this postmodern context now calls for a post-evangelicalism that can meet the challenges of the day.

Tomlinson finds a kind of inevitability in his proposal. Postmodern sensitivities will quite readily lead to a post-evangelical ethos, just as evangelicalism was in a certain sense the product of modernity. The postmodern world, therefore, is for post-evangelicals what the modern era was to their evangelical forebears. Hence, he declares that post-evangelicals "are people who relate more naturally to the world of postmodernity, and consequently this is the cultural environment which influences the way they think about and experience their faith." But not only are post-evangelicals shaped by postmodern sensitivities, the postmodern world is "the context in which the integrity and credibility of their faith must be tested."[79]

76. Ibid., 67.
77. Ibid.
78. Although largely unknown in North America, *The Post-Evangelical* triggered a vigorous debate in the global evangelical community, especially in Britain. For a highly critical response to Tomlinson's proposal, see Alister McGrath, "Prophets of Doubt," *Alpha* (August 1996): 28–30. A helpful interchange between Tomlinson and Derek Tidball appeared as "To Be or Not to Be . . . a Post-Evangelical," *New Christian Herald* (19 October 1996): 10–11. See also the collection of critical essays published in Graham Cray et al., *The Post-Evangelical Debate* (London: Triangle, 1997). I am in substantial agreement with the appraisal offered by David Parker in his review of *The Post-Evangelical* in *Evangelical Review of Theology* 21 (July 1997): 273.
79. Tomlinson, *Post-Evangelical*, 8–9.

Wells and Tomlinson stand at opposite poles of a spectrum of opinion on the vexing issue of the relationship of evangelicalism to culture. Wells is convinced that by taking seriously the call to openness to culture that the first generation of neo-evangelicals had articulated, contemporary evangelicals have capitulated to culture and in the process lost their theology, their relevance, and even their own soul. His proposed solution is for evangelicals to recapture the orthodox theology that characterized evangelicals in the past. Tomlinson, in contrast, worries that evangelicalism is in fact stuck in the past, that is, in a theological program shaped by modernity. His call, therefore, is for evangelicals to move forward into the postmodern context and articulate their faith in that context.

Evangelical Theology and the Postmodern Condition

This survey of paradigmatic third-generation evangelical thinkers has indicated two significant aspects of the ferment that characterizes contemporary evangelical theology. Some thinkers, typified by Grudem and Sanders, are about the business of carrying into the future the trajectories charted by their forebears, while engaging with what they see as the pressing theological questions of the day. Other participants, including Wells and Tomlinson, are asking questions about the impact of evangelicalism, and hence the form of evangelical theology, within the wider culture.

What all these writers share, albeit to differing degrees, is a realization that the context in which the theological enterprise must be advanced is changing. While neo-evangelicals were debating the best manner to engage the modern world, Western society has been moving "beyond" modernity. Although there are a variety of designations for this changing ethos, the term that seems to have gained the widest use is *postmodern*. Tomlinson's call for a "post-evangelical" move is surely ill-advised and unnecessary; yet by calling on evangelicals to take the postmodern condition seriously he is at least pointing in the right direction. The postmodern world has emerged as the context toward which evangelical theology must look.

The Postmodern Condition

Postmodernism defies definition. It is a complex phenomenon encompassing a variety of elements. Whatever else it may mean, however, postmodernism is, as the designation itself indicates, "post-modern." The postmodern ethos is on the one hand *modern*; it retains the modern. Rather than calling for a return to some premodern situation, the postmodern outlook accepts the Enlightenment, especially its elevation of skeptical rationality. On the other hand, the postmodern ethos is *post* modern; it sees the dangers inherent in the very skeptical rationality it accepts. For this reason, it seeks to live in a realm of chastened rationality.

The goal of this section is not to provide a detailed exposé of the cultural transition from the modern to the postmodern or offer a lengthy description of postmodernism itself.[80] Rather, what follows is a sketch of two dimensions of the postmodern condition that are especially important for the future of evangelical theology.

The Move from a Realist to a Constructionist View of Truth[81]

The reigning understanding of truth and knowledge throughout much of the modern era has been a viewpoint generally known as "realism." At the heart of the realist perspective are two interrelated assumptions: the objectivity of the world, and the epistemological prowess of human reason. Modern realism assumes that the world is a given reality existing outside the human mind. This objective world is permeated by order which is intrinsic to it, is displayed by it, and functions quite independently of human knowing activity. In addition, realism assumes that human reason has the capacity of discerning this objective order, especially insofar as it manifests itself in the "laws" of nature. That is, the human mind is capable of more or less accurately mirroring the external, objective nonhuman reality. As the product of the human mind, language provides an adequate means of declaring what the world is like.

These two assumptions, in turn, lead almost inevitably to what is called the correspondence theory of truth. According to this theory, truth is primarily a quality of propositions or assertions. "True" or "false" are above all judgments about statements. And the veracity of any particular statement is to be determined by comparing it with the dimension of the objective world about which it purports to speak. An assertion is true, therefore, if it "corresponds" to—that is, represents accurately or describes correctly—the world.

In a sense, realism emerges quite naturally out of day-to-day experience. "Common sense" itself seems to confirm its validity. And the realist assumption works quite well in many aspects of life. Certain realist philosophers, however, do not stop with the mundane. They extend the limits of the "re-

80. For the author's fuller treatment of these topics, see Stanley J. Grenz, *A Primer on Postmodernism* (Grand Rapids: Eerdmans, 1996).

81. See, for example, Walter Truett Anderson, *Reality Isn't What It Used to Be: Theatrical Politics, Ready-to-Wear Religion, Global Myths, Primitive Chic, and Other Wonders of the Postmodern World* (San Francisco: Harper and Row, 1990), x–xi, 8; Hilary Lawson, "Introduction" to "Stories about Truth," in *Dismantling Truth: Reality in the Post-Modern World*, ed. Hilary Lawson and Lisa Appignanesi (New York: St. Martin's Press, 1989), 4.

ality" that human reason can fathom, thereby universalizing the realist approach into a general theory of truth. These thinkers are convinced that the human mind can grasp, at least theoretically, reality as a whole, and consequently the human epistemological program can potentially devise the one true and complete description of the world as it actually is.

Although philosophical realism has been on the retreat for some time, in recent years it has come under full-scale attack.[82] In part, this challenge has been philosophical. Against the realist conception of the objectivity of knowledge, critics argue that knowledge is necessarily participatory. They deny that humans enjoy an Archimedean vantage point from which to gain a purely objective view of reality "out there." Rather, humans structure their world through the concepts they bring to it. Further, critics of realism deny that a simple, one-to-one relationship exists between language and the world or that any single language can provide an accurate "map" of the world. Instead, languages are human social conventions that map the world in a variety of ways, depending on the context of the speaker. Or to use another image, all linguistic signifiers (e.g., words) are embedded in "language games," each of which is a system of rules that govern the way words are used within that context.[83] These various language games color and alter the way humans experience their world.

In addition to these philosophical developments, the phenomenon known as "globalization" has also posed a challenge to realism.[84] Globalization has led postmodern thinkers to give up the modern dream of discovering the one, universal symbolic world that unites all humankind. Instead, they acknowledge that humans inhabit a globe that is home to "multiple realities." As different groups of people construct different "stories" about the world they encounter, these different languages facilitate differing ways of experiencing life. As a result, people do not merely espouse different political opinions and religious beliefs; for all practical purposes they live in different worlds.

82. For a concise critique of realism, see Hugh Tomlinson, "After Truth: Post-Modernism and the Rhetoric of Science," in *Dismantling Truth*, 46–48.

83. The "language game" terminology was proposed by Ludwig Wittgenstein, who is discussed in chapter 6. The definition offered here is based on Lyotard's description; Jean-Francois Lyotard, *The Postmodern Condition: A Report on Knowledge*, trans. Geoff Bennington and Brian Massumi (Minneapolis: University of Minnesota Press, 1984), 10.

84. Anderson writes, "The collapse of belief we have been witnessing throughout the twentieth century comes with globalism. The postmodern condition is not an artistic movement or a cultural fad or an intellectual theory—although it produces all of those and is in some ways defined by them. It is what inevitably happens as people everywhere begin to see that there are many beliefs, many kinds of belief, many ways of believing. Postmodernism *is* globalism; it is the half-discovered shape of the one unity that transcends all our differences." Anderson, *Reality Isn't What It Used to Be*, 231.

Considerations such as these have led some thinkers to what is called a "critical realist" stance. Others abandon realism in favor of a constructivist epistemology. Constructivists emphasize the role of language in providing access to the world. Radical constructivists declare that the so-called "real world" is merely an ever changing, social creation, and what humans inhabit is a "symbolic world," a social reality that people construct through language. Consequently, all explanations of reality are constructions. Such constructions may be useful, but they are not objectively true.

Moreover, radical constructivists elevate to a quasi-ontological status the insight, noted earlier, that different people, by devising different theories or accounts of the world, create and inhabit differing worlds.[85] Further, because humans lack the ability to step outside their constructions of reality,[86] they cannot measure any of these particular theories and propositions by comparison to a supposedly objective, external world.[87] In fact, insofar as there is no single objective world as such, only the many worlds people create, nothing can function as the final basis for thought and knowledge.[88] The result is a type of pluralistic stance toward knowledge that allows competing and seemingly conflicting constructions to exist side by side.[89] In the end, the "truth question" is no longer, "Is the proposition or theory correct?" but, "What does it do?"[90] or, "What is its outcome?"

The Move from the Grand Metanarrative to Local Stories

In *The Post-Evangelical*, Tomlinson characterizes the postmodern situation as the demise of "the big story." He explains that in the modern or Enlightenment version of reality, a big story or epic "not only tells us how things are but how they were and how they should be; it explains the whole thing."[91] Now, however, Tomlinson adds, "The big stories and the storytellers are losing credibility and fewer people want to gather around

85. Lawson explains, "Through language, theory, and text, we close the openness that is the world. The closures we make provide our world. . . . We do not have different accounts of the same 'thing,' but different closures and different things." Hilary Lawson, *Reflexivity: The Post-Modern Predicament* (London: Hutchinson, 1985), 128–29.

86. Anderson, *Reality Isn't What It Used to Be*, 255.

87. Thomas S. Kuhn, *The Structure of Scientific Revolutions*, 2d ed. (Chicago: University of Chicago Press, 1970), 206.

88. Robert P. Scharlemann, "Introduction," in *Theology at the End of the Century: A Dialogue on the Postmodern*, ed. Robert P. Scharlemann (Charlottesville: University Press of Virginia, 1990), 6.

89. A typical postmodern conclusion is offered by Anderson: "Lacking absolutes, we will have to encounter one another as people with different information, different stories, different visions—and trust the outcome." Anderson, *Reality Isn't What It Used to Be*, 183.

90. H. Tomlinson, "After Truth," 55.

91. D. Tomlinson, *The Post-Evangelical*, 76.

to listen."[92] Essentially, Tomlinson is repackaging Jean-Francois Lyotard's tersely stated and widely quoted characterization: "Simplifying to the extreme, I define *postmodern* as incredulity toward metanarratives."[93]

The modern project arose in part out of the desire to move beyond the wars and conflicts that were, according to the early Enlightenment intellectuals, the inevitable result of beliefs in myths and religious dogmas. They set themselves to the task of exploring the world "as it really is." In their estimation this meant discovering the universal laws that govern action and that comprise true, objective knowledge of the world.

In the twentieth century, however, anthropologists became increasingly aware of the foundational importance of myths to human society. Rather than being merely silly stories that primitive peoples tell, myths embody a central core of values and beliefs that in some sense are fundamentally religious.[94] Further, each society is bound together by a system of myths that sustains social relations within it[95] and forms the basis for its claim to legitimacy. And every such system carries its own force apart from argumentation and proof.[96] The contemporary term for a system of legitimizing myths, or, more specifically, for the overarching motif that unifies the collection of myths into a system, is *metanarrative*.

Postmodern thinkers such as Lyotard point out that in the name of science the Enlightenment outlook claimed to dispel from the realm of knowledge the "prescientific" beliefs, myths, and stories that primitive peoples use to speak about the world. Nevertheless, this outlook was itself dependent on an often unacknowledged appeal to variations on the metanarrative of progress.[97] Each of these variants, in turn, legitimated technological invention and economic development as the means of creating a better world for all humans. But more importantly, the metanarrative of the progress of science served to unite the smaller stories of the sciences into one, unified history.[98]

According to Lyotard the grand narratives of scientific progress that have legitimated modern society are losing their credibility and power.[99]

92. Ibid., 77.

93. Lyotard, *Postmodern Condition*, xxiii–xxiv.

94. Ferre speaks of "religious world models." A RWM is "any image suggesting how *all things fundamentally should be thought* which also *expresses or evokes profound value responses*." Frederick Ferre, *Hellfire and Lightning Rods: Liberating Science, Technology, and Religion* (Maryknoll, N.Y.: Orbis, 1993), 75.

95. See, for example, R. M. MacIver, *The Web of Government* (New York: Macmillan, 1947), 4.

96. See, for example, Lyotard, *Postmodern Condition*, 27.

97. Ibid., 29, 31–36.

98. Ibid., xxiii–xxiv.

99. Ibid., 37.

The demise of the scientific metanarrative marks the end of the age of unified inquiry as well. The one scientific enterprise subdivided into well-defined parallel disciplines has been replaced by a multiplicity of ill-defined and constantly shifting areas of inquiry.[100] Moreover, scholars no longer legitimate their work by appeal to their participation in the quest for scientific knowledge. And "performativity" has replaced "truth" as the goal, so that the question, "Is it true?" has given way to, "What use is it?"[101] In *No Place for Truth*, David Wells perceptively brings to light the presence of this aspect of postmodernism within many segments of contemporary evangelicalism,[102] thus suggesting that evangelicals are often more "postmodern" than they realize.

Lyotard acknowledges that history has repeatedly known times when the older narratives waned, only to be replaced by newer myths. The postmodern condition is not merely marked by the loss of the particular myths of modernity. Rather, the postmodern ethos entails the end of the appeal to any central legitimating myth whatsoever. Not only have all the reigning metanarratives lost their credibility, the idea of a grand narrative is itself no longer credible. Not only are people aware of a plurality of conflicting legitimating stories,[103] everything is "delegitimized." And consequently, the postmodern outlook demands an attack on any claimant to universality; it has declared "war on totality."[104] In his review of Jean-Francois Lyotard's book *Le Postmoderne expliqué aux enfants*, Terry Eagleton offers the following description of the postmodern mood:

> Post-modernism signals the death of such "meta-narratives" whose secretly terroristic function is to ground and legitimate the illusion of a "universal" human history. We are now in the process of awakening from the nightmare of modernity, with its manipulative reason and fetish of the totality, into the laid-back pluralism of the post-modern, that heterogeneous range of life-styles and language games which has renounced the nostalgic urge to totalize and legitimate itself. . . . Science and philosophy must jettison their

100. Ibid., 39–41.

101. Ibid., 51.

102. For example, Wells declares, "Being practical now substitutes for being theological." David F. Wells, *No Place for Truth*, 112.

103. Anderson somewhat erroneously states that six stories are vying for loyalty in the postmodern world. To the typical Western stories of human progress, Marxist revolution, and Christian social reconstruction, he adds the Islamic fundamentalist story about a return to a society governed on the basis of Islamic values and koranic belief; the Green story about rejecting the myth of progress and governing societies according to ecological values; and the "new paradigm" story about a sudden leap forward to a new way of being and a new way of understanding the world; Anderson, *Reality Isn't What It Used to Be*, 243–44.

104. Lyotard, *Postmodern Condition*, 82.

grandiose metaphysical claims and view themselves more modestly as just another set of narratives.[105]

The demise of the grand narrative means that postmoderns no longer search for the one system of "truth," the one metanarrative, that can unite humans into one people or the globe into one "world." Nevertheless, narratives still function in the postmodern world. But the narratives postmoderns tell are "local" rather than universal. Postmoderns continue to construct models (or "paradigms") to illumine their experience. And because they perceive life itself as a drama or narrative lived out within a socially constructed world, they engage in the process of fabricating stories that can define personal identity and give purpose and shape to social existence.[106] In this process, however, postmoderns remain dispossessed of the modernist illusion. They realize that rather than representing reality, all such models are "useful fictions."

As a result of the loss of the big story, many people are increasingly realizing the subjective nature of descriptions of the world; hence, they are suspicious of claims of objectivity, and they distrust assertions of certainty. This, in turn, is connected to the pluralism and relativism of the postmodern ethos. The new relativism, however, is less a return to individualistic variety, as propagated in late modernity, than an embracing of a new, communal relativism.

The consciousness that the "global village" encompasses great cultural diversity disposes many people to a radically pluralist mindset that goes beyond mere tolerance for other practices and viewpoints to the actual affirmation and celebration of diversity. The celebration of cultural diversity does not merely lead to eclecticism as the "style" of postmodernity; more importantly, it overthrows the whole notion of a common standard by which people can measure, judge, or value ideas, opinions, or even aspects of lifestyle. The result is a "centerless" society, one that lacks any clear focus that unites the diverse and divergent elements within it into a single whole. As the center dissolves, the former mass society devolves into a conglomerate of societies, which may have little in common apart from geographic proximity. Postmoderns, then, appear to live in self-contained social groups—or "tribes"—each of which has its own language, beliefs, and values. Beliefs, in turn, are matters of social context. The older individualistic relativism elevated personal choice as the "be all" and "end all." Its maxims were: "Each to his own," and, "Everyone has a right to her own opinion." Postmoderns, in contrast, espouse a communal relativism, expressed in maxims such as, "What is right

105. Terry Eagleton, "Awakening from Modernity," *Times Literary Supplement* (February 20, 1987): 194.
106. Anderson, *Reality Isn't What It Used to Be*, 108.

for us, may not be right for you," and, "What is wrong in our context, may in your context be okay or even preferable."

The advent of the postmodern ethos carries far-reaching implications for evangelicalism and evangelical theology. Subsequent chapters will explore several of these. The current chapter will conclude by sketching how the postmodern turn spells the end of theology within evangelicalism.

The Question of Evangelical Boundaries

In 1997 Jon Stone concluded that neo-evangelicalism is "captivated by the issue of defining its boundaries." In his estimation, the "flood of books and articles" that has flowed from evangelical pens since World War II "documents a sustained effort at defining the limits of evangelicalism by affirming and reaffirming its boundary differences with both liberalism and fundamentalism."[107] Over a decade earlier, William Abraham reached a similar conclusion. He observed that evangelicalism is an "essentially contested" tradition, characterized by an "intense debate and contest about how best to develop and explain its essential ingredients."[108]

The Inward Turn

As Stone's comment indicates, the debate over boundaries has been part of the neo-evangelical movement from the beginning. Yet in the postmodern context, it has taken on a new intensity. More importantly, the current interest in evangelical boundaries marks a turning inward. The first-generation pioneers were initially concerned about providing a third way in the larger intellectual arena. Hence they wanted to draw a circle wide enough to encompass as many of those who shared their basic program as possible. Many contemporary evangelicals concerned about theological boundaries, in contrast, have become increasingly absorbed with determining what constitutes proper credentials for participation in the movement and, by extension, with scrutinizing the credentials of some within the camp.

The ongoing conversation between Millard Erickson and Clark Pinnock offers a case in point. In *The Evangelical Left*, Erickson notes that Pinnock has questioned the evangelicalism of theologians who differ with him regarding the fate of those who have not heard the gospel.[109] Erickson is in fact making a veiled reference to an ill-conceived remark in *A Wideness in*

107. Jon R. Stone, *On the Boundaries of American Evangelicalism: The Postwar Evangelical Coalition* (New York: St. Martin's Press, 1997), 179.

108. William J. Abraham, *The Coming Great Revival: Recovering the Full Evangelical Tradition* (San Francisco: Harper and Row, 1984), 9–10.

109. Millard J. Erickson, *The Evangelical Left: Encountering Postconservative Evangelical Theology* (Grand Rapids: Baker, 1997), 145–46.

God's Mercy, in which Pinnock raises the question with respect to Erickson himself. After citing Erickson as one who doubts the possibility of becoming saved through general revelation, Pinnock asks, "What does 'evangelical' mean when applied to those who seem to want to ensure that there is as little Good News as possible?"[110]

Erickson returns the favor in *The Evangelical Left*. In fact, he broadens his brush stroke to color all the theologians who may be characterized as "left." In the closing paragraphs of the book he raises the internal boundary question, i.e., "how far one may move, or how many times one may halve the distance between things, and still claim to be within the original group."[111] Erickson interjects a folksy illustration, wondering how gooselike a duck can become and still remain a duck. He cautions, "There must come some point where the line has been crossed." Erickson closes his study of the "evangelical left" by magnanimously concluding, "It does not yet appear that these theologians have moved so far as to surrender the right to be called evangelicals, but such movement cannot be unlimited."[112]

Apart from the question of whether the theologians cited really do constitute a self-conscious, definable group as Erickson suggests—an assumption that John Stackhouse, to cite one example, rightly questions[113]— boundary-guarding attempts such as his suffer from several debilitating difficulties. First, setting theological boundaries for the evangelical movement runs the obvious risk of assuming that theology—or more particularly, a definitive list of doctrinal formulations—can function as the final arbiter as to who is "in" and who is "out." Although not completely misguided, this approach is ultimately of only limited value. As William Abraham notes, the practice of drawing up "a list of essentials or fundamentals that are the essence or heart of the tradition" is superficial.[114] While doctrine is crucial to evangelical identity, no one set of doctrines in fact defines the genius of the movement, namely, its connection to the "convertive piety" that emerged out of the coalescence of Puritanism and Pietism in the early eighteenth century (see chapter 1). In addition, theological boundaries are out of place as the ultimate defining markers of evangelicalism, because the movement is in fact a coalition and not an ecclesial tradition. Ultimately, only such traditions comprise bona fide confessional communities, and hence only they can be essentially creedal.

Second, theologians who set up a theological boundary in order to define evangelicalism by a particular set of doctrines tend to elevate their

---

110. Pinnock, *Wideness in God's Mercy*, 163.
111. Erickson, *Evangelical Left*, 146.
112. Ibid., 147.
113. Stackhouse, "Perils of Left and Right," 59.
114. Abraham, *Coming Great Revival*, 8–9.

own theology to the status of sine qua non. Rather than asking what evangelicals in fact believe, they all too readily fall into the temptation of setting up themselves as the standard for evangelical belief. In so doing, these evangelical theologians exchange the descriptive for the prescriptive; they substitute the imperative for the indicative.

Not only is this a questionable move in itself, it sets in motion an unfortunate consequence. When the focus shifts from the descriptive to the prescriptive, the boundary almost inevitably becomes subject to an arbitrary narrowing. The theological battles they are waging lead those who see themselves as the true evangelicals to add to the list of essentials. An example of this is the manner in which certain voices today claim that true evangelicalism is marked by opposition to the ordination of women, even though many prominent neo-evangelical theologians in the first and second generations were proponents of an egalitarian stance on this issue.

Third, theologically oriented boundary keepers all too often set up a linear continuum running from right to left. Proponents place theologians at particular points along this continuum and then draw a line indicating where the boundary of evangelicalism lies. Everyone to the right of the line is ipso facto an evangelical, in their estimation, whereas everyone to the left is branded "neo-orthodox" or "liberal." More importantly, by means of this grid a further group of theologians can be deemed as standing, as Erickson puts it, "partway between the evangelical view and some nonevangelical position."[115] Once in place, the right-left continuum can also be used to raise questions about the motivation of this third group of thinkers. They can be characterized as seeking to position themselves as close to the "nonevangelical position" as possible while still attempting to remain within the evangelical fold.

In his 1998 presidential address to the Evangelical Theological Society, Norman Geisler applied this suspicion to certain evangelical biblical scholars. He suggested that the tendency of some to "flirt with the latest critical methodology" is motivated by a subtle pride. According to Geisler, the antidote to this temptation lies in a refusal to "dance on the edges." Hence, he warned society members, "Do not see how far the borders of evangelicalism can be stretched to accommodate the latest scholarly fad."[116] And to indicate on which side of the continuum this danger lies, he added the additional admonition, "Steer right to go straight," for "the only way to keep on the straight orthodox path is to keep turning to the right."[117]

Warnings such as these do have their place, to be sure. Evangelical theologians need to remain vigilant, guarding "the good deposit" en-

---

115. Erickson, *Evangelical Left*, 146.

116. Norman L. Geisler, "Beware of Philosophy: A Warning to Biblical Scholars," *Journal of the Evangelical Theological Society* 42, no. 1 (March 1999): 15.

117. Ibid., 16.

trusted to them (2 Tim. 1:14). At the same time, self-appointed guardians of the boundary need to be careful that they not too hastily impugn the motives of those with whom they have theological differences.

Finally and perhaps most importantly, the attempt to establish evangelicalism's theological boundary fails to acknowledge the great diversity within the movement. Here the postmodern turn offers assistance, in that it marks the questioning of totalizing systems. Within the neo-evangelical movement, the "totalizing system" most often invoked has been one particular expression of the Reformed paradigm. However, the postmodern situation provides a context to discover once again the theological breadth that the evangelical trajectory encompasses, and how much broader it is than many "card-carrying" post-fundamentalist neo-evangelicals suggest.

This theological breadth goes back to the genesis of the movement itself. From the beginning, the convertive piety that emerged through the confluence of Puritanism and Pietism formed the heart of evangelicalism. This coalition of adherents of convertive piety was sufficiently broad to include both George Whitefield and John Wesley. In the nearly three hundred years that have transpired since the awakenings that gave birth to evangelicalism, the diversity present within the movement has only increased. As a result, the song of convertive piety is intoned by a great choir of voices who sometimes sing in tune and sometimes appear to troll at variance with each other. Today representatives of a variety of perspectives are engaging in the conversation within the evangelical movement about the nature of evangelicalism.[118] And in a manner that typifies the postmodern situation, voices from beyond the neo-evangelical establishment are now clamoring to be heard. As Tomlinson notes, "Postmodernity is what happens when marginalized peoples refuse to keep quiet anymore."[119]

These voices from the margins include representatives of ethnic minorities, including African-American thinkers who are raising the question of the relationship of their religious tradition to evangelicalism,[120] and, more recently, contributions from the budding Hispanic evangelical community. Also becoming increasingly important is the introduction into the conversation of impulses from beyond the British and North American

118. For an attempt to raise this question from a variety of perspectives, see Donald W. Dayton and Robert K. Johnston, eds., *The Variety of American Evangelicalism* (Downers Grove, Ill.: InterVarsity, 1991).

119. D. Tomlinson, *The Post-Evangelical*, 89.

120. For a sketch of the relationship of the African-American Christian tradition to evangelicalism, see Milton G. Sernett, "Black Religion and the Question of Evangelical Identity," in *The Variety of American Evangelicalism*, 135–47. See also William Pannell, "The Religious Heritage of Blacks," and William H. Bentley, "Bible Believers in the Black Community," in *The Evangelicals: What They Believe, Who They Are, Where They Are Changing*, ed. David F. Wells and John D. Woodbridge, rev. ed. (Grand Rapids: Baker, 1977), 116–41.

evangelical heartland, in particular, from the global evangelical movement that is burgeoning in Africa, South America, and Asia.[121]

To date, however, the most vocal voices from the margins have come from the constellation of traditions within evangelicalism that looks to John Wesley as its progenitor. Thus, in recent years Wesleyan,[122] holiness, and above all Pentecostal[123] and charismatic[124] contributions have been added to the evangelical theological conversation. These traditions are now shaping evangelicalism. Speaking of the extent of the influence of this trajectory in Britain, Tomlinson declares, "It is now clear that the whole centre ground of evangelicalism has become gradually charismaticized, adopting the style and ethos of the charismatic movement."[125] Joel Carpenter goes so far as to conclude, "We are now entering a new chapter of evangelical history, in which the pentecostal-charismatic movement is quickly supplanting the fundamentalist-conservative one as the most influential evangelical impulse at work today."[126]

Evangelicalism as a Mosaic of Local Theologies

Awareness of the variety of impulses and traditions that comprise the evangelical movement suggests that evangelicalism is a "big tent" that encompasses a wide diversity. It is a patchwork quilt of variegated subnarratives. Evangelical theology, in turn, is not a monolithic entity. It is not a given, static reality that can be neatly summarized by a set of universally held doctrines capable of being invoked as marking its boundaries, even though there is broad consensus among evangelicals on certain doctrines. Evangelical theology is instead a mosaic of local theologies. And the real-

121. For a helpful summary of some of these impulses, see William A. Dyrness, *Learning about Theology from the Third World* (Grand Rapids: Zondervan, 1990). See also William A. Dyrness, ed., *Emerging Voices in Global Christian Theology* (Grand Rapids: Zondervan, 1994); William A. Dyrness, *Invitation to Cross-Cultural Theology: Case Studies in Vernacular Theologies* (Grand Rapids: Zondervan, 1992).

122. See, for example, Henry H. Knight III, *A Future for Truth: Evangelical Theology in a Postmodern World* (Nashville: Abingdon, 1997).

123. See, for example, Land's attempt at constructing "a more . . . theologically responsible Pentecostalism." Steven J. Land, *Pentecostal Spirituality: A Passion for the Kingdom* (Sheffield: Sheffield Academic Press, 1993). The work of Miroslav Volf ought to be cited here as well, although Volf appears to be moving away from his Pentecostal heritage. See Miroslav Volf, *Exclusion and Embrace: A Theological Exploration of Identity, Otherness, and Reconciliation* (Nashville: Abingdon, 1996); Miroslav Volf, *After Our Likeness: The Church as the Image of the Trinity* (Grand Rapids: Eerdmans, 1998).

124. For an example, see J. Rodman Williams, *Renewal Theology: Systematic Theology from a Charismatic Perspective*, 3 vols. (Grand Rapids: Zondervan, 1988–92).

125. D. Tomlinson, *The Post-Evangelical*, 15.

126. Joel A. Carpenter, *Revive Us Again: The Reawakening of American Fundamentalism* (New York: Oxford, 1997), 237.

ization of the local nature of evangelical theology spells the end of theology. Insights from postmodern social anthropology provide the background for understanding in what sense this is the case.

In contrast to the older assumption that culture is a preexisting social-ordering force that is transmitted externally to members of a cultural group[127] and binds individuals to society, postmodern anthropologists focus on the disjunctures within culture. Hence, although cultures are wholes, these wholes are not monolithic but internally fissured.[128] Culture is "that which *agg*regates people and processes, rather than *int*egrates them," to cite Anthony Cohen's description.[129] Further, postmodern anthropologists speak of culture as the outcome and product of social interaction.[130] A society is an aggregate of people engaged in an ongoing struggle to determine the meaning of public symbols and thereby to build a consensus.[131] Consequently, as Alain Touraine points out, what binds people together is not so much a general framework of social relations, a clearly understood body of beliefs and values, or a dominant ideology, as much as "a set of resources and models that social actors seek to manage, to control, and which they appropriate or whose transformation into social organization they negotiate among themselves."[132]

Viewed from this perspective, the evangelical movement consists of a people who share a group of symbols that serve as both building blocks and conveyers of meaning. These symbols include a particular religious language, as well as specific images and rituals. While they share many symbols in common, evangelicals are not necessarily in agreement about the meaning these symbols are to convey. On the contrary, meaning-making is an ongoing task that involves lively conversation, intense discussion, and often heated debate among participants. What makes a particular group "evangelical" is the participants' desire to engage in the process of meaning-making from a particular vantage point that includes, among other things, the convertive piety and the historical trajectory they share, as well as the set of symbols this constellation of traditions mediates to them.

Theology is linked to the meaning-making activity found in all cultures. Evangelical theology, in turn, is related to the various symbols and activities

127. Roy G. D'Andrade, *The Development of Cognitive Anthropology* (Cambridge: Cambridge University Press, 1995), 250.

128. Kathryn Tanner, *Theories of Culture: A New Agenda for Theology* (Minneapolis: Fortress, 1997), 56.

129. Anthony P. Cohen, *Self Consciousness: An Alternative Anthropology of Identity* (London: Routledge, 1994), 118–19.

130. Ibid.

131. Tanner, *Theories of Culture*, 56.

132. Alain Touraine, *Return of the Actor*, trans. Myrna Godzich (Minneapolis: University of Minnesota Press, 1988), 8, 26–27, 54–55.

in their function as building blocks and conveyers of the particular cultural meaning characteristic of evangelicals. To this end, theology engages with church practices, but more importantly it involves with the explication of the meaning of the symbols evangelicals share. In this manner, the evangelical theological enterprise becomes—to cite Kathryn Tanner's succinct characterization of theology in general—"a material social practice that specializes in meaning production."[133] Evangelical theologians attempt to set forth their understanding of the particular "web of significance," "matrix of meaning," or "mosaic of beliefs" that lies at the heart of the evangelical community. This involves a process of give and take, as evangelical theologians converse about the shared cultural meanings connected to the symbols they hold in common. Further, evangelical theology is by its very nature "local." That is, it is the reflection and articulation of this particular group of participants in this particular Christian tradition at this particular moment of its ongoing existence in the world. In short, evangelical theology is not merely a shared deposit; it entails a shared task.

In this sense, then, the postmodern turn spells the end of theology. No longer can any one group, tradition, or subnarrative claim without reservation and qualification that their particular doctrinal perspective determines the whole of evangelicalism. Rather, the ongoing evangelical theological task includes (among other endeavors) a never-ending conversation about the meaning, in the contemporary context, of the symbols that as evangelicals they are committed to maintaining and that form the carriers of meaning for all.

Crisis or Opportunity—The Question of the Postmodern Context

This chapter began with Roger Olson's taxonomy of the current state of evangelical theology. All such taxonomies are intrinsically problematic if for no other reason than that they are by necessity reductionistic. They reduce to a few categories what is in fact a complex and variegated phenomenon. Further, all taxonomies that reduce their subject to a duality are additionally problematic in that they necessarily polarize what they purport to observe.

These inherent difficulties notwithstanding, the flow of this chapter suggests an alternative set of lenses through which to view the current discussion within evangelical theology. As the writings of a variety of thinkers from David Wells to Dave Tomlinson suggest, evangelical theology is at a crossroads. And one key aspect in the contemporary conversation is how evangelicals view the emerging postmodern ethos. Stated in the form of a question, Is the postmodern condition a crisis or an opportunity?

133. Tanner, *Theories of Culture*, 72.

Many theological voices within contemporary evangelicalism either discount the significance of the intellectual and cultural changes transpiring in our society or view the advent of postmodernism as an intellectual crisis. Convinced that evangelicalism itself is in danger, these thinkers believe that evangelical theologians must maintain the course their forebears charted, especially in the nineteenth and twentieth centuries. More specifically, they urge evangelicals to continue to engage in theological reflection on the basis of the questions and assumptions that arose out of the Enlightenment. Advocates of this program may be termed "evangelical modernists."[134]

Other evangelical theologians, in contrast, believe that Christians ought to take seriously their presence in the emerging milieu. As a result, these thinkers seek to engage the thought forms of the postmodern context and even draw insight for their theological work from certain impulses within contemporary postmodern writers or their precursors. Some go so far as to suggest the new context provides the occasion to move beyond the older conservative/liberal divide that so profoundly influenced theological thinking throughout much of the twentieth century. Those who believe that the modern project has run its course and who favor a critical appropriation of postmodern insights could rightly wear the designation "postmodern evangelicals."[135]

If the postmodern evangelicals are correct, then the era into which evangelicalism is moving is characterized by the end of theology. Evangelicalism is entering the post-theological era. This phrase ought not to be understood in the sense of the demise of theology, however. Nor does it necessarily spell the evacuation of theology from the life of the church as David Wells fears. The emerging context is post-theological, insofar as it is characterized by the end of the older theological style that has characterized not only the neo-evangelical movement but much of Christian theology in the Middle Ages and from the seventeenth century to the present. This older style elevated the solitary theological hero producing the great Summa on a foundationalist epistemological base. Theology as the quest for the one, timeless, objectivist system may be dying. But theology itself remains alive and well.

The post-theological era is one in which theology is released from the academic prison to which it had been banished. It is a time when theology returns to the context in which it rightly belongs: the community of faith, the church. As Timothy George notes in his appraisal of the current divide in evangelical theology, "The more important distinction is between those

---

134. For this characterization, see, for example, George M. Marsden, "Evangelicals, History, and Modernity," in *Evangelicalism and Modern America*, ed. George M. Marsden (Grand Rapids: Eerdmans, 1984), 98.

135. For this characterization, see Nancey C. Murphy, *Beyond Liberalism and Fundamentalism: How Modern and Postmodern Philosophy Set the Theological Agenda* (Valley Forge, Pa.: Trinity Press International, 1996), 90.

who see theology connected intrinsically to the life of the church, and those who see theology as an academic discipline whose basic norms and values come from the secularized academy."[136]

What is needed in the post-theological situation, to return to Olson's categories, is not a resurgence of the type of traditionalist mentality that would define clearly the boundary of evangelicalism and launch a campaign to oust from the movement any reformists whom they judge to have moved beyond the pale of evangelical orthodoxy. Nor does the current situation call for the kind of thorough revising of evangelical theology that gives scant attention to the great legacy of which the contemporary generation is the recipient. Instead, what is needed today is a continuation, a transferring into the present situation, of the program that the architects of the neo-evangelical movement inaugurated, namely, the creation of an apologetic theology that brings classic orthodoxy into conversation with the contemporary situation. For this to occur, however, requires that the theological task be advanced by traditional reformists and reforming traditionalists, by reform-minded theologians who value the tradition and tradition-anchored thinkers who are zealous for ongoing reform.

In short, the postmodern situation calls for a theology that is truly evangelical after the manner of the Reformation-Puritan-Pietist genesis of evangelicalism. At the heart of this theology is a commitment to the gospel as viewed through the lens of convertive piety. Such a theology is by its very nature apologetic, in that it seeks to engage the contemporary context for the sake of the mission of the church which theology must always serve. As it does so, it will fulfill in the contemporary context the vision of a new evangelical theology that in 1968 Millard Erickson hailed as the invigorating insight of the first-generation neo-evangelical pioneers.

---

136. Timothy George, "Theology to Die For," *Christianity Today* 42, no. 2 (February 9, 1998): 49.

six

Evangelical Theological Method
AFTER THE Demise
OF Foundationalism

❖

The last several years have witnessed a lively conversation among evangelicals. In fact, so tumultuous and at times even fractious has this discussion been that several chroniclers have warned that the evangelical movement itself may be imperiled. The ferment evident within evangelical theology is not unique to evangelicalism. Rather, in some respects it may be merely one instance of the growing fragmentation in the wider theological realm, and indeed, throughout contemporary society. In the eyes of some thinkers today, this splintering is in a great measure bound up with the postmodern condition. Princeton theologian J. Wentzel van Huyssteen, for example, observed, "Even the briefest overview of our contemporary theological landscape reveals the startling fragmentation caused by what is often called 'the postmodern challenge' of our times."[1]

In a sense that he may not have intended, van Huyssteen's comment is directly applicable to evangelical theology. The spirited theological engagement that has characterized it in recent years has increasingly focused on the question of the most appropriate response to the contemporary postmodern context. Hence, Nancey Murphy[2] and other observers are

---

1. J. Wentzel van Huyssteen, "Tradition and the Task of Theology," *Theology Today* 55, no. 2 (July 1998): 213.

2. Nancey C. Murphy, *Beyond Liberalism and Fundamentalism: How Modern and Postmodern Philosophy Set the Theological Agenda* (Valley Forge, Pa.: Trinity Press International, 1996), 90. See also Stanley J. Grenz, "An Agenda for Evangelical Theology in the Postmodern Context," *Didaskalia* 9, no. 2 (Spring 1998): 1–16.

surely correct in suggesting that any parting of ways evident in theology today, whether evangelical or mainline, arises largely from how thinkers engage the postmodern condition.

One especially far-reaching impact of the emerging postmodern situation is upon the realm of epistemology. The postmodern turn has been accompanied by a widespread rejection of the foundationalism that characterized the Enlightenment epistemology and the resultant quest for a nonfoundationalist, or even a postfoundationalist,[3] approach. This transition raises crucial questions for the manner in which evangelical theologians understand their discipline, as well as for the method they devise for engaging in theological construction. This chapter explores the move beyond epistemological foundationalism, with the goal of discerning its implications for an evangelical theological method that attempts to take postmodernism seriously and to engage critically yet sympathetically with postmodern sensitivities.

From Foundationalism to a Postfoundationalist Theology

The contemporary rejection of foundationalism offers evangelical theologians a great challenge, as well as a providential opportunity. The dislocation of the present together with the quest to move beyond the older foundationalist epistemology place them in a position to realize how dependent neo-evangelical theology has been on an Enlightenment paradigm, and how decreasingly appropriate this approach is in a world that is increasingly post-theological. To bring this challenge into clearer focus I will trace the rise and demise of foundationalism in philosophy and theology before offering a constructive proposal.

Enlightenment Foundationalism and Modern Theology

In the modern era, Protestant theologians across the theological spectrum were deeply influenced by the Enlightenment problematic, as well as the solutions proposed by thinkers in the Age of Reason. At the heart of the Enlightenment outlook was a specific understanding of the nature of human knowledge. This epistemology has often been termed "foundationalism."

Epistemological Foundationalism

In its broadest sense, foundationalism is merely the acknowledgment of the seemingly obvious observation that not all beliefs (or assertions) are

---

3. Hence, van Huyssteen, "Tradition and the Task of Theology."

on the same level, but that some beliefs (or assertions) anchor others. Stated in the opposite manner, certain beliefs (or assertions) receive their support from other beliefs (or assertions) that are more "basic" or "foundational."[4] Defined in this manner, nearly every thinker is in some sense a foundationalist.

In philosophical circles, however, "foundationalism" refers to a much stronger epistemological stance than is entailed in this observation about how beliefs intersect. At the heart of the foundationalist program is the desire to overcome the uncertainty generated by our human liability to error and the inevitable disagreements that follow. Foundationalists are convinced that the only way to solve this problem is to find a means of grounding the entire edifice of human knowledge on something that is unquestionably certain.[5] This quest for complete epistemological certitude is often termed "strong" or "classical" foundationalism.

Foundationalist epistemological proposals routinely draw from the metaphor of a building to conceive how human knowledge arises.[6] According to foundationalists, the acquisition of knowledge ought to proceed in a manner somewhat similar to the construction of a building. Like a physical edifice, knowledge must be built upon a sure foundation. Proponents see this epistemological foundation as consisting of either a set of incontestable beliefs or a number of unassailable first principles, on the basis of which the pursuit of knowledge can proceed. These basic beliefs or first principles are supposedly universal, context-free, and available— at least theoretically—to any rational person. The foundationalist's initial task, then, becomes that of establishing an epistemological foundation for the construction of the human knowing project by determining, and perhaps even demonstrating, the foundational beliefs or principles upon which knowledge rests. Viewed under the foundationalist rubric, therefore, reasoning moves in only one direction—from the bottom up, that is, from basic beliefs or first principles to resultant conclusions.

Actually, there are three primary aspects to the foundationalist picture of knowledge: the basic or immediate beliefs (or first principles), which form the bedrock undergirding everything else we are justified in believing; the mediate or nonbasic beliefs derived from these; and the basing relation, that is, the connection between the basic beliefs (or first principles) and the nonbasic beliefs, which specifies how the epistemic certainty of the former can

4. For this definition, see, for example, W. Jay Wood, *Epistemology: Becoming Intellectually Virtuous* (Downers Grove, Ill.: InterVarsity, 1998), 78–79.

5. Ibid., 84.

6. For the use of this metaphor in Descartes's writings, see René Descartes, *Selected Philosophical Writings*, trans. John Cottingham, Robert Stoothoff, and Dugald Murdoch (New York: Cambridge University Press, 1988), 23–24, 26–27, 76, 80.

be transferred to the latter.[7] Strong foundationalists demand that the foundations of human knowledge be unshakably certain. The only way this certitude can be transferred to nonbasic beliefs, they add, is by the ordinary logical relations of either deduction—such as inferring other truths from innate ideas (e.g., Descartes)—or induction—such as deriving truths from sense impressions caused by the material world (e.g., Locke).

Finally, in addition to distinguishing between basic and nonbasic beliefs, foundationalists generally relegate religious beliefs to the latter status. Hence, foundationalism often moves beyond description, beyond merely describing the difference between basic and nonbasic beliefs, to prescription, i.e., dictating what sorts of belief are properly basic.[8] Similarly, foundationalism becomes a prescription determining what constitutes a correct, acceptable, or rightly structured system of beliefs.[9]

Enlightenment Foundationalism

In a sense, foundationalism, understood as the quest for epistemological certitude in the face of the problem of error, boasts a long pedigree dating to the ancient Greek philosophers. But in Western philosophical history, this epistemological difficulty became acute in the Enlightenment. Historians routinely look to the French philosopher René Descartes as the progenitor of modern foundationalism.[10] In contrast to premodern Western philosophers who tended simply to assume the foundations for philosophical inquiry, Descartes began his philosophical work by attempting to establish that foundation.[11]

Descartes lived in troubled times. In the aftermath of the Reformation which had divided "Christ's seamless garment" and resulted in the Thirty Years War, questions about religion and morality could no longer be settled by appeal to a commonly acknowledged tradition. Further, through his travels Descartes discovered how culturally based and culturally dependent beliefs actually are.[12] His response to this situation was to seek certitude within the mind of the knowing subject. To accomplish this task, Descartes brought all his beliefs and assumptions under scrutiny. He doubted every-

7. This is delineated in Wood, *Epistemology*, 84.

8. Merold Westphal, "A Reader's Guide to 'Reformed Epistemology,'" *Perspectives* 7, no. 9 (November 1992): 10–11.

9. Alvin Plantinga, "Reason and Belief in God," in *Faith and Rationality: Faith and Belief in God*, ed. Alvin Plantinga and Nicholas Wolterstorff (Notre Dame, Ind.: University of Notre Dame Press, 1983), 48.

10. See, for example, Wood, *Epistemology*, 79.

11. See, for example, John E. Thiel, *Nonfoundationalism* (Minneapolis: Fortress, 1994), 4.

12. René Descartes, *Discourse on Method*, vol. 1 of *Philosophical Works of Descartes*, trans. Elizabeth Haldane and G. R. T. Ross (New York: Dover, 1955), 90–91.

thing until he arrived at a belief he could not doubt, namely, that he was doubting. This led him to the dictum, "I think; therefore, I am."

In this manner, Descartes claimed to have established the foundations of knowledge by appeal to the mind's own experience of certainty. On this basis, he began to construct anew the human knowledge edifice. Descartes was convinced that this epistemological program yields knowledge that is certain, culture- and tradition-free, universal, and reflective of a reality that exists outside the mind (this latter being a central feature of a position known as "metaphysical realism" or simply "realism").

Other philosophers took issue with specific aspects of the Cartesian proposal. John Locke, for example, rejected Descartes's view that our basic beliefs consist in innate ideas from which we deduce other beliefs. Locke argued that the foundation for human knowledge lies in sense experience, that is, in observations of the world, from which we induce conclusions (a proposal known as empiricism). Another proposed modification came from the Scottish philosopher, Thomas Reid, whose name surfaced in chapter 2. Reid pointed out that our psychological constitution draws us irresistibly to accept certain first principles as self-evident. Because we have no reason to suspect that these psychological processes are misleading, he added, we are epistemically entitled to accept and employ these first principles.[13] Reid's proposal (which, as I noted in chapter 2, played a crucial role in nineteenth-century conservative theology) led to a variant sometimes known as "soft" or "modest foundationalism." According to Jay Wood, "Modest foundationalists make no claims about the invincible certainty of one's basic beliefs or about a need to be reflectively aware of which beliefs have the status of basic. Instead of claiming that one's basic beliefs enjoy infallible certainty, modest foundationalists ascribe only prima facie certainty" [that is, such beliefs can be overridden but are acceptable unless one has good reasons for thinking that they have been undermined].[14]

Despite disagreements over particulars, however, most Enlightenment thinkers readily adopted Descartes's concern to establish some type of firm foundation for the human knowing project. And with this concern, the Enlightenment project assumed a realist metaphysic and evidenced a strong preference for the correspondence theory of truth, not only as an epistemological outlook focusing on the truth value of any individual proposition as reflecting some supposed "fact,"[15] but more importantly as a program for "mapping" the supposedly objective world as it really is.

13. Wood, *Epistemology*, 100.
14. Ibid., 98.
15. Bede Rundle, "Correspondence Theory of Truth," in *The Oxford Companion to Philosophy*, ed. Ted Honderich (New York: Oxford, 1995), 166.

Foundationalist Theology

The concerns of Descartes and other Enlightenment thinkers spilled over the boundaries of the philosophical guild. Indeed, the foundationalist problem challenged traditional viewpoints and reformulated thinking in every area of Western society, including theology. Soon theologians, swooning under the foundationalist spell, found themselves refashioning the theological edifice in accordance with the newly devised rationalist method.

The foundationalist impulse led to the Enlightenment theology, sketched in chapter 2, with its sharp distinction between natural religion and revealed religion. As the Age of Reason unfolded, the latter came increasingly under attack, for natural theology with its more certain foundation in the rationalist method of inquiry came to enjoy the exalted status of the true religion. The intellectual highway to the primacy of natural over revealed religion was paved by Locke's revolutionary thesis that when divested of its dogmatic baggage Christianity was the most reasonable form of religion. Other Enlightenment thinkers sought to reduce religion to its most basic elements, which they believed to be universal and therefore reasonable. In the process they constructed a theological alternative to orthodoxy, i.e., the deism that played such an important part in the founding of the American republic.

Yet, as the Age of Reason came to an end many intellectuals abandoned the religion of reason, concluding that reason is incompetent to answer the great metaphysical questions. These thinkers could see only two cogent alternatives: blindly accepting classical Christian doctrine by appeal to the Bible (or the church), or embracing the skeptical rationalism that seemed to be the final product of the enlightened mind.[16] In the nineteenth century, however, a new breed of theologians refused to be boxed in by these two options. With the Enlightenment thinkers, they assumed that there was no going behind the quest for certainty introduced by Descartes; there was no return to a seemingly irrational appeal to external religious authority. Still committed to the foundationalist agenda, these thinkers sought a new bedrock upon which to construct the theological house. In the end, the debate as to what might provide the proper foundation for theology netted two basic answers, liberalism and conservatism.

Liberal theologians constructed the house of theology upon the supposedly universal human experience of the religious, together with the religious or moral aspirations engraved, even if only in embryonic form, in (universal) human nature. More significant for neo-evangelicalism, however, was the conservative appeal to an inerrant Bible described in chapter 2. Under the impulse of the Princeton theologians, the "firm foundation" the hymn writer believed had been

16. See, for example, McGiffert's conclusion; Arthur Cushman McGiffert, *Protestant Thought Before Kant* (London: Duckworth, 1911), 253.

laid *in* God's "excellent Word" came to be equated with the words of the Bible themselves, the veracity of which was thought to be unimpeachable when measured by the canons of human reason. With such an incontrovertible foundation in place, conservative theologians were confident that they could deduce from Scripture the great theological truths that lay within its pages. Through the Princeton theologians, via fundamentalism, Enlightenment foundationalism seeped into neo-evangelical theology and became its reigning paradigm.

Theology after Foundationalism

Foundationalism, allied as it was with metaphysical realism and the correspondence theory of truth, was undeniably the epistemological king of the Enlightenment era. Today, however, it no longer commands the broad, unquestioned acceptance it once enjoyed. In fact, among philosophers foundationalism is in dramatic retreat.[17] As Merold Westphal observed, "That it [i.e., foundationalism] is philosophically indefensible is so widely agreed that its demise is the closest thing to a philosophical consensus in decades."[18] Wentzel van Huyssteen concurs with this judgment: "Whatever notion of post-modernity we eventually opt for, all postmodern thinkers see the modernist quest for certainty, and the accompanying program of laying foundations for our knowledge, as a dream for the impossible, a contemporary version of the quest for the Holy Grail."[19] And Nicholas Wolterstorff offers this sobering conclusion: "On all fronts foundationalism is in bad shape. It seems to me there is nothing to do but give it up for mortally ill and learn to live in its absence."[20]

The Quest for an Alternative Epistemology

Modern foundationalism has been the target of criticism since its genesis. As the nineteenth century gave way to the twentieth, certain philosophers, aware of the shortcomings of the Enlightenment epistemological program, became increasingly earnest in seeking a cogent alternative. These thinkers questioned the foundationalist assumption of the necessity of establishing the first principles of philosophy prior to engaging in the construction of knowledge, as well as the preoccupation with the quest for unassailable basic beliefs.[21] And they rejected the attendant understand-

17. For this judgment, see Thiel, *Nonfoundationalism*, 37.

18. Westphal, "Reader's Guide," 11.

19. Van Huyssteen, "Tradition and the Task of Theology," 216.

20. Nicholas Wolterstorff, *Reason Within the Bounds of Religion* (Grand Rapids: Eerdmans, 1976), 52.

21. For a helpful summary of the arguments against foundationalism, see Wood, *Epistemology*, 88–98. For an early twentieth-century critique of the correspondence theory of truth by a sympathetic critic who does not reject the theory completely, see Charles A. Campbell, *Scepticism and Construction* (London: George Allen and Unwin, 1931), 82–96.

ing of truth as the correspondence of individual assertions with the world, each of which—in the words of one critic of foundationalism—is thought to be "true per se absolutely and unalterably."[22]

At the turn of the twentieth century, two alternatives emerged almost simultaneously: coherentism and pragmatism. At the heart of coherentism is the suggestion that the justification for a belief lies in its "fit" with other held beliefs;[23] hence, justification entails "inclusion within a coherent system," to cite the words of philosopher Arthur Kenyon Rogers.[24] But what does it mean for a belief to cohere with other beliefs? Of course, noncontradiction must be an aspect of any coherence of beliefs. Coherentists, however, suggest that the "fitting together" of beliefs entails more than merely that the various assertions do not contradict each other. Rather, the corpus of beliefs must also be interconnected in some way. In other words, rather than remaining an aggregate of disjointed, discrete members that have nothing whatsoever to do with one another, the set of beliefs must form an integrated whole, and this whole must carry "explanatory power."

Coherentists, therefore, reject the foundationalist assumption that a justified set of beliefs necessarily comes in the form of an edifice resting on a base. In their estimation, the base/superstructure distinction is faulty, for no beliefs are intrinsically basic, and none are by their very nature superstructure.[25] Instead, beliefs are interdependent, each belief being supported by its connection to its neighbors and ultimately to the whole.[26] Rather than picturing human knowledge as a building, coherentists draw from the image of a network, in which beliefs come together to form an integrated whole. Hence, knowledge is a "web of belief,"[27] a "nest of beliefs,"[28] or to cite the more generic designation, a "conceptual scheme."[29]

---

22. Harold H. Joachim, *The Nature of Truth* (London: Oxford University Press, 1906, 1939), 72.

23. Wood, *Epistemology*, 114.

24. Arthur Kenyon Rogers, *What Is Truth?* (New Haven: Yale University Press, 1923), 12.

25. Jonathan Dancy, "Epistemology, Problems of," in *Oxford Companion to Philosophy*, 246.

26. Murphy, *Beyond Liberalism and Fundamentalism*, 94.

27. See, for example, W. V. Quine and J. S. Ullian, *The Web of Belief* (New York: Random House, 1970).

28. Wesley A. Kort, *Take, Read: Scripture, Textuality, and Cultural Practice* (University Park: Pennsylvania State University Press, 1996), 12.

29. Jack W. Meiland and Michael Krausz, "Introduction," in *Relativism: Cognitive and Moral*, ed. Jack W. Meiland and Michael Krausz (Notre Dame, Ind.: University of Nortre Dame Press, 1982), 7. In his critique of the concept, Donald Davidson offers the following summary of the typical definition: "Conceptual schemes, we are told, are ways of organizing experience; they are systems of categories that give form to the data of sensation; they are points of view from which individuals, cultures, or periods survey the passing scene." Donald Davidson, "On the Very Idea of a Conceptual Scheme," reprinted in *Relativism*, 66. The essay is also found in Donald Davidson, *Inquiries into Truth and Interpretation* (Oxford: Clarendon, 1984), 183–98.

In addition, whereas foundationalists tend to focus on the task of determining the truth value of each assertion independently of the others, coherentists find truth in the interconnectedness of beliefs. Truth is primarily a predicate of the belief system as a whole, rather than of particular assertions in isolation. Hence, the turn-of-the-century philosopher Harold H. Joachim criticizes the Cartesians for their preoccupation with what he describes as "the smallest and most abstracted fragment of knowledge, a mere mutilated shred torn from the living whole in which alone it possessed its significance." For him, the "ideal of knowledge . . . is a system, not of *truths*, but of *truth*."[30] Consequently, for coherentists, the quest for knowledge entails a "research program"[31] in which advances occur through "paradigm shifts."[32]

Despite this shift in emphasis, many modern coherentists remain committed to the quest for epistemological certainty. In fact, they embrace coherentism because they believe this approach provides a greater possibility of justifying beliefs. A. K. Rogers voices this illuminating appraisal:

> Mere logic never by any possibility can add more certainty to the conclusion than existed in the premises. Its ideal, is, therefore, to carry back proof to more and more general premises, until at last it finds something in its own right on which it can rest, and from which then a derivative certainty passes to the consequences. The idea of *system*, on the contrary, implies that certainty grows continually as new facts are added. . . . The conclusions, that is, have to be more certain than the premises. And the possibility of this depends, not on logical deduction from what is self-evident, but on a *coincidence* of evidence. In other words, when we see that two independent beliefs corroborate one another, the confidence we have in both is increased; and this is what we mean by their intellectual justification. For this to happen, logical processes are required, because to reinforce one another the two must come in contact in a connected system. But the essence of the validation lies not in the passing on of an equal measure of certainty due to the process of inference, but to the *increase* of certainty due to the confluence of evidence.[33]

At the same time, some coherentists acknowledge that rather than a present reality, absolute justification of beliefs belongs to the realm of the ideal. Yet this does not mean that the unattainable ideal is any less real.

30. Joachim, *Nature of Truth*, 73, 72.

31. Imre Lakatos, "Falsification and the Methodology of Scientific Research Programmes," in *Criticism and the Growth of Knowledge*, ed. Imre Lakatos and Alan Musgrave (Cambridge: Cambridge University Press, 1970), 132–33.

32. Thomas Kuhn, *The Structure of Scientific Revolutions*, 2d ed. (Chicago: University of Chicago Press, 1970).

33. Rogers, *What Is Truth?* 12–13 (italics in original).

Against those who argue that "finite experience is solid and fully real and clearly conceivable, an unshaken *datum* here and now; and that we must accept it without question," Joachim advocates a reversal in understanding: "In our view it is the ideal which is solid and substantial and fully actual. The finite experiences are rooted in the ideal. They share its actuality, and draw from it whatever being and conceivability they possess."[34] Thus, the coherentist move away from foundationalism entailed a shift not only from the part to the whole, but also from the actual to the ideal.

Turn-of-the-twentieth-century coherentists were joined in their critique of foundationalism by proponents of philosophical pragmatism. At first glance "pragmatism" may suggest nothing more than that truth is simply "what works," however that phrase may be understood. The modern pragmatist philosophers, especially Charles Peirce (1839–1914), however, had a specific understanding in view. In their estimation, the truth of any belief ought to be measured according to the belief's success in advancing "factual inquiry," that is, "the activity aimed at the discovery of truth."[35] The pragmatists' innovation, according to Arthur E. Murphy's judgment, was "their insistence that the meaning and worth of ideas is rightly judged, not by their conformity to a 'reality' set up in advance as the final standard of truth and reasonableness, but by the way they function in the context of responsible inquiry."[36]

Peirce, and pragmatists like him, did not differ significantly from the foundationalists about the *goal* of inquiry. Nor did he reject the reigning metaphysical realism of the day. Rather, Peirce's pragmatism was largely an attempt to clarify the *method* of scientific advance. In his estimation, truth emerges as we engage in prediction followed by testing, observation, and experimental confirmation. And in contrast to the here-and-now individualism of the Cartesian method, this process requires both a long-term horizon and the cooperative contributions of a community of scientific investigators. Peirce offers this lucid definition: "The opinion which is fated to be ultimately agreed to by all who investigate, is what we mean by the truth, and the object represented in this opinion is the real."[37]

As this remark suggests, although Peirce held to the objectivity of truth and the existence of reality independent of our subjectivity, he nevertheless posited an important connection between that reality and the human pursuit of truth: "The reality of that which is real does depend on the real fact that investigation is destined to lead, at last, if continued long enough,

34. Joachim, *Nature of Truth*, 82.

35. Arthur E. Murphy, *The Uses of Reason* (New York: Macmillan, 1943), 87.

36. Murphy, *Uses of Reason*, 85–86.

37. Charles S. Peirce, "How to Make Our Ideas Clear," in Charles S. Peirce, *Selected Writings (Values in a Universe of Chance)*, ed. Philip P. Wiener (New York: Dover, 1958), 133.

to a belief in it."[38] Yet, he rejected the suggestion that this conclusion makes reality dependent on thought. Peirce explains:

> The answer to this is that, on the one hand, reality is independent, not necessarily of thought in general, but only of what you or I or any finite number of men may think about it; and that, on the other hand, though the object of the final opinion depends on what that opinion is, yet what that opinion is does not depend on what you or I or any man thinks.[39]

William James explicitly advocated the connection between truth and the epistemological process implicit in Peirce: "Truth for us is simply a collective name for verification-processes, just as health, wealth, strength, etc. are names for other processes connected with life, and also pursued because it pays to pursue them. Truth is *made*, just as health, wealth and strength are made, in the course of experience."[40] In fact, James suggests that the pragmatists' central departure from foundationalism lies precisely here. In his estimation, "the great assumption of the intellectualists [i.e., the foundationalists] is that truth means essentially an inert static relation. When you've got your true idea of anything, there's an end of the matter. You're in possession; you *know*; you have fulfilled your thinking destiny." For the pragmatist James, in contrast, "The truth of an idea is not a stagnant property inherent in it. Truth *happens* to an idea. It *becomes* true, is *made* true by events."[41]

Coherentism and pragmatism provided ways to leave behind the foundationalist preference for the correspondence of truth. The means to overcome metaphysical realism, however, came from another source, the "turn to linguistics." Peirce himself was keenly interested in semiotics and language theory. But more significant for the quest for a nonfoundationalist epistemology via linguistics was the work of Ludwig Wittgenstein (1889–1951). In a sense, Wittgenstein completed the shift toward belief systems and the communal dimension of truth pioneered by the coherentists and the pragmatists.

Midway in his career, Wittgenstein came to realize that rather than having only a single purpose, to make assertions or state facts, language has many functions, e.g., to offer prayer, make requests, and convey ceremonial greetings. This discovery led to Wittgenstein's important concept of "language games." According to Wittgenstein, each use of language occurs within a separate and seemingly self-contained system complete with its own rules. Similar to playing a game, we require an awareness of the operative rules and sig-

38. Ibid., 134.

39. Ibid., 133.

40. William James, *Pragmatism: A New Name for Some Old Ways of Thinking* (1907; reprint, New York: Longmans, Green and Co., 1928), 218.

41. Ibid., 200–201.

nificance of the terms within the context of the purpose for which we are using language. Each use comprises a separate "language game," and each "game" may have little to do with the other "language games."[42]

Like the move to coherence and pragmatism, adopting the image of "language games" entailed abandoning the correspondence theory of truth. But unlike these two earlier proposals it also opened the door for the questioning of metaphysical realism. According to Wittgenstein, meaning and truth are not related—at least not directly or primarily—to an external world of "facts" waiting to be apprehended. Instead, they are an internal function of language. Because the meaning of any statement is dependent on the context—that is, on the "language game"—in which it appears, any sentence has as many meanings as contexts in which it is used. Rather than assertions of final truth or truth in any ultimate sense, all our utterances can only be deemed "true" within the context in which they are spoken.[43] Further, viewing language as a "game" presumes that language does not have its genesis in the individual mind grasping a truth or fact about the world and then expressing it in statements. Instead, for Wittgenstein, language is a social phenomenon, and any statement acquires its meaning within the process of social interaction.

Nonfoundationalist Theology

The Enlightenment quest for certitude served as a powerful molder of theology in the modern era. In recent years, however, several theologians have been looking to the insights of the nonfoundationalist philosophers in an effort to recast theology after the demise of foundationalism. Two of these theologians are especially significant as purveyors of a nonfoundationalist or postfoundationalist theological method.

Perhaps no theologian has exemplified more clearly the application to theology of the non-correspondence epistemological theories of the modern coherentists and pragmatists than Wolfhart Pannenberg.[44] At the heart of Pannenberg's theological agenda is the task of demonstrating the

42. See, for example the discussion in Ludwig Wittgenstein, *Philosophical Investigations*, 1.65, trans. G. E. M. Anscombe (Oxford: Blackwell, 1953), 32. See also Robert C. Solomon, *Continental Philosophy since 1750: The Rise and Fall of the Self* (Oxford: Oxford University Press, 1988), 150.

43. See Hilary Lawson, "Stories about Stories," in *Dismantling Truth: Reality in the Post-Modern World*, ed. Hilary Lawson and Lisa Appignanesi (New York: St. Martin's Press, 1989), xxiii–xxiv.

44. For my own lengthier treatment of Pannenberg's theological method, see Stanley J. Grenz, *Reason for Hope: The Systematic Theology of Wolfhart Pannenberg* (New York: Oxford, 1990), 11–43.

internal coherence of the doctrines and the external coherence of Christian doctrine with all knowledge.[45]

Pannenberg acknowledges that coherence is not a new idea in theological history. The scholastic theologians were concerned to show the truth of Christian doctrine through a presentation of its internal and external coherence. But, in a manner that at first glance appears to cast Pannenberg in a purely rationalist mode, he criticizes the tendency of the scholastic tradition, especially its Protestant form, to reduce the role of reason to that of illuminating truth already presupposed from revelation disclosed through what was assumed to be an inspired Bible.[46] Such a move, he maintains, led to several misguided tendencies. The scholastics unwittingly divided truth into autonomous spheres, attempted to shield the truth content of the Christian tradition from rational inquiry, and ended up placing the Bible in contradiction to every new discovery of truth, rather than integrating scientific discoveries into the truth claim of the Christian faith. In short, their doctrine of biblical inspiration failed to facilitate theologians in demonstrating the coherence of Christian doctrine with human knowledge.

Even more devastating, in Pannenberg's estimation, has been the proposal of what he refers to as "neo-Protestantism" (e.g., Pietism and liberalism) that places the focus of revelation in the act of faith itself.[47] In his estimation, this approach leads to a subjectivist understanding of truth which too easily borders on irrational fanaticism and ultimately fosters an unbiblical independence of the believing subject. Rather than being merely subjective, Pannenberg argues that truth is universal. Any valid "personal truth" must be, at least in principle, true for all. Pannenberg's task, therefore, is to chart an alternative to both of these widely held alternatives.

The basis for Pannenberg's reformulation of a coherentist theological method lies in his understanding of truth. Although he shares the older theological goal of discovering universal truth, he rejects the concept of truth the medieval scholastics inherited from the Greek philosophical tradition, namely, that truth is found in the constant and unchanging essences—or the eternal presence—lying behind the flow of time.[48] Rather, reminiscent of modern coherentists and pragmatists but drawing reso-

45. Wolfhart Pannenberg, *Systematic Theology*, trans. Geoffrey W. Bromiley (Grand Rapids: Eerdmans, 1991), 1:21–22.

46. Ibid., 1:28–38.

47. Ibid., 1:38–48.

48. In his early essay, "What Is Truth?" Pannenberg shows that the Hebrew and Greek conceptions of truth have certain common features, including that of constancy. At the same time the Hebrew conception includes and goes beyond the Greek; Wolfhart Pannenberg, *Basic Questions in Theology*, trans. George H. Kehm (Philadelphia: Fortress, 1971), 2:2–11.

lutely on what he sees as the biblical view, Pannenberg argues that truth is essentially historical. Truth is what shows itself throughout the movement of time, climaxing in the end event.[49] This end, he adds, is anticipated in the present, a point Pannenberg finds evident in general human life, for we continually modify our understandings in the light of subsequent experience.

At this point, Pannenberg applies the classical Augustinian linking of truth with God to his own dynamic view of the nature of truth: The truth that emerges in the end is the truth of God,[50] who is "the reality that determines everything."[51] Consequently, all truth ultimately comes together in God, who is the ground of the unity of truth. This, in turn, leads to a coherentist theological method. For Pannenberg, the goal of theology is to demonstrate the unity of truth in God, that is, to bring all human knowledge together in our affirmation of God. Or stated another way, theology seeks to show how the postulate of God illumines all human knowledge.[52]

Such an enterprise, however, is impossible to accomplish. The reality of God remains an open question in the contemporary world, and human knowledge is never complete or absolutely certain. To respond to this problem, Pannenberg appeals to the eschatological nature of truth. Because truth is historical, the focal point of certitude can only be the eschatological future. Only then will we know truth in its absolute fullness. Until the eschaton, truth will by its own nature always remain provisional, and truth claims contestable.[53]

This suggests that theological statements, like all human assertions, are hypotheses to be tested.[54] And we test our theological assertions as we seek to determine their internal and external coherence. In a manner resembling the modern pragmatists, therefore, Pannenberg maintains that the question of truth must be answered in the process of theological reflection and reconstruction. Like they, he remains optimistic about the ongoing quest to discover truth. Pannenberg is convinced that this testing process will confirm the power of the assertion of the reality of God to illumine the totality of human knowledge.

Pannenberg draws from a coherentist approach in his attempt to carve out a theological method that is nonfoundational, yet committed to a realist meta-

49. See "On Historical and Theological Hermeneutic," and "What is a Dogmatic Statement?" in Pannenberg, *Basic Questions*, 1:137–210.

50. Pannenberg, *Systematic Theology*, 1:53. See also, "What Is Truth?" 1–27.

51. For a statement of this foundational definition of God, which Pannenberg articulates repeatedly, see Wolfhart Pannenberg, "The Nature of a Theological Statement," *Zygon* 7, no. 1 (March 1972): 11.

52. Pannenberg, *Systematic Theology*, 1:59–60.

53. Ibid., 1:54.

54. Ibid., 1:56–58.

physic. What would theology look like if it not only rejected the correspondence theory of truth, but sought to follow Wittgenstein and move beyond realism as well? The program outlined by George Lindbeck provides a clue.

Similar to Pannenberg, Lindbeck's primary goal is to carve out an alternative to two rival—but in his estimation equally discredited—conceptions of doctrine, both of which are ultimately the results of the application of foundationalism to theological method. He terms these two the "cognitive-propositionalist" and the "experiential-expressive" approaches. The former erroneously assumes that theological statements (doctrines) make first-order truth-claims (that is, they assert that something is objectively true or false), thereby identifying religion too closely with its cognitive dimension. The latter sees doctrines as the outward expressions of the "inner feelings, attitudes or existential orientations"[55] related to personal religious experience, but in the process mistakenly assumes that there is some identifiable core experience common to all Christian traditions or even to all world religions.

Lindbeck's intent is to offer a third view, which he calls the "cultural-linguistic" approach. To this end, he not only follows the coherentist path but also gives it a Wittgensteinian twist. Lindbeck declares that doctrines are like rules of grammar. They constitute what we might call the rules of discourse of the believing community. Doctrines act as norms that instruct adherents how to think about and live in the world. Hence, like rules of grammar, church doctrine has a "regulative" function, serving as "community authoritative rules of discourse, attitude, and action."[56] They are "teachings regarding beliefs and practices that are considered essential to the identity or welfare of the group." As such "they indicate what constitutes faithful adherence to a community."[57] In short, Christian doctrines establish the ground rules for the "game" of Christian thinking, speaking, and living.

Lindbeck's use of Wittgenstein has far-reaching implications for the concept of truth. He notes that rules of grammar are routinely stated in the form of propositions; nevertheless, asking whether any one of them is objectively "true" or "false" involves a fundamental misunderstanding of the type of proposition the rule in fact is. It entails ripping the assertion out of its context and treating it apart from its regulative role within the language itself. These rules are not intended to say anything true about a reality external to the language they regulate. Hence, each rule is only "true" in the context of the body of rules that govern the language to which the rules belong. Lindbeck suggests that we might view doctrinal statements in a similar

55. George A. Lindbeck, *The Nature of Doctrine: Religion and Theology in a Postliberal Age* (Philadelphia: Westminster, 1984), 16.
    56. Ibid., 18.
    57. Ibid., 74.

manner. Seen from this perspective, such statements do not make "first-order" truth-claims; they do not assert something objective about reality. Instead, like rules of grammar, they are second-order assertions. This suggests that church doctrines are primarily rules for speech about God, rather than actual assertions about the divine reality.[58] Hence, they make "intrasystematic" truth-claims.[59] Doctrines are "true" primarily as "parts of a total pattern of speaking, thinking, feeling, and acting."[60]

His "third way" leads Lindbeck to call for an "intratextual theology" which "redescribes reality within the scriptural framework" and aims at "imaginatively incorporating all being into a Christ-centered world."[61] This theology draws from the text to explore what it means to articulate and live out the community's vision within a specific time and place.[62] Similar to Pannenberg, Lindbeck concludes that to this end, the theologian expounds the doctrinal core or framework of the Christian faith, determines that it coheres within itself, and indicates how doctrine illumines human existence.

Toward a Reconstructive Evangelical Theology

In recent years a growing number of evangelicals have become cognizant of the demise of foundationalism in philosophy and increasingly concerned to explore the implications of this philosophical development for theology. But in what sense, or to what extent, can the evangelical theological task move forward in the wake of the demise of foundationalism? How can evangelical theologians engage in the task of reconstructing evangelical theology by appropriating critically the insights of the non-foundationalist or postfoundationalist epistemology? In short, how can the descendants of Carl Henry and Millard Erickson incorporate—albeit critically[63]—aspects of the trajectory pioneered by thinkers like Wolfhart

58. Ibid., 69.
59. Ibid., 80.
60. Ibid., 64.
61. Ibid., 118.
62. Ibid., 113.
63. For the author's summary of a critical engagement with Pannenberg's thought from an evangelical perspective, see Stanley J. Grenz, "Pannenberg and Evangelical Theology: Sympathy and Caution," *Christian Scholars' Review* 20, no. 3 (February 1991): 272–85. For representative evangelical engagements with Lindbeck's proposal, see Timothy R. Phillips and Dennis L. Okholm, eds., *The Nature of Confession: Evangelicals and Postliberals in Conversation* (Downers Grove, Ill.: InterVarsity, 1996); Trevor Hart, *Faith Thinking: The Dynamics of Christian Theology* (Downers Grove, Ill.: InterVarsity, 1996), 81–89, 92–95; Alister E. McGrath, *The Genesis of Doctrine: A Study in the Foundation of Doctrinal Criticism* (Grand Rapids: Eerdmans, 1990), 14–34.

Pannenberg and George Lindbeck, in an attempt to develop a truly evangelical theological method that takes seriously the postmodern context?

Affirming a (Post)Foundation for Theology

As I noted earlier, the fundamental idea of foundationalism is that certain beliefs anchor other beliefs, i.e., certain beliefs are "basic," and other beliefs arise as conclusions from them. Enlightenment foundationalism, however, took the matter a step further. "Strong" foundationalists relegated religious beliefs to a nonbasic status, and sought to gain epistemological certitude by discovering an unassailable foundation of basic beliefs upon which to construct the knowledge edifice. Is there a way to avoid the error of foundationalism, on the one hand, without following Lindbeck's proposal to the bitter end?

(Re)Constructing a (Post)Foundationalist Epistemology

Perhaps the most helpful signpost along the way lies in the work of a group of philosophers sometimes known as the Reformed epistemologists.[64] These thinkers, whose ranks include Alvin Plantinga and Nicholas Wolterstorff, question strong foundationalism while not rejecting the basic foundationalist insight. Plantinga and Wolterstorff join other nonfoundationalists in claiming against the Enlightenment that there is no universal human reason. That is, there is no single, universal set of criteria by means of which we can judge definitively the epistemic status of all beliefs.[65] Further, according to the Reformed epistemologists reason is not the supposedly neutral medium in which human reflection takes place. Nor is it a purely formal and autonomous given that precedes and gives shape to intellectual reflection. Instead, they argue that reason is "person specific" and "situation specific,"[66] and that the nature of reason is itself a disputed topic.[67]

At the same time, the proponents of Reformed epistemology do not deny categorically the validity of the foundationalist search for a type of basic belief. Indeed, Plantinga goes so far as to agree that certain beliefs are in fact basic. What these thinkers reject as arbitrary and indefensible is the Enlightenment foundationalist restriction on which beliefs can count as properly basic, a restriction that assigns religious beliefs to the realm of

---

64. For this designation, see, for example, Nicholas Wolterstorff, "Introduction," in *Faith and Rationality*, 7. See also Plantinga, "Reason and Belief in God," 73–74.

65. Wood, *Epistemology*, 170.

66. Nicholas Wolterstorff, "Can Belief in God Be Rational If It Has No Foundations?" in *Faith and Rationality*, 155.

67. Westphal, "Reader's Guide," 12.

superstructure. Plantinga, in contrast, claims unequivocally that belief in God ought at times to be viewed as properly basic.[68]

In somewhat different yet complementary ways, Plantinga and Wolterstorff raise the question as to what, if anything, might be deemed "basic" for Christian theology: Does theological reflection and construction build upon something that we must presuppose? For the answer, these philosophers, like other nonfoundationalists, point to the believing community. In fact, this is in part what makes Reformed epistemology's seemingly weak brand of foundationalism at the same time nonfoundationalist and decidedly postmodern. Plantinga and Wolterstorff acknowledge the inevitability of our being situated in a particular community and the indispensable role our respective communities or traditions play in shaping our conceptions of rationality, as well as the religious beliefs we deem basic and thus by appeal to which we test new claims. And they readily admit the attendant loss of certitude involved with this acknowledgment, for they realize that these various communities may disagree as to the relevant set of paradigm instances of basic beliefs.

The difficulty this poses for any claims to universal truth ought not to be overlooked, a situation that will be addressed in chapter 7. Nevertheless, the communitarian turn marks an important advance. This focus returns theological reflection to its proper primary location within the believing community, in contrast to the Enlightenment ideal that effectively took theology out of the church and put it in the academy. More specifically, nonfoundationalist approaches see Christian theology as an activity of the community that gathers around Jesus the Christ. This has far-reaching implications for evangelical theology. As the British evangelical theologian Trevor Hart declares,

> Good theology . . . is the disciplined and critical reflection of the community of faith upon the gospel entrusted to it. It is reflection carried out within the community of faith, from the standpoint afforded by faith, and (though not exclusively certainly primarily) for the sake of the community of faith. Christian theology, then, is a pursuit of the church. It is the attempt on the part of those who belong to the church of Christ to explore and to comprehend more fully the shape and structure of the truth which they are called upon to profess and to live out in all its varied aspects.[69]

But in what sense is this so? More must be said about the nature of an ecclesially based, evangelical theology.

68. Westphal, "Reader's Guide," 11; Plantinga, "Reason and Belief in God," 73–78.
69. Hart, *Faith Thinking*, 11.

The Communitarian "Turn" and the Casting of Evangelical Theology

Despite their differences, evangelicals share a common vision as to what it means to be the Christ-focused community. Most evangelicals would agree that at the heart of their vision of the faith is an emphasis on an experience of being encountered savingly in Jesus Christ by the God of the Bible. This encounter is an identity-producing event. Through Christ, God constitutes us individually as believers and corporately as a community of believers. As a result, evangelicals are storytellers; we readily recite our "personal testimonies," narratives that recount our historical and ongoing personal encounter with God. These are cast in categories drawn from biblical narrative, as well as the didactic sections of Scripture. As evangelicals, therefore, we have come to see the story of God's action in Christ as the paradigm for our stories. We share an identity-constituting narrative.

This elevation of the role of experience ought not to be confused with the older Protestant liberalism. Two aspects separate the evangelical ethos as delineated here from the liberal project. First, liberalism transformed religious experience into a new foundationalism. Liberal theologians assumed—and sought to discern—a single, universal, foundational religious experience that supposedly lay beneath the plethora of religious experiences found in the various religious traditions. Rather than following liberalism in this direction, the evangelical theology proposed here avers that the various religions mediate religious experiences that are categorically different from each other. The encounter with the God of the Bible through Jesus, which is foundational to Christian identity, is shared only by those who participate in the Christian community (even though the experience is *potentially* universal, in that all persons might conceivably embrace the Christian faith). In fact, the commonality of this experience is the identifying feature of participation in this specific community, whereas a quite different experience would mark a person as a member of some other community.

Second, and providing the theoretical basis for the first, my proposal differs from liberalism in that the evangelical approach takes seriously the experience-forming dimension of interpretive frameworks. As Lindbeck has pointed out, the older liberal project tended to give primacy to experience and to view theological statements as expressions of religious experience. But this approach misunderstands the nature of experience. Experience does not precede interpretation. Rather experiences are always filtered by an interpretive framework that facilitates their occurrence.[70] Hence, re-

---

70. See, for example, Owen C. Thomas, "Theology and Experience," *Harvard Theological Review* 78, no. 1–2 (1985): 192.

ligious experience is dependent on a cognitive framework that sets forth a specifically religious interpretation of the world. In this sense, Lindbeck is correct in suggesting that religions produce religious experience rather than merely being the expression of it.[71]

The move away from classical liberalism must proceed a step farther than Lindbeck seems willing to go, however. There is no generic religious experience, only experiences endemic to specific religious traditions, i.e., experiences that are facilitated by an interpretive framework that is specific to that religious tradition. And any such interpretive framework is theological in nature, for it involves an understanding that sees the world in connection with the divine reality around which that tradition focuses. More specifically, Christian experience is facilitated by the proclamation of the Christian gospel. And every such proclamation comes clothed in a specifically Christian theological interpretive framework that views the world in connection with the God of the Bible.

Christian theology, in turn, is an intellectual enterprise by and for the Christian community. In this enterprise, the community of those whom the God of the Bible has encountered in Jesus Christ seeks to understand, clarify, and delineate the community's interpretive framework, which is connected with the gospel, as informed by the narrative—revealed in the Bible—of the action of this God on behalf of all creation. Theology delineates this interpretive framework not as residing as a given within the community as a particular visible, institutional reality. The task of theology is not purely *descriptive* (as is perhaps the case in Schleiermacher's view), but *prescriptive*. The theologian seeks to articulate what *ought* to be the interpretive framework of the Christian community. In this sense, the specifically Christian experience-facilitating interpretative framework, arising as it does out of the biblical gospel narrative, is "basic" for Christian theology.

Re-forming the Mosaic

At first glance, the suggestion that the Christian interpretive framework is "basic" for theology might appear to be simply a return to Enlightenment foundationalism. In fact, however, it marks a radical departure from the Enlightenment, while maintaining the central concerns of foundationalism. The cognitive framework that is "basic" for theology is not a given that precedes the theological enterprise; it does not provide the sure foundation upon which the theological edifice can in turn be constructed.

---

71. See, for example, Lindbeck, *Nature of Doctrine*, 34, where he states, "A religion is above all an external world . . . that molds and shapes the self and its world, rather than an expression or thematization of a preexisting self or of preconceptual experience."

Rather, in a sense the interpretive framework and theology are insepara-bly intertwined. Just as every interpretive framework is essentially theo-logical, so also every articulation of the Christian cognitive framework comes already clothed in a specific theological understanding. In fact, every such articulation is the embodiment of a specific understanding of the Christian theological vision; each embodies a specific understanding of the world as it is connected to the God of the Bible.

Consequently, the theologian's task is not to work from an interpretive framework to a theological construct. Instead, the theological enterprise con-sists in setting forth in a systematic manner a delineation of the Christian in-terpretive framework as informed by the Bible for the sake of the mission of the church in the contemporary context. By its very nature, the system-atic articulation of the Christian interpretive framework takes the form of an integrated (and prescriptive) statement of Christian doctrine. This leads inevitably to the kind of coherentist theological method Pannenberg has pioneered.

Commitment to the foundationalist approach, however, takes many neo-evangelical theologians in a quite different direction. Neo-evangelical systematicians routinely approach theological reflection in a somewhat piecemeal manner, indicative of an understanding that sees knowledge as the compiling of correct conclusions from a sure foundation. Indeed, once a theologian has set forth the proper foundation (which for the evangeli-cal modernist is often focused in an inerrant Bible), he or she is free to construct the house of theological knowledge in any order. As a conse-quence, the systematic theologies of many neo-evangelicals give the ap-pearance of being elaborate collections of loosely related facts, derived from a Bible which is "a store-house of facts," to cite Charles Hodge's de-scription.[72] Rather than *systematic* theologies, they tend to be what might be called "encyclopedias of theological knowledge." And even though the treatment of the various topics in these exhaustive works generally fol-lows a customary pattern—a pattern that has a certain logic to it—the au-thors often admit that the chosen order is in fact quite arbitrary, leading to a compilation of doctrine that looks quite like beads on a string. Wayne Grudem, to cite an especially illustrative example, writes:

> There is nothing to prevent us from going to Scripture to look for answers to *any* doctrinal questions, considered in *any sequence*. The sequence of topics in this book is a very common one and has been adopted because it is or-derly and lends itself well to learning and teaching. But the chapters could be read in any sequence one wanted and the conclusions should not be dif-ferent, nor should the persuasiveness of the arguments—if they are rightly

72. Charles Hodge, *Systematic Theology* (Grand Rapids: Eerdmans, 1975), 1:10.

derived from Scripture—be significantly diminished. . . . I have tried to write the chapters so that they can be read as independent units.[73]

Of course, Grudem is free to release the reader to read the chapters in any sequence because in the book's prolegomenon he has assumed the proper foundation for what follows. Once the foundation is laid, the theological construction engineer can erect the scaffolding of individual doctrines in any order.

The demise of foundationalism, however, calls into question the propriety of this paradigm. Coherentist philosophers assert that knowledge is not a collection of isolated factual statements arising directly from first principles. Rather, beliefs form a system in which each is supported by its neighbors and, ultimately, by its presence within the whole. If this is the case, theology can no longer model itself after the foundationalist metaphor of constructing an edifice. Theologians need no longer spin their wheels constructing elaborate prolegomena, thinking thereby they have laid a sure foundation for the compilation of seemingly separable units of biblical teaching subsequently elaborated.

The move to coherence suggests alternate images of the theological enterprise. Viewed from a perspective that takes the demise of foundationalism seriously, Christian doctrine comprises a "web of belief" or a "mosaic," and theology is the articulation and exploration of the interrelated, unified whole of Christian doctrine. Hence, a helpful image for the nature of theological work is that of articulating the belief-mosaic of the Christian community, a mosaic consisting of interlocking pieces forming a single pattern (in which, of course, some pieces are more central to the "picture" and others are more peripheral). This mosaic consists of the set of interconnected doctrines that together comprise what ought to be the specifically Christian way of viewing the world. This worldview is truly theological and specifically Christian, because it involves an understanding of the entire universe and of ourselves in connection with the God of the Bible, and the biblical narrative of God, at work bringing creation to its divinely destined goal.

However, not only does the theological task entail explicating this doctrinal mosaic, but as Pannenberg has argued, it also includes demonstrating the explicative power of the Christian faith, by indicating the value of the Christian worldview for illuminating human experience, as well as our human understanding of our world. In this manner, evangelical theology retains the apologetic focus that has characterized it since the 1940s. And the goal of doctrinal formulation is to facilitate both conversion and

---

73. Wayne Grudem, *Systematic Theology: An Introduction to Biblical Doctrine* (Grand Rapids: Zondervan, 1994), 32.

the pursuit of the convertive life. In short theology is a second-order conversation that seeks to serve the mission of the church, which is understood as a people who proclaim and live out the biblical narrative of God's saving action in Christ through the Spirit.

Evangelical Theology as Conversation

I noted above that a theology that seeks to be responsive to, and to take seriously, postmodern sensitivities after the demise of foundationalism views itself as a conversation. More specifically, theological construction—the attempt to delineate what ought to be the belief-mosaic of the Christian church—may be characterized as an ongoing conversation that the participants in the faith community share as to the meaning of the cultural symbols through which Christians express their understanding of the world they inhabit. These symbols include sacred texts, language, rituals, and practices. This constructive theological conversation requires the interplay, or perichoretic dance, of three sources of insight.

The Primary Voice in the Theological Conversation

At the heart of evangelical theology is the Bible; evangelicals pride themselves on being a "people of the book." In the modern era, however, a misunderstanding of Luther's principle of *sola scriptura* led many theologians to trade the ongoing reading of the text for their own systematic delineation of the doctrinal deposit that was supposedly encoded in its pages centuries ago. Thereby, the Bible was all too readily transformed from a living text into the object of the scholar's exegetical and systematizing prowess. The postmodern situation has laid bare the foundationalist presuppositions lying behind this modernist program. But what marks the way forward toward a reconstruction of evangelical theology in the wake of the demise of foundationalism?

Chapter 2 traced the development of the grand Reformation hallmark of *sola scriptura* through the Puritan and Pietist movements into the fledgling evangelical awakening. This trajectory took seriously the Protestant concern to bring Word and Spirit together in a living relationship, a desire that led to the "born again reader" who through the Spirit discerns the "spiritual meaning" of the biblical text. It also led to an emphasis on the practical goal of exegesis. The paradigmatic statement of this trajectory came in insightful description of the Protestant principle of authority found in the *Westminster Confession*. According to the Westminster divines, "The Supreme Judge, by which all controversies of religion are to be determined, and all decrees of counsels, opinions of ancient writers, doctrines of men, and private spirits, are to be examined, and in whose sentence we are to rest, can be no other than the Holy Spirit speaking in the Scripture."[74] When placed in the context of the theological movement from the Reformation to the evangelical awakening, this statement suggests the sense in which the Bible is the norming norm in theology. Scripture carries this lofty position in that it is the instrumentality of the Spirit.

Insights from contemporary speech-act theory suggest how this principle can be effectively understood in the postmodern, postfoundationalist context. The Bible is the instrumentality of the Spirit in that the Spirit appropriates the biblical text so as to speak to us today. Through Scripture the Spirit performs the illocutionary act of addressing us. This address can take several forms, in keeping with the manifold diversity of writings that constitute the Bible.[75] For example, the Pauline statement to Timothy suggests that through Scripture, the Spirit teaches, reproves, corrects, and instructs (2 Tim. 3:16). Also, through the text the Spirit even informs us as to how we might voice our thoughts, feelings, and emotions to God, as for example in certain of the Psalms.

As important as these dimensions are, however, they are only parts of a larger whole, namely, the *goal* or *product* of the Spirit's speaking. By appropriating the text, the Spirit seeks to perform a particular *perlocutionary* act. And the specific perlocutionary act the Spirit performs is the creation of "world." As the Life-giver, the divine power at work fashioning the universe, the Spirit creates through the Word a new world, a "centered" world, an eschatological world, a world that finds its cohesion in the Word who is Jesus the Christ (2 Cor. 5:17). And this world consists of a new community comprised of renewed persons.

Through the Bible, the Spirit orients our present on the basis of the past and in accordance with a vision of the future. The Spirit leads contemporary hearers to view themselves and their situation in the light of God's past and future, and to open themselves and their present to the power of that future, which is already at work in the world. Thereby they are drawn to participate in God's eschatological world. The task of theology, in turn, is to assist the people of God in hearing the Spirit's voice speaking through the text, so that we can live as God's people—as inhabitants of God's eschatological world—in the present.

74. *The Westminster Confession of Faith*, 1.10, in *The Creeds of the Churches*, ed. John H. Leith, 3d ed. (Atlanta: John Knox, 1982), 196.

75. For a helpful delineation of the Bible as comprising four basic types of materials, see John Goldingay, *Models for Scripture* (Grand Rapids: Eerdmans, 1994).

The Hermeneutical Trajectory of the Theological Conversation

The Spirit's goal in appropriating the biblical text is to fashion a community that lives the paradigmatic biblical narrative in the contemporary context. The goal of reading the text, therefore, is to hear the Spirit's voice and to be formed into that community. Consequently, reading the text is a community event.

This idea is not foreign to the evangelical movement. As a people, evangelicals tend to elevate the reading and proclamation of Scripture within the local congregational setting. We come to Scripture aware that we are participants in a concrete, visible fellowship of disciples. Ultimately, therefore, our desire is to hear what the Spirit is saying to this particular congregation and to these particular believers who share together the mandate to be a fellowship of disciples in this specific setting. Hence, most evangelicals would readily agree with the words of the Mennonite theologian Walter Klaassen, "The text can be properly understood only when disciples are gathered together to discover what the Word has to say to their needs and concerns."[76]

Reading within community also means, however, that we approach the text conscious that we are participants in the one faith community that spans the ages. This consciousness involves recognizing the theological heritage, the tradition, within which we stand as contemporary readers of the text. The use of the word *tradition* here ought not to be viewed as reintroducing the medieval Roman Catholic idea of a twofold source of truth. Rather, the term stands as a reminder that the evangelical tendency to summarize our doctrinal identity in the form of "confessions of faith" is not misguided. It bears witness to the fact that Christians in every generation read the text through the lenses provided by a particular hermeneutical context. And *tradition* indicates that luminaries of the past have an ongoing role in the contemporary theological conversation.

Understood properly, then, tradition plays an important albeit secondary role in theology. Like all Christians everywhere, we read the biblical text today conscious that we are part of an ongoing listening community and therefore that we are participants in a hermeneutical trajectory. We are not the first generation since the early church to seek to be formed into the community of Christ in the world. On the contrary we are the contemporary embodiment of a historical people, the people of God throughout the ages.

76. Walter Klaassen, "Anabaptist Hermeneutics: Presuppositions, Principles and Practice," in *Essays on Biblical Interpretation: Anabaptist-Mennonite Perspective*, ed. Willard M. Swartley (Elkhart, Ind.: Institute of Mennonite Studies, 1984), 10. For this idea, Klaassen cites John Howard Yoder, *Mennonite Quarterly Review* 41 (October 1967): 301.

Hence, our theological heritage provides a reference point for us today. This heritage offers examples of previous attempts to fulfill the theological mandate, from which we can learn. Looking at the past alerts us to some of the pitfalls we should avoid, some of the landmines that could trip us up, and some of the cul-de-sacs or blind alleys that are not worth our exploration. In addition to warning us of possible dangers, past theological statements can point us in directions that hold promise as we engage in the theological calling.

Theological heritage serves as a reference point in another way as well. Today we engage in theology conscious that we are members of a community of faith which spans the centuries. Because we come to the text as those who seek to understand the whole of Scripture as the instrumentality of the Spirit's speaking to us, we do well to keep in view what the church through the ages has considered this biblical "whole" to be. Further, consciousness of our participation in the one church of Jesus Christ also involves acknowledging that like others before us, we desire to read the Bible "Christianly." This process is advanced as we take seriously the attempts of our forebears to engage in the hermeneutical task that now occupies us. Because we participate in the one church of Jesus Christ, we desire to be in hermeneutical fellowship with all the people of God. One aspect of this true evangelical "ecumenism" is our attempt to retain continuity of outlook with the church throughout the ages. In short, we desire to participate in a truly "catholic" reading of the text, even in those instances when that reading leads us to differ with past luminaries on certain theological issues.

The Wider Context of the Theological Conversation

The ultimate authority in the church is the Spirit speaking through Scripture. The Spirit's speaking through Scripture, however, is always a contextual speaking; it always comes to its hearers within a specific historical-cultural context. This has been the case throughout church history, for the Spirit's ongoing provision of guidance has always come, and now continues to come, to the community of Christ as a specific people in a specific setting hears the Spirit's voice speaking in the particularity of its historical-cultural context. But the same principle was operative even during the biblical era. In fact, the canon itself was the product of the faith communities hearing the Spirit speaking within their changing contexts. This speaking often came through literary materials that they had gathered and preserved, and it led in turn to the composition of additional texts.

The specificity of the Spirit's speaking means that the conversation with culture and cultural context is crucial to the hermeneutical task. We seek to listen to the voice of the Spirit through Scripture, who speaks to us in the particularity of the historical-cultural context in which we live.

This hermeneutical process occurs in part as our theological construction is informed by contemporary "knowledge," the discoveries and insights of the various disciplines of human learning. For example, theories about addictions and addictive behavior can provide insight into the biblical teaching about sin. Likewise, current discoveries about the process of human identity formation can lead to a deeper or wider awareness of the many dimensions entailed in the new identity the Spirit seeks to create in us through our union with Christ. Our theological reflections can draw from the so-called "secular" sciences, because ultimately no discipline is in fact purely secular. Above all, because God is the ground of truth, as Wolfhart Pannenberg so consistently argues, all truth ultimately comes together in God. Theology therefore looks to all human knowledge, for in so doing it demonstrates the unity of truth in God.[77]

These considerations, however, have not yet pierced to the core of the pneumatological basis for hearing the Spirit's voice in culture. Much of Western theology has focused on the church as the *sole* repository of all truth and the *only* location in which the Holy Spirit is operative. The biblical writers, however, display a much wider understanding of the Spirit's presence, a presence connected to the Spirit's role as the Life-giver (Gen. 1:2; 2:7) and Life-sustainer (Ps. 104:29–30; Isa. 32:15; cf. Job 27:3; 34:14–15). Because the life-giving Spirit is present wherever life flourishes, the Spirit's voice can conceivably resound through many media, including the media of human culture. Because Spirit-induced human flourishing evokes cultural expression, Christians can anticipate in such expressions traces of the Creator Spirit's presence. Consequently, in the conversation that constitutes theology, evangelical theologians should listen intently for the voice of the Spirit, who is present in all life and therefore precedes us into the world, bubbling to the surface through the artifacts and symbols humans construct.

A cautionary note is in order here, however. Whatever speaking that occurs through other media does not come as a speaking against the text. To pit the Spirit's voice in culture against the Spirit speaking through Scripture would be to fall prey to the foundationalist trap. It would require that we elevate some dimension of contemporary thought or experience as a human universal that forms the criterion for determining what in the Bible is or is not acceptable.[78] Hence, while

77. Pannenberg, *Systematic Theology*, 1:59–60.

78. Darrell Jodock, "The Reciprocity between Scripture and Theology: The Role of Scripture in Contemporary Theological Reflection," *Interpretation* 44, no. 4 (October 1990): 377.

being ready to acknowledge the Spirit's voice wherever it may be found, evangelical theology must always give primacy to the Spirit's speaking through the biblical text. Even though we cannot hear the Spirit speaking through Scripture except by listening within a particular historical-cultural context, hearing the Spirit in the biblical text provides the only sure canon for hearing the Spirit in culture, because the Spirit's speaking everywhere and anywhere is always in concert with this primary speaking through the Bible. In fact, culture and biblical text do not comprise two different moments of communication; rather, they are but one speaking. And consequently we do not engage in two different "listenings," but one. We listen for the voice of the Spirit who speaks the Word through the word within the particularity of the hearers' context, and who thereby can speak in all things, albeit always according to the Word who is Christ.

Evangelical Theology as "Christian" Theology

The demise of foundationalism accompanying the postmodern situation opens the way for an evangelical theological method that views constructive theology as an ongoing conversation involving the interplay of Scripture, tradition, and culture.[79] The overarching goal of this conversation is to hear the Spirit's voice speaking to the faith community today, one important dimension of which is the task of delineating, articulating, and reflecting upon the Christian belief-mosaic.

This perspective, in turn, leads to the conclusion that ultimately all theology is, as the "postmodern condition" suggests, "local" or "specific." That is, it is the conversation involving, and the resultant articulation authored by, a particular group in a particular moment of their ongoing existence in the world. Despite the specificity of all theology, these various local theologies share in common "a similar pattern, shape or 'style' "[80] that makes them *Christian* theology. A postmodern local theology carries the designation *Christian*, then, insofar as it reflects the uniquely Christian "style." The explication of this style, in turn, provides the finishing touches of an evangelical theological method that can meet the postmodern challenge.

79. For the structure of the methodological proposal reflected in this section, I am indebted in part to John Franke, my coauthor in the writing of a book-length treatment of theological method.

80. According to Kroeber, culture provides "a far more natural and fit medium" for "style" to grow in than does "life"; Alfred L. Kroeber, *Style and Civilizations* (Ithaca, N.Y.: Cornell University Press, 1957), 76.

The Structural Motif of Evangelical Theology

Early in the twentieth century, Emil Brunner noted, "The ecclesiastical doctrine of the Trinity, established by the dogma of the ancient Church, is not a Biblical *kerygma*, therefore it is not the *kerygma* of the Church, but it is a theological doctrine which defends the central faith of the Bible and of the Church."[81] Brunner's point is well taken. The doctrine of the Trinity emerged as the result of a lengthy theological process during the patristic era. Once formulated, however, the understanding of God as triune became a nonnegotiable dimension of church teaching. Indeed, the concept of tri-unity lies at the heart of the unique biblical understanding of God, and therefore Christians through the years have seen it as crucial for maintaining the central message of the Bible.

While the confession of God as triune has become a standard component of the Christian faith, the question of its proper role in theology is the subject of considerable debate. Many theologians give little place to the doctrine of the Trinity. Although this tendency has been represented in the Christian tradition in every age, it was exacerbated in the Enlightenment as thinkers under the banner of "reason" called into question not only its centrality for theology but also its veracity. Then, in the wake of Kant, skepticism about the very possibility of providing an ontology of God served to diminish, if not altogether eclipse, the doctrine of the Trinity in theology. As a result, it has become marginalized, both by theologians who see it as an abstract and indefensible example of the excesses of speculative theology, and by Christians who view the doctrine as an inherited dogma that is of no relevance to the modern world or to daily life.[82]

Yet, by its very definition theology—the teaching about God—has as its central interest the divine reality, as well as God's actions in creation. The chief inquiry for any theology, Christian or otherwise, is the question of the identity of God. The Christian answer to the question, "Who is God?" ultimately surrounds the doctrine of the Trinity. The one God, Christians assert, is triune. God is, to cite the traditional theological designations, Father, Son, and Spirit. The confession of the triune God is the sine qua non of the Christian faith. Rather than being mere speculation, therefore, unpacking the eternal trinitarian relations is endemic to the theological task.

---

81. Emil Brunner, *The Christian Doctrine of God*, vol. 1 of *Dogmatics*, trans. Olive Wyon (Philadelphia: Westminster, 1950), 206.

82. Gunton states the matter bluntly: "Overall, there is a suspicion that the whole thing is a bore, a matter of mathematical conundrums and illogical attempts to square the circle." Colin Gunton, *The Promise of Trinitarian Theology*, 2d ed. (Edinburgh: T. and T. Clark, 1997), 2–3.

In keeping with this basic Christian understanding of God, both the Apostles' Creed and the Nicene Creed, those ancient and ecumenical symbols of the church, are ordered and divided into three articles that correspond to the three persons of the triune God: the Father (creation); the Son (reconciliation); and the Spirit (redemption and consummation). For much of the history of the church this creedal pattern gave rise to the classical trinitarian structure in theological construction. These ancient confessions of the church suggest that any truly Christian theology must be trinitarian theology. That is, because Christian theology is committed to finding its basis in the being and action of the triune God, it should be ordered and structured in a manner that reflects the primacy of this fundamental Christian confession. At its core the content of Christian theology consists of a witness to, as well as participation in, the narrative of the being and act of the triune God. As such, theology's structuring motif is rooted in the Christian confession of God as triune, and hence must be trinitarian.

This suggests that the centrality of God's tri-unity goes beyond the doctrine of God (or theology proper). It gives structure to other aspects of the Christian belief-mosaic as well. The link from theology proper to the other systematic-theological loci runs through the biblical teaching of humans as the *imago dei*. Ultimately, the "image of God" is connected with God's design for humankind, including our divinely given role as those who mirror for the sake of creation the nature of the Creator. As is evident throughout Scripture, the divine image is not primarily individual, but is shared or relational.[83] The doctrine of the Trinity indicates why this is the case. The God we know is the triune one, three trinitarian persons united together in perfect love. Because God is "community"— the fellowship of the three persons—the creation of humankind in the divine image must be related to humans in relationship as well. God's own character can only be mirrored by humans who love after the manner of the perfect love lying at the heart of the triune God. Only as we live in fellowship can we show forth what God is like. And as we reflect God's character—love—we also live in accordance with our own true nature and find our true identity.

In short, as biblical Christians we must be thoroughgoing trinitarians, looking to the divine life as the model for human life, so that it might reflect the very character of the God who is eternally love. When this fundamental Christian view of God as triune permeates the entire explication of the community's belief-mosaic, giving structure to the theological pre-

---

83. For a fuller discussion of the author's view of the relationship of sexuality and community, see Stanley J. Grenz, *Sexual Ethics: An Evangelical Perspective*, rev. ed. (Louisville, Ky.: Westminster John Knox, 1998), 35–37.

sentation in its entirety, a local theology becomes truly trinitarian and in this sense "Christian."

The Integrative Motif of Evangelical Theology

Understood from the perspective of a theological ecclesiology that takes its cue from the triune God, the church is a community. Indeed, community lies at the heart of the Christian concept of the church. But more importantly, all Christian theology is communitarian.

I noted earlier the work of the Reformed epistemologists who point out that to be human means to be situated in a particular community, so that our respective communities (or traditions) play an indispensable role in shaping our conceptions of rationality, as well as the religious beliefs we deem basic and to which we appeal to test new claims. However, following the lead of the Reformed epistemologists, i.e., by declaring that the church is "basic" in theology, can lead to a new "foundationalism of the church." This danger requires a nuanced understanding of the Reformed epistemological insight.

Viewed from one perspective, what is "basic" for theology is not the church itself, but the specifically Christian experience-facilitating interpretative framework, which in turn is connected to the gospel, and by extension to the biblical narrative. At the same time, there is a sense in which the church *is* basic for theology. In fact, only by viewing the church as basic can evangelical theology avoid the foundationalism of modern theology, in both its liberal and conservative forms. The church is basic in that participation in the faith community calls forth theological reflection. Theology is "faith seeking understanding," to cite the classic definition. Therefore, the very existence of the faith community, the community in which faith is present, leads naturally to the reflection on faith that is called *theology*.

For this reason, theological construction needs no elaborate, foundation-setting, certainty-gaining prolegomenon. Instead, it arises out of the life of the discipleship community, persons who are joined together by the Spirit and who join together in living out the mandate they share. Therefore, presence within the Christian community itself leads to the theological task. And the existence of this community provides the only rationale necessary for launching into the process of delineating and determining the shared Christian belief-mosaic, or explicating its interpretive framework.

The focus on the communal nature of theology opens the way for introducing *community* as theology's integrative motif. That is, community—or more fully stated, persons-in-relationship—is the central, organizing concept of theological construction, the theme around which a systematic theology is structured. Community provides the integrative thematic perspective in light of which the various theological foci can be understood and significant theological issues explored.[84]

Christian theology must be communitarian, because it is linked to a particular community, namely, the community of the disciples of Jesus. As I noted above, theology has classically been understood as faith seeking understanding. At the heart of faith is personal response to the good news. Yet this does not mean that theology is solely the faith of the individual believer seeking understanding. Rather, as the Reformed philosophers remind us, our beliefs—and hence our faith—are dependent on the community in which we are situated. More specifically, being a Christian entails membership in the fellowship of those who have come to know the God of the Bible through Jesus Christ by the Spirit. Theology, in turn, is the community seeking to understand the faith they share. Thus, McClendon declares, "Theology is always theology of the community, not just of the individual Christian."[85] As the shared faith of the community seeking understanding, Christian theology is necessarily communitarian.

This same conclusion emerges as well from a parallel consideration. A central task of theology is to express communal beliefs and values as well as the meaning of the symbols of the faith community. Theological construction has as its goal that of setting forth an understanding of the mosaic of beliefs that lies at the heart of a particular community. More specifically, the task of *Christian* theology includes the determination and articulation of the belief-mosaic of the Christian faith, the interlocking doctrines that together comprise the specifically Christian way of viewing the world. As a result, Christian theology is by its very nature "church dogmatics," as Karl Barth describes it. As church dogmatics, as the faith of the community seeking understanding, theology is inherently communitarian.

Further, theology is communitarian because it is the explication of the Christian conception of God. In addition to being faith seeking understanding, theology is by definition the study of God. This study, however, is never generic. Rather it is always specific; it is always the explication of the understanding set forth within a particular community. Hence, *Christian* theology speaks about the God known in the Christian community. And the God to whom the Christian community bears witness is the triune God. The only true God, Christians declare, is social or communal. Christian theology is inherently communitarian, therefore, because it is

---

84. For a discussion of the idea of the integrative motif in theology, see Gerhard Sauter and Alex Stock, *Arbeitswesen Systematischer Theologie: Eine Anleitung* (Munich: Kaiser, 1976), 18–19.

85. James William McClendon, *Systematic Theology* (Nashville: Abingdon, 1986), 1:36.

the explication of the Christian understanding of the God who is the triune one.

This leads to a final reason why theology is inherently communitarian. Christian theology is the study of the narrative of this God fulfilling the divine purposes as disclosed in the Bible. The biblical narrative presents as the ultimate goal of the biblical God the establishment of community. Taken as a whole the Bible asserts that God's program is directed to the establishment of community in the highest sense of the word: a redeemed people, living within a redeemed creation, enjoying the presence of the triune God.[86] Theology, in turn, is the explication of this divine goal.

To summarize: as Josiah Royce declared, the "real world" means simply the "true interpretation" of our situation;[87] but "an interpretation is real only if the appropriate community is real, and is true only if that community reaches its goal."[88] Christian theology is the explication of the interpretation of God and the world in which the Christian community finds its identity. Theology engages in this task in order to help the fellowship of Christ's disciples to fulfill their calling to be the image of God, and thereby to be the biblical community God destines us to become. For this reason, theology is by its very nature communitarian. And as a local, trinitarian theology finds its integrative motif in the concept of community, it follows the Christian "style."

The Orientating Motif of Evangelical Theology

Royce's comment leads directly to the third in this triad of motifs in a method that seeks to reconstruct evangelical theology in the wake of the postmodern condition: eschatology. The basis for this aspect of the Christian theological "style" flows almost as a matter of course from what has been said already about theology's connection to the biblical narrative. Simply stated, Christian theology is inherently eschatological, because it is the teaching about the promising God, who is bringing creation to an eternal *telos*. Theology finds its orientation in eschatology, therefore, not so much as the compilation of what God has told us in Scripture "about the major events yet to come in the history of the universe,"[89] but because of its connection to the narrative of God at work in creation as disclosed in Scripture. Taken as a whole, the biblical story is directed toward a *telos*. It speaks of the God who is bringing creation to its divinely intended goal.

---

86. See, for example, Paul D. Hanson, *The People Called: The Growth of Community in the Bible* (San Francisco: Harper and Row, 1986), 510.

87. Josiah Royce, *The Problem of Christianity* (New York: Macmillan, 1913), 2:264.

88. Ibid., 2:269.

89. Grudem, *Systematic Theology*, 1091.

The eschatological motif leads to a theology that is theocentric, rather than anthropocentric. In contrast to "totalizing"[90] modernist metanarratives, against which postmodernism rightly rebels, an eschatological theology views the God of the Bible, and not humankind, as the acting subject who unites the diverse moments of time into a single story. It rejects the modernist idea that history is *our* story (i.e., the story of Man, or the tale of the progress of humankind), and it denies that the goal of history is a humanly devised utopia. Instead Christian theology declares that history's goal is nothing less than the realization of God's purposes for creation, which will arrive only because the God who stands at the end of the human story is already graciously ordering the cosmic story toward its intended goal.

The eschatological motif leads likewise to a theology that takes its orientation from the perspective of our human *telos* together with the *telos* of creation as a whole. It engages all theological questions from the perspective of the future consummation. It looks to the completion of God's creative work—that is, to the biblical narrative in its eschatological culmination—for the revelation not only of who God is, but also of who we are and of what creation is, as well as the revelation of God's purposes for all creation including humankind. In this manner, an eschatological theology anticipates the future within the present. It finds our human identity, as well as the identity of all creation, in the God who promises to make everything new (Rev. 21:5). And it speaks about the in-breaking of this new creation (2 Cor. 5:17) into our lives in the here and now.

By speaking about a world invading the present from the future, the eschatological motif moves the discussion from epistemology to ontology. It introduces the question of the "objective" truth of what Christian theology explicates, which is the topic of the next chapter.

90. Terry Eagleton, "Awakening from Modernity," *Times Literary Supplement* (February 20, 1987), 194.

seven

Theology AND Science AFTER THE Demise OF Realism

❖

While part of an "away team" exploring the subterranean religious sanctuary of another civilization, the overly exuberant Kess dashed into a sacred shrine and as a result became deathly ill. In a bid to save her crew member, Kathryn Janeway, captain of the starship *Voyager* (of *Star Trek: Voyager* fame), following the advice of one of the spiritual leaders of the alien people, engaged in a grueling physical and mental "purification" ordeal. Despite her successful completion of the test, however, Janeway learned that the only possible way to save Kess would be to put aside her dependence on her personal abilities and commit her dying friend to the ancestral spirits who inhabit the shrine Kess violated. Faith finally prevailed over scientific rationality, as Janeway carried the unconscious Kess across the shrine's threshold. With the miraculous healing accomplished, Kess safely on board *Voyager,* and the routine medical examination completed, the ship's doctor offered the captain his theory as to how reentering the shrine's court had reversed the young woman's terminal condition, an explanation that spoke about biogenic fields and biological reactions, but omitted any reference to the possible role of the spirits in sparing her life. Asked to respond to the doctor's reconstruction of the events, Janeway, whose deep reflection had been interrupted by the query, remarked just before she left the room, "It's a perfectly sound explanation, Doctor, very . . . *scientific.*"

From the beginnings of the movement in the 1940s to the present, neo-evangelicals have been deeply interested in the relationship between faith, or theology, and science.[1] Although this interest boasts a long pedigree in church history, neo-evangelicals inherited the concern to bring faith into critical conversation with science from the trajectory that begins with the evangelical revival, runs through their nineteenth-century Princeton forebears, and leads more immediately to fundamentalism. What sets neo-evangelical theologians apart from their fundamentalist predecessors has been their abandonment of an adversarial stance. Instead, they cultivate the apologetic interest in bringing theology into constructive engagement with science in general and current scientific findings in particular. Chapter 3 sketched the important work of Bernard Ramm in this aspect of the neo-evangelical theological program, as was evident in his widely hailed book, *The Christian View of Science and Scripture*.[2]

In recent years, this evangelical concern has coincided with similar interests among mainline theologians.[3] In fact, a growing chorus of voices consisting of both scientists and theologians is calling for new styles of engagement characterized by the kind of dialogue that can lead to mutual interaction or a new integration of the two. This impulse has led many thinkers to look to the territory where theology and science supposedly overlap for the focal point of a potential rapprochement.[4] Initially cosmology emerged in the minds of many as an area of promising dialogue and mutually beneficial integration,[5] and that approach continues to gain ad-

---

1. One example of this is the renewed interest of evangelical thinkers in Darwinian theories of human origins. See, for example, Michael J. Behe, *Darwin's Black Box: The Biological Challenge to Evolution* (New York: Free, 1996); Philip E. Johnson, *Defeating Darwinism by Opening Minds* (Downers Grove, Ill.: InterVarsity, 1997); David N. Livingstone, *Darwin's Forgotten Defenders: The Encounter between Evangelical Theology and Evolutionary Thought* (Grand Rapids: Eerdmans, 1987); J. P. Moreland and John Mark Reynolds, eds., *Three Views on Creation and Evolution* (Grand Rapids: Zondervan, 1999); Delvin Lee Ratzsch, *The Battle of Beginnings: Why Neither Side is Winning the Creation-Evolution Debate* (Downers Grove, Ill.: InterVarsity, 1996).

2. Bernard L. Ramm, *The Christian View of Science and Scripture* (Grand Rapids: Eerdmans, 1954).

3. According to Ian Barbour, there are four ways of relating science and religion: conflict, independence, dialogue, and integration. See Ian G. Barbour, *Religion in an Age of Science* (San Francisco: Harper and Row, 1990), 3–30. In the recent past, relations between the Christian faith and modern science have more often than not been characterized by either conflict or the assumption that each is independent from the other. For an example of the conflict model, see Bertrand Russell, *Religion and Science* (New York: Oxford, 1935, 1961).

4. Barbour proposes that this engagement be facilitated through a renewed theology of nature, Barbour, *Religion in an Age of Science*, 30. Arthur Peacocke, in contrast, advocates a new critical realism; Arthur Peacocke, *Theology for a Scientific Age: Being and Becoming—Natural, Divine, and Human*, enlarged edition (Minneapolis: Fortress, 1993), 21. For a discussion of six other, more recent proposals, see Niels Henrik Gregersen and J. Wentzel van Huyssteen, eds., *Rethinking Theology and Science: Six Models for the Current Dialogue* (Grand Rapids: Eerdmans, 1998).

5. See, for example, Ernan McMullin, "How Should Cosmology Relate to Theology?" in *The Sciences and Theology in the Twentieth Century*, ed. Arthur R. Peacocke (Stocksfield, England: Oriel, 1981), 17–57.

herents.[6] More recently, however, attention has shifted to the larger question of method,[7] as certain thinkers have sought to determine whether there is a fundamental methodological overlap between practitioners in the two fields.[8]

The attempt to discover a connection in method between the disciplines is not new. Christian theologians throughout the history of the church have engaged in the task of relating their discipline methodologically to science and the scientific endeavor. Moreover, many theologians have not only understood their enterprise as standing in a positive relationship to science but have seen themselves as practitioners of science in some sense of the word. This leads, however, to the question: In *what* sense? Exactly *how* are theologians scientists?

This chapter sketches three paradigmatic Christian theological answers to the question. The immediate purpose of this critical interaction is to outline a methodological approach for an engagement between theology and science that takes the postmodern condition seriously. But the overarching goal lies deeper. The discussion seeks to provide an answer to the question of ontology left hanging in the previous chapter. That is, it sets forth an evangelical theological response to the problem of the "objectivity" of the world introduced by the demise of foundationalism and the retreat from realism that characterizes the postmodern condition, as was briefly outlined in chapter 5.

The Modern Paradigm: Theology Is like a Science

The understanding of the relationship between theology and science that reigned from the seventeenth century to the 1970s, and hence that cradled the evangelical movement since its genesis, looks to science for the methodological model for all intellectual endeavor, including theological construction. Lying behind this program is the assumption that theology is like a science and hence that theologians are actually aspiring scientists. Theologians need to be scientists, therefore, because their discipline is governed by the scientific method.

Enlightenment Science

Francis Bacon (1561–1626) and Galileo (1564–1642) stand at the beginning of a long shift in thinking away from the Aristotelian ap-

6. For example, see J. Wentzel van Huyssteen, *Duet or Duel?: Theology and Science in a Postmodern World* (Harrisburg: Trinity Press International, 1998), 30.

7. See, for example, Alister E. McGrath, *The Foundations of Dialogue in Science and Religion* (Oxford: Blackwell, 1998), 34.

8. An important example of this is Nancey Murphy, *Theology in the Age of Scientific Reasoning* (Ithaca, N.Y.: Cornell University Press, 1990).

proach of the Middle Ages to the empirical science that characterizes modernity. Bacon inaugurated the focus on experimentation. He was convinced that the experimental process would not only lead to individual discoveries, but would also show the interrelations of the sciences themselves, thereby bringing them into a unified whole. To this end, Bacon placed at the foundation of the sciences a body of truths he called "first philosophy," consisting of the axioms shared by the various sciences, together with the laws of reasoning.[9] Bacon looked to this fledgling enterprise not only as a way of discovering nature's secrets, but also as providing the means to exercise power over nature and thereby alter nature for human benefit.

Galileo's innovation consisted in his focus on a strictly quantitative perspective from which to understand the universe. Hence, he pioneered the mathematical approach to experimentation, a program that yields quantifiable results (i.e., numbers rather than nonnumerical qualities). The great advantage of this focus on numerical measurement is its ability to give the impression of exact and unambiguous knowledge of the world.

Lying between these thinkers and the full flowering of the new empirical science was the methodological revolution inaugurated by René Descartes (1596–1650), who is often characterized as the father of modern philosophy.[10] As I noted in chapter 6, Descartes was concerned about the problem of error and in response sought to devise a method of investigation to facilitate the discovery of those truths that were absolutely certain, that is, when viewed in accordance with the pattern of mathematical certitude. To pursue this goal, Descartes introduced "doubt" as the first principle of reasoning. When the mind doubts everything, he noted, something certain emerges, knowledge of the reality of the doubting subject. Thus, Descartes concluded that the existence of the thinking self is the first truth which doubt cannot deny.[11] In this manner, Descartes claimed to have established the foundations of knowledge by appeal to the mind's own experience of certitude. On this basis, he began to construct anew the human knowledge edifice.

Descartes's foundationalism, together with the work of innovators such as Bacon and Galileo, opened the way for the scientific revolution

9. W. L. Reese, *Dictionary of Philosophy and Religion* (Atlantic Highlands, N.J.: Humanities Press, 1983), 48.

10. This opinion is voiced, for example, by Descartes's translator. Laurence J. Lafleur, "Translator's Introduction," in René Descartes, *Discourse on Method and Meditations*, trans. by Laurence J. Lafleur (Indianapolis: Bobbs-Merrill, 1960), vii, xvii. See also Stuart Hampshire, *The Age of Reason: The 17th Century Philosophers* (New York: New American Library, 1956), 12.

11. René Descartes, *Discourse on the Method* 4, in *The Essential Descartes*, ed. Margaret D. Wilson (New York: New American Library, 1969), 127–28.

that marked the break with the Middle Ages.[12] Thinkers in the Age of Reason rejected as metaphysical speculation the medieval preoccupation with "natural tendencies," *telos*, and "inner purpose," and hence the driving assumption of medieval science that every object followed a "natural" tendency to fulfil its own inner purpose. Instead, the Enlightenment theorists drew from the mathematical, quantifying view pioneered by Galileo over a century earlier. They believed that precise methods of measurement and the acceptance of mathematics as the purest mode of reason formed the tools for the proper approach to the study of natural processes. Scientific observers, in turn, were to describe phenomena in accordance with laws of nature which, the Enlightenment foundationalists believed, yielded quantifiable results and hence knowledge that carried indubitable certitude.

Although T. F. Torrance argues that the basis for the new empirical science lay in the theological gains of the Reformation,[13] more directly instrumental in the development of the emerging scientific method was the work of the British philosopher John Locke (1632–1704). Locke's goal was to develop a universal method of inquiry that would be applicable to all intellectual disciplines, theology as well as science. He rejected Descartes's view that our basic beliefs consist of innate ideas from which we deduce other beliefs. Rather, Locke argued that the foundation for demonstrative knowledge, characterized by universality and certainty, and which can be stated in the form of assertions, lies in sense experience, i.e., observations of the world, from which we abstract ideas and induce conclusions. His proposal, known as empiricism, provided the methodological program for the foundationalist turn in science.

12. Nicholas Wolterstorff offers this helpful summary of the shift in the understanding of science: "The Enlightenment practice and understanding of the newly emergent natural sciences represented a significant break with the practice and understanding of the antecedents of these in the High Sciences (*scientiae*) of the Middle Ages. After much debate on the matter, hypotheses began to occupy a central place in the new science; they were rigorously excluded from medieval *scientia*. Predictions became an important part of the new science; though medievals naturally wanted predictions, they did not look to the *scientiae* to provide them. The new science was, from the very beginning, praised and pursued for its technological potentials; medieval *scientia* was regarded as more relevant to the life of contemplation than to the pursuits of the technologist. The Enlightenment theorists gradually came to see their science as eliciting the contingent causal structure of nature; the medievals were after essences in their *scientia*. Probability, in our modern sense of that term, was granted a place in the new science. . . . Aquinas allowed only demonstrative inferences in *scientia*." Nicholas Wolterstorff, "Theology and Science: Listening to Each Other," in *Religion and Science: History, Method, Dialogue*, ed. W. Mark Richardson and Wesley Wildman (New York: Routledge, 1996), 97–98.

13. Thomas F. Torrance, *Theological Science* (London: Oxford University Press, 1969), 59–76.

The picture of this empirical world was supplied through the work of Isaac Newton (1642–1727), who conceived of the universe as a grand, orderly machine whose movements could be known, because they followed certain observable laws. In this manner, Newton provided the impetus for replacing the organic view of the world, which dominated the ancient understanding, with a mechanistic understanding that reduces reality to a set of basic elements or elementary particles (plus continuous fields such as electromagnetism and gravity). Each particle embodies an essence that determines its nature and value; each is what it is apart from the other particles. These autonomous particles interact with each other; they "push each other around," as it were. But such interactions do not affect their inner natures.[14]

The work of these thinkers resulted in what Arthur Peacocke terms the "standard account" or "received view" of the structure of scientific theories,[15] which in turn was connected to a particular understanding of science and the world. Mary Hesse summarizes the twentieth-century form of this position (which she rejects) in the following manner:

> There is an external world which can in principle be exhaustively described in scientific language. The scientist, as both observer and language-user, can capture the external facts of the world in propositions that are true if they correspond to the facts and false if they do not. Science is ideally a linguistic system in which true propositions are in one-to-one relation to facts, including facts that are not directly observed because they involve hidden entities or properties, or past events or far distant events. These hidden events are described in theories, and theories can be inferred from observation, that is, the hidden explanatory mechanism of the world can be discovered from what is open to observations. Man as scientist is regarded as standing apart from the world and able to experiment and theorize about it objectively and dispassionately.[16]

Enlightenment thinkers applied the new method to all disciplines of knowledge. Not only the natural, but also the human sciences—politics, ethics, metaphysics, and even philosophy and theology—came under the purview of the new science. In this way all fields of the human endeavor became, in effect, branches of natural science as it had been reoriented under the rubric of Cartesian foundationalism and Lockean empiricism.

14. David Bohm, "Postmodern Science and a Postmodern World," in *The Reenchantment of Science: Postmodern Proposals*, ed. David Ray Griffin (Albany: SUNY Press, 1988), 60–62.

15. Arthur Peacocke, *Intimations of Reality: Critical Realism in Science and Religion* (Notre Dame, Ind.: University of Notre Dame Press, 1989), 16. Peacocke observes that this view "held way from the 1920s to the 1970s"; yet its genesis lies in the work of Locke.

16. Mary Hesse, *Revolutions and Reconstructions in the Philosophy of Science* (Brighton: Harvester Press, 1980), vii.

In the world that emerged from the Enlightenment, theology found it-self losing the exalted place it once enjoyed, as the central role formerly played by the theologian became the prerogative of the scientist. This world assumes that the doctor aboard the *Voyager* gave the correct and only true diagnosis of what had actually saved Kess's life. If theology is to find a place in this world, it must fit in with the canons of empirical sci-ence. It must be able to present itself as scientific and scientifically credi-ble. From the seventeenth century to the 1970s, theologians took up this challenge.

"Scientific" Theology

I noted in chapter 2 that this new situation led to the ascendancy of "natural religion" accompanied by the attempt on the part of the Protes-tant scholastics to maintain the appeal of Christian theology by devising a rational foundation for it. Borrowing from Locke's claim that Christianity was the most reasonable religion[17] as well as the assumption that God was the author of all truth, these theologians drew readily from reason and philosophy.[18] Other Enlightenment theologians constructed an alterna-tive to orthodoxy in the form of Enlightenment deism. But when the waning of the Age of Reason led many intellectuals to abandon religion in the name of skeptical reason, early nineteenth-century theologians re-sponded by seeking new measures to ensure a place for theology within the realm of science.

The Nineteenth-Century Alternatives and the Neo-Evangelical Paradigm

The liberal proposal, with its focus on Christianity as the embodiment of the universal aspirations of humankind, once again opened avenues for conversation between theology and science. Looking back on the liberal program, Claude Welch concludes,

> The really interesting theologies of the nineteenth century . . . were fully committed to positive mediation between the "gospel" and modern thought, to building bridges in the modern world, including bridges between theol-ogy and science. . . . This endeavor . . . called specifically for profound re-spect for science and the scientific method, which was recognized as being

17. Hence, Locke sought to demonstrate the existence of God in such a manner that this postulate carried mathematical certainty. See Gillian R. Evans, Alister E. McGrath, and Allan D. Galloway, *The Science of Theology* (Grand Rapids: Eerdmans, 1986), 191.

18. On this endeavor, see Evans et al., *Science of Theology*, 161.

rooted in the same Enlightenment spirit of criticism that had to characterize religious thinking.[19]

As this summary suggests, theologians assumed that the bridge-building task required that they continue the pattern, set in the Enlightenment, of taking their cue from the scientists. Hence, Welch admits that this massive nineteenth-century effort at mediation or synthesis was accompanied by "a demythologizing within theology, whereby theological assertions take on new kinds of meaning,"[20] meanings, I might add, that in the end were determined above all by their compatibility with the modern scientific mind.

Like their liberal antagonists, conservative theologians also searched for a foundation for theology that could stand firm when subjected to the canons of empirical science. To this end, they appealed to what they saw as an incontrovertible Bible, whose special status could be justified by appeal to rational, scientific arguments, such as empirical evidence that the Bible contains prophecies that were subsequently fulfilled or that the various facts the biblical writers present are completely accurate. Conservative theologians also looked to the modern scientific method to provide the clue to the proper *theological* method. Consequently, like many conservatives of his day, Charles Hodge patterned his approach after that of the scientist. Just as the natural scientist uncovers the facts pertaining to the natural world, he asserted, so the theologian brings to light the theological facts found within the Bible.[21] The conservatives' infatuation with the reigning scientific model led them to view the theological propositions they drew from the Bible as "facts" and to view themselves as theological scientists busily compiling these various facts.

The empirical-scientific foundationalism of the nineteenth-century conservatives set the tone for what would become the reigning theological program of fundamentalist and neo-evangelical theology throughout much of the twentieth century. It is exemplified, for example, in the *Integrative Theology* of Gordon Lewis and Bruce Demarest, with its sophisticated attempt to apply to theology a method reminiscent of that found in Enlightenment empirical science. According to Lewis and Demarest, theology introduces and then tests hypotheses so as to amass true statements,[22] i.e., factual propositions,[23] each of which is true in its own

19. Claude Welch, "Dispelling Some Myths about the Split between Theology and Science in the Nineteenth Century," in *Religion and Science*, ed. Richardson and Wildman, 33.

20. Ibid., 37.

21. Charles Hodge, *Systematic Theology* (Grand Rapids: Eerdmans, 1975), 1:18.

22. See, for example, Gordon R. Lewis and Bruce A. Demarest, *Integrative Theology* (Grand Rapids: Zondervan, 1987), 1:25.

23. Ibid., 1:26–27.

right.[24] To this end, the theologian applies the scientific method, assisted by the canons of logic, to the data of the theological enterprise, which for Lewis and Demarest lies within the pages of Scripture. Similarly, the understanding of the Bible as a compendium of truths unlocked through "scientific" induction is evident in Wayne Grudem's definition of systematic theology as the attempt to determine what the whole Bible teaches about any given topic.[25]

Certain specific assumptions about the nature of God and humans lies behind this long-standing attempt to apply to theology the method arising from Enlightenment empirical science. Lewis and Demarest offer an illuminating insight into these working theological presuppositions. They claim that their theological enterprise "assumes (from the argumentation of apologetics and evidence concerning revelation) that God can reveal information to people who are created in his image to think his thoughts after him."[26] The principles of logic, in turn, facilitate the human process of thinking God's thoughts because these principles, which conservative "modernists" assume to be universal, are "rooted ultimately in the mind and nature of the Creator."[27]

Remnants of the Scientific Method in Contemporary Theology

As I noted in chapter 6, the postmodern critique has all but demolished the foundationalist program launched in the Enlightenment. Nevertheless, it has not stopped theologians from following the Pied Piper of empirical science in providing the method for their own work. Remnants of the modern view are evident, for example, in Thomas F. Torrance's "theological science," with its focus on the "facts." He writes,

> In our day . . . there has taken place a powerful rehabilitation of *dogmatics* in the proper and original sense in which it can be applied to pure physics as well as to pure theology—i.e., the kind of knowledge that is forced upon us when we are true to the facts we are up against, and in which we let our thinking follow the witness of those facts to their own nature and reality, together with the kind of statements we are compelled to make in sheer recognition and acknowledgment of the nature of those facts.[28]

Yet, Torrance's position is not simply that of the neo-evangelical modernists, such as Lewis and Grudem. Although speaking the language of

24. Ibid., 1:25–27.
25. Wayne Grudem, *Systematic Theology: An Introduction to Biblical Doctrine* (Grand Rapids: Zondervan, 1994), 21.
26. Lewis and Demarest, *Integrative Theology*, 1:27.
27. Ibid., 1:33.
28. Torrance, *Theological Science*, 341.

facts and divine logic to which we have access as humans, his understanding of these terms and the ensuing theological task reveals a decidedly Barthian influence. Rather than looking to the canons of Western logic, Torrance states categorically that the "logic of God" can only refer to Jesus Christ who is "the eternal *Logos* of God become flesh . . . the incarnate *Logic* of God, the Logic of God's Grace and Truth toward us."[29]

More significant is the lingering presence of the modern program in the work of several self-declared postmodern, postfoundationalist theologians who consciously attempt to bring into the theological enterprise methodological insights from contemporary science. Although differing in substance, these thinkers follow the lead of their modern predecessors in that they too give primacy to science and view the role of theologians in the ongoing interdisciplinary conversation as that of relating theology to science.[30]

A particularly lucid example of this tendency is Nancey Murphy's appropriation of Imre Lakatos's method of scientific research programs as the paradigm for theological inquiry. Lakatos argues that what we call science entails the process of testing particular hypotheses that are themselves members of a larger network held together by a overarching program that consists of certain methodological rules that guide the research process. Some of these rules indicate paths of research that ought to be avoided (the "negative heuristic" or "hard core" of the program), and others indicate directions the research should pursue (the "positive heuristic" or "protective belt" surrounding the "hard core"). At the center of a research program is a core theory such as "the mechanistic theory of the universe—according to which the universe is a huge clockwork [and system of vortices] with push as the only cause of motion."[31] This core is not subject to direct testing. What researchers do instead is articulate auxiliary hypotheses that surround and preserve the core. These auxiliary hypotheses, in turn, connect with empirical data, to which we appeal to confirm or disconfirm them. Hence, the hypotheses "bear the brunt of tests and get adjusted and re-adjusted, or even completely replaced."[32] In short, a research program is an ongoing endeavor to preserve a core theory that lies at its heart, and can be evaluated by its ability to explain the known facts and to anticipate new, novel facts.[33]

29. Ibid., 205–6.
30. For an example of this tendency, see van Huyssteen, *Duet or Duel?* 132.
31. See Imre Lakatos, "Falsification and the Methodology of Scientific Research Programmes," in *Criticism and the Growth of Knowledge*, ed. Imre Lakatos and Alan Musgrave (Cambridge: Cambridge University Press, 1970), 132–33.
32. Ibid., 133.
33. Murphy, *Theology in an Age of Scientific Reasoning*, 59–60.

According to Murphy, the application of this model to theology requires that the theologian identify the theological research program's core theory and auxiliary hypotheses, as well as the empirical data that we might use to test the hypotheses.[34] The empirical grounding that can help confirm the core theory, Murphy argues, is behavior that indicates that God is at work. She asserts that such theological, behavioral facts are objective and replicable, and as such they resemble the empirical facts to which science appeals to confirm scientific hypotheses.[35]

The modern paradigm, which looks to empirical science as providing the method for theology, has yielded impressive results. By borrowing the scientific method, conservative theologians have constructed systems of Christian doctrine that have assisted apologists in responding to the challenge posed by a world that, from their perspective, appears to deify science and is enamored with the scientific method. Similarly, by employing this method liberal theologians have been able to make intellectual peace with what they perceive to be a thoroughly secularized modern world. And thinkers of various theological affinities have artfully demonstrated the credibility of faith to a culture in which doubt has become the first principle of knowing.

Yet those who would adopt wholesale a method derived from science do well to realize that scientists are no longer agreed as to what "the scientific method" in fact entails. Hence, John Polkinghorne notes, "It has proved impossible to distil the essence of the scientific method. Proposals such as making refutable conjectures (Popper), pursuing progressive research programmes (Lakatos), attaining empirical adequacy (van Fraassen) or pragmatic success (Rorty), capture aspects of the complex practice of science, but each falls far short of an adequate account."[36]

Further, in the process of paying homage to empirical science, theologians may be guilty of too readily conceding the autonomy of a particularly Western understanding of human rationality. This is occurring at a time when the hegemony of Western scientific rationality appears to be waning, as increasing numbers of thinkers are becoming aware of the local, rather than universal, nature of both theology and science. J. Wentzel van Huyssteen notes this well: "'Theology' and 'science' never exist in such a generalized, abstract sense, but always only in quite specific social, historical, and intellectual contexts."[37] And Polkinghorne concludes that

34. Ibid., 183–92.

35. See, for example, ibid., 168.

36. John Polkinghorne, *Belief in God in an Age of Science* (New Haven: Yale University Press, 1998), 105–6.

37. Van Huyssteen, *Duet or Duel?* 163.

"the study of science encourages the recognition that there is no universal epistemology."[38]

There is, however, an even more problematic aspect of this approach. The attempt to gain some semblance of intellectual credence in a conversation whose ground rules have been determined by the scientific enterprise has actually robbed theology of its own "soul."[39] It is therefore not surprising that a growing number of theologians today are looking for alternatives to the reigning modern paradigm that looks to science for the method of theological inquiry and believes that theology is a valid intellectual endeavor only to the extent that it is able to take its place among the sciences.

The Medieval Paradigm: Theology Is the Queen of the Sciences

The demise of the naive realism that characterized modern empirical science has left theologians scurrying for alternative models of the relationship between theology and science, and hence for the devising of a proper method for the construction of a scientific theology. The contemporary "shaking of the foundations" has occasioned some thinkers to go behind the rise of the empirical scientific method and resurrect an older paradigm that dates to the Middle Ages. Under the impulse of this older medieval model, these theologians have reversed the order of methodological dependency, replacing the modern movement from science to theology with the proposal that theology assert its rightful place as setting the tone for the scientific endeavor and integrating human knowledge into a composite whole. Proponents of the refurbished medieval paradigm argue that theologians need to be scientists because theology is the "queen of the sciences."

To return to the *Star Trek: Voyager* episode, according to this model what proved crucial in saving Kess's life was Janeway's faith and the power of the ancestral spirits. The ship's doctor merely indicated the physical means through which this miracle was accomplished.

The Paradigm in the Middle Ages

The view that theology is the queen of the sciences boasts a long history. While its roots lie earlier, its heyday came in the high Middle Ages in

---

38. Polkinghorne, *Belief in God in an Age of Science*, 108.

39. See, for example, Ellen T. Charry, *By the Renewing of Your Minds: The Pastoral Function of Christian Doctrine* (New York: Oxford, 1997).

connection with the revival of Aristotelian thought.[40] Building from Aristotelian anthropology, the medieval thinkers viewed knowledge (*scientia*) as an enduring cognitive orientation and dexterity of the soul (*habitus*). Theology in turn, they argued, is also a *habitus*, a disposition of the soul that entails knowledge of God and is oriented toward personal salvation. But rather than being given directly to the soul, knowledge of God emerges through a deliberate, intellectual exploration. For the medieval thinkers, then, theology is the cognitive discipline that gives rise to salvific knowledge of God.

Further, the medieval thinkers asserted that theology qualifies as a science in the Aristotelian sense. Like other cognitive disciplines, it works from "first principles," and it attains knowledge through the process of demonstrating conclusions from such principles. For this reason, in the emerging medieval universities, theology took its place among the Aristotelian scientific disciplines that yield knowledge, such as law, medicine, and the arts. Yet theology's place was not merely to be one science alongside the sciences. Rather, the medieval theologians argued that theology deserves primacy over the others, because theology's first principles are of supernatural origin, and its subject matter is God. In short, theology is the queen of the sciences.

The Thomistic Model

The grand exponent of this model was Thomas Aquinas, who is routinely hailed as the greatest of the medieval theologians. The relationship between theology and what he calls the philosophical sciences is the first issue that Aquinas explores in his *Summa Theologica*. Theology (*sancta doctrina*), understood as the quest for knowledge arising from divine revelation, is necessary in addition to the philosophical sciences, which focus on knowledge that can be obtained through reason, because the eternal truths required for human salvation exceed human reason and come to us only through revelation.

Despite its source in divine revelation, theology is to be numbered among the sciences, Aquinas maintains, because like the other sciences, it proceeds from first principles. At the same time, theology differs from the other sciences in one crucial aspect. Unlike sciences such as optics (whose principles are established by geometry) and music (which proceeds from principles established by arithmetic), the principles out of which theology emerges are "made known by the light of a higher science, namely, the science of God and the blessed," that is, theology "accepts the principles revealed by God."[41]

40. For a helpful summary of the medieval understanding, see Edward Farley, *Theologian: The Fragmentation and Unity of Theological Education* (Philadelphia: Fortress, 1983), 35–38.

41. Thomas Aquinas, *Summa Theologica*, 1.1.2, in *Introduction to St. Thomas Aquinas*, ed. Anton C. Pegis (New York: Random House Modern Library, 1948), 6.

This distinction leads to theology's superiority over the philosophical sciences. It is superior, Aquinas argues, because of the "higher dignity" of its subject matter; it is the pursuit of knowledge of what transcends human reason (i.e., knowledge of God). Theology is also superior because of its greater certitude. Theology derives its certainty from "the light of the divine knowledge," which cannot err, in contrast to the errant "natural light of human reason." Finally, theology is superior because it is directed toward the highest practical goal, eternal beatitude, which is itself the ultimate end toward which "the ends of all the practical sciences are directed."[42] Hence, theology treats the scientific topics in relation to the way in which the sciences bring humans to the perfect knowledge of God, which Aquinas, following Aristotle, believes entails human happiness.

For Aquinas, theology is both practical and speculative. Yet it is, in his words, "more speculative than practical." Theology has this speculative bent because it is "more concerned with divine things than with human acts," and even when it deals with human acts it does so with a view toward our eternal beatitude, which is perfect knowledge of God.[43] Aquinas's emphasis on theology as a speculative science paved the way for subsequent thinkers to elevate the speculative aspect to the loss of the practical. This tendency was exacerbated as the Aristotelian conception of science gave way to the empirical science pioneered by Bacon and developed by Locke. As the new science rose in prominence, theology—now increasingly understood as a speculative discipline—was dethroned from its lofty position as the queen of the sciences.

The Retrieval of the Medieval Model

The contemporary interest in the interface between theology and science in the wake of the demise of foundationalism, however, has given the medieval proposal a new lease on life. But what kind of renewal of theology as the queen of the sciences might fit in the postmodern context? Few thinkers today follow Aquinas in his baptizing of Aristotle, nor do many build upon his distinction between revelation and reason. Likewise, few theologians advocate continuing the medieval legacy in the ordering of the sciences. As T. F. Torrance declares,

> Certainly theology cannot and must not claim to be queen of the sciences in the old medieval sense, in which she is thought of as presiding over a hierarchy of *scientias speciales*, and therefore as supreme over all the sciences

42. Thomas Aquinas, *Summa Theologica*, 1.1.5.
43. Ibid., 1.1.4.

through which man seeks to understand and rule over the natural world in which God has placed him and given him his duties and tasks.[44]

Yet several prominent theologians have returned to another aspect of the medieval proposal, namely, the idea that theology brings the sciences together into a unified whole. In their view, theology serves as the queen of the sciences insofar as it explores how all human knowledge is unified and illumined through the Christian conception of God, and the universe as the creation of God.

This aspect of the medieval model is evident, for example, in the British mathematical physicist turned Anglican priest John Polkinghorne, who speaks of theology as "the great integrative discipline."[45] Philosophical theologian J. Wentzel van Huyssteen betrays a similar stance in his attempt to carve out a method of integrating theology and science in the emerging postmodern context. He writes,

> For Christian theology the ultimate postmodern challenge to its rationality and its credibility as a belief system can be stated as follows: do we still have good enough reasons to stay convinced that the Christian message does indeed provide the most adequate interpretation and explanation of our experience of God, and of our world as understood by contemporary science? Put differently: does it still make sense within a postmodern context to be committed to the fact that our evolving, expanding universe, as we have come to know it through science, ultimately makes sense only in the light of Sinai and Calvary?[46]

Yet the most thoroughgoing contemporary exposé of theology as the queen of the sciences comes in the work of the German theologian Wolfhart Pannenberg.

Pannenberg and the Medieval Legacy

At the basis of Pannenberg's theological agenda is his commitment to the public nature of theology. As I noted in chapter 6, Pannenberg resolutely rejects the turn toward the believing subject he finds in much modern theology. He avers that theological statements cannot be grasped merely by "a decision of faith," for faith is not a way of knowing in addition to reason. Instead, theology is grounded in public, historical knowledge. For this reason Pannenberg declares that theology cannot be rele-

---

44. Torrance, *Theological Science*, 283.
45. John Polkinghorne, *Scientists as Theologians: A Comparison of the Writings of Ian Barbour, Arthur Peacocke, and John Polkinghorne* (London: SPCK, 1996), 1.
46. Van Huyssteen, *Duet or Duel?* 21–22.

gated to a private, sheltered sphere of life. Rather, theological affirmations are to be subjected to the rigor of critical inquiry into the reality on which they claim to be based. Theology, in other words, must be evaluated on the basis of critical canons, just as the other sciences.

Pannenberg's understanding of the public nature of theology is motivated by certain crucial theological suppositions central to his thinking. He believes that in whatever form it is found, the human quest for truth is ultimately the quest for God. Here Pannenberg builds upon the Augustinian linking of truth with God.[47] Because God is truth, all human inquiry has God as its ultimate subject matter. In proposing that God is the truth of the world, Pannenberg sees himself as standing in a long tradition, dating to the early Christian apologists, equating the God of the Bible with the philosophical idea of God as the source of the unity of the world.[48] This stance, in turn, leads to an engagement with science. If God is this unifying source, all truth must cohere in God. Hence, Pannenberg is convinced that the Christian understanding of God is crucial to the pursuit of knowledge.

The public nature of theology arises as well out of Pannenberg's innovative assertion that because God is the power that determines everything, God's deity is connected to the demonstration of God's lordship over creation. This means that the idea of God, if it corresponds to an actual reality, must be able to illumine not only human existence but also our experience of the world as a whole. In this way, the idea of God can provide unity to all reality. Pannenberg believes that in a secular world, this quest makes dialogue between theology and the scientific account of the universe inevitable. If God is the Creator of the universe, the world can be properly understood only when it is seen as the creation of God. This leads Pannenberg to see the overarching task of theology as that of showing the illuminating power of the Christian conception of God.

Following the medieval scholastics, Pannenberg undertakes the task of demonstrating the truth of Christian teaching through a representation of its coherence both internally (the relation of the various topics of systematic theology to each other) and externally (its relation to other knowledge).[49] His belief that the theologian's task includes showing the coherence of Christian teaching with all human knowledge drives Pannenberg to engage with science. He believes that in a certain sense the failure to bring to light the illuminating power of the idea of God for scientific

47. Wolfhart Pannenberg, *Systematic Theology*, trans. Geoffrey W. Bromiley (Grand Rapids: Eerdmans, 1991), 1:53.

48. Ibid., 1:70.

49. Ibid., 1:21–22.

knowledge would mark the failure of the Christian vision of God and, consequently, the failure of the Christian God.[50]

Rather than following the Greek understanding of truth as the constant and unchanging essences—the eternal presence—lying behind the flow of time, Pannenberg draws from the Hebrew idea that truth is essentially historical and ultimately eschatological. Truth is what shows itself throughout the movement of time climaxing in the end event.[51] Consequently, prior to the eschaton all human knowledge will remain provisional and all human truth-claims contestable. All human attempts to set forth a coherent articulation of truth, he avers, remain an incomplete "thinking after" the divinely grounded unity of truth. Consequently, Pannenberg looks to the eschatological future as the focal point of ultimate truth.

The provisionality of knowledge leaves us in a situation in which alternative claims to truth compete with each another. In such a situation, Pannenberg concludes, theology takes on an apologetic dimension. He believes that the systematic reconstruction of Christian doctrine is itself a way of testing and verifying the truth-claims of Christian revelation.[52] Thus, the best apologetic for the truth of the Christian faith is the demonstration of both the internal and the external coherence of Christian teaching, that is, the demonstration of the power of the Christian conception of God to illumine our understanding of reality.

Pannenberg, however, pushes the matter further. He argues that the focal point of divine revelation is the historical process. On the world historical stage, conflicting truth-claims are struggling for supremacy. And at their core, these claims are ultimately religious. Consequently, he anticipates that the religious orientation that best illumines the experience of all reality will in the end prevail, and thereby demonstrate its truth value. For him, therefore, it is in the specifically *religious* history of humankind that truth emerges.[53]

Pannenberg's reintroduction of the medieval focus on theology as informing the sciences has much to commend it. Yet at one point it seems to carry overtones of the modern paradigm. Despite his focus on the indeterminacy of knowledge, Pannenberg conceives of theology as adding to our knowledge of empirical reality.[54] In so doing, his proposal appears, at

---

50. See, for example, Wolfhart Pannenberg, "Theological Questions to Scientists," in *Sciences and Theology in the Twentieth Century*, 4.

51. Pannenberg, *Systematic Theology*, 1:54.

52. Ibid., 1:257.

53. Ibid., 1:167–71.

54. Philip Hefner, "The Role of Science in Pannenberg's Theological Thinking," in *Beginning with the End: God, Science, and Wolfhart Pannenberg*, ed. Carol Rausch Albright and Joel Haugen (Chicago: Open Court, 1997), 100.

least at first glance, to retain a potentially problematic objectivist orientation;[55] his vision of a public theology seems to require that thinkers bracket their faith stance when they enter the halls of the academy. Van Huyssteen puts his finger on the potential tension here. Pannenberg, he argues, "fails to confront the vital question of the intrinsic role of the theologian's subjectivity (his *ultimate commitment* and its conceptualization) in the theorizing of this theological reflection."[56] Hence, van Huyssteen suspects that Pannenberg may be caught in a dilemma between critical rationalist demands for non-commitment and the theologian's subjective religious commitment.

Despite this possible difficulty, Pannenberg indicates certain crucial aspects of the way forward. While he does not take this seemingly obvious step, his perspective suggests that in a sense the scientific portrayal of the universe is also fundamentally religious in tone. Taking this insight a step further suggests that the dialogue between theology and science does not pit faith against reason, or the religious against the secular. Rather, it entails a discussion between alternative (if not rival) views of reality. Philip Clayton recently asserted that "theology is one of many semantic worlds or 'meaning-complexes' that individuals and societies can draw on in their attempt to understand human existence."[57] Clayton's description would characterize science equally well.

The Postmodern Paradigm: Science Is Theology

One of the most far-reaching developments in recent intellectual history is the widespread questioning, and even wholesale dismantling, of the assumption of the objectivity and neutrality of the scientific method that reigned in the modern era. Van Huyssteen pinpointed the situation aptly: "The theology and science discussion in our time has been characterized . . . by a rejection of reductionism and a new awareness of the hermeneutical dimension of science."[58] Indeed, the twentieth century has witnessed the emergence of a post-empirical philosophy of science, a development that requires a rethinking of the query, Why do theologians need to be scientists?

55. Joel Haugen, "Introduction: Pannenberg's Vision of Theology and Science," in *Beginning with the End*, 3.

56. Wentzel van Huyssteen, "Truth and Commitment in Theology and Science: An Appraisal of Wolfhart Pannenberg's Perspective," in *Beginning with the End*, 369.

57. Philip Clayton, "From Methodology to Metaphysics: The Problem of Control in the Science-Theology Dialogue," in *Beginning with the End*, 402.

58. Van Huyssteen, *Duet or Duel?* 41. Here he consciously echoes Polkinghorne, *Belief in God in an Age of Science*, xi.

Post-Empirical Philosophy of Science

Armed with the scientific method, modern scientists busied themselves with the task of unlocking the mysteries of the universe and, in the process, celebrated discovery after discovery. Yet even as science was enjoying its greatest triumphs, certain aspects of the modern scientific worldview were shaken from within.[59] The most far-reaching internal challenge came from physics, the discipline that had hitherto provided the firmest foundation for the modern scientific edifice. Developments in the early twentieth century—such as quantum theory, relativity theory, and Heisenberg's uncertainty principle—undermined not only the mechanistic model of the world but also earlier assumptions about scientific objectivity and certitude,[60] together with the ability of science to delve into the "deepest secrets" of creation[61] or to gain unambiguous knowledge of the universe.[62]

The findings that subverted the older understandings of the nature of the universe led as well to a shaking of once sacrosanct views of the scientific method itself, as a chorus of philosophers of science challenged scientific positivism as well as the linear conception of the rise of scientific knowledge. Many voices have been involved in this critique,[63] including Norwood Hanson[64] and Paul Feyerabend.[65] But perhaps the most seminal work has been Thomas S. Kuhn's *The Structure of Scientific Revolutions* (1962).[66]

Science and Paradigm Shifts

Kuhn argues that foundational shifts in theory are not simply logical modifications or reinterpretations of past knowledge. Nor do scientists simply add one fact to another. Rather, science is a dynamic historical phenomenon. Shifts

59. For a succinct summary, see Peacocke, *Intimations of Reality*, 57.

60. A perplexing illustration of this is the famous Paradox of Schrodinger's Cat. See Robert Matthews, *Unravelling the Mind of God* (London: Virgin Books, 1992), 148–49.

61. James B. Miller, "The Emerging Postmodern World," in *Postmodern Theology: Christian Faith in a Pluralist World* (San Francisco: Harper and Row, 1989), 10.

62. Tito Arecchi, "Chaos and Complexity," reprinted in *The Post-Modern Reader*, ed. Charles Jencks (New York: St. Martin's Press, 1992), 351.

63. Although commonly associated with positivism, Karl Popper pointed out that science is not simply a rational enterprise but ultimately depends upon the exercise of the creative human imagination, which often works in a nonlogical manner. See Miller, "The Emerging Postmodern World," 11–12. For a helpful critical analysis of the movement away from positivism, see Derek Stanesby, *Science, Reason and Religion* (London: Croom Helm, 1985).

64. Norwood Russell Hanson, *Patterns of Discovery: An Inquiry into the Conceptual Foundations of Science* (Cambridge: Cambridge University Press, 1958).

65. Paul Feyerabend, *Against Method* (London: New Left Books, 1975).

66. Thomas S. Kuhn, *The Structure of Scientific Revolutions*, 2d ed. (Chicago: University of Chicago Press, 1970).

in theory come as radical transformations in the way scientists view the world. Hence, science lurches ahead in sudden creative bursts or "paradigm shifts."

The work of Kuhn and others has resulted in an increased recognition that the foundations of scientific discourse, and hence scientific "truth," are in some sense communally determined. Science is not merely the neutral observation of data.[67] Nor does science lead us to definitive statements about the world as an objective reality "out there." In fact one recent theory, the Duhem-Quine thesis, denies that an experiment can test a theoretical prediction in any final way. Because the test itself depends on the validity of the various theories that support it,[68] any experiment rests ultimately on a network of theories, opinions, ideas, words, and traditions—that is, on the culture[69] or the community—in which it transpires. Scientific knowledge, therefore, is a collection of research traditions borne by particular communities of inquirers. Any scientific paradigm involves the constellation of beliefs, values, and techniques shared by the members of a given community. More specifically, it is the belief system that prevails in a certain scientific community at a certain time in history. And scientific discourse—the scientific "language game" to use Wittgenstein's well-known phrase[70]—is largely unintelligible outside the lived practice of such communities.[71]

67. Ibid., 126.

68. See H. M. Collins, "The Meaning of Experiment: Replication and Reasonableness," in *Dismantling Truth: Reality in the Post-Modern World*, ed. Hilary Lawson and Lisa Appignanesi (New York: St. Martin's Press, 1989), 88.

69. Walter Truett Anderson, *Reality Isn't What It Used to Be: Theatrical Politics, Ready-to-Wear Religion, Global Myths, Primitive Chic, and Other Wonders of the Postmodern World* (San Francisco: Harper and Row, 1990), 77.

70. See, for example, Ludwig Wittgenstein, *Philosophical Investigations* 1.65, trans. G. E. M. Anscombe (Oxford: Blackwell, 1953), 32.

71. Robert N. Bellah, "Christian Faithfulness in a Pluralist World," in *Postmodern Theology: Christian Faith in a Pluralist World*, ed. Frederic B. Burnham (San Francisco: Harper and Row, 1989), 76. Van Huyssteen offers this summary of the direction philosophy of science has been moving in the days since Kuhn's landmark book: "Postmodern science, however, finds its best expression in postpositivist, historicist and even post-Kuhnian philosophies of science, which have revealed the theory-ladenness of all data, the underdetermination of scientific theories by facts, and the shaping role of epistemic and non-epistemic value-judgments in the scientific process. Postmodern philosophy of science also reveals the narrative and hermeneutical dimension of science to us by acknowledging that science itself is a truly cultural and social phenomenon. This not only results in the cross-disciplinary breakdown of traditional boundaries between scientific rationality and other forms of rational inquiry, but also in the inevitable move from being objective spectators to being participants or agents in the very activities that were initially thought to be observed objectively. . . . Epistemologically this is ultimately recognized as the turn from foundationalism to holism, but also as the move away from a modernist notion of individualism to the indispensable role of the community in postmodern thought." Van Huyssteen, *Duet or Duel?* 15–16.

Kuhn adds yet another important twist. Paradigms do not merely direct the scientific enterprise; they also constitute the world of the scientist.[72] The reigning paradigm determines what scientists see when they look at the world, and influences even the operations and measurements that scientists choose in conducting experiments.[73] Kuhn writes, "Examining the record of past research from the vantage of contemporary historiography, the historian of science may be tempted to exclaim that when paradigms change, the world itself changes with them."[74]

Science and Constructionism

From this statement it is only a short jump to the conclusion that a paradigm entails a social construction of reality.[75] Indeed, Kuhn's work occasioned an attempt to apply insights from sociology, especially the newer sociology of knowledge, to the scientific enterprise. The result was an upstart enterprise known as "the sociology of scientific knowledge," which explores the socially contextualized nature of scientific theories.

Some proponents of this approach have drawn radically relativistic conclusions from their findings. Michael Mulkay, to cite one example, declares,

> Scientific knowledge, then, necessarily offers an account of the physical world which is mediated through available cultural resources; and these resources are in no way definitive. The indeterminacy of scientific criteria, the inconclusive character of the general knowledge-claims of science, the dependence of such claims on the available symbolic resources all indicate that the physical world could be analysed perfectly adequately by means of language and presuppositions quite different from those employed in the modern scientific community. *There is, therefore, nothing in the physical world which uniquely determines the conclusions of that community.* It is, of course, self-evident that the external world exerts constraint on the conclusions of science. But this constraint operates through the meanings created by scientists in their attempt to interpret that world. These meanings, as we have seen, are inherently inconclusive, continually revised and partly dependent on social context in which interpretation occurs. If this view, central to the new philosophy of science, is accepted, there is no alternative but to regard the products of science as social constructions like all other cultural products.[76]

72. Kuhn, *Structure of Scientific Revolutions*, 110.
73. Ibid., 126.
74. Ibid., 111.
75. Ibid., 175.
76. Michael Mulkay, *Science and the Sociology of Knowledge* (London: George Allen and Unwin, 1979), 60–61.

He then adds, "Of course, we would hardly expect any other conclusion, for one of the central claims of the revised view is that scientific assertions are socially created and not directly given by the physical world as previously supposed."[77]

Since the 1970s, appraisals of the sociologists of science such as Mulkay have been rightfully contested.[78] Yet in the emerging post-empirical understanding, science no longer looms as a haven of objectivity in a sea of cultural relativity. Few contemporary philosophers of science today deny that there is both a personal and a social dimension in the scientific enterprise. The scientist is no longer seen as merely a passive receptor of data, but as one who comes to the noetic situation with a particular preunderstanding. Werner Heisenberg anticipated this conclusion early in the twentieth century, "Natural science does not simply describe and explain nature; it is part of the interplay between nature and ourselves; it describes nature as exposed to our method of questioning."[79] And scientists' observations will be colored and affected by their own perspective, including social location, culture, ideological commitments, prior experiences, and even gender. Thus, as Thomas Guarino lucidly concluded, "Even the scientist must always be called an interpreter and creator as well as an observer."[80] In short, post-empirical philosophy of science has led to a "chastened" view of science. No longer tempted by the naive realism that characterized the modern era, scientists now generally view their proposed theories and models as "candidates for reality," to cite Arthur Peacocke's descriptor,[81] rather than as simply reflections of reality itself.

We might say that the post-empirical understanding has led to the realization that scientists resemble theologians. As biochemist Jeffrey Wicken poignantly declared, "Everyone who does theoretical science seriously *is* a theologian."[82] This observation leads to a third paradigmatic answer to our question, Why do theologians need to be scientists? Theologians need to be scientists because scientists are theologians. But in what sense?

77. Ibid., 62.

78. See, for example, Ernan McMullin, "Comments," in *Sciences and Theology in the Twentieth Century*, 301–2.

79. Werner Heisenberg, *Physics and Philosophy* (London: George Allen and Unwin, 1959), 75.

80. Thomas Guarino, "Contemporary Theology and Scientific Rationality," *Studies in Religion* 22, no. 3 (1993): 316.

81. Peacocke, *Intimations of Reality*, 25.

82. Jeffrey S. Wicken, "Toward an Evolutionary Ecology of Meaning," in *Beginning with the End*, 256.

The Scientist as Theologian

The post-empirical understanding has led to the realization that the scientific enterprise is not simply the accumulation of facts that are "out there" waiting to be discovered by neutral, dispassionate observers. Rather, scientists must, and quite naturally do, bring a type of "faith" to their endeavors. T. F. Torrance, echoing the important work of Michael Polanyi, describes what he sees as a significant turn in science, a turn to viewing the discipline as "faith seeking understanding." In this new view, "Faith is . . . recognised again as the very mode of rationality adopted by reason in its fidelity to what it seeks to understand, and as such it constitutes the most basic form of knowledge from which all subsequent inquiry proceeds."[83] Similarly, a variety of thinkers now acknowledge that religious convictions play a role in the development and assessment of scientific theories.[84]

Scientists are theologians, then, in that personal "stance" affects, even directs, their research, as theorists such as Polanyi suggest.[85] Like theologians, scientists engage in their discipline as persons of "faith." They bring a certain type of personal commitment, i.e., faith, to their work.

Of course, this assumes that theologians engage in their discipline from a faith perspective. In the modern era this perspective was overshadowed by the assumption that theology was an academic discipline after the pattern of the sciences and therefore could be practiced by anyone who displayed the necessary intellectual skills. One of the ironies of recent intellectual history is that just when scientists are increasingly becoming theologians, many theologians are struggling even harder to remain scientists. The post-empirical context, however, provides an appropriate occasion to rediscover the faith dimension in both science and theology.

The common element of faith in all human intellectual endeavors leads to a second conclusion arising out of post-empirical philosophy of science. Scientific knowledge and religious knowledge are not diametrically opposite, mutually exclusive genres, but are of the same order.[86] This conclusion

---

83. Thomas F. Torrance, *The Christian Frame of Mind: Reason, Order, and Openness in Theology and Natural Science* (Colorado Springs: Helmers and Howard, 1989), 75. Likewise, Paul Davies concluded, "Even the most atheistic scientist accepts as an act of faith that the universe is not absurd, that there is a rational basis to physical existence manifested as a lawlike order in nature that is at least in part comprehensible to us. So science can proceed only if the scientist adopts an essentially theological worldview." Paul Davies, "Physics and the Mind of God," *First Things* 55 (August–September 1995): 32.

84. Wesley J. Wildman, "The Quest for Harmony: An Interpretation of Contemporary Theology and Science," in *Religion and Science*, ed. Richardson and Wildman, 52.

85. Michael Polanyi, *Personal Knowledge* (Chicago: University of Chicago Press, 1958).

86. W. Mark Richardson and Wesley J. Wildman, "Introduction to Part II," in *Religion and Science*, ed. Richardson and Wildman, 85.

initially came as the outworking of the realization that the universe is a more "mysterious" place than the empirical scientists of the modern era realized. Because the natural world is not a simple, closed network of causal relations, the older model of science is not capable of explaining it completely.[87] For this reason, in offering their models of the universe, scientists repeatedly cross over the boundaries that traditionally divided their discipline from the realm of theologians.[88] In essence, they *become* theologians.

This realization has led many thinkers to call for a new partnership between theology and science in the task of understanding the world.[89] In this new engagement, theologians and scientists bring to the table their own unique contribution without either discipline attempting to provide the standard for the other. Through this conversation, scientists and theologians offer insights that enrich each other's work.[90] Some thinkers even see signs of a new "physico-theology" taking shape.[91]

As significant as these two observations are, however, they do not go to the heart of the manner in which scientists are theologians, and therefore why theologians must be scientists. To do so, we must consider again the installment of *Star Trek: Voyager* that I cited earlier. The episode provides an interesting postmodern twist to the discussion of the relationship between theology and science, for it characterized the aliens and the ship's doctor as inhabiting two distinct worlds. Being the product of cultural myths and religious beliefs, the world of the aliens quite naturally included spiritual entities who had the power to affect physical beings. The doctor, in contrast, inhabited the supposedly "objective" world of modern science, which has room only for physical beings and physical causation. The episode leads the viewer to conclude, however, that the second world is no less a "created" realm than the first.

At this point, many scientists would likely demur from this analysis by claiming that they do not devise social constructions of the world, but really *are* engaging in the task of discovering a universe that is an objective, external reality. While perhaps admitting the social dimensions of scientific theories,

---

87. Ibid., 86.

88. Torrance noted one obvious, albeit elementary, aspect of this: "We have now moved beyond the old idea that natural science is concerned only with the *how* and not with the *why*; that is, with mechanical processes and not with ends; whereas theology is concerned only with *why-questions*: that is, questions about beginnings and ends. . . . It is now evident . . . that the *how* questions and the *why* questions cannot be finally separated." Torrance, *Christian Frame of Mind*, 24–25. Examples of this "invasion" of theology by contemporary scientists include Robert Jastrow, Stephen Hawking, Frank Tipler, and John Polkinghorne.

89. Richardson and Wildman, "Introduction to Part II," 86.

90. For a summary of how physics offers challenges to theology, see Mark William Worthing, *God, Creation, and Contemporary Physics* (Minneapolis: Fortress, 1996), 199–206.

91. Ibid., 204.

contemporary "critical realists" adamantly maintain that scientific theories seek to approximate a natural world that actually exists apart from scientific descriptions of it. Ernan McMullin, to cite one example, maintains that "the long term success of a scientific theory gives reason to believe that something like the entities and structure postulated by the theory actually exist."[92]

Critical realists do have a point. There is, of course, a certain undeniable givenness to the universe apart from the human linguistic-constructive task. Indeed, the universe predates the appearance of humans upon the earth. To assume that this observation is sufficient to relegate all the talk of social construction to the trash heap, however, is to miss the point. We do not (yet) live in the universe as a given, external reality. We do not inhabit the "world-in-itself." This principle operates on several levels.

Norwood Hanson points out that we live in a world of our own construal. He indicates that seeing and construing are not two separate epistemological moments, but that "the construing is there in the seeing." As an example, Hanson sets up an imaginary scene in which two astronomers, Johannes Kepler (who regarded the sun as fixed) and Tycho Brahe (who following Ptolemy believed the earth was fixed), watch the dawn from a hill. Hanson asks, "Do Kepler and Tycho see the same thing in the east at dawn?" In response he declares,

> Tycho sees the sun beginning its journey from horizon to horizon. He sees that from some celestial vantage point the sun (carrying with it the moon and planets) could be watched circling our fixed earth. . . . Kepler will see the horizon dipping, or turning away, from our fixed local star. The shift from sunrise to horizon-turn is . . . occasioned by differences between what Tycho and Kepler think they know.[93]

Not only do we inhabit a world of our construal, we also live in a linguistic world of our own making. Hence, scientists engage in world construction because they offer linguistic models and expect others to inhabit a world of their descriptions.

Although Wittgenstein introduced the phrase "language game" into popular parlance, the Swiss linguist, Ferdinand de Saussure (1857–1913), provided the basis for the turn to linguistics. In contrast to his predecessors who viewed language as a natural phenomenon that develops according to fixed and discoverable laws, Saussure proposed that a language is a social phenomenon[94] and that a linguistic system is a product of social con-

---

92. Ernan McMullin, "A Case for Scientific Realism," in *Essays on Scientific Realism*, ed. J. Leplin (Berkeley: University of California Press, 1984), 26.

93. Hanson, *Patterns of Discovery*, 23–24.

94. David Holdcroft, *Saussure: Signs, System and Arbitrariness* (Cambridge: Cambridge University Press, 1991), 7–8.

vention.[95] Structuralists, such as the anthropologist Claude Levi-Strauss (b. 1908), and the proponents of the sociology of knowledge built on Saussure's insight. The result was an awareness of the role of culture, including language, in both personal identity formation and the construction of linguistic worlds.[96]

Basically, sociologists argue that culture generates a shared context in which a people engage in the construction of meaning and in the task of making sense out of the world. Hence, Peter Berger, to cite a formative example,[97] argues the world we inhabit is not simply given, not merely prefabricated for us. Rather, we are world-builders. We live in a social-cultural world of our own creation. This constructed world attains for us the character of objectivity, in the sense both of seeming to be external to our personal consciousness and of being experienced with others.[98] According to Berger, world construction entails above all the imposition of a meaningful order (a "nomos") upon our variegated experiences. The ordering of experience involves language and "knowledge," the latter of which Berger understands not as objective statements about the universe as it actually is, but the "common order of interpretation" that a society imposes upon experience.[99]

In this process culture is important. Raymond Williams points out that culture functions as a "*signifying system* through which necessarily . . . a social order is communicated, reproduced, experienced and explored."[100] Language, which we inherit from our social context—together with nonlinguistic modalities, such as metaphorical images and symbols—provides the conceptual tools through which we construct the world we inhabit, as well as the vehicles through which we communicate and thereby share meaning with others. In the words of Peter Berger and Thomas Luckmann, "Language objectivates the shared experiences and makes them available to all within the linguistic community, thus becoming both the basis and the instrument of the collective stock of knowledge."[101] The "universe" we inhabit, then, "is a socially constituted reality, which an individual member of society learns to take for granted as 'objective' knowl-

95. Ibid., 10.

96. See, for example, Peter L. Berger and Thomas Luckmann, *The Social Construction of Reality: A Treatise in the Sociology of Knowledge* (Garden City, N.Y.: Anchor, 1967), 99–104. For a fuller statement of Berger's views, see Peter L. Berger, *The Sacred Canopy: Elements of a Sociological Theory of Religion* (Garden City, N.Y.: Doubleday, 1969), 3–51.

97. For a summary and appraisal of Berger's contribution, see Robert Wuthnow, *Rediscovering the Sacred: Perspectives on Religion in Contemporary Society* (Grand Rapids: Eerdmans, 1992), 9–35.

98. Berger, *Sacred Canopy*, 3–13.

99. Ibid., 20.

100. Raymond Williams, *The Sociology of Culture* (New York: Schocken Books, 1982), 13.

101. Berger and Luckmann, *Social Construction of Reality*, 68.

edge about the world."[102] And the language of empirical science, like the language of religious myth, is one such world-constructing grammar.

But we must take this insight one step farther. As a world-constructing grammar, the language of science is not merely *like* the language of religious myth; ultimately it functions *as* such a language. Berger argues that throughout human history religion, defined sociologically as "the human enterprise by which a sacred cosmos is established,"[103] has played "a decisive part in the construction and maintenance of universes."[104] Religion legitimates the socially constructed world that participants in any society inhabit. Religion does so by locating a society and its institutions within a sacred and cosmic frame of reference, by bestowing on participants in a society a sense of being connected to ultimate reality, and by giving cosmic status to the nomoi (or common orders of interpretation) of that society.[105]

This world-constructing and legitimating function is not limited to religious traditions, however. To allude again to the *Star Trek: Voyager* episode, the scientific realm of the doctor is no less the construction of a religious vision than is the realm of the alien religionists. Thus, science both legitimates its socially constructed world and mediates cosmic status to the nomoi of a scientifically oriented society. In this manner, science fulfills sociologically a religious role. In short, post-empirical philosophy of science leads to the conclusion that the empirical world of the scientist is a construction, and this constructed world is "religious" in orientation. In constructing a "scientific universe,"[106] the scientist *is* a theologian.

Theology, Science, and the Construction of the World

This conclusion—that both theologians and scientists are involved in the process of constructing "world"—leads back to the question left dangling at the end of chapter 6, namely, the thorny issue of the objectivity of the world. Actually, the question is twofold. First, can Christian theology continue to talk about an actual world in the face of the postmodern condition characterized by the demise of realism and the advent of social constructionism?[107]

---

102. Peter L. Berger and Thomas Luckmann, "Sociology of Religion and Sociology of Knowledge," *Sociology and Social Research* 47 (1963): 421.

103. Berger, *Sacred Canopy*, 25.

104. Berger and Luckmann, "Sociology of Religion and Sociology of Knowledge," 422.

105. Berger, *Sacred Canopy*, 32–36.

106. For an early statement, see Carl Friedrich von Weizsäcker, *The World View of Physics*, trans. Marjories Grene (Chicago: University of Chicago Press, 1952), 123.

107. See, for example, J. Wentzel van Huyssteen, "Postfoundationalism in Theology and Science: Beyond Conflict and Consonance," in *Rethinking Theology and Science*, 39.

And second, can Christian theology make any claim to speak "objective truth" in a context in which various communities offer diverse paradigms, each of which is ultimately theological? That is, does Christian theology speak about anything objective, or does it content itself with merely determining, delineating, and articulating the interpretive framework of a particular religious tradition?

Lindbeck's proposal introduced in chapter 6 provides a lucid example of how this question readily arises once a shift is made to a nonfoundationalist theology. His suggestion that theological statements are second-order assertions and his close linking of doctrine with the construction of a coherent vision of the world seem to beg the sticky question as to whether such assertions and such a vision somehow reflect a reality beyond themselves.[108] Further, his intimation that theological assertions are "in house" statements potentially results in a "sectarian" church, one that no longer assumes any role in the public realm.[109] In short, Lindbeck's work raises the question, Does the move to nonfoundationalism entail a final and total break with metaphysical realism?[110]

Formulated in this manner, the question is both improper and ultimately unhelpful. It might be better stated, How can a postfoundationalist theological method lead to statements about a world beyond our formulations?

Theology and the "Real" World

Similar to the so-called "critical realists,"[111] Christian theology maintains a certain undeniable givenness to the universe. But this givenness is

108. This was a central point of contention in the encounter between Carl F. H. Henry and Hans Frei at Yale; see Carl F. H. Henry, "Narrative Theology: An Evangelical Appraisal," *Trinity Journal* 9 (Spring 1987): 19. For a similar critique, see Alister E. McGrath, "An Evangelical Evaluation of Postliberalism," in *The Nature of Confession: Evangelicals and Postliberals in Conversation*, ed. Timothy R. Phillips and Dennis L. Okholm (Downers Grove, Ill.: InterVarsity, 1996), 35–39.

For a sympathetic treatment of this issue, see Bruce D. Marshall, "Absorbing the World: Christianity and the Universe of Truths," in *Theology and Dialogue: Essays in Conversation with George Lindbeck*, ed. Bruce D. Marshall (Notre Dame, Ind.: University of Notre Dame Press, 1990), 69–102. Clark Pinnock notes this objection but then (erroneously) concludes that Lindbeck is not denying that doctrines make first-order truth claims. *Tracking the Maze: Finding Our Way through Modern Theology from an Evangelical Perspective* (San Francisco: Harper and Row, 1990), 59.

109. See, for example, David H. Kelsey, "Church Discourse and Public Realm," in *Theology and Dialogue*, 7–34.

110. For a reading of Lindbeck that suggests that his program is not inherently antirealist, see Jeffrey Hensley, "Are Postliberals Necessarily Antirealists? Reexamining the Metaphysics of Lindbeck's Postliberal Theology," in *Nature of Confession*, 69–80.

111. See, for example, David Elton Trueblood, *General Philosophy* (New York: Harper and Row, 1963), 38–45. See also Peacocke, *Theology for a Scientific Age*, 21.

not that of a static actuality existing outside of, and co-temporally with, our socially and linguistically constructed reality. It is not the objectivity of what some might call "the world as it is." Rather, seen through the lenses of the gospel, the objectivity set forth in the biblical narrative is the objectivity of the world as God wills it, as is suggested in the petition of the Lord's Prayer, "Your will be done on earth as it is in heaven" (Matt. 6:10).[112]

However, the universe as God wills it, the realm in which the divine will is actualized, is primarily a future, rather than a present, reality. It is the world as it will be (e.g., Isa. 65:17–19; Rev. 21:5). Therefore, ultimately the "objectivity of the world" about which we can truly speak is an objectivity of a *future*, eschatological world. Seen from this perspective, the objective universe is the universe that one day will be. It is nothing short of a *new* creation. Because this future reality is God's determined will for creation, as that which cannot be shaken (Heb. 12:26–28) it is far more real, and hence more objective, than the present world, which is even now passing away (1 Cor. 7:31). This biblical perspective leads to what we might call an "eschatological realism." Viewed through Christian lenses, there is indeed a real universe "out there." But this reality lies "before," rather than "beneath" or "around" us. And it is discovered through anticipation, and not merely via experimentation,[113] or I should say, it is discovered through anticipatory experimentation. Therefore, the only ultimately valid "objectivity of the world" is that of a *future*, eschatological world, and the "actual" universe is the universe as it one day will be.

Rather than being antithetical to the constructionist insight, the "eschatological realism" indicative of the Christian theological style actually takes social constructionism a crucial step forward. Eschatological realism gives shape to a social constructionist understanding of our shared human task. As God's image-bearers, we have a divinely given mandate to participate in God's work of constructing a world in the present that reflects God's own eschatological will for creation. Because of the role of language in the world-constructing task, this mandate has a strongly linguistic dimension. We participate with God as, through the constructive power of language, we inhabit a present linguistic world that sees all reality from the perspective of the future, real world that God is bringing to pass.

112. For the author's delineation of the nature of prayer as viewed from an eschatological perspective, see Stanley J. Grenz, *Prayer: The Cry for the Kingdom* (Peabody, Mass.: Hendrickson, 1988).

113. It is for this reason that scientific eschatology needs the counterbalance of theological eschatology. For a summary of eschatology as a topic of conversation—and divergence—between theology and science, see Worthing, *God, Creation, and Contemporary Physics*, 159–98.

This divine eschatological world is the realm in which all creation finds its connectedness in Jesus Christ (Col. 1:17) who is the *logos* or the Word (John 1:1), that is, the ordering principle of the cosmos as God intends it to be. The centrality of Christ in the eschatological world of God's making suggests that the grammar that constructs the "real" world focuses on the narrative of Jesus given in Scripture. Further, the dynamic in the construction of this linguistic world is the Holy Spirit, who by speaking through Scripture creates the eschatological world in, among, and through us. The Spirit seeks to bring us to view all of life in accordance with God's creative program in fashioning a universe in accordance with Jesus Christ, the eternal Word, so that we might inhabit a world that truly reflects God's purposes for creation. In short, in contrast to the driving vision of much of modern science, the Christian faith refuses to posit a universe without recourse to the biblical God who is "the Creator of the heavens and the earth." And the only ultimate perspective from which that universe can be viewed is the vantage point of the eschatological completion of God's creative activity.

In the task of viewing the universe from a theocentric perspective, both theology and science play important roles. Through the use of linguistic models[114] that they devise, explore, and test, practitioners of both disciplines construct a particular world for human habitation. For its part, theology sets forth and explores the world-constructing, knowledge-producing, identity-forming "language" of the Christian community. The goal of this enterprise is to show how the Christian belief-mosaic offers a transcendent vision of the glorious eschatological community God wills for creation, and how this vision provides a coherent foundation for life-in-relationship in this penultimate age. In so doing, theology assists the community of Christ in its mission to be the sign in the present, anticipatory era of the glorious age to come, and to anticipate that glorious future in the present.

But how does science fit into this program? Because the scientist, as well as the theologian, creates a particular world, the question then becomes, What kind of a world ought science to be creating? The clue to the answer lies in the widely held conclusion that ours is an evolving universe and hence that scientists study a universe that is in the process of being created.[115] Viewed from the perspective of Christian theology, this sug-

114. For a helpful summary of the contemporary discussion of models in both science and theology, see Peacocke, *Intimations of Reality*, 29–34, 40–44; Barbour, *Religion in an Age of Science*, 41–51.

115. For an example of a theological appropriation of this contemporary understanding, see Karl Schmitz-Moormann, *The Theology of Creation in an Evolutionary World* (Cleveland: Pilgrim, 1997), 27–49.

gests that science devises models of a present universe that is the "embryo" of the eschatological new creation. In so doing, science speaks about the present, embryonic universe that is en route to the fullness of the divine will for creation, and science likewise gives evidence to proleptic experiences and dimensions within the present of the future new creation that God is already in the process of fashioning.

This offers the final answer to the question, Why do theologians need to be scientists? Because theologians, together with scientists, are in the construction business. They engage in the work of linguistic world construction. Theologians and scientists draw from their unique grammars to build a linguistic world for human habitation in the present. Understood in the context of Christian eschatological realism, the world they construct finds its basis in the new creation that God is already bringing to pass, even as they speak about the world as a present "reality." As they engage in this task in unique yet complementary ways, scientists are theologians, and theologians in turn must be scientists.

The connection between theology and science outlined here addresses the first question raised at the beginning of this section, namely, How is it possible to speak about a real world after the demise of realism? But the second question, the critical question of truth, remains: Why give primacy to the world-constructing language of the Christian community? As evangelical Christians we would likely respond by asserting that we believe that the Christian theological vision is *true*. But on what basis can we make this claim? Must we now finally appeal to some court beyond the Christian faith itself, some rational "first principle" that supposedly carries universality? In the end, must we inevitably retreat to a foundationalist epistemology? The response to this question requires a shift in focus away from the natural sciences and toward the religions of the world. And that is the task of the next chapter.

eight

Evangelical Theology
AND THE Religions

As I indicated in chapter 5, evangelical theologians are increasingly realizing that they carry on their work in a postmodern context, that is, in a situation characterized by a chastened rationality involving a shift from a realist to a constructionist view of truth and a rejection of the metanarrative in favor of local stories. One far-reaching result of the sensitivity to the local nature of all narratives is the cultural pluralism indicative of the postmodern ethos. Under the impulse of globalization, postmoderns have concluded not only that they are citizens of one planet, but also that humans live within a plurality of communities, each of which gives shape to the identities of its participants.

This "global" awareness has exercised a great impact on contemporary attitudes toward the world's religions, even among Christians. In contrast to the wholesale dismissal of other religions that predominated in the past,[1] many Christians now grant that there is some truth or revelation in every religion, even though they may differ radically as to the degree that it is present beyond the pale of Christianity. So widespread is this acknowledgment that D. A. Carson declares, "That there is 'revelation' in *some* sense in all religions few Christian thinkers ... would want to deny."[2]

1. Ken Gnanakan, *The Pluralist Predicament* (Bangalore, India: Theological Book Trust, 1992), 25.
2. D. A. Carson, *The Gagging of God: Christianity Confronts Pluralism* (Grand Rapids: Zondervan, 1996), 31.

The question of the status of the religions of the world is of special concern to evangelicals. Not only does evangelicalism take its name from the *euangelion*, the gospel, but from the beginning it has been characterized by a globally oriented evangelistic fervor to the extent that David Bebbington cites the missionary spirit as one of evangelicalism's defining characteristics.[3]

Of course, a missionary impulse is inherent in Christianity itself. All Christian traditions share the claim that God's action in Christ is somehow intended for all people. Christians agree that the purposes of the God of the Bible overflow the boundaries of nation, language, culture, and religion, and that these purposes are uniquely revealed in Jesus of Nazareth who is the Christ. In this sense, all Christians proclaim a faith that arises out of a "scandal of particularity," i.e., the belief that the eternal reality of God (or eternal truth) is disclosed in one historical human life. Yet, evangelicals are the bearers of the Christian claim to universality-in-particularity in a special way. Their commitment to convertive piety leads them to seek the conversion of the nations. To this end, evangelicals proclaim to people everywhere the message of the new birth, the good news of a personal salvation experience that evangelicals believe God intends for all people.

The evangelical dedication to the task of evangelizing the entire world one person at a time leads almost inevitably to the kind of apologetic theology that has been indicative of neo-evangelicalism since the 1940s. This apologetic orientation places evangelicals at odds with the relativistic spirit of the times, for it thrusts upon evangelical thinkers the task of articulating the seemingly offensive, yet undeniably Christian, claim to uniqueness in a pluralist context. If this message, which lies at the heart of the evangelical movement, is to retain its voice today, evangelical theologians must bathe it in a theology of the religions that takes seriously a context characterized by globalization.

The aim of this chapter is to interact with this problem. Doing so, however, eventually takes us back to the truth question left hanging in chapter 7, namely, How can evangelicals "privilege," or give primacy to, the world-constructing language of the Christian community? Therefore, the goal of the ensuing pages is to pursue the task of developing an evangelical theology of the religions, so as to bring to a fitting conclusion the discussion of the contours of a renewed apologetic evangelical theology that began in chapter 6.

---

3. Bebbington describes the missionary spirit as "activism." See David Bebbington, *Evangelicalism in Modern Britain: A History from the 1730s to the 1980s* (Grand Rapids: Baker, 1992), 2–3, 10–12.

The Religions and Personal Salvation

Although contemporary thinkers respond to the question of the universality and particularity of God's salvific work from a variety of vantage points, the most widely followed approach seeks to carve out a theology of the religions through a consideration of the question of personal participation in eternal salvation. Christian theologians who follow this approach focus on the difficult problem of bringing together the biblical teaching about God's universal salvific will with the equally strong scriptural emphasis on the particularity and finality of the salvation available in Jesus.[4] Viewed from this perspective, the main task of a theology of the religions becomes that of determining whether or not adherents of other religions can be fitting recipients of eternal life, and then charting the biblical and theological basis for this determination.

Contemporary Christian Approaches to the Religions

Few theological questions have distributed contemporary thinkers into more competing options than the question about the eternal destiny of the adherents of the world's religions. In fact, so varied are the theological proposals that observers of the debate cannot even agree as to how many viewpoints are currently being fielded. Thus, whereas Mark Heim cites six distinct positions,[5] Klaas Runia collapses the various options into two basic alternatives.[6] More popular is the tendency to posit four distinct categories,[7] a view preferred by a wide range of thinkers including the Roman Catholic pluralist theologian Paul Knitter[8] as well as evangelicals Dennis Okholm and Timothy Phillips, editors of the "four views" volume dealing with this topic.[9] Although it is not without de-

---

4. This is the manner in which John Sanders sets up the problem of the unevangelized; *No Other Name: An Investigation into the Destiny of the Unevangelized* (Grand Rapids: Eerdmans, 1992), 25–30.

5. S. Mark Heim, *Is Christ the Only Way?* (Valley Forge, Pa.: Judson, 1985), 111–27.

6. Klaas Runia, "The Gospel and Religious Pluralism," *Evangelical Review of Theology* 14, no. 4 (October 1990): 363–67.

7. Examples include J. Peter Schineller, "Christ and Church: A Spectrum of Views," *Theological Studies* 37, no. 4 (December 1976): 545–66; Michael G. Fonner, "Christology: The Central Issue in Christian Theologies of Religions," *Asia Journal of Theology* 2, no. 2 (1988): 327–341; Ivan Satyavrata, "God Has Not Left Himself without Witness," *AETEI Journal* 5, no. 2 (December 1992): 2–9; Gnanakan, *Pluralist Predicament*.

8. Paul F. Knitter, *No Other Name? A Critical Survey of Christian Attitudes Toward the World Religions* (Maryknoll, N.Y.: Orbis, 1985). He presents four models: conservative Evangelical, mainline Protestant, Catholic, and theocentric.

9. Dennis L. Okholm and Timothy R. Phillips, eds., *More Than One Way? Four Views on Salvation in a Pluralistic World* (Grand Rapids: Zondervan, 1995).

tractors,[10] the taxonomy that has gained widest use[11] divides participants in the discussion into three categories: exclusivism, inclusivism, and pluralism.[12] This classification dates at least to the early 1980s and the work of Alan Race, a student of John Hick, published as *Christians and Religious Pluralism*.[13]

Carson's succinct definition of the three terms reveals the orientation toward the question of "eternal destiny" that is generally linked to this threefold categorization. He writes,

> Exclusivism is the view that only those who place their faith in the Christ of the Bible are saved; inclusivism is the view that all who are saved are saved on account of the person and work of Jesus Christ, but that conscious faith in Jesus Christ is not absolutely necessary: some may be saved by him who have never heard of him, for they may respond positively to the light they have received. And pluralism is the view that all religions have the same moral and spiritual value, and offer the same potential for achieving salvation, however "salvation" be construed.[14]

This same orientation is evident in Mark Heim's characterization of the standard typology (which he himself critiques):

> Exclusivists believe the Christian tradition is in sole possession of effective religious truth and offers the only path to salvation. Inclusivists affirm that salvation is available through other traditions because the God most decisively acting and most fully revealed in Christ is also redemptively available within or through those traditions. Pluralists maintain that various religious traditions are independently valid paths to salvation.[15]

Exclusivism: Salvation through Christianity Alone

Exclusivism is not a uniquely Christian phenomenon. Rather, as the Roman Catholic scholar J. A. DiNoia notes, "The alleged 'exclusiveness' of traditional Christian doctrines is an expression of a particularistic claim to

10. See, for example, Ian Markham, "Creating Options: Shattering the 'Exclusivist, Inclusivist, and Pluralist' Paradigm," *New Blackfriars* 74, no. 867 (January 1993): 33–41; Tim Perry, "Beyond the Threefold Typology: The End of 'Exclusivism, Inclusivism and Pluralism'?" *Canadian Evangelical Review* 14 (Spring 1997): 1–8.

11. For this judgment, see Perry, "Beyond the Threefold Typology," 1–2.

12. For an example of its use, see Gavin D'Costa, *Theology and Religious Pluralism: The Challenge of Other Religions* (Oxford: Blackwell, 1986).

13. Alan Race, *Christians and Religious Pluralism: Patterns in the Christian Theology of Religions* (London: SCM, 1983).

14. Carson, *The Gagging of God*, 278–79.

15. S. Mark Heim, *Salvations: Truth and Difference in Religion* (Maryknoll, N.Y.: Orbis, 1995), 4.

universality, with cognates in other religious traditions."[16] At the same time, in the eyes of many people, both advocates and critics, Christianity seems to be inherently, and perhaps uniquely, exclusivistic.

At the foundation of the exclusivist position is the assumption that the biblical trajectory, which since Pentecost is focused on the church, is the sole vehicle of God's saving work in history. This idea lies behind the variously interpreted traditional formula, *extra ecclesiam nulla salus.* Exclusivists argue that if there is indeed "no salvation outside the church," then other religions have no role in the divine program of effecting salvation. Many contemporary exclusivists go so far as to conclude from this principle that only those who stand in conscious relationship to Christ in this life may hope for salvation in the next.

Throughout most of its history (at least until the Enlightenment), the church has taken a basically exclusivist posture,[17] as even certain of its contemporary opponents acknowledge.[18] Christians have understood God's action in Christ as unique to the extent that the Christian faith is "the true and unique religion," to cite Luther's description. As the Indian theologian Ken Gnanakan notes, "For many centuries this claim went unchallenged within the church, which sounded out its proclamation of the claims of salvation in Jesus and denied any truth in other religions."[19]

In the twentieth century, exclusivism has been prominent in certain circles within the wider Protestant tradition. For example, the exclusive claim of the Christian gospel in the face of contemporary pluralism has been championed in no uncertain terms by the Lutheran theologian Carl Braaten in his *No Other Gospel!*[20] Yet commentators routinely highlight Barth as the most significant modern exclusivist. For example, Kenneth Surin declares, "Karl Barth is the foremost modern exponent of the view that Jesus Christ is the decisive, unrepeatable and unsurpassable 'locus' of divine revelation, and that consequently it is only by following the way of Christ that we can possibly hope for the ultimate salvation of mankind."[21]

Barth's exclusivism arose out of his concern to maintain the uniqueness of God's self-disclosure in Jesus Christ in the face of the challenge of liberalism. In contrast to God's coming to humans through divine revela-

---

16. J. A. DiNoia, *The Diversity of Religions: A Christian Perspective* (Washington, D.C.: Catholic University of America Press, 1992), 164.

17. See, for example, James G. Sigountos, "Did Early Christians Believe Pagan Religions Could Save?" in *Through No Fault of Their Own? The Fate of Those Who Have Never Heard,* ed. William V. Crockett and James G. Sigountos (Grand Rapids: Baker, 1991), 229–41.

18. See, for example, Race, *Christians and Religious Pluralism,* 24.

19. Gnanakan, *Pluralist Predicament,* 25.

20. Carl E. Braaten, *No Other Gospel! Christianity among the World's Religions* (Minneapolis: Fortress, 1992).

21. Kenneth Surin, "Revelation, Salvation, the Uniqueness of Christ and Other Religions," *Religious Studies* 19, no. 3 (September 1983): 323.

tion, Barth declared, all attempts to know God from the human stand-point "are wholly and entirely futile."[22] So thoroughly was he committed to this principle that Barth not only relegated all religions to the realm of futility, but he also saw religion as "the contradiction of revelation,"[23] and he declared that "in religion man bolts and bars himself against revelation."[24] For this reason, Barth added,

> Revelation does not link up with a human religion which is already present and practised. It contradicts it, just as religion previously contradicted revelation. It displaces it, just as religion previously displaced revelation; just as faith cannot link up with a mistaken faith, but must contradict and displace it as unbelief, as an act of contradiction.[25]

For Barth, the divine revelation that contradicts religion is exclusively in Jesus Christ. Rather than filling out and improving human attempts to think about God, Barth adds, "as the self-offering and self-manifestation of God" Jesus replaces all such attempts. In addition, as the one in whom God reconciles the world to himself, Jesus replaces "all our human efforts at justification and sanctification, at conversion and salvation."[26]

Although his *Church Dogmatics* laid the foundation for exclusivism, Barth himself did not devote his attention to addressing the issue in a book-length treatment. The honor of providing the most significant twentieth-century treatise defending the exclusivist position, therefore, does not belong to Barth but to the Dutch missionary Hendrik Kraemer, who delineated his views in his controversial book, *The Christian Message in a Non-Christian World*.[27] Drawing from a christocentrism[28] similar to Barth's, Kraemer argues that because the uniqueness of Christ is central to the entire message of the church, Christians remain obligated to proclaim it.[29] Further, the great discontinuity between human religions and God's revelation in Christ means that to decide for Christ requires "a break with one's religious past."[30]

22. Karl Barth, *Church Dogmatics*, trans. G. T. Thomson and Harold Knight (Edinburgh: T. and T. Clark, 1956), 1:2:301

23. Ibid., 1:2:302–303.

24. Ibid., 1:2:303.

25. Ibid.

26. Ibid., 1:2:308.

27. Hendrik Kraemer, *The Christian Message in a Non-Christian World* (London: Harper and Brother, 1938).

28. See, for example, Hendrik Kraemer, *Why Christianity of All Religions?* (London: Lutterworth, 1962), 15–16.

29. Kraemer, *Christian Message*, 107.

30. Ibid., 291.

While following the basically Barthian line, Kraemer moves beyond Barth at one crucial point, namely, by positing a dialectical relationship between God's self-disclosure in Christ and the world's religions. Of course, this revelation pronounces a no upon all human religion. When placed under the searchlight of Christ, Kraemer declares, "All religious life, the lofty and degraded, appear to lie under the divine judgement, because it is *misdirected*."[31] Yet, this great no is also accompanied by a yes arising out of the conclusion that the misguided human searching for God is prompted by a religious consciousness within humans. Kraemer summarizes his dialectical position in this manner:

> The religious and moral life of man is man's achievement, but also God's wrestling with him; it manifests a receptivity to God, but at the same time an inexcusable disobedience and blindness to God. . . . Man seeks God and at the same time flees from Him in his seeking, because his self-assertive self-centredness of will, his root-sin, always breaks through.[32]

The exclusivist position finds echo today in voices representing all Christian traditions. But it is especially widespread among evangelical theologians. According to Ronald Nash, evangelical exclusivism affirms two principles: "(1) Jesus Christ is the only Savior, and (2) explicit faith in Jesus Christ is necessary for salvation."[33] Actually to round out evangelical exclusivism a third principle ought to be added to these two: Such explicit faith in Christ can only occur in this life.[34]

At Lausanne in 1974 a representative group of evangelicals gave quasi-official expression to at least the first principle of exclusivism, while offering a categorical rejection of pluralism. The Lausanne Covenant declares,

> We affirm that there is only one Saviour and only one gospel. . . . We recognise that all men have some knowledge of God through his general revelation in nature. But we deny that this can save, for men suppress the truth by their unrighteousness. We also reject as derogatory to Christ and to the gospel every kind of syncretism and dialogue which implies that Christ speaks equally through all religions and ideologies. Jesus Christ being him-

---

31. Ibid., 136.

32. Ibid., 126–27.

33. Ronald H. Nash, *Is Jesus Christ the Only Savior?* (Grand Rapids: Zondervan, 1994), 11; Harold Lindsell, *A Christian Philosophy of Missions* (Wheaton: Van Kampen, 1949), 117. See also the implicit assumption of this principle in Carl F. H. Henry, *Answers for the Now Generation,* formerly titled *Giving a Reason for Our Hope* (1949; reprint, Chicago: Moody, 1969), 21–24.

34. See, for example, Carl F. H. Henry, *God, Revelation and Authority* (Waco: Word, 1976–1983), 6:511.

self the only God-man, who gave himself as the only ransom for sinners, is the only mediator between God and man. There is no other name by which we must be saved. . . . To proclaim Jesus as "the Saviour of the world" is not to affirm that . . . all religions offer salvation in Christ. Rather it is to proclaim God's love for a world of sinners and to invite all men to respond to him as Saviour and Lord in the wholehearted personal commitment of repentance and faith.[35]

The Lausanne statement reflects the main theological themes that lie at the foundation of evangelical exclusivism. Evangelicals are concerned to maintain a high Christology that underscores the finality of Jesus Christ and his atoning work as God's provision for human salvation. But the Lausanne Covenant alludes to another theological grounding as well. Most evangelical exclusivists acknowledge the presence in the world of "general revelation." All humans are aware of God, because the Creator has left the divine imprint in creation and in human reason or conscience. Nevertheless, proponents deny that such revelation is sufficient for salvation.

Some evangelicals reach this conclusion on the basis of their understanding of the purpose of general revelation as "noetic" rather than "salvific." In contrast to special revelation, general revelation is only intended to mediate knowledge of God as Creator rather than to bring humans into a reconciled, saving relationship with God as Savior.[36] Others blame human sin for the inability of people to be saved through general revelation. On the basis of texts such as Romans 1:18–23, they conclude that sin both obscures the divine self-disclosure in creation and blinds humans from seeing it or leads them to suppress it.

In either case, the result is the same. Rather than providing a means to salvation, exclusivists argue, general revelation only serves to condemn humankind. In the words of Bruce Demarest,

> General revelation thus performs the function of rendering man judicially accountable before God. If God were not discernable in His works, if general revelation were invalid or failed to mediate knowledge of God, then the masses of people who have never heard the gospel would be innocent of their ungodliness and irreligion. But since knowledge of God is mediated to

35. Lausanne Covenant (1974), clause 3. See, for example, C. René Padilla, ed., *The New Face of Evangelicalism: An International Symposium on the Lausanne Covenant* (Downers Grove, Ill.: InterVarsity, 1976), 49.

36. The classic expression of this view was articulated in B. B. Warfield, *Revelation and Inspiration*, reprint edition (Grand Rapids: Baker, 1972). For a recent restatement of Warfield's position, see Bruce Demarest, "Revelation, General," in the *Evangelical Dictionary of Theology*, ed. Walter A. Elwell (Grand Rapids: Baker, 1984), 944.

all by general revelation, human accountability to God is firmly established. Hence in practice, general revelation becomes a vehicle not for salvation but for divine judgement.[37]

In the view of many evangelical exclusivists, this understanding of the results of general revelation implies that humans have no hope of salvation unless they come in contact with special revelation. The focal point of special revelation, in turn, is Christ and, by extension, located in the Bible. Beyond the pale of the gospel of Jesus Christ, therefore, lies darkness. The other religions, which at best find their genesis in general revelation, are expressions of this darkness. Hence, they promote error and falsehood, for they are the outgrowth of human idolatry.

This bleak assessment of the human situation often forms the context for evangelical missions. The few who possess special revelation must take the good news of salvation in Christ to the rest of humankind, so that others can be rescued from the fate of perdition that otherwise awaits them.[38]

Exclusivists have not always been able to maintain consistently their rejection of the presence of revelation in other religions. Even Kraemer seemed to soften his position in his later writings. In recent years certain evangelicals have also joined the growing chorus of theologians who question the traditional exclusivist theme or at least the "hard exclusivism" often articulated by evangelicals.

Some evangelical revisionists begin their reflections with the bedrock belief that in his grace God grants everyone a genuine opportunity to participate in the salvation available through Christ. Because of their commitment to the evangelical focus on convertive piety, these thinkers see no hope for salvation apart from a personal encounter with the gospel. Consequently, they explore the question as to how such an encounter might occur. One possibility is that God sees to it that all individuals who seek him will in fact hear the gospel, such as in the case of Cornelius (Acts 10). Another possibly related eventuality is that those who did not hear the good news in life experience an evangelistic encounter with Christ at death (hence, 1 Pet. 3:19–20).[39] Or perhaps God, who knows our hearts, judges the unevangelized on the basis of how they would have responded had they heard the gospel.[40] Finally, God may use means other than human agents in general or preaching in particular to bring the gospel to the "unreached." Some evangelicals

---

37. Bruce A. Demarest, *General Revelation* (Grand Rapids: Zondervan, 1982), 246.

38. Heim styles this position "imperial particularity"; *Is Christ the Only Way?* 125–27.

39. For this position and its connection with the previous, see Clark H. Pinnock, *A Wideness in God's Mercy: The Finality of Jesus Christ in a World of Religions* (Grand Rapids: Zondervan, 1992), 168–75.

40. For a discussion of these positions, see Sanders, *No Other Name*, 151–214.

conclude from this biblical principle that divine salvation is not restricted to those who come under the church's missionary activity. Alister McGrath, to cite one prominent example, declares,

> So what about those who have never heard the gospel? Is the universality of the gospel compromised by the fact that, as a matter of history, the gospel has not been preached to all and its benefits made universally available? There can be no doubt that certain types of evangelical theology have caused considerable anxiety in this respect by their apparent insistence that only those who respond to the explicit verbal proclamation of the gospel will be saved. . . . But this is a flawed theology, which limits God's modes of action, disclosure, and saving power.[41]

Other thinkers seek to retain the term "exclusivist," while looking for the possibility of participation in salvation beyond the boundaries of the Christian gospel. For example, Robert H. Culpepper argues for an "open-ended exclusivism." On the basis of scriptural indications that God may be "working in undreamt ways among people who do not stand within the stream of Judeo-Christian history,"[42] Culpepper urges Christians to follow Jesus' example and present the gospel without "denigrating the faith of others."[43]

Inclusivism: Salvation through Christ Alone

Proposals such as McGrath's and Culpepper's appear to overflow the boundaries of exclusivism, or at least the "hard" exclusivism often propagated by evangelicals. These thinkers appear to have moved into what in recent years has become an increasingly prevalent alternative, "inclusivism."

While some suggest that patristic thinkers such as Justin Martyr[44] and Irenaeus[45] were early inclusivists, contemporary inclusivism has its more direct roots in the work of certain twentieth-century thinkers. Several of these theologians stand in the Roman Catholic tradition, and their influence is evident in the statements of the Second Vatican Council on salvation.[46] Yves Congar, for example, spoke about a "faith before Faith" or im-

---

41. Alister E. McGrath, "A Particularist View: A Post-Enlightenment Approach," in *More than One Way?* 178.

42. Robert H. Culpepper, "The Lordship of Christ and Religious Pluralism: A Review Article," *Perspectives in Religious Studies* 19, no. 3 (Fall 1992): 320.

43. Ibid., 321.

44. There are parts in Justin Martyr's *First Apology*, chapters 10 and 14, that suggest that non-Christians are accepted by God as long as they meet his moral standards. See, for example, Hernigild Dressler et al., eds., *Writings of Saint Justin Martyr*, trans. Thomas B. Falls (Washington, D.C.: Catholic University of America Press, 1948), 42–43, 46–47.

45. For this judgment, see Clark H. Pinnock, "An Inclusivist View," in *More Than One Way?* 118 n. 45.

46. See, for example, the inclusive stance of statement 16 on the church. Walter M. Abbott, ed., *The Documents of Vatican II*, trans. Joseph Gallagher (New York: Corpus, 1966), 35.

plicit faith.[47] Likewise, Edward Schillebeeckx speculated that an "anonymous supernatural revelation and faith" is present in every religion. In his estimation, an *"instinctus divinus"* lodges deep within the human religious psyche that is attracted to divine grace even before the person hears the gospel.[48] More generally viewed as the pioneer of inclusivism, however, is Karl Rahner,[49] who articulated the concept of "anonymous Christians."[50] In Rahner's words, "Christianity does not simply confront the member of extra-Christian religion as a mere non-Christian but as someone who can and must already be regarded in this or that respect as an anonymous Christian."[51]

Lying behind Rahner's inclusivism is his "transcendental method." Rahner is convinced that humans are transcendent, that is, they transcend nature and are open toward an infinite, mysterious horizon that Christians call God.[52] In this sense, God is universally present to all humans, and in his gracious self-communication "God in his own most proper reality makes himself the innermost constitutive element" in their very humanity.[53] While not completely indebted to Aquinas, Rahner's approach is nevertheless reminiscent of the Thomistic thesis[54] that "grace" does not destroy "nature," but perfects it, so that Christians can affirm world religions as the product of the natural human knowledge of God while adding that this natural knowledge needs completion or perfection through the gospel. Yet, for Rahner, this universal divine presence is not "natural" but gracious and hence supernatural. Consequently, Rahner held out the possibility that a non-Christian religion might also contain elements of a supernatural knowledge of God "arising out of the grace which is given to men as a gratuitous gift on account of Christ."[55] Hence, he concluded,

47. Yves Congar, *The Wide World My Parish: Salvation and Its Problems*, trans. Donald Attwater (Baltimore, Md.: Helicon, 1961), 103.

48. Edward Schillebeeckx, *Christ the Sacrament of the Encounter with God*, trans. Paul Barrett et al. (New York: Sheed and Ward, 1963), 8 n. 2.

49. For this judgment, see, for example, D'Costa, *Theology and Religious Pluralism*, 80.

50. See, for example, his essay "Christianity and the Non-Christian Religions," in Karl Rahner, *Theological Investigations*, trans. Karl-H. Kruger (New York: Crossroad, 1983), 5:115–34.

51. Ibid., 5:131.

52. Karl Rahner, *Hearer of the Word: Laying the Foundation for a Philosophy of Religion*, trans. Joseph Donceel (New York: Continuum, 1994), 53.

53. Karl Rahner, *Foundations of Christian Faith: An Introduction to the Idea of Christianity*, trans. William V. Dych (New York: Crossroad, 1978), 116.

54. See, for example, Walter H. Capps, "Toward a Christian Theology of the World's Religions," *Cross Currents* 29, no. 2 (Summer 1979), 159.

55. Rahner, *Theological Investigations*, 5:121.

If one believes seriously in the universal salvific purpose of God towards all men in Christ, it need not and cannot really be doubted that gratuitous influences of properly Christian supernatural grace are conceivable in the life of all men . . . and that these influences can be presumed to be accepted in spite of the sinful state of men and in spite of their apparent estrangement from God.[56]

More specifically, Rahner looks to the social nature of all religions to find a place for non-Christian religions as the context in which the salvation God intends for all reaches those who have not heard the gospel.[57] Rahner argues that as intrinsically social beings who are in a sense even constituted by their social location, humans can stand in positive relationship with God within the particular religion their society offers them, in that for its devotees such a religion is legitimate[58] and hence the means through which God's will for them actually reached them. In Rahner's words, "By the fact that in practice man as he really is can live his proffered relationship to God only in society, man must have had the right and indeed the duty to live this his relationship to God within the religious and social realities offered to him in his particular historical situation."[59]

Despite Rahner's influence in Roman Catholic circles, evangelical inclusivists routinely distance themselves from his position. Even as sympathetic a theologian as Clark Pinnock, for example, bemoans that Rahner has actually served to damage the cause. While applauding the Catholic inclusivist, Pinnock declares,

In a way he has discredited my point by extending it speculatively to an unreasonable extent. I appreciate Rahner's basic insight that God takes account of faith in any and all situations from anyone, but not his many extensions of it that make it sound as if being a Buddhist is perfectly all right. . . . We cannot say anything that would create the impression that there are some who do not need to repent and believe the gospel.[60]

Inclusivism among evangelicals dates at least to Augustus Hopkins Strong[61] who likened the situation of the unevangelized to that of the Old Testament era. In both situations people can "be saved by casting them-

---

56. Ibid., 5:125.
57. Ibid., 17:42.
58. Ibid., 5:129.
59. Ibid., 5:131.
60. Clark Pinnock, "The Finality of Jesus Christ in a World of Religions," in *Christian Faith and Practice in the Modern World: Theology from an Evangelical Point of View*, ed. Mark Noll and David F. Wells (Grand Rapids: Eerdmans, 1988), 164–65.
61. For this judgment, see Millard J. Erickson, *How Shall They Be Saved? The Destiny of Those Who Do Not Hear of Jesus* (Grand Rapids: Baker, 1996), 122–23.

selves as helpless sinners upon God's plan of mercy."[62] More significant in gaining a hearing for this idea, however, has been the work of Norman Anderson, especially his widely read book *Christianity and Comparative Religion*,[63] which was subsequently revised and retitled *Christianity and World Religions*.[64] In fact, so widespread has this position become that it has won the affirmation of prominent conservatives such as J. I. Packer. At the Evangelical Affirmations Consultation in 1989, Packer declared that at least in theory the unevangelized could be saved by casting themselves on the mercy of God:

> A British lay theologian, Sir Norman Anderson, poses an often-asked question as follows: "Might it not be true of the follower of some other religion that the God of all mercy had worked in his heart by his Spirit, bringing him in some measure to realize his sin and need for forgiveness, and enabling him, in his twilight as it were, to throw himself on God's mercy?" The answer surely is: yes, it might be true, as it seems to have been true for some non-Israelites in Old Testament times: think of Melchizedek, Job, Naaman, Cyrus, Nebuchadnezzar, the sailors in Jonah's boat, and the Ninevites to whom he preached, for starters. In heaven, any such penitents will learn that they were saved by Christ's death and their hearts were renewed by the Holy Spirit, and they will worship God accordingly. Christians since the second century have voiced the hope that there are such people, and we may properly voice the hope today.[65]

As this observation suggests, inclusivism is an exceedingly difficult position to define, and its boundary with exclusivism is fuzzy and fluid. The indeterminacy of the view is evident in the basic definition offered by the Roman Catholic thinker, J. A. DiNoia: "Inclusivists espouse some version of the view that all religious communities implicitly aim at the salvation that the Christian community most adequately commends, or at least that salvation is a present possibility for the members of other religious communities."[66]

Closest to the exclusivist position is the suggestion that holds out the possibility for salvation for members of other religious communities. Seen from this perspective, inclusivists remain firmly committed to the asser-

62. Augustus Hopkins Strong, *Systematic Theology: A Compendium Designed for the Use of Theological Students*, 3 vols. in 1 (Westwood, N.J.: Revell, 1907, 1967), 3:842.

63. James Norman D. Anderson, *Christianity and Comparative Religion* (London: Tyndale, 1970).

64. James Norman D. Anderson, *Christianity and World Religions: The Challenge of Pluralism* (Downers Grove, Ill.: InterVarsity, 1984).

65. James I. Packer, "Evangelicals and the Way of Salvation: New Challenges to the Gospel—Universalism, and Justification by Faith," in *Evangelical Affirmations*, ed. Kenneth S. Kantzer and Carl F. H. Henry (Grand Rapids: Zondervan, 1990), 121–23. For Carl Henry's argument to the contrary, see *God, Revelation and Authority*, 6:367–69.

66. DiNoia, *Diversity of Religions*, ix.

tion that Jesus is God's unique means of salvation, that is, that eternal life, whenever and to whomever it may come, arises only through Christ. What sets them apart from "hard exclusivists" is their willingness to affirm the possibility of salvation for those who lie beyond the pale of the Christian gospel in this life. As was noted earlier, some theologians agree that salvation requires that a person accept Jesus as Lord and Savior. Yet they look to the possibility that those who do not encounter the gospel in this life may do so at or beyond death, a position that in addition to its evangelical advocates enjoys the sympathy of mainline Protestants such as Richard Swinburne,[67] and Roman Catholics including J. A. DiNoia.[68]

More explicitly "inclusivist," however, is a second position. Many inclusivists argue that salvation is not dependent on *explicit* faith in Christ. Rather, salvation can also arise through personal commitment to the God who saves through the work of Jesus Christ.[69] Hence, those who never hear the gospel may nevertheless enjoy eternal life, if they respond in faith to the revelation they do have.

Some proponents of this "wider hope" retain a basically negative evaluation of the world's religions. Stephen Travis, for example, writes, "If a Hindu finds salvation, it is not by virtue of being a good Hindu, any more than a Christian is saved by being a good Christian. Whatever a person's religious background, 'saving faith' involves coming to an end of one's own 'religion' and abandoning oneself to the grace of God."[70] Other inclusivists take the wider hope a step farther. Reflecting the first part of DiNoia's definition, these thinkers conclude that other religions may be actual channels for God's salvific activity or revelation. Proponents of this understanding favor dialogue with other religious traditions on the basis of a recognition of God's presence in them, and with the goal of seeing how they are related to God's unique revelation in Christ.[71]

Despite their differences, inclusivists of all varieties (like exclusivists) remain committed to the unique veracity of the Christian vision of salva-

---

67. While holding firmly to the doctrine of *extra ecclesiam nulla salus*, he grants the possibility of a person participating in the saving benefit of the church "either here or *hereafter*." Richard Swinburne, *Responsibility and Atonement* (Oxford: Clarendon, 1989), 173.

68. In his estimation, "the concept of prospective salvation can also be employed to refer, by way of the theology of death and purgatory, to possibilities in the individual futures of non-Christian persons." DiNoia, *Diversity of Religion*, 74, 103–7.

69. Sanders, *No Other Name*, 215. See also Stephen H. Travis, *I Believe in the Second Coming of Jesus* (Grand Rapids: Eerdmans, 1982), 204.

70. Travis, *I Believe in the Second Coming of Jesus*, 204.

71. Vinay Samuel and Chris Sugden, "Dialogue with Other Religions—An Evangelical View," in *Sharing Jesus in the Two Thirds World*, ed. Vinay Samuel and Chris Sugden (Grand Rapids: Eerdmans, 1983), 128. Samuel and Sugden represented the Indian view in the First Conference of Evangelical Missions Theologians from the Two Thirds World, Bangkok, Thailand, March 22–25, 1982.

tion and to the finality of Jesus Christ in procuring salvation. Hence, Di-Noia declares,

> When inclusivist theologians assert that non-Christian persons can attain salvation, or that their communities aim at salvation, "salvation" designates all or much of what Christians understand it to comprise: complete well-being in the life to come, in eternal fellowship with the Blessed Trinity and with other human beings, won for us by Jesus Christ through whom grace is given.[72]

Pluralism: Salvation through God Alone

For some thinkers even the inclusivist approach is insufficient, in that in their estimation it retains the imperialistic overtones of exclusivism.[73] For this reason, many voices are now calling for a move beyond inclusivism to pluralism and an acknowledgment of the essential truth status of all religions. Rejecting the traditional Christian conviction about the finality or definitive normativity of Christ, pluralists find God at work salvifically in all religions. Each tradition can be a valid means toward the one ultimate goal. Advocates are quick to dispel the common stereotype that equates pluralism with relativism, however.[74] To embrace the relativity of all truth-claims, they argue, does not preclude commitment to a particular statement of truth. Hence the proclamation of the importance of Christ as a universal truth for all religions does not necessitate a negation of the importance of universal truth in other religions.

Although contemporary pluralists often look to the work of Ernst Troeltsch,[75] the actual beginnings of contemporary pluralism appear to lie more directly in the World Missions Conferences of the early twentieth century.[76] The report of the second conference (Jerusalem, 1928) declared that although there is only one way of salvation, rays of light are found in other religions. In preparation for the third conference (Tambaram, 1938), Harvard professor W. E. Hocking compiled a report of a lay tour of mission fields in India, Burma, China, and Japan. The group's findings were published in a volume entitled *Re-Thinking Missions*,[77] which set forth the thesis that all religions are ways to God and that the religions should engage to-

72. DiNoia, *Diversity of Religions*, 37.

73. For an example of this charge, see Chester Gillis, "Evangelical Inclusivism: Progress or Betrayal?" *Evangelical Quarterly* 68, no. 2 (April 1996): 148.

74. Knitter, *No Other Name?* 93.

75. See Braaten, *No Other Gospel!* 34–40.

76. See Runia, "The Gospel and Religious Pluralism," 347–48.

77. William Ernest Hocking et al., *Re-Thinking Missions: A Laymen's Inquiry after One Hundred Years* (New York: Harper and Brothers, 1932).

gether in a common search for truth. Lying behind the conclusion was the group's positive appraisal of what they saw as a monumental transition in theological outlook among Christians: "Western Christianity has in the main shifted its stress from the negative to the affirmative side of its message, it is less a religion of fear and more a religion of beneficence . . . it has become less concerned in any land to save men from eternal punishment than from the danger of losing the supreme good."[78]

An impulse toward pluralism came as well through responses to Kraemer's work. One significant critique was voiced by A. G. Hogg, an English missionary in India who served at the Madras Christian College. Hogg's position was triggered in part by his contact with such Hindu leaders as S. Radhakrishnan,[79] which led him to differentiate between non-Christian *faiths* and non-Christian *faith*. Hogg called on Christians to come to grips not only with "those complexes of spiritual, ethical, intellectual and social elements which we call the non-Christian 'religions' but also with the question of the right Christian attitude to what I have called 'non-Christian faith.'" Then, alluding to the Christian teaching that the religious life is a life "hid with Christ in God," Hogg asked, "Can there be, within the non-Christian religions, in those for whom their religion is a living personal possession, a life which, although without Christ, is yet somehow a life 'hid in God'?"[80] Hogg not only believed that this question demanded an affirmative answer, he also held out the possibility that such non-Christian faith could be enriching for Christians. Hence, Hogg posed the additional rhetorical question, "In non-Christian faith may we meet with something that is not merely a seeking but in real measure a finding, and a finding by contact with which a Christian may be helped to make fresh discoveries in his own finding of God *in Christ*."[81]

These views gained momentum in the 1970s and 1980s, as a variety of thinkers including Wilfred Cantwell Smith, John Hick, Paul Knitter, and Stanley Samarthas joined the chorus calling for a new outlook toward the presence of truth in other religions.

Although the position itself by no means originated with him, Hick is often cited as the one who brought pluralism into mainstream contemporary Christian theology.[82] Hence, the Roman Catholic pluralist Paul Knit-

---

78. Ibid., 19.

79. For this judgment, see Gnanakan, *Pluralistic Predicament*, 39.

80. Eric Sharpe, *The Theology of A. G. Hogg* (Madras, India: Christian Literature Society, 1971), 206. Sharpe here reproduces Hogg's paper, delivered at the Tambaram Conference of 1938, as printed in the Conference Proceedings, *The Authority of the Faith*, Tambaram Series, Vol. 1 (London, 1939), 102–25.

81. Sharpe, *Theology of A. G. Hogg*, 207.

82. This is evident in the number of treatments of the topic of Christianity and the religions that treat Hick as the quintessential pluralist. For an unsympathetic treatment of the development of Hick's thought, written by an exclusivist, see Nash, *Is Jesus Christ the Only Savior?* 29–52.

ter declared already in 1985, "Hick is the most radical, the best-known, and therefore the most controversial of the proponents of a theocentric [i.e., pluralistic] model for Christian approaches to other religions."[83] In a series of books beginning with *God and the Universe of Faiths*[84] and more recently in his *A Christian Theology of Religions*,[85] Hick has championed what he calls a "Copernican revolution" in the Christian outlook toward the religions. In addition to offering his own writings, he served as editor in several joint projects, including *The Myth of God Incarnate*[86] and *The Myth of Christian Uniqueness*.[87] In his presentation in the latter collection of essays, John Hick offers the highly controversial thesis[88] that lying behind the aims of the various religions is a goal they all share, namely, the quest to overcome self-centeredness in favor of "Reality-centeredness,"[89] an understanding he reiterates in his subsequent defense of pluralism.

Although in agreement that God is active in the various religions, pluralists differ as to the means of that presence. While acknowledging that truth comes through all religions, the older pluralism nevertheless viewed Christianity as superior. Many contemporary pluralists, in contrast, seek to place the religions on an equal plane. Some claim that there is a common core within the religions, a universal faith that forms the quest of religious dialogue.[90] More widely advocated today, however, is the suggestion that the religions are all partial reflections of the one divine reality. Each religion sees a specific dimension of God's nature. Consequently, devotees can learn from each other, and the encounter of the religions is mutually edifying for all. For some pluralists, the final goal of such dialogue is the construction of one global theology to which the insights of all religions contribute.[91] Others seek a more human-centered goal, such as the discovery of a "true *humanitas*" which "reflects and participates in *divinitas*."[92]

83. Knitter, *No Other Name?* 147.

84. John Hick, *God and the Universe of Faiths* (London: Macmillan, 1973).

85. John Hick, *A Christian Theology of Religions: The Rainbow of Faiths* (Louisville: Westminster John Knox, 1995), 18.

86. John Hick, ed., *The Myth of God Incarnate* (London: SCM, 1977).

87. John Hick and Paul Knitter, eds., *The Myth of Christian Uniqueness: Toward a Pluralistic Theology of Religion* (Maryknoll, N.Y.: Orbis, 1987).

88. For an engagement with this thesis, see DiNoia, *Diversity of Religions*, 34–64.

89. Hick describes religions from the perspective of pluralism as contexts "within which the transformation of human existence from self-centeredness to God- or Reality-centeredness is occurring . . . to about the same extent." Hick and Knitter, *Myth of Christian Uniqueness*, 23.

90. For a description of this position, see Heim, *Is Christ the Only Way?* 111–14.

91. See, for example, Wilfred Cantwell Smith, *Towards a World Theology: Faith and the Comparative History of Religion* (Philadelphia: Westminster, 1981), 108. Cantwell Smith envisions a Christian theology of the religions that views Christianity as one religion among many others.

92. R. T. Simpson, "The New Dialogue between Christianity and Other Religions," *Theology* 92, no. 746 (March 1989): 102.

Reflecting on the rise of pluralism, Knitter concludes that it is the result of a gradual evolution in the Christian consciousness since the early part of the century, from ecclesiocentrism to christocentrism and finally to theocentrism.[93] Pluralists, he concludes, "are placing God, not the church or Jesus Christ, at the center of things." Such a shift, of course, is based on the supposition that theology encompasses Christology, that is, that God is not, in the words of Mark Heim, "*exhausted* in Christ or totally confined to Christ."[94]

In recent years, many pluralist theologians have sought to deepen their own work and thereby develop further the basic pluralist impulse.[95] Other theologians, in contrast, have grown uneasy over certain aspects of the pluralist position and therefore have endeavored to go "beyond" pluralism.[96] Such attempts have met with varying success,[97] many promising more than they deliver.[98]

The Eternal Fate of Non-Christians

Evangelical theologians have been practically unanimous in their rejection of the pluralist position advocated by Hick, Knitter, and others. They have shown less unanimity, however, on the remaining two basic options. The majority of evangelical thinkers would likely classify themselves as exclusivists, although the number who are inclusivists in sympathy if not in actual self-designation appears to be growing. This overall ambivalence among evangelicals is understandable, for evangelical theologians sincerely desire to uphold the universality-particularity of the Christian gospel as they find it in Scripture.

The particularity of the gospel is a theme sounded clearly in Scripture. The New Testament contains various claims that Jesus is the way—and the only way—to God (John 14:6; 17:3; Acts 4:12). Further, one finds in Scripture repeated statements to the effect that salvation comes through a personal response to Jesus (Acts 16:31; Rom. 10:9), as well as the parallel warning that rejecting Christ brings condemnation (Mark 16:16; John

93. Knitter, *No Other Name?* 166.
94. Heim, *Is Christ the Only Way?* 132.
95. One such example is Paul Knitter, *Jesus and Other Names: Christian Mission and Global Responsibility* (Maryknoll, N.Y.: Orbis, 1996).
96. See, for example, Schubert M. Ogden, *Is There Only One True Religion or Are There Many?* (Dallas: Southern Methodist University Press, 1992), where he proposes a "fourth option" of "*pluralistic* inclusivism."
97. For one of the more interesting proposals, see Pamela Dickey Young, *Christ in a Post-Christian World: How Can We Believe in Jesus Christ When Those around Us Believe Differently—Or Not at All?* (Minneapolis: Fortress, 1995).
98. For this appraisal of Ogden's proposal, see Carson, *The Gagging of God*, 149–50.

3:16–18, 36; 1 John 2:23; 5:11–12). This outlook is coupled with clear statements indicating that all humans are sinful and therefore are desperately in need of God's provision of salvation in Christ (Rom. 3:23–24; 6:23). Finally, the New Testament writers declare that God's salvation is made available through the proclamation of the gospel (Rom. 10:14, 17).

Scripture also articulates the theme of universality. Indeed, the saving intent of the God of the Bible is directed toward all people (e.g., Luke 13:29; Rom. 11:32; 1 Tim. 2:4; 2 Pet. 3:9). While Scripture appears to teach the necessity of conscious faith in Christ as the norm and general rule, certain texts give some evangelicals hope that the number of persons who participate in God's eternal community could possibly overflow the boundaries of the church. Thus, the Old Testament narrative includes servants of God, such as Melchizedek (Gen. 14:17–24), and people who apparently feared God, including Abimelech (Gen. 20:1–18) and Jethro (Exod. 18:10–12), who stood outside the main line of salvation history. To this list, the New Testament adds Cornelius (Acts 10:2). Examples such as these lead certain evangelical theologians to cling to the hope that God will save all who on the basis of the light they have received respond in faith toward God. These thinkers note that God is merciful to those whose mistaken piety arises out of ignorance (e.g., 1 Tim. 1:13), and they argue that faith in God (Heb. 11:6), and not hearing and responding to the gospel of Jesus Christ, is what is ultimately crucial.[99]

In 1991 in his dialogue with David Edwards, John Stott offered this advice to all who engage in the debate about the final destiny of those beyond the boundaries of the church:

> I believe the most Christian stance is to remain agnostic on this question. When somebody asked Jesus, 'Lord, are only a few people going to be saved?', he refused to answer and instead urged them 'to enter through the narrow door' (Luke 13:23–24). The fact is that God, alongside the most solemn warnings about our responsibility to respond to the gospel, has not revealed how he will deal with those who have never heard it. We have to leave them in the hands of the God of infinite mercy and justice, who manifested these qualities most fully at the cross.[100]

Fidelity to their heritage as a gospel people requires that evangelicals reject any theological position that fails to foster zealous obedience to the evangelistic mandate Christ has given to his church[101]—a zealous obedi-

---

99. See, for example, Pinnock, *Wideness in God's Mercy*, 157–58, 163.

100. David L. Edwards and John Stott, *Evangelical Essentials: A Liberal-Evangelical Dialogue* (Downers Grove, Ill.: InterVarsity, 1991), 327.

101. See, for example, John C. Barrett, "Does Inclusivist Theology Undermine Evangelism?" *Evangelical Quarterly* 70, no. 3 (1998): 243.

ence, I quickly add, that must always be guided, and at times even tempered, by knowledge. While maintaining a strong missiological stance, evangelical thinkers do well to accept Stott's words as a helpful reminder of the limits of our human ability to discern the mind of God. Of course, such an acknowledgment of the boundary beyond which theological reflection may not be able to penetrate cannot become an excuse for theological lethargy. As John Sanders points out in calling evangelicals to reject what he calls "reverent agnosticism," "We must not adopt an agnostic stance before we have made a thorough investigation."[102] Nevertheless, evangelical scholarship to date has not provided overwhelming rationale for jettisoning the cautious stance of thinkers such as Stott.

To summarize the current situation: The evangelical heart, it seems, would deeply desire to hold out hope that the eternal community will include persons who have been found by the God of the Bible even though they appeared to live beyond the reach of Christian evangelists. At the same time, given the scanty information available in Scripture about such persons, evangelical zeal rightly keeps before the church the crucial task of carrying the good news to persons who have not yet heard Jesus' blessed name.

God's Program and the Religions

As important as the question of the final destiny of those outside the church is, coming to a stated position on this issue does not provide the most helpful basis for theological engagement with the globalized context in which evangelicals now live.[103] As Ken Gnanakan declared, "Even if the 'exclusive' position is biblically tenable, the challenge that comes is whether one can continue to merely reiterate the position without rethinking some contextual aspects that will help us respond more effectively to the challenge."[104] In this task, focusing on the unresolved matter of eternal salvation may actually head theologians in a wrong direction.[105] While the question, Will those who do not believe in Jesus Christ be lost forever? may at times be motivated by a concern that all persons hear the gospel so that they can enjoy life with God, Lesslie Newbigin points out

102. Sanders, *No Other Name*, 18.
103. For another example of the suggestion that Christian theologians set aside, at least temporarily, the question of individual salvation in constructing a theology of the religions, see George Lindbeck, "The Gospel's Uniqueness: Election and Untranslatability," *Modern Theology* 13, no. 4 (October 1997): 424–25.
104. Gnanakan, *Pluralistic Predicament*, 42.
105. Runia, "The Gospel and Religious Pluralism," 362.

that it all too often "starts with the individual and his or her need to be assured of ultimate happiness, and not with God and his glory."[106] Rather than seeking a definitive answer to questions of eternal destinies, an evangelical apologetic theology of the religions ought to focus on the query as to whether or not the religions play what DiNoia calls a "providential role" in the divine economy. Do the religions of the world participate in any way in God's purposes in the penultimate age in which we are living?[107]

The Religions in the Bible

This question is of far-reaching importance. The possibility of a role of human religious expressions in the overarching plan of God provides a basis for a mutually enriching theological engagement between evangelical thinkers and adherents of other traditions. Any evangelical theology of the religions, however, must by necessity take its cue from the Bible. Therefore, the beginning point for the search for a helpful answer to the question of a providential role of the religions lies in the attitude toward the religions evident in the biblical texts.[108]

The Theological Context of the Biblical Narrative

The Bible narrates the salvific activity of God, especially as God has acted in the history of Israel and in Jesus the Christ. The particularity of the biblical sweep of salvation history, in turn, transpires within a broader context, namely, the universal human situation.

The biblical depiction of the universality of the human situation begins in the opening chapters of Genesis with the creation narrative. The curtain rises on the cosmic drama with God's act in bringing the world into existence and in forming humankind. This overarching context of creation gives a theocentric cast to the human reality. In the primordial garden, God speaks to the first humans and calls them to respond to the divine address. Human life, therefore, is always life before God. To be human means to be addressed by the Creator and as a consequence to be unavoidably accountable to the Maker of heaven and earth.

The theme of the universal divine address carries important implications for the biblical attitude to the religions. Religious expression arises as a human response to the God before whom every human stands. In this

106. Lesslie Newbigin, *The Gospel in a Pluralist Society* (Grand Rapids: Eerdmans, 1989), 179.

107. See, for example, Per Lonning, *Creation—An Ecumenical Challenge* (Macon, Ga.: Mercer University Press, 1989), 58.

108. For a helpful summary of the biblical material, see Jacques Dupuis, *Toward a Christian Theology of Religious Pluralism* (Maryknoll, N.Y.: Orbis, 1997), 29–52.

broad sense, to be religious is indicative of being human; humans are "incurably religious."[109] Insofar as it is a response to God's address to humans, the religious impulse is positive. Foundational to an evangelical theology of the religions, therefore, must be the recognition that the development of religions is a sign that humans are aware that they are addressed by the divine reality.

Although "creation" is the first biblical theme guiding a theology of the religions, this initial positive appraisal of religion must be tempered by a second foundational theme, the fall. According to the Genesis narrative, from the beginning failure and the fracture of relationships have characterized all dimensions of human existence. Nowhere is this fracture more obvious than in the human conscious response to God, that is, in the religious life. The dialectic of creation and fall lies behind the biblical authors' ambivalent attitude toward the religions. Religion is both a positive aspect of creaturely life and a flashpoint for human error.[110] Because of this ambiguity and potential for error, we must approach all religious traditions, practices, and institutions—including those associated with the Christian church—with caution, knowing the uncanny human ability to deface and defile what was originally intended for good.

More important than either creation or fall as the context for the biblical salvation narrative is the vision of the new creation as reflecting the goal of God's program. Consequently, the new creation forms a third foundational theme for a theology of the religions. In fact, the final perspective from which an evangelical theology ought to view religion is from the vantage point of God's ultimate intention for creation, namely, the establishment of community,[111] and the potential role of religion in advancing that intention.

The Universal Focus of God's Saving Activity

If the reality of creation and fall together with the vision of the establishment of community form the context for the biblical drama, salvation history is its content. The Bible narrates the story of God at work overcoming the fall with the purpose of bringing creation to its goal. Salvation history as narrated in Scripture has a universal intent. God's purposes overflow the boundaries of any one people to encompass all humankind.

109. J. Blauw, "The Biblical View of Man in His Religion," in *The Theology of the Christian Mission*, ed. G. H. Anderson (London: SCM, 1961), 32.

110. Christopher J. H. Wright, "The Christian and Other Religions: The Biblical Evidence," *Themelios* 9, no. 2 (1984): 5.

111. For a fuller articulation of this position, see Stanley J. Grenz, *Revisioning Evangelical Theology* (Downers Grove, Ill.: InterVarsity, 1993), 147–61.

The universal intent of God's purposes forms the point of the early narratives of Genesis. Already at the fall, God promises that the offspring of Eve—whose name means "the mother of all the living" (Gen. 3:20)—will eventually crush the serpent (Gen. 3:15). After the flood, God enters into another covenant with all humankind through Noah (Gen. 9:1–17). But of greatest significance is God's covenant with Abraham, through whom God promises to bless "all peoples on earth" (Gen. 12:3). The Genesis narratives point out that God's universal promises form the backdrop for the particular covenant with Israel. From the beginning, therefore, God's election of Israel has a universal intent. God chose this nation for the sake of all peoples. Through Israel the electing God desires to bless humankind. At the same time, while the election of Israel is universal in intent, it is particular in content. As Lindbeck notes, "There is not the slightest suggestion in the Old Testament that any nation beside Israel is especially beloved of God as means of blessing to all peoples."[112]

The biblical authors repeatedly sound the theme of a universal intent for particular election. Although it was primarily set in the context of the elected people of God, Jesus also directed his ministry toward the nations, as is evidenced, for example, in his healing of Gentiles (e.g., Mark 7:24–30). Simeon underlined the universal salvific purpose of Jesus' mission and its link to Israel's election. Upon encountering the Christ child, he declared, "For my eyes have seen your salvation, which you have prepared in the sight of all people, a light for revelation to the Gentiles and for glory to your people Israel" (Luke 2:30–32). Joseph Ratzinger is surely correct, therefore, in declaring summarily, "Election is always, at bottom, election for others."[113]

Not only is election directed toward the nations, God is active among all peoples. Perhaps the most radical Old Testament articulation of this idea came through the prophet Amos. In warning the haughty nation of impending judgment, God declared, "Are not you Israelites the same to me as the Cushites? . . . Did I not bring Israel up from Egypt, the Philistines from Caphtor and the Arameans from Kir?" (Amos 9:7). Hence, in the face of Israel's tendency toward self-righteousness, God reminded the covenant nation that other peoples have also been the recipients of providential guidance.

God's wider activity suggests that some type of faith in the true God may be present beyond the particular boundaries of the covenant people. Jesus reserved the highest praise for the faith he found in a Roman centurion, a Gentile (Luke 7:9). The conversion of Cornelius convinced Peter

---

112. Lindbeck, "The Gospel's Uniqueness," 445.

113. Joseph Ratzinger, *The Meaning of Christian Brotherhood*, trans. W. A. Glen-Doepel (New York: Sheed and Ward, 1966), 79.

that "God does not show favoritism but accepts men from every nation who fear him and do what is right" (Acts 10:34–35). These aspects of the biblical narrative lead some evangelicals to conclude that people of any nation who humbly seek to serve God and who depend upon God's grace may find divine favor. Even certain exclusivists sense the importance of such considerations. Ken Gnanakan, for example, concludes,

> There is no total justification for such a closed attitude to the world even in the Bible and this is what is urgently needed to be explored. Why did Jesus commend the 'faith' of the Gentiles if that faith did not matter at all? Why did Paul build from the worship of the 'unknown God' when he dealt with the people in Athens? These questions will need to be answered with reference to the totality of the revelation of God through Jesus Christ.[114]

Whether or not such faith leads to eternal life, an evangelical theology of the religions must give place to the faith-producing divine activity at work beyond the central trajectory of salvation history, Israel, and the church.

The Worship of Yahweh and the Religions

The prophets of Israel and the apostles of Christ declare that God's intent is that all nations join together in worship of the only true God (e.g., Zech. 14:16; Rev. 21:24–25). Jesus himself articulated this vision: "I say to you that many will come from the east and the west, and will take their places at the feast with Abraham, Isaac and Jacob in the kingdom of heaven" (Matt. 8:11). But how does this promise of a universal worship of God fit with the practices of the religions? Here the biblical writers offer two quite different appraisals.

Certain texts suggest that true worship is not limited to those who join the covenant people in paying homage to the God of Israel. The narratives of the early patriarchs that indicate some connection between Yahweh and El form an illuminating example. According to Christopher Wright, these texts suggest that the patriarchs worshiped the Mesopotamian and West Semitic high god, El, who entered into covenant with them. Although the biblical narrator identifies El with Yahweh, the God of Israel, he continues to use the old name in the dialogue sections. During Moses' confrontation with Pharaoh, God explains to his servant: "I appeared to Abraham, to Isaac and to Jacob as God Almighty [El-Shaddai], but by my name the Lord [Yahweh] I did not make myself known to them" (Exod. 6:3). From this phenomenon Wright concludes,

114. Gnanakan, *Pluralistic Predicament*, 46.

What we have here, then, is a situation where the living God is known, worshipped, believed and obeyed, but under divine titles which were common to the rest of contemporary semitic culture, and some of which at least, according to some scholars, may originally have belonged to separate deities or localizations of El.[115]

A similar phenomenon is evident elsewhere in Israel's early history. The Hebrew historians indicate that certain individuals stood in a positive relationship to the one God, even acting as his mouthpieces, although they were not directly members of Israel. Perhaps the most prominent examples are Melchizedek (Gen. 14:18–19; cf. Heb. 7:1–10), Jethro (Exod. 18:1, 9–12, 27), and Balaam (Num. 22). Certain persons beyond the lineage of Israel also received God's blessings through the prophets. Included among them were the widow in Sidon who provided hospitality for Elijah (1 Kings 17:7–24) and Naaman, who through Elisha was cured of leprosy (2 Kings 5:1–19; cf. Luke 4:25–27). Such acts of blessing served to confirm Yahweh's power. In the case of Naaman, the healing also led the recipient to join in the worship of Yahweh (2 Kings 5:17). Yet such worship neither required that he attach himself to the nation of Israel nor precluded his participation in the pagan religious rituals that his position required (e.g., 2 Kings 5:18–19).

A similar wider understanding of the worship of God is evident in the New Testament as well. Cornelius forms the most obvious example, for his prayers and acts of charity were accepted by God before he heard the message about Christ (Acts 10:4). The same idea lies behind Paul's astounding connection between the unknown deity worshiped by the Athenians and the true God whom the apostle declared to them (Acts 17:22–23). Perhaps Jesus himself hinted at this principle when he cautioned his disciples that the stranger who casts out demons in his name is an instrument of God's healing love (Luke 9:49–50). Clearly, then, the biblical authors did not limit the ranks of those who are offering acceptable worship to the circle of devotees who attach themselves to Israel or to Jesus' followers.

At the same time, the writers also voice a biting critique of the religions. Apart from the possible exception of Naaman, the biblical authors never encourage participants in other traditions to continue permanently in these structures. Rather, the goal of the gospel proclamation consistently seems to be that of bringing people to a full relationship with the God whom they may already have come to know in a partial manner. A turning point in attitude toward the religions of the Near East occurred at the covenant renewal at Shechem. There Joshua challenged the people to "throw away the gods your forefathers worshiped beyond the River and

---

115. Wright, "Christian and Other Religions," 6.

in Egypt, and serve the LORD [Yahweh]" (Josh. 24:14). From this point on, worship in Israel was to be exclusively Yahweh-centered.

Not only do the biblical writers admonish all people to worship the God of Israel and of Jesus Christ, they also call into question the gods of the nations. Mark Heim notes that their contemporaries "were not surprised that Jews and Christians rejected gods and cults other than their own, but that they rejected them as *false*." He then explains: "People could understand refusal to recognize gods on the ground that they belonged to other cities or tribes or professions, but they were surprised at rejection on general principle."[116] Franz Jozef vam Beeck sums up appropriately the situation of the biblical peoples:

> The New Testament shows the Christian Church at its beginning, coming into a world of religious pluralism and profiting from it, yet confidently claiming that its faith involves a call, to be issued to all alike, to turn away from all the local gods, lords, spirits and demons, in order to find salvation in the one true God, and in the man Jesus Christ, God's unique Son.[117]

The biblical rejection of other religions took two avenues. The most obvious was to acknowledge the reality of other gods, but to characterize them as evil and malicious. The Old Testament writers continually warned against idolatry, occasionally even connecting the gods with the demonic[118] (note the Hebrew words *shed* [Deut. 32:17; Ps. 106:37] and *saʾir* [2 Chron. 11:15]), a theme that finds echo in the New Testament (e.g., 1 Cor. 10:19–20). The other avenue was to deny any objective reality to the gods. Until the time of the exile, the Hebrews attributed to the rule of God events—even tragic experiences—that other peoples would have viewed as caused by other deities (e.g., 2 Sam. 24:15; also compare v. 1 with 1 Chron. 21:1).[119] Because Yahweh alone is sovereign, the Old Testament prophets proclaim, the gods of the nations are nothing, except perhaps members of the heavenly court. The most lucid statement of the denial of the objective reality of other deities comes from Paul:

> So, then, about eating food sacrificed to idols: We know that an idol is nothing at all in the world and that there is no God but one. For even if there are so-called gods, whether in heaven or on earth (as indeed there are many "gods" and many "lords"), yet for us there is but one God, the Father, from

116. Heim, *Is Christ the Only Way?* 35–36.

117. Franz Josef vam Beeck, "Professing the Uniqueness of Christ," *Chicago Studies* 24, no. 1 (1985): 29.

118. The Old Testament gives little place to the concept of demons. See, for example, Werner Foerster, "Δαίμων κτλ," in Gerhard Kittel, ed., *Theological Dictionary of the New Testament*, trans. and ed. Geoffrey W. Bromiley (Grand Rapids: Eerdmans, 1964), 2:10–11.

119. Ibid.

whom all things came and for whom we live; and there is but one Lord, Jesus Christ, through whom all things came and through whom we live. But not everyone knows this. . . . (1 Cor. 8:4–7a)

This denial of the existence of the gods forms the context for the New Testament claim that salvation comes solely through Christ (e.g., John 14:6; Acts 4:12).

The two avenues of rejection find resolution in Paul's statement, "But not everyone knows this." The power of the gods lies in the ignorance of humans apart from Christ. As they pay homage to the gods, devotees of the religions allow these deities to exercise power over their lives. Thereby such realities gain objective existence.

An Evangelical Apologetic Theology in the Context of the Religions

Evangelicals often conclude that Christianity is the only legitimate expression of special revelation, thereby denying any positive significance for all other religions.[120] The survey of the biblical material, however, indicates that the Bible allows no such unequivocal rejection of the possibility of either faith or true worship beyond the central salvation-historical trajectory of Israel and the church. This, in turn, leads to the suggestion that human religious traditions may indeed participate in some meaningful manner in the divine program for creation, even if only in the present penultimate age. The religions may have a providential role in the work of God in history en route to the culmination of the divine program. Yet, the question remains, What exactly is that role?

Community: The Foundation for a Theology of the Religions

The previous discussion of the biblical themes led to the suggestion that an evangelical theology of the religions involves a yes/no attitude toward the religions. The yes dimension arises out of indications that human religious traditions might play some providential role in the divine program in the present era. The task of an evangelical theology of the religions includes, therefore, the attempt to understand what this providential role might be. The appropriate beginning point for such reflection is God's

120. For an example of this approach, see David F. Wells, *God the Evangelist* (Grand Rapids: Eerdmans, 1987), 24.

overarching intent for creation in general and humankind in particular, an intent that may be summarized in the word "community."

The biblical visionaries anticipate the establishment of the eternal community of a reconciled humankind dwelling within the renewed creation and enjoying the presence of the redeeming God. While the fullness of community comes only as God's gift at the culmination of history, the writers also assert that we can enjoy foretastes of the future reality in the present. This suggests that the providential place of human religious traditions may lie with their role in fostering community in the present.

While the concept of community arises immediately from the biblical vision, certain contemporary sociologists offer insight into its significance. These thinkers speak about the importance of the "social web" or the experience of "community" to human existence. The stage for such an understanding was set in part by the French sociologist Emile Durkheim (1858–1917), who theorized that social cohesion is facilitated by "collective representations," the group-based symbols with which individuals identify. In his estimation, a "conscious collective," a pre-given solidarity of shared meanings and values, is a prerequisite to social diversification.[121] George Herbert Mead (1863–1931), in turn, showed the importance of community for identity formation. According to Mead, meaning is no individual matter but is interpersonal or relational. The mind, therefore, is not only individual but also a social phenomenon,[122] and the self—the maturing personality or one's personal identity—is socially produced.[123]

Building on the work of these pioneers, contemporary thinkers assert that a sense of personal identity develops through the telling of a personal narrative[124] which is always embedded in the narrative of the communities in which the person participates.[125] The transcending story that gives meaning to a personal narrative is mediated to the individual by the community, which transmits traditions of virtue, common good, and ultimate meaning.[126] The community is likewise important to the sustaining of character, virtue, and values. And it provides the necessary foun-

121. Emile Durkheim, *The Division of Labor in Society*, trans. George Simpson (New York: Macmillan, 1964), 277.

122. George Herbert Mead, *Mind, Self and Society*, ed. Charles W. Morris (1934; reprint, Chicago: University of Chicago Press, 1967), 133, 164, 186–92.

123. For Mead's cumulative case for the social theory of the self, see ibid., 135–226.

124. Robert N. Bellah et al., *Habits of the Heart: Individualism and Commitment in American Life* (Berkeley: University of California Press, 1985), 81.

125. See, for example, Alisdair MacIntyre, *After Virtue*, 2d ed. (Notre Dame: University of Notre Dame Press, 1984), 221.

126. E.g., George A. Lindbeck, "Confession and Community: An Israel-like View of the Church," *Christian Century* 107 (May 9, 1990), 495.

dation for involvement in public discourse about matters of worldview. Consequently, community is also crucial to the well-being of the broader society.

It is within this context that religion plays a significant role. As sociologists since Durkheim have noted, religion creates and maintains social solidarity, for it provides the symbols by means of which people understand their world. By providing the foundation for the social community in which we live, religion mediates to us the framework for group and personal identity formation. As contributors to the worldview of their devotees, religions are not merely systems of beliefs but rather are integrally related to the entire socio-economic and political structures of the lives of their adherents.[127]

The seemingly universal quest for community and the social role of religion in human life suggests a criterion by which an evangelical theology of the religions can view all religious traditions. The human religious phenomenon carries a positive intent. Whatever their ultimate vision of reality may be, all religious traditions contribute to identity formation and social cohesion. Their immediate goal is to mediate to their adherents a sense of identity as persons standing in some type of relationship to something "larger" than the individual, however that encompassing reality may be understood. In this sense, religions fulfill a divinely sanctioned function. Because God's ultimate purpose is the establishment of community, an evangelical theology of the religions can affirm each religious tradition in its intent to promote social cohesion among human beings, for in this manner each contributes to the present experience of community.[128] As DiNoia notes, "Other religions are to be valued by Christians, not because they are channels of grace or means of salvation for their adherents, but because they play a real but as yet perhaps not fully specifiable role in the divine plan to which the Christian community bears witness."[129]

This basically positive appraisal must be balanced by a cautionary attitude. Although directed toward a divinely sanctioned purpose, religion readily becomes an expression of human fallenness, even falling prey to the demonic. The Roman Catholic ecumenist Eugene Hillman articulates this two-sided Christian appraisal of all religions: "The fallibility and peccability of fallen humankind are reflected in religions no less than in all the other human systems and institutions which can also, in various surprising ways, serve God's purposes.[130] The potential for evil is bound up

127. Wright, "The Christian and Other Religions," 8.

128. A biblical parallel to this positive appraisal of religion lies in Paul's affirmation of government as God's agent in promoting good and punishing evil (Rom. 13:1–6).

129. DiNoia, *Diversity of Religions*, 91.

130. Eugene Hillman, *Many Paths: A Catholic Approach to Religious Pluralism* (Maryknoll, N.Y.: Orbis, 1989), 51.

with the specificity of religion. Religion never occurs in the abstract. Instead the human response to God always takes a specific form. And because humans are by nature social beings, rather than responding to God in isolation, the human response always has a social character,[131] coming to expression as a specific religion characterized by certain beliefs, practices, and structures.

As was noted earlier, religion plays a role in personal identity formation and provides the sanction for specific societal forms. Further, the social structures that a particular religion sanctions and the type of personal identity it fosters arise out of the worldview convictions the religion propounds. This connection means that any religion can be assessed according to both the personal identity/social structures it fosters and the underlying belief system that sanctions the social order. The primary question in appraising any religion, therefore, concerns the extent to which religious beliefs and practices lead to a personal identity and to social structures that cohere with God's intent for human life. Indeed, just as in the Old Testament setting, to choose the true God is to opt for the truly human as well, whereas the worship of false gods leads to injustice.[132]

This process of critical appraisal cannot allow any religion in its institutional form—including Christianity—a privileged exemption. History indicates that the various religious traditions have sanctioned deeply ingrained oppressive social structures. Although Christians may easily point to injustices perpetrated by other major religions, the record of institutionalized Christianity is far from spotless. This critical, interactive attitude opens the way to interreligious dialogue.

According to John V. Taylor, dialogue is "a sustained conversation between parties who are not saying the same thing and who recognize and respect the differences, the contradictions, and the mutual exclusions, between their various ways of thinking."[133] The process of critical appraisal provides the context for determining the value of interreligious dialogue. Because we must assume that all human religions are mixtures of truth and error, the study of other religious traditions and discussions with devotees can be mutually enriching, even for Christians who often shun such exercises.[134] At the very least, such interaction offers a vantage point from which to determine the extent to which we as participants in a specific tra-

131. Arnulf Camps, *Partners in Dialogue*, trans. John Drury (Maryknoll, N.Y.: Orbis, 1983), 47.

132. Wright, "The Christian and Other Religions," 8.

133. Taylor stated this in the first Lambeth Interfaith Lecture on November 2, 1977. John V. Taylor, "The Theological Basis for Interfaith Dialogue," in *Christianity and Other Religions: Selected Readings*, ed. John Hick and Brian Hebblewaite (Philadelphia: Fortress, 1981), 212.

134. For a helpful delineation of this point, see James L. Fredericks, *Faith among Faiths: Christian Theology and Non-Christian Religions* (Mahwah, N.J.: Paulist, 1999), 139–80.

dition are living up to the religious principles we espouse. As Alister McGrath declares, "Dialogue is important . . . because it acts as a gadfly, inviting us to reassess our understanding of our own faith by forcing us to reexamine its various aspects in the light of its foundational sources."[135] Pinnock takes the idea a step further. He offers as the first element in good dialogue "the willingness to appreciate other religions, to honor their truth and to learn from them," admitting that "other religions have positive contributions to make and a wealth to share."[136]

While this dimension is crucial, dialogue cannot stop here. Such discussions must also move to questions about the nature of ultimate reality and the final purpose or goal of existence. While there may be great similarities, at this point genuine differences inevitably emerge among the religious traditions. Postmodern thinkers have laid to rest the modern idea that the term *religion* denotes an overarching category that subsumes the "great religions of the world" or a phenomenon of which they are all examples.[137] Despite what some pluralists suggest, therefore, the world's religions are not simply the guises worn by the one, hidden religion.

Also suspect is the modern notion that all the so-called religions are merely seeking the same goal. In fact, to suggest that all religions are seeking the same goal is to presume that we know the truth of a religion better than its own devotees.[138] Rather than being variations on the same theme, the religions have differing conceptions of the nature of God and salvation. The world's religions may be attempting to provide answers to the human predicament, but they understand that predicament, and hence its solution, quite differently.[139] Grace Jantzen therefore rightly cautions theologians to avoid the assumption that "all religions have a concept of salvation at all, let alone that they all mean the same thing by it or offer the same way to obtain it: it is misleading to assume that there is some one thing that is obtained when salvation is obtained."[140] And DiNoia notes the explicitly Christian focus bound up with the concept of salvation:

> "Salvation" is not a term that encompasses what all religions seek, but is a properly Christian designation for that which should be sought above all

---

135. McGrath, "Particularist View," 159.

136. Pinnock, *Wideness in God's Mercy*, 139.

137. See, for example, John Milbank, "The End of Dialogue," in *Christian Uniqueness Reconsidered: The Myth of a Pluralistic Theology of Religions*, ed. Gavin D'Costa (Maryknoll, N.Y.: Orbis, 1990), 176–81.

138. Heim, *Is Christ the Only Way?* 29–30.

139. Ibid., 138.

140. Grace M. Jantzen, "Human Diversity and Salvation in Christ," *Religious Studies* 20 (1984): 579–80.

else in life. Salvation has a distinctively Christian content: transformation in Christ with a view to ultimate communion with the triune God.[141]

This difference in the conception of the human situation and its remedy produces an exclusivist impulse in all religions and provides the context in which Christians rightly maintain the finality of Christ.

The Finality of Christ in a Pluralist Context

The appeal to a universal criterion such as the promotion of social cohesion appears to provide the basis for an evangelical theology of the religions in the postmodern world. But the acknowledgment of "difference" offered in the previous paragraphs introduces a potentially debilitating problem. Despite their common quest for social cohesion (or "community"), the various communities espouse differing visions and embody differing understandings of what actually constitutes true community. This, in turn, leads to the crucial question, Why give primacy to the world-constructing language of the Christian community?

Of course, some theologians might opt here for a pluralism that limits the truth-value of any religious vision, including the Christian, to the particular religious community that embodies it. Yet this approach is ultimately unsatisfying. Pamela Dickey Young pinpoints the problem:

> If religious traditions make no claims to truth beyond themselves they become trivial. As merely innocuous expressions of one point of view alongside another, they would carry no power or depth to invite or command participation. Reasons for adhering to a religious tradition would not include that it told the truth about the way the world and its inhabitants are.[142]

Considerations such as these, as well as their commitment to the heritage of convertive piety, lead most evangelicals to respond to the query, Why privilege the Christian vision? by asserting that this theological vision is in fact *true*. But on what basis can we make this claim? Must we now finally appeal to some court beyond the Christian faith itself, some rational "first principle" that supposedly carries universality? In the end, must we inevitably retreat to a foundationalist epistemology? Here Mark Heim points the way forward: "The discussion of religious differences shifts then from a sole focus on flat issues of truth and falsehood, or degrees of these, to include consideration of alternatives: not 'Which religion alone is true?' but 'What end is most ultimate, even if many are

---

141. J. A. DiNoia, "Jesus and the World Religions," *First Things* 54 (June/July 1995): 25.
142. Young, *Christ in a Post-Christian World*, 68.

real?'"[143] More particularly, the wedding of the communitarian perspective with the theological method outlined in chapters 6 and 7 offers assistance.

The communitarian reminder that the goal of all social traditions is to construct a well-ordered society (although the various communities might well differ from each other as to what that society entails) suggests that the truth question is better formulated: Which theologizing community articulates an interpretive framework that is able to provide the transcendent vision for the construction of the kind of world that the particular community itself is in fact seeking? Hence, rather than settling for the promotion of some vague concept of community, the communitarian insight leads to the question, Which religious vision carries within itself the foundation for the community-building role of a transcendent religious vision? Which vision provides the basis for community in the truest sense?

Like other community-based visions, a central goal of the Christian message of salvation is the advancement of social cohesion, which it terms "community" or "fellowship." At the heart of the Christian message is the declaration that the goal of life is community: fellowship with God, with others, with creation, and in this manner with oneself. Taken as a whole, the biblical narrative speaks of God at work establishing community. God's *telos* is nothing less than gathering a reconciled people, nurtured in a renewed creation and enjoying fellowship with the eternal God (Rev. 21:1–5).

Of course, all human religious traditions contribute in some way to the building of society. All offer some semblance of "community," even when viewed from this specifically Christian perspective. And reminiscent of the Melchizedek story, many do so by appeal to a transcendent vision that includes the conception of a Most High God. Consequently, the Christian message does not necessarily deny the presence of divine knowledge beyond the boundaries of the church. Just as in the biblical era, so also today, wherever people are drawn to worship the Most High God, there the true God is known. And wherever God is truly known, the God who is known is none other than the one who is revealed through Jesus Christ.

But the Christian message does not stop here. Evangelicals firmly believe that the Christian vision sets forth more completely the nature of community that all human religious traditions seek to foster. Christians humbly conclude that no other religious vision encapsulates the final purpose of God as they have come to understand it. Other reli-

---

143. Heim, *Salvations*, 160.

gious visions cannot provide community in its ultimate sense, because they do not embody the highest understanding of who God actually is.

Foundational to the specifically Christian theological vision is not only the acknowledgment of God as the Most High, but also as the triune one. We declare that the only true God is none other than the triune God, the eternal community of Father, Son, and Spirit. The Christian vision speaks of humankind, in turn, as "created in God's image." The divine design is that we mirror within creation what God is like in God's own eternal reality. The goal of human existence has been revealed most completely in Jesus Christ, who in his life, death, and resurrection modeled the divine principle of life, namely, life in intimate fellowship with his heavenly Father by the Holy Spirit who indwelt him.

Viewed from this perspective, the Christian principle of the finality of Christ means that Jesus is the vehicle through whom we come to the fullest understanding of who God is and what God is like. Through the incarnate life of Jesus we discover the truest vision of the nature of God. Specifically, the encounter with Christ reveals that God is the triune one. The one whom the nations may worship as the Most High God is one we know as Father, Son, and Spirit. Because he has brought this more complete picture of God, Jesus mediates a more complete salvation. Through him we enter into a fuller relationship with the eternal God. Through Jesus, we know God in his triune personhood, rather than merely as the Most High God. And by the power of the Holy Spirit, we share in the fellowship that the Son enjoys with the Father. By means of the Spirit who was poured out into the world at the exaltation of Jesus, therefore, we enter into a fuller community with God than is enjoyed in any other religious tradition.

The Christian vision, a vision of God as triune and of our creation to be the *imago dei*, provides the transcendent basis for the human life-in-community that all belief systems in their own way and according to their own understanding seek to foster. It looks to the divine life as the basis for understanding what it means to be human persons-in-community. Just as God is a plurality-in-unity, so also to be human means to be persons-in-community. This glorious vision leads us to realize that the task of human society is to bring together the multiplicity of individuals into a higher unity, as is reflected so well in the motto of the United States: *e pluribus unum*, "out of the many, one." In short, the biblical vision of God at work establishing community is not merely a great idea that God devised in eternity. Instead, it is an outworking of God's own eternal reality. As a result, the human quest for community is not misguided. At its heart it is nothing less than the quest to mirror in the midst of all creation the eternal reality of God, and thereby to be the image of God. In this manner, the

Christian vision stands as the fulfillment of the human religious impulse as the early church fathers recognized, and as J. N. Farquhar[144] reintroduced into the contemporary discussion. In keeping with this insight DiNoia concludes, "According to traditional Christian doctrines, no theology of religions could be fully consistent with the Christian scheme unless it incorporated some version of the claim that other religions are superseded or fulfilled by Christianity."[145]

This leads to a final statement about the reconstruction of evangelical theology in a post-theological era, one that fits with the apologetic focus neo-evangelical theology has always reflected. Systematic theology seeks to show how the Christian belief-mosaic offers a transcendent vision of the glorious eschatological community God wills for creation, and how this vision provides a coherent foundation for life-in-relationship in this penultimate age, which life ought to be visible in the community of Christ as the sign of the age to come. Implicit in the construction of a coherent presentation of the Christian vision is a claim to "validity," a claim that, however, does not look to a universally accessible present reality for confirmation, but awaits the eschatological completion of the universally directed program of the God of the Bible.

Christian Universality

One problem still remains, however. The community-based approach followed throughout this section seems to undercut any claim to universality. It appears to leave us imprisoned within the "incredulity toward metanarratives" that Lyotard sees as characteristic of the postmodern condition[146] and that therefore views the Christian vision as merely one among the many. In such a situation, how can we claim that the Christian vision is not merely a tribal ethic but in fact is for everyone? How can we say that the Christian conception of salvation is universal in any sense of the word? What forms the connection between the particularity of the Christian vision and the universality of the human phenomenon?

A first connection lies in the universality of the divine intent. God's eschatological goal is not designed for only a select few but for all humans. Regardless of whether all will in fact eventually participate in God's eternal community, the God who wants all "to be saved and to come to a knowledge of the truth" (1 Tim. 2:4) desires that all participate in the divine goal for creation. The universal intent of the divine work forms the

144. J. N. Farquhar, *The Crown of Hinduism* (London: Oxford University Press, 1913).

145. DiNoia, *Diversity of Religions*, 75.

146. Jean-Francois Lyotard, *The Postmodern Condition: A Report on Knowledge*, trans. Geoff Bennington and Brian Massumi (Minneapolis: University of Minnesota Press, 1984), iv.

basis for understanding election. Similar to Israel in the Old Testament, the church is the elect people of God for the sake of the world. We seek to be a people who embody God's intention for all humankind. Thus, we view the vision of salvation we proclaim as more than merely the way of life of a specific religious tradition. Rather than huddling together as the "chosen few" who live unto themselves, our desire is to live according to God's will in the midst of, and for the sake of, the many. We long that the many might join with us—become part of "the few" as it were—so as to actualize God's intentions for all humankind. In this manner, we can correctly claim that the Christian message of salvation is nothing less than God's desire for all people everywhere.

A second connection between particularity and universality arises from the link the Bible forges between creation and new creation. Although God's intention is not derived completely from creation, it nevertheless is closely connected with original creation, because it marks the completion of creation. The same universe that God called into existence "in the beginning," God will transform into the eschatological new creation. In the same way, the very people who now exist in this world God will make perfect through the resurrection after the pattern of the resurrected Lord Jesus Christ, for through faith they are united to Christ.

Insofar as this is God's intention, we can rightly say that the eschatological new creation is present in embryonic form in creation, and the seed that will blossom into the renewed inhabitant of the eternal community lies within our human nature as created by God "in the beginning." And this is a design or purpose that all humans share. This universal divine purpose for humankind means that insofar as it arises from an understanding of God's intent for us, the Christian vision is for all.

The Christian understanding offers an even more concrete bridge between creation and new creation: Christ. The New Testament writers boldly assert that God created the world through Christ (Col. 1:15–16), who is the divine Word (John 1:3). Christ's role in creation is cosmic in extent, for he is the one in whom all things find their center (Col. 1:17). But Christ is also the one through whom God reconciled the world (2 Cor. 5:18–19). It is through connection with Jesus that we, together with the entire cosmos, participate in God's new creation.[147] This eschatological reality is not a new divine act of creation *ex nihilo*, but the transformation of *this* universe which God called into existence out of nothing "in the beginning."

---

147. See Helmut Thielicke, *Theological Ethics*, trans. John W. Doberstein, ed. William H. Lazareth (Philadelphia: Fortress, 1966), 1:383–451; Dietrich Bonhoeffer, *Ethics*, trans. Neville Horton Smith (New York: Macmillan, 1965), 120–213.

The implication of this Christological focus is vividly portrayed in Paul's typology between the First Adam and the Second Adam (Rom. 5:12–21; 1 Cor. 15:21, 45). Through this typology, the Apostle asserts that the goal of our very existence as the children of Adam is that we might experience eschatological transformation after the pattern of the resurrected Christ. For this reason, all human beings meet at the foot of the cross and at the door into the empty tomb. Through his death and resurrection Christ is the "life-giving Spirit" (1 Cor. 15:45) who seeks the transformation of what was begun in the creation of the First Adam.[148] The ultimate basis for the Christian claim to universality, therefore, rests in the fact that the goal it announces is in reality nothing else than God's goal for all creation.[149]

Conclusion: The Gospel and the Religions

As Christians we have come to see that the salvation God is effecting is the establishment of community in the highest sense. Although other religions can contribute to the divine program, the vision of community—with its focus on fellowship with the triune God—that we have received through our relationship to Christ constitutes a more complete appraisal of the human situation and the divine intention.

As the bearers of this more complete vision—as the sign of the future community—we are the people of the triune God. That is, we are a people who seek to serve God's purposes by modeling the divine intention of establishing community. According to the New Testament, we fulfill this purpose through our worship of the triune God, through mutual edification as we act as community to each other, and through outreach, i.e., service to the world and proclamation in the world.

Our witness in the world is based on the universal intention of God's activity in human history. Just as God elected Israel to serve the nations, so also God's Spirit has gathered us into the community of Christ in order to announce and embody—that is, to make explicit—God's desire that all persons participate in the fellowship God offers, which ultimately includes nothing less than the unity of humankind in fellowship with God (Eph. 4:4–6). This means that we must engage in the task of evangelism unto the end of the age. But we must avoid making the reality of judgment the sole motivation for our proclamation. It is simply not our prerogative to

148. For a similar attempt to connect believers and nonbelievers together through the Adam-Christ typology, see Paul L. Lehmann, *Ethics in a Christian Context* (New York: Harper and Row, 1963), 154–55.

149. For a similar conclusion, see Brian Hebblethwaite, *Christian Ethics in the Modern Age* (Philadelphia: Westminster, 1982), 136.

speculate as to the final outcome of the eschatological judgment, which will be a day of surprises. Rather, we continue to carry out the evangelism mandate, sometimes to bear the truth into realms of darkness, sometimes to bring to light the truth that is already hidden, and sometimes to bring to explicit confession of Christ the implicit covenant with God already present in our hearers. In the end, the gospel is the only gift we have to offer our world. More importantly, however, our obedience in announcing the gospel in word and action is the only gift we can offer to God. Indeed, the proclamation of the story of God's mercy in Christ is our act of worship of the one with whom we enjoy fellowship through Jesus our Lord and by the power of the indwelling Spirit.

nine

Evangelical Theology
AND THE Ecclesiological Center

The constructive proposal for a renewed evangelical theology sketched in the preceding chapters embodies a strong ecclesiological orientation. At its genesis, this proposal seeks to take seriously the contemporary insight that humans are inevitably situated in particular communities, which play a formative role in shaping not only one's personal convictions but also one's conception of rationality. Being a Christian likewise entails membership in a specific community, namely, the fellowship of those who have come to know the God of the Bible through Jesus Christ by the Spirit. Building from this insight, chapter 6 presented Christian theology as a communal activity. Theology emerges as Jesus' disciples seek to understand the faith they share. Christian theology, in other words, entails the determination and articulation of the belief-mosaic of the Christian faith.

Chapter 8 brought this perspective into conversation with the contemporary globalized context. Many people today are convinced that a world characterized by the presence of a plurality of communities, each of which gives shape to the identities of its participants, leads almost inevitably to the kind of pluralism that dominates the contemporary intellectual landscape. In this context, the theological significance of the Christian community gains a new and potentially profound importance. The conversation with other religious traditions provides the occasion for the Christian community to come to terms with its significance as a people who embody a theological vision that sees the divine goal for humankind as that of being the bearers of the image of the God who is triune. This self-awareness occasions a reaffirmation of the universality and uniqueness of Jesus Christ as the one who has not only revealed most completely but who also has effected the divinely given goal for human existence. Jesus gains this distinction, in that through his life, death, and resurrection he mediates salvation, understood as life in intimate fellowship with his heavenly Father, by the indwelling Holy Spirit.

The orientation to ecclesiology indicative of the proposal sketched in chapters 6, 7, and 8 was anticipated already in chapter 5, which concluded that the postmodern context requires a theology developed by, within, and for the community of faith, the church. In that chapter, I noted Timothy George's distinction between thinkers "who see theology connected intrinsically to the life of the church, and those who see theology as an academic discipline whose basic norms and values come from the secularized academy."[1] In applauding the former and rejecting the latter, George expresses the important postmodern insight that all intellectual reflection, and hence theology itself, is by its very nature always embedded within a particular (faith) community.

The turn toward community evident in much of contemporary thought raises a question that has simmered beneath the surface of evangelical theology throughout its history, namely, the question of ecclesiology. George Marsden recently noted, "One of the striking features of much of evangelicalism is its general disregard for the institutional church."[2] The goal of this chapter is to bring the discussion of the future of evangelical theology to a conclusion by engaging explicitly with its ecclesiological dimension. In so doing, the chapter brings squarely into view what has been implicit throughout the preceding pages: Evangelical theology must recapture a credible ecclesiology.

The "Problem" of Ecclesiology in Evangelicalism

In his sketch of the evangelical movement, the British evangelical Baptist Derek Tidball quipped, "From the very beginning . . . evangelicals have differed over the Church."[3] Evangelicals have indeed differed over the church, but this is at least in part because as a movement evangelicalism has never developed or worked from a thoroughgoing ecclesiology. The lack of a full-orbed ecclesiological base is related to the "parachurch"

1. Timothy George, "Theology to Die For," *Christianity Today* 42, no. 2 (February 9, 1998): 49.
2. George M. Marsden, *Understanding Fundamentalism and Evangelicalism* (Grand Rapids: Eerdmans, 1991), 81.
3. Derek J. Tidball, *Who Are the Evangelicals? Tracing the Roots of the Modern Movements* (London: Marshall Pickering, 1994), 156.

character of evangelicalism, which in turn has shaped the movement's particular ecumenicity.

Ecclesiology and Evangelical "Parachurchicity"

In many respects, the face of evangelicalism—globally but especially in North America—is that of a parachurch organization. As was evidenced even in the theological pilgrimages of the paradigmatic neo-evangelical theologians sketched in chapters 3, 4, and 5, the evangelical ethos is embodied in a variety of organizations and "ministries" that exist alongside of the ecclesiastical structures within which evangelicals hold membership. Thus, R. Albert Mohler is surely correct when, setting the context for his description of the life and theology of Carl Henry, he notes,

> The evangelical movement itself, while including many within the established churches, was largely a parachurch movement. The momentum and defining characteristics of the movement came from the parachurch institutions which shaped the evangelical consciousness.[4]

Viewing the situation largely from a British context, Tidball offers a similar assessment. He writes, "In contrast to the churches and denominations which, given their mixed natures, are often viewed with some suspicion by evangelicals, these agencies are often taken to be the true home of authentic evangelicalism."[5]

The parachurch nature of evangelicalism has resulted in an unmistakable minimizing of ecclesiology. Evangelical leaders routinely display no indication that they have given serious, extended attention to questions about the nature of the church. In the estimation of his biographer James Findlay, D. L. Moody, to cite one extreme example, had no doctrine of the church whatsoever.[6] More telling is the relatively insignificant place given to ecclesiology, at least historically, in the work of evangelical theologians. This is not to suggest that evangelicals ignore ecclesiology. A quick look at evangelical systematic theologies indicates that these treatises routinely include a section on the topic. Likewise, evangelical theologians repeatedly produce book-length treatments explicating the doctrine.[7] And evan-

---

4. R. Albert Mohler, "Carl F. H. Henry," in *Baptist Theologians*, ed. Timothy George and David S. Dockery (Nashville: Broadman and Holman, 1990), 530.

5. Tidball, *Who Are the Evangelicals?*, 161.

6. For this point and how Moody substituted a doctrine of "work" for a doctrine of the church, see James F. Findlay, Jr., *Dwight L. Moody: American Evangelist 1837–1890* (Chicago: University of Chicago Press, 1969), 246–48.

7. One recent example is Edmund P. Clowney, *The Church* (Downers Grove, Ill.: InterVarsity, 1995).

gelicals sporadically call together consultations on the church and even publish their results.[8] Rather, the point touches on a deeper dimension of the evangelical psyche. Evangelicalism's parachurch ethos works against the ability of the movement to develop a deeply rooted ecclesiological base from which to understand its own identity and upon which to ground its mission, whether it sees that mission as being as, to, or on behalf of the body of Christ.

Symbolic of the situation is Donald Bloesch's two-volume attempt "to spell out the core of the historic Christian faith from an evangelical and Reformed perspective" published in the late 1970s under the seemingly comprehensive title, *Essentials of Evangelical Theology*.[9] In the second installment of the work, Bloesch tackles three ecclesiological issues: the priesthood of all believers, the two kingdoms, and the church's spiritual mission. Yet nowhere in the nearly six hundred pages that comprise the composite treatise does the author engage in a sustained discussion of the evangelical understanding of the church itself. Whether or not it reflects Bloesch's actual intention, the message the work conveys is that ecclesiology per se does not belong to the movement's essential theology.

This perceived irrelevancy of the deeper issues of ecclesiology is not endemic solely to evangelicalism, however. Rather, it typifies Protestantism itself, at least in the modern era. In 1959, George S. Hendry bemoaned this situation. He wrote, "Where the Protestant principle has been popularly understood as an assertion of the spiritual independence of the individual against the authority of the Church, there has been a tendency in the Protestant reading of the Bible either to ignore the Church or to relegate it to a secondary or peripheral place."[10] While winds of change have begun to blow over the landscape in the decades since Hendry voiced this judgment, the situation has not been substantially altered, especially among evangelicals.

The Shaping of Evangelicalism's (Non)Ecclesiology

The roots of evangelicalism's inattention to the church lie in the theological trajectory that formed the movement.

As I noted in chapter 1, ecclesiology as such was not Luther's central theological issue. Instead, the German Reformer's concern was to restore the gos-

8. See, for example, D. A. Carson, ed., *The Church in the Bible and the World: An International Study* (Grand Rapids: Baker, 1987).

9. Donald G. Bloesch, *Essentials of Evangelical Theology*, 2 vols. (San Francisco: Harper and Row, 1978–1979).

10. George S. Hendry, "The Theological Context of the Church Today," in *The Ecumenical Era in Church and Society: A Symposium in Honor of John A. Mackay*, ed. Edward J. Jurji (New York: Macmillan, 1959), 38–39.

pel to the church. Consequently, his engagement with the question of the nature of the church emerged out of this restorative desire. By contending for the gospel, he hoped to bring into being a truly gospel church, that is, to establish the church once again upon the foundation of the gospel.[11]

With the Puritans, ecclesiology moved out of the shadows and into the limelight, for the Puritan program—namely, the quest for a duly constituted church—focused directly on ecclesiological issues. However, as the desire for a church of visible saints led to a concern to determine who are the truly elect, ecclesiology was eclipsed by soteriology or, more specifically, by the question of assurance of one's elect status. Hence, the kind of Puritanism that most directly fed into the rise of the evangelical movement had traded its earlier ecclesiological orientation for a concern for the kind of experiential religion that would in fact readily transcend confessional distinctives.

Equally significant in determining the shape of early evangelicalism was the movement's Pietist heritage. The Pietists were even more disinterested in matters pertaining to ecclesiology than were their late Puritan co-religionists. Unlike the early Puritans who voiced serious misgivings about the status of the Church of England, the Pietists never suggested that the Lutheran church was anything but a true church of Jesus Christ. Rather than engaging the ecclesiological question of the nature of a true church, the Pietists, under the rubric of a concern for authentic Christianity, turned their attention to the individual, that is, to the inner life of the regenerate believer and to the personal practice of the Christian faith. In setting the new birth as the principle article of faith while challenging the efficacy of churchly rites such as baptism and mere adherence to church doctrine, the Pietists inaugurated a new vision of what it means to be Christian. When it was later removed from its original context within confessional Lutheranism and Lutheran ecclesiology, this Pietist vision effectively relegated the church to the sidelines.

The Pietists bequeathed their vision of true Christianity to the fledgling evangelical movement. The personal experience of new birth became the sine qua non of authentic Christianity, a move that occasioned the development of a benign neglect of the church, if not a certain anti-church bias, among many evangelicals. Committed to the primacy of the new birth, early evangelical leaders such as George Whitefield bemoaned the nominalism they found in the established churches of their day. In their estimation, such churches were filled with persons baptized by water but bereft of the regenerative work of the Spirit, which alone counted for salvation. Hence, in the wake of the Great Awakening formerly nominal

11. Paul D. L. Avis, *The Church in the Theology of the Reformers* (Atlanta: John Knox, 1981), 13.

church members who had been dramatically converted began calling into question the ecclesiastical structures that in their view not only allowed the unconverted into the church but also placed unconverted clergy in authority over the church. To cite one example, in Norwich, Connecticut, in 1745 those who had been touched by the evangelical awakening, the so-called New Lights, proposed that the local parish church adopt a new membership requirement stipulating that no one be admitted into fellowship without first giving oral testimony to a conversion experience. When this proposal was defeated, the New Lights began holding separate worship services and a year later organized a separate congregation.[12]

Not only did the early evangelicals look askance at the nominal Christianity characteristic of the churches of the day, as those who had experienced the new birth they sensed a special, spiritual kinship with each other. In their eyes, all truly converted souls constituted the fellowship of true Christians, and this true, spiritual fellowship transcended the particularity of ecclesiastical affiliation (or lack thereof). Consequently, born-again evangelicals often sensed a deeper bond with kindred spirits in other confessional bodies than they did with those within their own ecclesiastical fold. John Wesley represented this evangelical spirit when he declared,

> I, and all who follow my judgment, do vehemently refuse to be distinguished from other men by any but the common principles of Christianity—the plain, old Christianity that I teach, renouncing and detesting all other marks of distinction. . . . But from real Christians, of whatsoever denomination they be, we earnestly desire not to be distinguished at all. . . . 'Is thy heart right, as my heart is with thine?' I ask no farther question. 'If it be, give me thy hand.' For opinions, or terms, let us 'not destroy the work of God.' Dost thou love and serve God? It is enough. I give thee the right hand of fellowship.[13]

And for Wesley that sole basis by which to determine another's status as a "real Christian" was the person's evangelical experience, a point capsulized in the question Wesley enunciated both in this sermon and elsewhere: "Is thine heart right, as my heart is with thy heart?"[14]

Moreover, the experience of regeneration that the evangelicals shared forged a unity among them that transcended differences over points of doctrine that had hitherto not only proven divisive but divided Christians

---

12. For a fuller account, see Stanley J. Grenz, *Isaac Backus—Puritan and Baptist*, NABPR Dissertation Series No. 4 (Macon, Ga.: Mercer University Press, 1983), 67–68.

13. John Wesley, "The Character of a Methodist," in *The Works of John Wesley*, ed. Albert C. Outler et al. (Nashville: Abingdon, 1984), 9:41–42.

14. John Wesley, "Catholic Spirit," *Forty-Four Sermons, or, Sermons on Several Occasions* (London: Epworth, 1944), 448.

into differing confessional groups. Hence, Winthrop Hudson reports that during one of his sermons George Whitefield looked toward heaven and declared, "Father Abraham, whom have you in heaven? Any Episcopalians? No! Any Presbyterians? No! Any Independents or Methodists? No, no, no! Whom have you there? We don't know those names here. All who are here are Christians."[15] Because of the primacy they gave to the new birth, Whitefield and Wesley could close ranks for the purpose of fostering the evangelical revival, despite their differing understandings on such matters as the workings of divine grace.

The Visible Form of Evangelicalism's (Non)Ecclesiology

The sense of spiritual unity among evangelicals of differing ecclesiastical and doctrinal loyalties that emerged in the eighteenth century soon took on quasi-institutional, "visible" form, a tendency that came to full flowering in the nineteenth century. At the heart of the institutional expression of evangelicalism was a new model of Christian cooperative engagement, the voluntary society.

The societal model was in part the natural extension of the congregational polity pioneered by certain so-called "left wing" Puritans in England and transported to colonial New England. The roots of Puritan congregationalism lay in the underground churches that emerged during the 1560s and 1570s. Not only were these congregations necessarily independent, but many of their leaders also came to the conclusion that the church was a voluntary association of believers standing in covenant with God. This understanding led early congregationalists such as Robert Browne to conclude that the church is by its very nature solely congregational; that is, it consists of the local bodies of the people of God and not the hierarchy of officers, as in episcopal polity. Further, Browne believed that Christ's will for the church is to be discerned by the local congregation as a whole, as guided by their elders.[16]

Congregationalism, therefore, honored no ecclesiastical authority above the local church. Nevertheless, later congregationalists favored the construction of voluntary associational structures. This is evident, for example, in the emergence by the 1650s of associations of Baptist churches in England.[17] The rise of the associational principle raised as a crucial issue in congregational life the question of the relationship of associations to local churches. A century later, the Philadelphia Association worked

15. As quoted by Winthrop S. Hudson, *American Protestantism* (Chicago: University of Chicago Press, 1961), 45.

16. Barrington R. White, *The English Separatist Tradition from the Marian Martyrs to the Pilgrim Fathers* (London: Oxford University Press, 1971), 56–63.

17. H. Leon McBeth, *The Baptist Heritage* (Nashville: Broadman, 1987), 95.

out what came to be the standard position of Baptists in the United States. Each congregation was viewed as having complete power and authority from Christ to administer the ordinances, receive and expel members, and select and ordain leaders. The association, in turn, carried the power of advising its member congregations, as well as of withdrawing fellowship from a wayward congregation.[18] Insofar as the association was a fellowship of congregations, it retained an ecclesiastical nature and an ecclesiological grounding. Yet the voluntary aspect of the associational model paved the way for a new type of voluntarism that later emerged and eventually developed into the parachurch approach characteristic of evangelicalism.

Initially the congregationalists, like other Puritans, were concerned almost exclusively with proper church order; theirs was the task of determining the nature of a truly constituted church. As the eighteenth century began giving way to the nineteenth, however, the evangelical impulse resulted in the emergence of other interests among Browne's successors. More particularly, congregationalists debated the question as to how the evangelistic work of the church might best be pursued. Especially significant was the commissioning and supporting of workers for the newfound task of home and foreign missions. Some, maintaining the strict congregational focus on the local church, resisted the creation of institutional structures of any kind beyond the local church. Whatever evangelistic activities that Christ had commissioned his people to do, they argued, the Lord had mandated to the congregations, which alone constituted the church of Jesus Christ. Others, however, considered the task too great for the congregations to do in isolation from each other. American evangelicals came to believe that the winning of the West and the conversion of the world required concerted action not only on the part of clusters of churches but also across confessional lines. The method that emerged for engaging in this greater work became that of the voluntary society, which in turn blazed the trail for the parachurch aspect of the evangelical movement.

An illuminating example of the societal model at work was the development of mission societies by Baptists first in England and then in the United States. Many historians date the beginnings of the modern missionary movement to the May 1792 meeting of the Northampton Association at which William Carey preached his memorable sermon on Isaiah 54:2. In response to his plea, the delegates passed a resolution calling for the formation of "a Baptist society for propagating the gospel among the Heathen."[19] Armed with this directive, a group of fourteen Baptists

18. Ibid., 243–46.
19. As quoted in ibid., 184.

met and voted to form what came to be known as the Baptist Historical Society.

This basic model, interested Baptists forming a voluntary society apart from but with the blessing of local churches or associations of churches, was repeated on the American side of the Atlantic during the nineteenth century. During the first third of the century, Baptists engaged in the formation first of regional mission agencies, such as the Massachusetts Baptist Missionary Society (1802), and then of what Leon McBeth calls the "Three Great Societies,"[20] which were devoted to foreign missions (1814), publications (1824), and home missions (1832). Actually, the formation of these national agencies among the Baptists was preceded by the founding by Congregationalist leaders of the American Board of Commissioners for Foreign Missions (1810), which McBeth cites as "the first organized foreign mission body in America," and which garnered support from non-Congregationalist contributors as well.

The societal model of cooperation was a stroke of genius, for it set the ecclesiological form for the visible or institutional functioning of the budding evangelical movement. Voluntary societies provided the vehicle through which evangelicals from a variety of denominations could band together on a variety of projects. As a result, church-based, confessionally oriented agencies were joined by a host of evangelical, transdenominational voluntary societies, as varied as the American Bible Society (1816), the American Sunday School Union (1824), and the Young Men's Christian Association (1855), as well as the Evangelical Alliance itself (1846). The stage was set for the dawn of the era of the parachurch organization, which in the twentieth century became both the molder and the incarnation of the evangelical ethos.

The Ecclesiological Basis of Evangelical "Parachurchicity"

The development of evangelicalism as a transconfessional movement imbuing a basically parachurch ethos emerged out of a constellation of factors: the focus in Pietism and late Puritanism on the new birth together with the bracketing of the question of the true church, the expansion of congregational polity and the attendant associational principle, and finally the advent of the voluntary society composed of concerned, like-minded Christian individuals as the means of carrying out the broader mandate of the church. But this historical sketch has not yet pinpointed the deeper ecclesiological assumptions that lay behind and gave impetus to the development of these innovations in church polity.

20. Ibid., 344.

The emergence of evangelicalism as a transconfessional movement was facilitated by a far-reaching ecclesiological compromise worked out in the eighteenth and nineteenth centuries: denominationalism. Actually, the flowering of evangelicalism and the widespread acceptance of denominationalism went hand in hand. As historian Winthrop Hudson indicates, both in name and in content denominationalism was the creation of the leaders of the evangelical revival on both sides of the Atlantic.[21]

Basically, denominationalism is the outlook that refuses to acknowledge any ecclesiastical body as comprising the whole church on earth. Instead, Christ's church is "denominated" into the various confessional groups, each of which constitutes only a part of the one church of Christ. Hudson offers a fuller explanation:

> The word "denomination" implies that the group referred to is but one member of a larger group, called or denominated by a particular name. The basic contention of the denominational theory of the church is that the true church is not to be identified in any exclusive sense with any particular ecclesiastical institution. The outward forms of worship and organization are at best but differing attempts to give visible expression to the life of the church in the life of the world.[22]

In a sense, denominationalism offers its proponents the best of both worlds. Each confessional group can continue to see itself as the best or most biblically faithful visible expression of the church. Yet, rather than evidencing a sectarian attitude, the group eschews the claim to be the only legitimate expression of the church, seeing itself instead as but one denomination among many. On this basis, members of any denomination are able to maintain their confessional loyalties while both affirming other denominations as expressions of the one church and cooperating with Christians across denominational lines in various tasks and ministries.[23] For evangelicals committed to convertive piety, the Christians of other denominations whom they might well affirm and with whom they might therefore cooperate were those who, like they, had experienced the new birth and consequently were bona fide regenerated believers.

Since its inception, denominationalism has been a powerful ecclesiological principle among Protestants, above all in the United States. It has been especially helpful in the advancement of the evangelical cause. How-

21. Hudson, *American Protestantism*, 33–34.
22. Winthrop S. Hudson, "Denominationalism as a Basis for Ecumenicity: A Seventeenth Century Conception," *Church History* 24, no. 1 (March 1955): 32. See also Hudson, *American Protestantism*, 34.
23. D. G. Tinder, "Denominationalism," in *Evangelical Dictionary of Theology*, ed. Walter A. Elwell (Grand Rapids: Baker, 1984), 311.

ever, the denominationalism of evangelicals has generally been coupled with another ecclesiological assumption, through which the evangelical form of denominationalism has functioned. The operative principle of evangelical ecclesiology from its inception has been the distinction between the invisible church of the truly converted and the church as a visible institution, whose members include both true believers and nominal Christians.[24]

The idea of a distinction between the invisible church and the visible church predates the evangelical movement itself, of course. A contrast between the two may be found in many of the church fathers from Irenaeus to Augustine, as well as medieval theologians such as Bonaventure and Thomas Aquinas. According to Avery Dulles, these thinkers all viewed the true church as a mystical communion that is operative wherever the Holy Spirit brings people together into a fellowship of faith and love.[25] The resultant differentiation between a spiritual fellowship and the institutional church has been echoed by Protestant theology into the present. Paul Tillich, to cite one prominent twentieth-century example, draws a sharp distinction between the disunited human institutions called "churches" and the mystical, undivided "Spiritual Community" latent in and lying behind them.[26]

More important in providing the basis for evangelical ecclesiology, however, is the legacy of a particular Augustinian understanding of the invisible church as reformulated by the Puritans under the influence of Calvin. As was noted in chapter 1, the Puritans borrowed the concept of the invisible church understood as the full number of the elect known only to God, but who can be made visible, at least in part, through the preaching of the gospel. While drawing from this theological trajectory, the evangelical focus on convertive piety gave the older distinction a new twist. Evangelicals came to view the invisible church not as the elect as known only to God, but as the fellowship of the truly converted, a fellowship that transcends the visible church in its various institutional forms. In 1851, Edward Litton capsulated this foundational aspect of evangelical ecclesiology when he declared,

> The one true Church, the holy catholic Church of the Creed, is not a body of mixed composition, comprehending within its pale both the evil and the good: it is the community of those who, whatever they may be, are in living union with Christ by faith, and partake of the sanctifying influences of His Spirit.

24. For a recent restatement of this view, see Rex A. Koivisto, *One Lord, One Faith: A Theology for Cross-Denominational Renewal* (Wheaton: Victor, 1993), 269–74.

25. Avery Dulles, *Models of the Church* (Garden City, N.Y.: Image Books, 1978), 150.

26. Paul Tillich, *Systematic Theology* (Chicago: University of Chicago Press, 1963), 3:162–72.

Litton then concluded that the true church cannot be confused with any earthly ecclesiastical institution: "The true Church is so far invisible as that it is not yet manifested in its corporate capacity; or, in other words; there is no one society, or visible corporation here on earth, of which it can be said that it is the mystical Body of Christ."[27]

Litton's distinction finds echo in neo-evangelical theologians such as Millard Erickson, who likewise acknowledges—albeit somewhat grudgingly—a distinction between "the visible or empirical church and the invisible or spiritual fellowship."[28] Perhaps more pronounced is Wayne Grudem's use of this distinction. In typical evangelical fashion, he declares, "In its true spiritual reality as the fellowship of all genuine believers, the church is invisible." This spiritual fellowship, Grudem adds, must be distinguished from the visible church, which "includes all who profess faith in Christ and give evidence of that faith in their lives," but by its very nature "will always include some unbelievers."[29]

Although Grudem claims the Reformation and the Puritans as providing the background for this distinction, he in fact follows neither in his delineation of the classical differentiation. The Reformers reintroduced the invisible church as the means to combat the Roman Catholic tendency to equate the true church with the visible organization headed by the Pope, as well as to indicate how the Roman Catholic Church could retain some semblance of being a true church. In response, Luther argued that the spiritual character of the church, while connected to the visible institution, is ultimately hidden in Christ, and therefore is simply not identical to any empirical reality. Similarly, the Calvinist approach that typified the Puritans lodged the invisible nature of the true church in the mind of God who alone knows who the elect are. For Calvin, this distinction was intended to underscore the divine lordship over the church, in that "it is . . . the special prerogative of God to know those who are his. . . ."[30] In contrast to these earlier understandings, Grudem follows the more evangelical focus on the converted heart, which only God can see. Hence, he explains, "We cannot see the spiritual condition of people's hearts. We can see those who outwardly attend the church, and we can see outward ev-

---

27. Edward A. Litton, *The Church of Christ* (1851), 48 ff., as quoted in Peter Toon, *Evangelical Theology 1833–1856: A Response to Tractarianism* (Atlanta: John Knox, 1979), 178. That Litton also held to the concept of the visible church is evident in his extended treatment of the topic in the second edition of the work (London: Nisbet, 1898), 58–72.

28. Millard J. Erickson, *Christian Theology* (Grand Rapids: Baker, 1985), 3:1048.

29. Wayne Grudem, *Systematic Theology: An Introduction to Biblical Doctrine* (Grand Rapids: Zondervan, 1994), 855–56.

30. John Calvin, *Institutes of the Christian Religion*, 4.1.8, trans. Henry Beveridge (Grand Rapids: Eerdmans, 1989), 288.

idences of inward spiritual change, but we cannot actually see into people's hearts and view their spiritual state—only God can do that."[31]

Their understanding of the distinction between the invisible church and the visible church led evangelicals to elevate the invisible church, often to the expense of the visible church.[32] If the true church is the invisible church, the "fellowship of all genuine believers" understood as those who are truly born again, participation in the visible church ultimately becomes soteriologically irrelevant. Dallas Seminary theologian Robert Lightner takes this tendency to the extreme when he declares that the "company of the redeemed is called the church without consideration of whether or not those who are a part of it are members of local churches."[33] If the visible church is soteriologically irrelevant, participation in it can quickly become, at best, motivated more by pragmatic concerns than by a sense of necessity, and at worst, merely a matter of personal preference.

The focus on the invisible church of the truly converted, together with the implied de-emphasis upon the visible or institutional church, provided the ecclesiological basis for the parachurch ethos of the evangelical movement. By invoking the invisible church as the true church, evangelicals were freed from excessive concern with matters of church order. As Edmund Clowney noted, "Evangelicals have often excused a deep neglect of the order of the church by emphasizing its invisibility."[34] In this manner, a distinction that in the Reformation was intended "to expose the tensions and responsibility of the visible Church," to cite G. C. Berkouwer's description, now was invoked to "'solve' those tensions."[35]

The elevation of the invisible church also allowed evangelicals to unite across denominational boundaries with others among the truly converted and hence with those whom they viewed as co-members of the true (i.e., invisible) church, so as to engage together in what they perceived to be the true task of Christ's church. As a result, the parachurch displaced the confessional church. Clowney articulates the typical evangelical affirmation of this ecclesiological development. After noting the evangelical neglect of the institutional church (quoted above) he quickly adds, "All this has been less disastrous than might be supposed. . . . Parachurch groups

---

31. Grudem, *Systematic Theology*, 855.

32. The loss of the visible church has been augmented by the influence of dispensational thinking among evangelicals. In dispensational theology, the visible church is of negligible importance. See Michael D. Williams, "Where's the Church? The Church as the Unfinished Business of Dispensational Theology," *Grace Theological Journal* 10, no. 2 (1989): 167.

33. Robert P. Lightner, *Evangelical Theology* (Grand Rapids: Baker, 1986), 228.

34. Clowney, *The Church*, 110.

35. G. C. Berkouwer, *The Church*, trans. James E. Davison (Grand Rapids: Eerdmans, 1976), 38.

have often accomplished what the Lord designed the church to do, providing nurture and encouraging evangelism."[36]

Evangelical Ecumenicity

By redefining the invisible church as the company of the truly converted known only to God, while acknowledging the various confessional groups as denominations of the one church, evangelicals were able to affirm one another within existing visible structures and join hands across ecclesiastical boundaries. By uniting together with all who were born again and therefore members of the invisible church, evangelicals seemed to have found a practical solution to the perplexing problem of ecclesiology. Nevertheless, the problem of the visible church did not immediately evaporate. The ongoing disunity within a church divided along confessional lines occasioned the drive toward ecumenicity that dominated the agenda of the mainline churches in the twentieth century.

The ecumenical movement has been widely hailed as one of the greatest accomplishments of the church in the twentieth century, perhaps even to the point of being the defining mark of the church today.[37] Despite the accolades ecumenism has garnered among mainline theologians and church leaders, neo-evangelicals have been almost unanimous in voicing skepticism of the direction the movement has pursued and in remaining aloof toward the institutional forms that it has spawned, especially the World Council of Churches. Already in 1973, Donald Bloesch noted what he termed "the ambivalent position of the new evangelicalism toward ecumenism."[38] While evangelicals routinely articulate both theological and pragmatic concerns,[39] Geoffrey Wainwright finds something distinctively American in such reticence. He writes,

> The varied escapes from Europe, the hard-won development of internal tolerance, and the effort of building one nation from the many peoples have all contributed to a semicompetitive, semicooperative denominationalism whose strongly voluntaristic character is seen as an acquisition not lightly to be set at risk for the sake of a unity that might mean restrictive uniformity.[40]

36. Clowney, *The Church*, 110.

37. See, for example, Donald G. Miller, *The Nature and Mission of the Church* (Richmond: John Knox, 1957), 128.

38. Donald G. Bloesch, *The Evangelical Renaissance* (Grand Rapids: Eerdmans, 1973), 43.

39. For a helpful delineation of some of these concerns, written from a Baptist perspective, see William R. Estep, *Baptists and Christian Unity* (Nashville: Broadman, 1966), 168–94. Erickson incorporates Estep's concerns, which he sees as having broader evangelical appeal, into his own response to the ecumenical movement. Erickson, *Christian Theology*, 3:1142–46. For a critique from the perspective of a chastened ecumenist, see Thomas C. Oden, *Life in the Spirit*, vol. 3 of *Systematic Theology* (San Francisco: Harper Collins, 1992), 309–11.

40. Geoffrey Wainwright, *The Ecumenical Movement: Crisis and Opportunity for the Church* (Grand Rapids: Eerdmans, 1983), 192.

The ecumenical movement triggered a resurgence in ecclesiological reflection among Roman Catholics,[41] mainline Protestants[42] and even Eastern Orthodox theologians,[43] bringing to fulfillment, as it were, Otto Dibelius's prediction, voiced in 1927, that the twentieth would be "the century of the Church."[44] Evangelical thinkers, however, remained largely on the sidelines and as a consequence fell woefully behind in the task of engaging with ecclesiology. The situation, however, is showing signs of change. As Carl Braaten noted in his mid-1990s survey of recently published evangelical systematic theologies, "Evangelicalism, like other forms of Protestantism, may now be facing the ecclesiological crisis that ecumenism has brought home to us."[45]

The Ecumenical Challenge

Although widely rejected by neo-evangelicals, the modern ecumenical movement was to a large degree the product of the rise of evangelicalism itself. Many thinkers among evangelicalism's Puritan and Pietist forebears were characterized by what might be denoted as a proto-ecumenical spirit. Richard Baxter, for example, evidenced just such a spirit when he declared, "I would . . . recommend to all my brethren, as the most necessary thing to the Church's peace, that they unite in necessary truths, and bear with one another in things that may be borne with; and do not make a larger creed and more necessaries than God hath done."[46] Similarly, Pietism carried within itself what Donald Bloesch calls an "ecumenical thrust." He points out that the Pietists "were quick to seek spiritual unity with other Christians" and adds that some, such as Zinzendorf, held that "friendly cooperation is not a substitute for unity."[47]

Standing more directly at the genesis of modern ecumenism were the evangelical revivals of the eighteenth and nineteenth centuries, which, as was noted above, brought together persons committed to convertive piety across confessional lines. Not only did these evangelicals share a common experience, the new birth, but their common focus on convertive piety led them to realize that they also shared a

41. For a helpful summary of Roman Catholic ecclesiology in the twentieth century, see Avery Dulles, "A Half Century of Ecclesiology," *Theological Studies* 50 (1989): 419–42.

42. See, for example, Colin W. Williams, *The Church*, vol. 4 of *New Directions in Theology Today*, ed. William Hordern (Philadelphia: Westminster, 1968), 12.

43. Petros Vassiliadis, "Orthodox Theology Facing the Twenty-first Century," *Greek Orthodox Theological Review* 35, no. 2 (Summer 1990): 140.

44. Otto Dibelius, *Das Jahrhundert der Kirche* (Berlin: Furche, 1927).

45. Carl E. Braaten, "A Harvest of Evangelical Theology," *First Things* 63 (May 1996): 46.

46. Richard Baxter, *The Reformed Pastor*, ed. Hugh Martin (Richmond: John Knox, 1956), 101.

47. Bloesch, *Evangelical Renaissance*, 121.

common task, that of evangelizing the world.[48] In the spirit of William Carey's call for a "general association of all denominations of Christians from the four quarters of the world,"[49] evangelicals launched a series of interdenominational missions conferences that spanned the nineteenth century and spilled over into the twentieth. The climactic event was the World Missionary Conference held in Edinburgh in 1910. In response to a plea from an Asian colleague, the delegates committed themselves to using "every possible means" to remove the scandal of importing denominational distinctions and divisions into the mission fields of the world. On that day, the modern ecumenical movement was born.[50]

Nearly all Protestant theologians, ecumenists and critics alike, begin their discussion of the question of ecumenicity with the same affirmation: Christian unity is a divine gift. The evangelical thinker Millard Erickson, for example, launches his interaction with ecumenism by declaring, "We need to realize that the church of Jesus Christ *is* one church. All who are related to the one Savior and Lord are indeed part of the same spiritual body (1 Cor. 12:13)."[51] Similarly, ecumenist Donald Miller writes,

> It is always to be remembered . . . in our striving after unity, that it is a gift of God, not a human achievement. We cannot, by human decision and organizational effort, make the church one. The church is already one, made so by the creative act of God. It is ours merely to *realize* the unity which we already have in Christ, and to *manifest* it by word and deed to the world.[52]

Despite this common starting point, the ecumenical and evangelical paths quickly diverge. The point of contention between the two groups focuses on the question as to how this fundamental unity ought to be expressed. In 1947 Henry Van Dusen pinpointed the issue dividing the antagonists as "the extent, if any, to which the realization of Christian unity as God intends it requires the achievement of *church union*—that is, whether the ideal of Christian unity may be fulfilled merely through the

---

48. For this point, see Kenneth Scott Latourette, "Ecumenical Bearings of the Missionary Movement and the International Missionary Council," in *A History of the Ecumenical Movement, 1517–1948*, ed. Ruth Rouse and Stephen Charles Neill, 2d ed. (Philadelphia: Westminster, 1968), 353.

49. The call is found in a letter from Carey to Andrew Fuller dated May 1806. See Eustace Carey, *Memoir of William Carey* (London: Jackson and Walford, 1836), 481.

50. Maurice Villain, *Unity: A History and Some Reflections*, trans. J. R. Foster from the third revised and augmented edition (London: Harvill, 1961), 30.

51. Erickson, *Christian Theology*, 3:1146.

52. Miller, *Nature and Mission of the Church*, 127.

fellowship of individual Christians, or whether it requires new relationships between the organized churches."[53]

When cast in this form, ecumenists are convinced that the question can engender only one credible answer. The underlying Christian unity must come to visible expression. Geoffrey Wainwright, for example, declares, "Spiritual unity and visible unity are not truly alternatives: the alternative to visible unity is visible *dis*unity, and that is a witness against the gospel."[54] Wainwright's declaration reflects the pragmatic or missiological argument for visible unity that motivated the modern ecumenical movement at its genesis, namely, the concern for the gospel in the world.[55] Drawing from the idea of scandal as "something that hinders reception of faith," the Methodist ecumenist Albert Outler cast the argument in these terms: "The scandal of disunity, then, lies in its effect on our witness to the world."[56]

Other proponents have offered a more specifically theological grounding for ecumenical endeavors. T. F. Torrance, to cite one lucid example, declares, "Unity belongs to the very essence of the Church as the community of people who have been reconciled to God, and to one another, through the life and passion of the Incarnate Son."[57] On this basis, Torrance concludes that disunity violates the very nature of the church:

> Hence, failure on the part of the Church to realise the dynamic unity by which it lives would inevitably call in question its ontological grounding in the unity of God given to it through Christ and in the Spirit, and any division arising within the Church would have the effect of introducing a contradiction into its very existence, for it would mean that the Church had fallen into disagreement with its innermost nature by sinning against its own reconciliation with God and therefore against the unity in and through which it is constituted the people of God, the Body of Christ.[58]

Considerations such as these lead ecumenists to link division with sin. They argue that the lack of organizational unity within the visible church is the result of human failure and consequently that to perpetuate disunity is tantamount to remaining in sin. Donald Miller, for example, as-

---

53. Henry P. Van Dusen, *World Christianity: Yesterday, Today, Tomorrow* (New York: Abingdon-Cokesbury, 1947), 209.

54. Wainwright, *Ecumenical Movement*, 4.

55. For a similar point, see Berkouwer, *The Church*, 46–48.

56. Albert C. Outler, *That the World May Believe: A Study of Christian Unity and What It Means for Methodists* (New York: Joint Commission on Education and Cultivation, Board of Missions of the Methodist Church, 1966), 10–11.

57. Thomas F. Torrance, *Theology in Reconciliation: Essays towards Evangelical and Catholic Unity in East and West* (Grand Rapids: Eerdmans, 1976), 20.

58. Ibid., 21–22.

serts, "When the church divides at any place, it is the result of sin, either on the part of those who leave it or those who thrust them out, or both." From this assumption, Miller draws the stark conclusion:

> This means that we should not glory in our divisions, but repent of them, and work for their healing. To accept our present divisions as right, or to seek to perpetuate them, or even to go so far as deliberately to foster new divisions, is to try to destroy the Body of Christ, and is thus a thrust at Christ Himself.[59]

This assumption about the presence of denominational divisions within the one church lies behind the controversial practice sometimes followed in ecumenical gatherings of offering a prayer beseeching divine forgiveness for the sin of schism.[60]

"Believer Ecumenicism"

In the face of the ecumenical challenge, evangelicals have not spoken with one voice. Some have articulated basic agreement with the theological concerns that motivate the ecumenical movement. One prominent example is the British evangelical Anglican, David Watson.

Watson agrees with his ecumenical colleagues that "the plethora of churches in almost every place presents a continuing and conflicting headache which cannot be brushed under the carpet of special conventions and united services."[61] He is convinced that divisions among the churches "seriously weaken the worldwide mission of the church."[62] But Watson does not leave the matter on the pragmatic missiological level. Reminiscent of T. F. Torrance, he sees a deeper theological issue at stake:

> Most of all, the disunity within the church is a constant offence to God, who, in his love, naturally longs to see his family united; it is an affront to Christ who, by his death, broke down all those walls of hostility that divide us, so as to reconcile us all to God in one body; and it constantly grieves the Holy Spirit who has come to dwell within us to produce the fruit and gifts that are necessary for a truly united church.[63]

Like thinkers across the theological spectrum, Watson grounds the unity of the church in the unity of God.[64] But unlike many evangelicals,

---

59. Miller, *Nature and Mission of the Church*, 123.
60. For a critique of this practice, see Estep, *Baptists and Christian Unity*, 176.
61. David Watson, *I Believe in the Church* (Grand Rapids: Eerdmans, 1978), 337.
62. Ibid., 337.
63. Ibid., 340–41.
64. Ibid., 342.

he adamantly asserts that this spiritual unity must come to concrete expression. This leads him to challenge a widely held evangelical assumption: "The time has come when we can no longer excuse our disunity by appealing to the invisible unity of all true Christians." Watson is convinced that "any concern for fresh spiritual life that is in accordance with the teaching of the New Testament must also lead to a concern for the unity of the church."[65]

Watson's admonitions echo a declaration drafted at about the same time by a group of evangelical thinkers on the American side of the Atlantic. In this statement, known as *The Chicago Call* (1977), the signatories deplored "the scandalous isolation and separation of Christians from one another," claiming that "such division is contrary to Christ's explicit desire for unity among his people and impedes the witness of the church in the world."[66] While stating their rejection of "church union-at-any-cost," the group voiced disapproval of "mere spiritualized concepts of church unity." Convinced that "unity in Christ requires visible and concrete expressions," the signatories called on evangelicals to "cultivate increased discussion and cooperation, both within and without their respective traditions, earnestly seeking common areas of agreement and understanding."[67]

A similar spirit of ecumenicism was given expression more recently by the Methodist convert to evangelicalism Thomas Oden. Taking stock of the first two millennia of Christian experience, Oden remarked, "The third millennium faces the task of once again practically embodying the unity that we already have juridically in Christ."[68]

Despite voices such as Watson, Oden, and the architects of *The Chicago Call*, neo-evangelical theologians have tended to offer cautious and somewhat ambiguous responses to the ecumenical challenge. On the one hand, evangelicals do not want to appear opposed to closer ties among confessional traditions. Indeed, the evangelical movement is itself "ecumenical" in the sense that it brings together believers from many ecclesiastical loyalties and seeks to foster a united face for the sake of the mission of the church.

On the other hand, skepticism toward grandiose plans of organizational union seems almost inherent in the evangelical ethos. This skepticism is in part the result of the commitment to convertive piety that defines the movement. As has been noted already, from the beginning born-again evangelicals have been suspicious of the nominal Christianity that they

65. Ibid., 351.

66. *The Chicago Call*, reprinted in *The Orthodox Evangelicals: Who They Are and What They Are Saying*, ed. Robert E. Webber and Donald Bloesch (Nashville: Thomas Nelson, 1978), 16.

67. *Chicago Call*, 16.

68. Oden, *Life in the Spirit*, 307.

find rampant in the mainline churches. This perceived nominalism leads more separatistic evangelicals to shy away from engaging in common cause, let alone contemplating organizational union, with these churches. Other evangelicals, especially those within mainline churches, tend to view ecumenical endeavors as sidelining the church from what ought to be its true focus, namely, internal renewal and evangelism.

The ambiguity that typifies evangelicals in general is evident in Erickson's treatment of church unity. The evangelical theologian boldly asserts that the underlying spiritual unity Christians share ought to come to expression "in goodwill, fellowship, and love for one another."[69] But the "fellowship" he envisions appears to be quite ad hoc and narrow in focus. Nowhere does Erickson even hint that Christian unity makes it incumbent on believers to take steps toward organizational union. Instead, the strongest statement he can muster is the declaration that "Christians of all types should work together whenever possible" but especially in the church's evangelistic task.[70]

The typical neo-evangelical ambiguity is perhaps even more pronounced in the short discussion Wayne Grudem devotes to the question of unity in his lengthy *Systematic Theology*. On the one hand, Grudem admits that the New Testament teaching on church unity means that "we are also to work for the unity of the visible church."[71] But on the other hand, he is clearly not disturbed by the current lack of unity. Going against the standard ecumenical appraisal of the situation, Grudem asserts that "the existence of different denominations, mission boards, Christian educational institutions, college ministries, and so forth is not necessarily a mark of disunity of the church."[72] Moreover, he defends such diversity both historically ("There are sometimes reasons why the outward or visible unity of the church cannot be maintained")[73] and pragmatically ("There may be a great deal of cooperation and frequent demonstrations of unity among such diverse bodies as these").[74] Grudem is quite sure that the kind of visible unity the New Testament enjoins on believers does not entail organizational union, especially in the form of "one worldwide church government over all Christians."[75] Rather, for valid expressions of "the unity of believers," Grudem looks to such things as "voluntary cooperation and affiliation among Christian groups" as well as such grassroots enterprises as the charismatic movement and neighborhood Bible

69. Erickson, *Christian Theology*, 3:1146.
70. Ibid.
71. Grudem, *Systematic Theology*, 877.
72. Ibid.
73. Ibid., 878.
74. Ibid., 877.
75. Ibid.

study groups. Such enterprises have been a more potent force for unity than the ecumenical movement, which in his estimation has been "without noteworthy success."[76]

Evangelicals have not stood alone in questioning either the value or the theological basis of modern ecumenism. Some mainline Protestant theologians, for example, have rejected the official, church-sponsored form it has assumed, calling instead for a practical, missional, or "secular" ecumenism that is directed outward rather than inward and whose focus is on the world rather than on the churches. John Macquarrie explains:

> The primary aim of the secular ecumenist is the unity of mankind. This type of ecumenism therefore comes as a timely reminder that the end of history, according to Christian belief, is not the church but the kingdom of heaven, and this is a more inclusive concept, gathering up both church and world in an eschatological unity. Our primary aim should not be the unity of the church. We look beyond that to the unity of mankind.[77]

Critics likewise claim that in his prayer that his disciples "may be one" (John 17:21), Jesus could not have had organizational unity in view.[78] On the contrary, they argue that Jesus' explanatory statement, "as we are one," indicates that the desired unity is of a personal and hence spiritual nature. To cite Macquarrie once again,

> The unity is personal unity, and it is personal unity of the most perfect kind, the unity of the Father and the Son. Carrying the argument a step further, it is the unity of the persons of the Trinity. Leaving aside the question of how exactly we are to understand the word "person" in the context of trinitarian discourse, we can at least say that the divine Triunity represents the ultimate fulfilment of diversity-in-unity and unity-in-diversity and that the imperfect personal and social unities of human life afford some dim prefiguring of that ultimate unity of the Three-in-One.[79]

For a variety of reasons, then, neo-evangelicals are generally not interested in the kind of modern ecumenism that focuses on the task of creating institutional union. But this does not mean that the evangelical movement is completely devoid of an ecumenical impetus. On the contrary, as a coalition that draws adherents from a variety of confessional bodies, evangelicalism is inher-

76. Ibid., 879.

77. John Macquarrie, *Christian Unity and Christian Diversity* (Philadelphia: Westminster, 1975), 25.

78. Rudolf Bultmann, *The Gospel of John: A Commentary*, trans. G. R. Beasley-Murray et al. (Philadelphia: Westminster, 1971), 512–13.

79. Macquarrie, *Christian Unity and Christian Diversity*, 43.

ently ecumenical. But the movement displays a unique type or style, one that might be termed a "believer ecumenicism" rather than the "church ecumenism" that typifies the modern ecumenical movement. Instead of seeing the ecumenical task as directed primarily toward confessional bodies, evangelical ecumenism generally concentrates on believers, in keeping with its focus on the invisible church. Rather than seeking the mutual recognition of the major church traditions, evangelical ecumenism—often informed by a commitment to the principle of denominationalism—attempts to bring about the mutual recognition of believers of differing confessional loyalties. And by uniting Christians of various denominational affiliations through involvement in endeavors of common interest to them all, the evangelical movement has become what Gerald Bray calls "an ecumenical church on the ground."[80]

Toward a Renewal of Evangelical Ecclesiology

The parachurch nature of evangelicalism as an "ecumenical church on the ground" has been undergirded by the denominationalism evangelicals developed in the eighteenth and nineteenth centuries focused on the invisible church. The contemporary context, however, occasions the reopening of the ecclesiological question that evangelicals have been seemingly quite happy to ignore. As the discussion in chapter 8 intimates, postmodern pluralism has elevated the apologetic role of the religious community within the context of interreligious conversation. The postmodern situation looks to the church to be the practical demonstration of the reality of its message, that is, to be the embodiment of the gospel invitation to enter into fellowship with God in the divine triune fullness. In such a situation, the ecclesiological question can no longer be answered merely by appeal to the true church as an invisible, spiritual reality, together with the denominationalist compromise. Rather, the postmodern, pluralist context calls for an apologetic evangelical theology that reaffirms the place of the church as a people and, in a certain sense, as a soteriologically relevant reality.

The Marks of the True Church

The way to begin the development of such an ecclesiology is by looking again at the Reformation understanding of the relationship between the invisible church and the visible church. More particularly, the ecclesiolog-

---

80. Gerald Bray, "What Is the Church? An Ecclesiology for Today," in *Restoring the Vision: Anglican Evangelicals Speak Out*, ed. Melvin Tinker (Eastbourne: MARC, 1990), 208.

ical engagement necessary for a renewed evangelical apologetic theology finds its orientation point in the Reformers' use of the traditional concept of the "marks" of the church, the *notae ecclesiae*.

The Reformation "Marks"

In describing the true church in accordance with its essential characteristics, i.e., the *notae*, the Reformers were not charting new territory. On the contrary, they were merely appealing to a theological tradition that Christians shared since the formulation of the Nicene-Constantinopolitan Creed. This creed bequeathed to subsequent generations what by the time of the Reformation had been the standard approach to the question of ecclesiology, namely, the practice of describing the church by appeal to four adjectives: the church is "one, holy, catholic, and apostolic."[81]

The Reformers did not reject outright the use of these four adjectives as appropriate descriptors for the church; indeed, they accepted these creedal marks as comprising its essential "notes" or characteristics. What raised their ire was the use to which Roman Catholic theologians had put these terms. Specifically, in claiming that the Roman Catholic Church was the true church, the Catholic theologians predicated the characteristics of the institution centered in Rome. Avery Dulles underscores the institutional focus of Roman Catholic ecclesiology in the wake of medieval theology:

> In Roman Catholic apologetics from the fifteenth to the mid-twentieth century, the notes were usually understood in function of a highly institutional concept of the Church. The Church was statically viewed as a society having certain attributes definitively given to it by Christ.[82]

In keeping with this focus, Dulles adds, Roman Catholic thinkers understood the four marks as characterizing a visible society. Hence, unity referred to the subordination of all the faithful to the same spiritual jurisdiction and teaching magisterium. Catholicity meant that the one Church spread throughout the world shared the same creed, worship, and system of canon law. Holiness focused on the life of the visible community and especially on the sanctity of the means that fostered holiness, such as the sacramental system and the moral guidance of an infallible magisterium. And apostolicity referred to the legitimate succession of pastors, as well as their approval by Rome.[83]

---

81. See, for example, John H. Leith, ed., *Creeds of the Churches*, 3d ed. (Atlanta: John Knox, 1982), 33.

82. Dulles, *Models of the Church*, 133.

83. Ibid., 133–34.

The Reformers steadfastly rejected the Roman Catholic premise. One means they used to avoid what they perceived as the error of equating the church with the visible institution was by appeal to the concept of the invisible church and to the resultant contrast between the invisible nature of the church and its earthly institutional form. Yet for Luther at least, the designation "invisible church" referred primarily to the hidden nature of the believers' relationship to God in Christ and not to some Platonic idea of a heavenly reality disembodied from the church in the world. Luther's intention was not to suggest that the true church is only "invisible," but that its deepest meaning as a christological reality is hidden with Christ in God.[84] The church, he added, can never be completely invisible, for it always becomes visible in a physical manifestation. For Luther the marks, in turn, provided the vital link between these two aspects of the church.

Luther's followers, and perhaps even Luther himself, later lost this nuanced understanding of the *notae* as the linchpin connecting the two aspects of the church. The Protestant temptation was to link the creedal marks, understood as the essential characteristics of the true church, solely with the invisible church, viewed as the number of the elect, or, in the case of evangelicalism, as the company of the truly converted, known only to God. In 1846 Hugh McNeile, to cite one example, offered a typically evangelical interpretation of the creedal marks. In his book, *The Church and the Churches*, he asserted that the true church is the invisible church composed of the elect of all ages and places. He then articulated an understanding of the *notae* in keeping with his linking of the true church with the invisible company of the regenerate. The church is "one," McNeile explained, in that the elect are united with Christ by the one Holy Spirit; "holy" because each member is indwelt by the Holy Spirit and being made holy by the power of God's grace; "catholic" in that the elect represent every age of world history and every country of the world's geography; and "apostolic" insofar as believers continue steadfastly in apostolic doctrine and fellowship as described in Scripture.[85]

This viewpoint has not been the sole domain of non-conformist or free church evangelicals. On the contrary, even evangelical Anglicans have been known to run to the invisible church when the conversation turns to the *notae ecclesiae*. Above all, the true unity of the church is often predicated of the invisible, in contrast to the visible, church. Church of England vicar Melvin Tinker typifies this tendency. In his presentation of

---

84. Avis, *Church in the Theology of the Reformers*, 5.

85. Hugh McNeile, *The Church and the Churches; or, The Church of God in Christ, and the Churches of Christ Militant Here on Earth* (London: J. Hatchard and Son, 1846), 70, 128, 220, 224.

what he sees as a solidly evangelical ecclesiology, Tinker writes, "The fact is, all true believers *are* one (we are back to the invisible church again)."[86] Further, in Tinker's estimation the spiritual unity that characterizes the invisible church finds its proper visible expression within the local church. In fact, he goes so far as to reject the modern tendency to equate "church" with "denomination," a tendency that he sees as the source of the confusion abounding in the ecumenical movement. Reminiscent of certain congregationalists, Tinker suggests that rather than being churches, denominations are actually parachurch institutions, "ideally organized to facilitate and encourage the work of the local church."[87]

Although the Reformers clearly accepted the creedal marks as *notae ecclesiae*, in their conflict with Rome they did not focus their attention on these four adjectives. In their estimation, such an appeal did not actually solve the ecclesiological problem, for describing the nature of the church as one, holy, catholic, and apostolic did not delineate where that true church was in fact to be found.[88] For the answer to this question, the Reformers turned to other marks, which they found better suited as determinative characteristics of the true church in its visible form.

The most consistent Reformation answer to the question, Where can the true church be found? entailed an appeal to Word and sacrament. To cite Calvin's well-known formulation, "Wherever we see the Word of God sincerely preached and heard, wherever we see the sacraments administered according to the institution of Christ, there we cannot have any doubt that the Church of God has some existence. . . . "[89] Other Reformers, such as Bucer, added discipline as a third mark, a step that Luther avoided and Calvin did not take explicitly, perhaps because he saw discipline as intrinsic to the proclamation of the Word.[90] Actually, Luther at times went in the opposite direction, reducing the marks to one—the preaching of the Word—insofar as he believed that through the preached Word Christ reigns. In Luther's words,

> These are the true marks whereby one can really recognize the kingdom of the Lord Christ and the Christian Church: namely, wherever this scepter is, that is, the office of the preaching of the Gospel, borne by the apostles into

86. Melvin Tinker, "Towards an Evangelical Ecclesiology (Part One)," *Churchman* 105, no. 1 (1991): 25.

87. Melvin Tinker, "Towards an Evangelical Ecclesiology (Part Two)," *Churchman* 105, no. 2 (1991): 143.

88. Avis, *Church in the Theology of the Reformers*, 8.

89. Calvin, *Institutes of the Christian Religion*, 4.1.9, 289.

90. For this judgment, see Timothy E. Fulop, "The Third Mark of the Church?—Church Discipline in the Reformed and Anabaptist Reformations," *Journal of Religious History* 19, no. 1 (June 1995): 35.

the world and received from them by us. Where it is present and maintained, there the Christian Church and the kingdom of Christ surely exist, no matter how small or negligible the number of the flock.[91]

The "Marks" and the Local Character of the Church

Taken as a whole, the predominant impulse of the Reformation elevated the community gathered around Word and sacrament. In the appraisal of J. S. Whale, even Calvin, who conceived of the church primarily as the invisible company of the elect, also viewed it "as the visible body of believers recognizable by their corporate participation in the preached and heard Word, and in the Sacraments."[92] In fact, this focus set the Reformers' ecclesiology apart from the medieval Roman Catholic emphasis on the clergy, which had effectively devalued the gathered fellowship. According to Whale, "For Protestantism, the community of believers is the constitutive essence of the Church; its *sine qua non*. The faith, worship and life of the Church are meaningless without the *societas fidelium*, a fellowship of those who are gathered in the Spirit and united by love."[93]

This Reformation principle has recently led to a new focus on the local nature of the church, from which, in turn, emerges the universal church as the interconnection of all local congregations. In the words of the Gospel and Our Culture project team, "The movement toward missional connectedness should be centrifugal, starting from particular communities and expanding to the global dimensions of the church, the community of communities."[94]

When the universal church is viewed as the "community of communities," the unity of the one church in the world can no longer imply complete uniformity in all aspects of church life. The plurality of the one church is a theme that finds echo among many ecumenists today. Avery Dulles, for example, claims that the Vatican II Decree on Ecumenism "takes pains to stress that unity does not imply uniformity, and that there is room for an enormous variety of rites and procedures within the Catholic family."[95] According to Donald Miller, not only can the churches display diversity in ritual and church structure, but even uniformity of doc-

---

91. Martin Luther, *Luther's Works*, ed. Jaroslav Pelikan et al. (St. Louis: Concordia, 1955–86), 13:272. Here Luther is commenting on Ps. 110:2 regarding the "scepter of the Lord's kingdom."

92. J. S. Whale, *Christian Reunion: Historic Divisions Reconsidered* (Grand Rapids: Eerdmans, 1971), 28.

93. Ibid., 25–26.

94. Darrell L. Guder et al., *Missional Church: A Vision for the Sending of the Church in North America* (Grand Rapids: Eerdmans, 1998), 265.

95. Avery Dulles, *The Dimensions of the Church: A Postconciliar Reflection* (Westminster, Mich.: Newman, 1967), 40.

trine "is not of the essence of the church," a point that must be revisited in chapter 10.[96]

Despite diversity, the various churches also display an essential commonality that marks them as specifically Christian. A central feature of the commonality shared by all Christian congregations emerges from a consideration of another emphasis that has paralleled the contemporary rediscovery of the local nature of the church, namely, the church as "community." Avery Dulles provides an illuminating summary of the implications of the turn to community for a proper understanding of the creedal marks of the church, that is, of the "notes":

> In the community model of the Church, the notes are no longer interpreted as the visible marks of a given society, but rather as qualities of a living community. The Church is no longer exclusively identified with any one society or institution, but is seen as a mystery operative both within and beyond the borders of any given organization.[97]

When seen from the perspective of the church as community, the *notae ecclesiae* no longer are the exclusive property of any particular institution. Instead, they encapsulate "a task for every Christian community." In short, according to Dulles, "The Church must aspire to be ever more fully one, holy, catholic, and apostolic."[98]

To Dulles's appraisal might be added the suggestion that being community is likewise not a given condition, but a shared task. In that it is in a sense the goal of the fellowship of Christ's disciples, viewing the church as a community offers a central motif that could potentially lead to the delineation of a renewed evangelical ecclesiology.

To speak of the church as fundamentally community is not to suggest that the biblical writers themselves thought in terms of this category. As Stephen C. Barton rightly declares, "Paul was not a sociologist before his time trying to understand what 'community' is." Indeed, "Paul's talk is not about 'community' but about how Jews and Gentiles, men and women, slave and freeborn can embody and celebrate the eschatological life of the kingdom of God."[99] The sociological word *community* nevertheless offers a conceptual tool for understanding the essential nature of the church.

A truly helpful community-focused ecclesiology takes seriously the evangelical commitment to convertive piety, while looking to the Refor-

---

96. Miller, *Nature and Mission of the Church*, 126.
97. Dulles, *Models of the Church*, 135–36.
98. Ibid.
99. Stephen C. Barton, "Christian Community in the Light of 1 Corinthians," *Studies in Christian Ethics* 10, no. 1 (1997): 15.

mation principle of the visible church as community gathered around Word and sacrament.

The Church as Community

The Enlightenment brought in its wake an individualist impulse that elevates the human person as the logical *prius* of all forms of social life, and views the contract between individuals as the basis of all social interaction. Individualism promotes such values as personal freedom, self-improvement, privacy, achievement, independence, detachment, and self-interest.[100] It sees society, in turn, as the product of autonomous selves who enter into voluntary relationship with each other. More particularly, the state is the creation of a "social contract" in which individuals agree to give up a certain amount of their personal prerogatives to the whole for the sake of personal advantage.

Voluntarist contractualism finds its ecclesiological counterpart in the view of the church as the voluntary association of individual believers. Rather than constituting its members, the church is constituted *by* believers, who are deemed to be in a sense complete "spiritual selves" prior to, and apart from, membership in the church. In this manner, the (visible) church, which is by necessity concretized in separate congregations, becomes an aggregate of the individual Christians' "contract" with each other to form the "society" of Christians.[101] In evangelical ecclesiology, this concept of the visible church routinely provides the counterpart to the parallel understanding of the invisible church as the total number of the truly regenerate. Evangelicals tend to speak of individual Christians as being members of the true, invisible church, prior to and apart from their contracting with each other to form local congregations.

In recent years, radical individualism has been under attack. Voices from a variety of disciplines have been calling for a rediscovery of the communal tradition, while maintaining the valid and helpful insights of individualism. The postmodern situation has led likewise to a questioning of an individualistically oriented contractual ecclesiology. Properly understood, the contractual understanding of the church can embody and protect the principle of the priesthood of all believers. Nevertheless, under the impulse of individualism, it all too easily reduces the community of

100. Gerry C. Heard, *Basic Values and Ethical Decisions: An Examination of Individualism and Community in American Society* (Malabar, Fla.: R. E. Krieger, 1990), 3.

101. Bloesch is an example of those thinkers who bemoan the "appalling neglect" of ecclesiology in evangelicalism, which he believes is due in part to the emphasis on individual decision, as evangelicals give priority to the decision of faith rather than to nurture; Donald G. Bloesch, *The Future of Evangelical Christianity* (Garden City, N.Y.: Doubleday, 1983), 127.

Christ's disciples to little more than what Robert Bellah calls a "lifestyle enclave," a group of individuals united by their shared interest in certain practices, or who believe that membership in this particular group will contribute to their personal good.[102] The way forward for evangelical ecclesiology in the contemporary context requires a rediscovery of the sense of the church as community.

The Church as a Community of Word and Sacrament

Chapter 8 drew from George Herbert Mead and others in noting that personal identity is socially produced and that communities play a crucial role in the process. Contemporary narrative thinkers[103] theorize that identity emerges as a person selects certain events from one's past and uses them as a basis for interpreting the significance of the whole of one's life. This identity, however, requires an "interpretive scheme" that provides the "plot" through which the chronicle of a person's life makes sense, an interpretive framework that arises from one's social context or "tradition."[104] By mediating the communal narrative necessary for personal identity formation, a community shapes the identity of its participants and thereby functions as a "reference group"[105] or a "community of reference." This perspective provides a vantage point from which to understand both the church as a fellowship of the converted and the Reformation insight that the church is a community of believers gathered around Word and sacrament.

Ultimately, the church is the product of the work of the Spirit. As was noted in chapter 6, the Spirit creates the church by speaking through the biblical text and thereby brings into being a converted people, that is, a people who forsake their old lives so as to inhabit the new, eschatological world centered on Jesus Christ who is the Word. For this reason, rather than being merely the aggregate of its members, the church is a people imbued with a particular "constitutive narrative," namely, the biblical narrative of God at work bringing creation to its divinely intended goal. The church is a community of the converted, therefore, because the biblical narrative provides its participants with the interpretive framework

102. Robert N. Bellah et al., *Habits of the Heart: Individualism and Commitment in American Life* (Berkeley: University of California Press, 1985), 72.

103. For a lucid statement of this theory, see George W. Stroup, *The Promise of Narrative Theology* (Atlanta: John Knox, 1981), 101–98.

104. Here narrative thinkers like Stroup are in substantial agreement with social constructionist sociologists, such as Peter Berger. See, for example, Peter L. Berger, *The Sacred Canopy: Elements of a Sociological Theory of Religion* (Garden City, N.Y.: Doubleday, 1969), 20.

105. Peter L. Berger, *Invitation to Sociology: A Humanistic Perspective* (Harmondsworth, England: Penguin, 1963), 118.

through which they individually and corporately find their identity as those who are "in Christ" and through which they view life and the world.

Although the church is constituted by the Spirit, the proclamation of the Word is the vehicle through which the Spirit engages in this constituting work, and such proclamation is ultimately an activity of the church viewed as a community of reference. As the faith community retells the biblical narrative that constitutes it as a people, it mediates to its members the interpretive framework—the narrative plot—through which they find meaning in their personal and communal stories.

Contemporary community theory provides additional insight into this process. The role of any group as a community of reference is connected with its ability to forge a link both to the past and to the future, that is, with its ability to function as what Josiah Royce called a "community of memory" and a "community of hope."[106] Every community has a history; in fact, it is in an important sense constituted by that history. This constitutive narrative begins "in the beginning," with the primal event(s) that called the community into being. Rather than forgetting its past, a community retells the story of its genesis and of the crucial milestones and struggles that have marked its subsequent trajectory.[107] Recalling the narrative past places the contemporary community within the primal events that constituted their forebears as this particular community. By retelling the narrative, the community retrieves its past—i.e., brings the past into the present—and thereby the narrative reconstitutes the present participants as the contemporary embodiment of a communal tradition that spans the years.

Rather than ending in the past, the narrative history extends into the future. By expectantly looking to the ideal or "eschatological" future when its purpose and goals, its *telos*, will be fully actualized, a community turns the gaze of its members toward the future. This expectation of a glorious future serves as an ongoing admonition to participants to embody the communal vision in the present. It stands as a reminder that they are to be in the here-and-now the anticipatory manifestation of the reality that will one day characterize their community in its fullness.

By narrating an overarching, "cosmic" story that spans the ages, the community's constitutive narrative provides a transcendent vantage point for life in the present. It bestows a qualitative meaning upon life, upon time and space, and upon community members as they inhabit their world. The recited narrative provides the overarching plot through which members of the community can view their lives and the present moment

---

106. Josiah Royce, *Problem of Christianity* (New York: Macmillan, 1913), 2:50–51.
107. Bellah et al., *Habits of the Heart*, 152–55.

in history as a part of a stream of time that transcends every particular "now." Likewise, it supplies a context of meaning that allows community members to connect their personal aspirations with those of a larger whole, and facilitates them in seeing their efforts as contributions to that whole. In this manner, as the community retells its constitutive narrative it functions as an "interpretive community," to borrow Royce's term.[108]

The church is a community in this sense. By proclaiming the biblical narrative, the church links the present with the entire history of God's action, a history that begins "in the beginning" (Gen. 1:1) and spans the ages, climaxing in "a new heaven and a new earth" (Rev. 21:1). Through their connection with the community that is constituted by this narrative, believers find their lives linked with something greater, something transcendent, namely the work of the biblical God in history. And finding one's life within the salvific work of God is in this sense the essence of conversion. Moreover, by proclaiming the biblical narrative of God at work in history centered in Jesus Christ, the church becomes a people focused on the Word and gathered around the Word.

A functioning community does not only retell its constitutive narrative. Rather, the "Word" is accentuated through sacred practices or "rites of intensification." These rituals "bring the community together, increase group solidarity, and reinforce commitment to the beliefs of the group," to cite the description of Christian cultural anthropologists Stephen Grunlan and Marvin Mayers.[109] Such "practices of commitment" define the community way of life, as well as the patterns of loyalty and obligation that keep the community alive.[110] Through their participation in these acts, members come to sense that they comprise a community.[111]

"Practices of commitment," to use Bellah's phrase,[112] lead directly to the "sacrament" side of the Reformation couplet of "Word and sacrament." As many Christian thinkers from Augustine to the Reformers have suggested, baptism and the Lord's supper are visual sermons; they constitute the Word of God symbolically proclaimed.[113] More particularly, these acts are visual, symbolic embodiments of the constitutive narrative of the Christian community. By linking participants with the biblical narrative, at the heart of which is the life, passion, and resurrection of Jesus and the

108. Royce, *Problem of Christianity*, 2:211.

109. Stephen A. Grunlan and Marvin K. Mayers, *Cultural Anthropology: A Christian Perspective*, 2d ed. (Grand Rapids: Zondervan, 1988), 222.

110. Bellah et al., *Habits of the Heart*, 152–54.

111. Robert A. Nisbet, *The Sociological Tradition* (New York: Basic Books, 1966), 48.

112. Bellah et al., *Habits of the Heart*, 152–54.

113. See, for example, Calvin, *Institutes of the Christian Religion*, 4.14.4, 493–94, where he insists on linking the Word with the external signs, so the participant may understand and believe in their significance.

sending of the Spirit, these acts function together with the proclamation of the Word in the Spirit's identity-forming, community-building work.

Baptism and the Lord's supper are visual sermons in that they recount in a dramatic, symbolic manner the Christian declaration that "God was in Christ reconciling the world unto himself" (2 Cor. 5:19 KJV). To this end, these practices serve as vivid memorials, recalling Christ's accomplished work on behalf of humankind. Their meaning goes beyond mere memorial, however. Participation in the acts facilitates symbolic participation in the saving events that form the foundation for Christian identity as persons united with Christ. As visual sermons, the acts of commitment symbolically transport the faith community into the narrative past. Through these symbols believers reenact the story of Christ's death and resurrection, as well as their conversion, that is, their own death and resurrection with Christ. Thereby the Spirit vividly confirms in their hearts their identity as new persons in Christ (2 Cor. 5:17).

Baptism and the Lord's supper bring not only the narrative past, but also the eschatological future into view. These acts symbolically announce the promise that God will one day bring the divine creative work to completion, but more importantly that this completion constitutes the true identity of the believer, the believing community, and even all creation. Not only do baptism and the Lord's supper announce this truth, through these acts believers symbolically take part in that grand event, as participants in the rites of the community are drawn to celebrate in the midst of the brokenness of the present the glorious fullness of a future reality that is already at work in their midst and in the world by the Spirit.

In short, "sacrament" is integrally connected to "Word." Baptism and the Lord's supper comprise vivid, symbolic declarations of the gospel narrative. Like the proclamation of the Word itself, its symbolic embodiment connects the contemporary believing community with the biblical story that it presents. As participants symbolically experience the foundational events of Christ's death and resurrection and are gathered into the vision of God's future, their lives are linked to God's creative-salvific action, the narrative of which is the plotline of all of history. And this transcendent vantage point, in turn, becomes the vehicle through which the Spirit empowers the community for the task of living as the eschatological community, founded upon their union with Christ, in the here and now.

Viewing the church as community in this manner indicates how the church is essentially local and yet universal. The church is primarily local, for it is, of course, the local fellowship that gathers faithfully around Word and sacrament. It is in the context of the local fellowship of believers that the biblical narrative is proclaimed and ritually embodied. At the same time, the constitutive biblical narrative is neither the invention nor the exclusive possession of any one congregation. It is rather a shared story, a story shared by all who in every place gather around Word and sacrament, and hence a story that transcends all local congregations. Further, the proclaimed Word and the administered sacraments also transcend the local gathering, for they belong to each faithful congregation of believers. The shared nature of the narrative and of its proclamation in Word and sacrament not only brings together the many believers into a local congregation, therefore, but also unites each local gathering of believers with all other congregations of the faithful. For this reason, the church, which is fundamentally the particular, local congregation gathered around Word and sacrament, nevertheless simultaneously transcends any one local congregation and all local congregations.

The Creedal Marks and the Missional Church

The Reformation effectively substituted Word and sacrament for the creedal marks as the focus for understanding the *notae ecclesiae*. Yet this shift did not mean that the Reformers had no place for the traditional adjectives. On the contrary, they agreed that the true church was to be characterized by unity, holiness, catholicity, and apostolicity. Yet they saw these four traits more as eschatological goals to be sought than as attributes that can be realized by the church on earth.[114] In this sense, the four adjectives became for the Reformers the essential marks of the true church hidden within the ecclesiastical institution and thus the attributes of the church in its invisible fullness. Yet, ecclesiology would go astray if the "ideal" status of the marks were allowed to lead to the conclusion that they are the prerogative solely of some invisible church that is totally disjointed from the church in the world.

In keeping with the Reformation emphasis on the eschatological direction of the creedal marks, some theologians view these traits as essentially dynamic, rather than static. Rather than characterizing any one particular institution, they set forth the task shared by the people of God. The dynamic reading of the marks readily fosters a missiological ecclesiology, which arises in part out of an innovative interpretation of the church's apostolicity as declaring that the church is *sent* (from *apostello* meaning "send out") into the world with the gospel and thus is by its very nature a missionary church.[115] Missiologist Charles Van Engen takes this insight a step farther. He suggests that the marks are better read as adverbs rather than adjectives so as thereby to capture the dynamic character of the church's mission faithfulness. In his estimation, the *notae ecclesiae* describe

---

114. Avis, *Church in the Theology of the Reformers*, 8.
115. See, for example, Tinker, "Towards an Evangelical Ecclesiology (Part One)," 25.

the missional ministry of the church as unifying, sanctifying, reconciling, and proclaiming. He boldly asserts the missional essence of the church when he answers his own question,

> What is the Church? It is the unifying, sanctifying, reconciling, and proclaiming activity of Jesus Christ in the world. Mission cannot be something separate from or added to the essence of the Church. The essential nature of the local congregation is, in and of itself, mission, or else the congregation is not really the Church.[116]

A missional view of the church opens the way for a return to the missional ecumenism that motivated the inauguration of the modern ecumenical movement. It also facilitates an ecclesiology that keeps the primary focus on the local community of believers gathered around Word and sacrament, but gathered for the sake of the church's mission. The goal of ecumenism, in turn, becomes the mutual affirmation and cooperation in mission of the global network of local congregations.

The Faith and Our Culture work group, however, offer an additional and immensely helpful suggestion: The four marks ought to be placed in reverse order. Consequently, the missional church is called to be a "proclaiming, reconciling, sanctifying and unifying" community.[117] This reversal in order stands as a reminder of the directedness of the church's missional task and hence its ultimate goal. Seen from this perspective, the four creedal marks paint a picture of a church active in mission.

First, the church active in mission is apostolic, i.e., it is a proclaiming community. The church, then, is truly apostolic not only as it stands in continuity with the apostles' doctrine. Rather an apostolic church is one that takes seriously its calling in the divine program to be a fellowship that continually proclaims through Word and sacrament the good news of God's action in Christ and in so doing patterns its life after the example of Jesus, the one sent from God, as well as the apostles whom he in turn sent into the world.

Second, the church in mission is truly catholic, insofar as it is a reconciling community. Essentially reconciliation involves bringing into wholesome relationships those whose differences readily occasion hostilities. The missional church engages continually in the work of being an agent of the divine reconciliation. This includes, of course, seeking fervently and untiringly to bring into the fellowship of Word and sacrament—both locally and, by extension, globally—people in all their diversity. But catholicity in the sense of carrying

---

116. Charles Van Engen, *God's Missionary People: Rethinking the Purpose of the Local Church* (Grand Rapids: Baker, 1991), 70.

117. Guder et al., *Missional Church*, 255.

on a reconciling mission entails as well acting to foster wholesome relationships among humans in every dimension of life and existence.

The third mark, holiness, has several dimensions, but at the heart of its biblical meaning are the twin aspects of being set apart for God's use (e.g., Exod. 28:41)[118] and attempting to pattern human life after the example of God (hence, Matt. 5:43–48; 1 Pet. 1:15–16). This provides the context to picture the church as a sanctifying community. The church's sanctifying mission is both internal and external. As the *ecclesia semper reformanda*, the faith community continually reforms its own pattern of life, of course, and this as it repeatedly gathers to hear the Word anew and to celebrate the sacraments afresh. But it also seeks to be a people whose presence in the world results in God's name being "hallowed," in accordance with Jesus' own prayer (Matt. 6:9).

Finally, the church is one in that the mission of the church is intended to exert a unifying effect. This unifying mission begins, of course, with "the house of God" (1 Pet. 4:17 KJV). The church's quest to foster unity is to be operative primarily within the local congregation (e.g., Phil. 2:2), among those who gather together around the unifying participation in word and sacrament (1 Cor. 12:13; 10:17), and then by extension among all congregations that share the same Word and the same sacred acts. But as John Macquarrie and others have noted, the unifying impulse of the missional church extends beyond itself. As it gathers around Word and sacrament in this penultimate age, the community bears witness to, and seeks to anticipate—in celebration as well as in concrete ways—the Spirit's fashioning of one new humanity in Christ (Eph. 2:15) and the eschatological day when God will dwell with the redeemed in the renewed creation (Rev. 21:1–5; 22:1–5).

Theological Ecclesiology and the Church Visible/Invisible

The church is a people mandated with a mission, and this missional community is one, holy, catholic, and apostolic in that it engages in a mission that is proclaiming, reconciling, sanctifying, and unifying. As helpful as the missional approach is, the descriptions outlined above do not fully explicate the ecclesiology needed for an apologetic evangelical theology. One additional dimension is required, namely, ecclesiology's theological context.

Reflection on the *notae ecclesiae* has led some theologians in recent years to the recognition that ultimately the church's character is determined by its connection with its Lord. This means that the creedal marks must be predi-

118. Robert G. Girdlestone, *Synonyms of the Old Testament* (1897; reprint, Grand Rapids: Eerdmans, 1973).

cated first of the triune God active in and through the church, and then by extension to the church as the people through whom God works. According to Jürgen Moltmann, for example, "The church receives the attributes named from the activity of Christ in the workings of the Spirit for the coming kingdom."[119] Moltmann then draws out the implications for the *notae*:

> If the church acquires its existence through the activity of Christ, then her characteristics, too, are characteristics of Christ's activity first of all. The acknowledgment of the 'one, holy, catholic and apostolic church' is acknowledgment of the uniting, sanctifying, comprehensive and commissioning lordship of Christ.[120]

Moltmann's insight stands as a reminder that ecclesiology must ultimately arise out of theology, rather than anthropology or cosmology. Viewed as a missional community, then, the church finds its central qualities in the mission of the triune God. The church's true nature as a community sent by God arises from its mandate to be the bearer of the divine mission in the world, a mission that is directed not merely toward all humankind, but toward all creation. But even more significant, the church's identity as a community must emerge out of the identity of the God it serves and in whom its life is hidden, to allude to Luther's description of the invisible church. This theological ecclesiology provides the final link between the church in the world (i.e., the so-called "visible church") and the church in its essential nature (or the "invisible church").

At the heart of the biblical narrative is the story of God bringing humankind to be the *imago dei*, that is, to be the reflection of the divine character, love (1 John 4:8, 16). Because God is the triune one, the three persons-in-relationship, the *imago dei* must in some sense entail humans in relationship as well, i.e., humans who through their relationships reflect the divine love (1 John 4:7–8).[121] The church's calling is related to this universal human design to be the divine image.[122] The church is to be a people who reflect in relation to each other and to all creation the character of the Creator and thereby bear witness to the divine purpose for hu-

---

119. Jürgen Moltmann, *The Church in the Power of the Spirit: A Contribution to Messianic Ecclesiology*, trans. Margaret Kohl (New York: Harper and Row, 1977), 338.

120. Ibid.

121. For a discussion of the implications of the social Trinity for the concept of the image of God, see Cornelius Plantinga, Jr., "Images of God," in *Christian Faith and Practice in the Modern World*, ed. Mark A. Noll and David F. Wells (Grand Rapids: Eerdmans, 1988), 59–67.

122. For a recent exploration of this theme, see Miroslav Volf, *After Our Likeness: The Church as the Image of the Trinity* (Grand Rapids: Eerdmans, 1998). See also Miroslav Volf, "Kirche als Gemeinschaft: Ekklesiologische Überlegungen aus freikirchlicher Perspektive," *Evangelische Theologie* 49, no. 1 (1989): 70–76; Kilian McDonnell, "Vatican II (1962–1964), Puebla (1979), Synod (1985): *Koinonia/Communio* as an Integral Ecclesiology," *Journal of Ecumenical Studies* 25, no. 3 (Summer 1988): 414.

mankind. This fundamental calling to be the foretaste of the *imago dei*, in turn, determines the church's proclaiming, reconciling, sanctifying, and unifying mission in the world.

Ultimately, however, this divine calling to be the *imago dei* does not find its source in God's design for humankind, but in the church's fundamental existence "in Christ." According to the New Testament, Christ is the true image of God (2 Cor. 4:4; Col. 1:15; Heb. 1:3), and through their union with Christ believers share in this designation (Rom. 8:29; 1 Cor. 15:49) by the transforming presence of the Holy Spirit (2 Cor. 3:18). But being in Christ by the Holy Spirit carries far-reaching ecclesiological implications. It suggests that the church gains its true identity through participation in the fountainhead of community, namely, the life of the triune God. The facilitator of this participation is the Holy Spirit, who is the agent of the new birth—conversion—through which event believers become co-heirs with Christ in the family of God (Rom. 8:14–17). By placing believers "in Christ," therefore, the Spirit brings them to participate in the fellowship of the eternal Son with the eternal Father (e.g., Gal. 4:6). As J. M. R. Tillard poignantly declared, "The reality which the Christians have in common and which lays the foundation of their communion is not merely salvation nor even a deep mystical experience. It is another, more fundamental, *koinonia*; the divine communion of the Father and his Son."[123] For this reason, the communal fellowship Christians share is nothing less than a shared participation—a participation together—in the perichoretic community of trinitarian persons.[124]

In the end, participation in the perichoretic dance of the triune God as those who by the Spirit are in Christ is what constitutes community in the highest sense and hence marks the true church. And being a people whose life is hidden in Christ (and hence are the invisible church) even as they live in the world (and therefore remain the visible church) is the present calling of those whose lives have been, and are being, transformed by the Spirit.

The theological ecclesiology outlined here provides the final response to the question of interreligious dialogue raised in chapter 8. The demise of foundationalism endemic to the postmodern condition undercuts any illusion of gaining access to some universal reality called "community" against which every particular embodiment of community (including the church) might be judged. On the contrary, every such judgment can only be made from the perspective of a particular community or tradition. So also Christians can engage in the conversation about the nature

123. J. M. R. Tillard, "What Is the Church of God?" *Mid-stream* 23, no. 4 (October 1984): 371.
124. Ibid., 372–73.

of true community and the truly communal dimension present in human social institutions or expressions only by reference to Christian theological ecclesiology.[125]

Christians declare that the touchstone of community is the eternal triune life and God's gracious inclusion of humans in Christ by the Spirit, constituting them as participants in the perichoretic trinitarian life. This theological-ecclesiological perspective leads Christians to view every social reality in accordance with its potential for being a contribution to, prolepsis of, or signpost on the way toward the participation in the divine life that God desires humans to enjoy. And even while the community of Christ, under the Spirit's guidance, seeks to enhance community in its various forms, believers nevertheless wait expectantly for God to complete the divine work of bringing creation into the enjoyment of the fullness of fellowship as the divinely fashioned eschatological community.

125. Nicholas Lash, *A Matter of Hope: A Theologian's Reflections on the Thought of Karl Marx* (London: Darton, Longman and Todd, 1981), 75.

ten

Renewing
THE Evangelical
"Center"

In a 1987 response to Carl Henry's critique of narrative theology, Hans Frei declared, "My own vision of what might be propitious for our day, split as we are, not so much into denominations as into schools of thought, is that we need a kind of generous orthodoxy which would have in it an element of liberalism . . . and an element of evangelicalism."[1] Later in the short essay, Frei indicated that more than merely a blending of the two traditions, in at least one respect he was actually groping for a way to transcend what he saw as an outmoded liberal-evangelical dichotomy. Hence he mused, "But it may also be that I am looking for a way that looks for a relation between Christian theology and philosophy that disagrees with a view of certainty and knowledge which liberals and evangelicals hold in common."[2]

Viewed from one perspective, this volume is an extended call to evangelicals to take seriously a concern evident within Frei's vision. These pages have emerged out of a sense that the time is ripe to reflect on the type of theological program that might result in a "generous orthodoxy" after the manner that Frei wished to see. The implementation of this vision, however, requires more than merely that liberals see some truth in the conservative position and that conservatives reciprocate the feeling

---

1. Hans Frei, "Response to 'Narrative Theology: An Evangelical Appraisal,'" *Trinity Journal* 8 (Spring 1987): 21.
2. Ibid., 24.

toward liberals. Such a program is as unworkable as it is naive. Rather, what the present situation demands, and in a sense even evokes, is the renewal of a "generous orthodoxy" that is as "orthodox" as it is "generous." The goal of this final chapter is to indicate what "more" might be entailed in the emergence of a theologically attuned generous orthodoxy that could facilitate the church as it seeks to be faithful to its divinely given mandate, and that could enhance the mission of the church as it moves into the future.

Evangelicalism and the "Center"

Despite his farsighted call for a move beyond the liberal-evangelical impasse, Frei's words indicate that he remained captive to the predilection to talk in the categories of the two-party model that appears so pervasive in characterizations of Protestantism, and even Christianity in general, in the United States. This widely used taxonomy suggests that the American scene is monopolized by two opposing camps, the liberal/mainline and the fundamentalist/evangelical, which are at war with each other. The renewal of theology and the creation of a "generous orthodoxy" in our day requires, however, that theologians move beyond this outmoded schema.

The Two-Party Taxonomy and the Impending "Culture Wars"

In the introduction to the collection of essays entitled *Re-Forming the Center* (1998), editors Jacobsen and Trollinger assert that the roots of the "two-party" paradigm lie in the modernist-fundamentalist controversy, which so powerfully shaped American Protestantism in the twentieth century. They report that at the height of this conflict in the early decades of that century, church leaders used two-party language "to depersonalize and demonize their opponents, and to advance their own standing and agendas within their respective denominations or parachurch organizations."[3] Around 1970, the two-party taxonomy invaded the academy, as interpreters of American religious history used the categories of bipolar confrontation to provide the framework for understanding Protestantism in the United States.

Jacobsen and Trollinger cite as one of the first such treatments Martin Marty's *Righteous Empire*,[4] in which the author theorized that two Protes-

---

3. Douglas Jacobsen and William Vance Trollinger, Jr., "Introduction," in *Re-Forming the Center: American Protestantism, 1900 to the Present*, ed. Douglas Jacobsen and William Vance Trollinger, Jr. (Grand Rapids: Eerdmans, 1998), 2.

4. Martin E. Marty, *Righteous Empire: The Protestant Experience in America* (New York: Dial Press, 1970).

tant parties—the "private" and the "public"—have dominated the American religious landscape since the late nineteenth century. Ten years later, in *Fundamentalism and American Culture*,[5] George Marsden imported the two-party framework in its more widely known form into evangelical historical scholarship. Marsden advanced the theory that the unified evangelicalism of the late nineteenth century divided into the liberal-conservative bipolar split characteristic of the twentieth.

Beginning in the late 1980s, sociologists took up the theme. Robert Wuthnow, to cite one significant proponent, argued in *The Restructuring of American Religion*[6] that since World War II, rather than separating entire denominations from each other, the polarization of American Protestantism into "liberal" and "conservative" factions has run right through the middle of almost all mainstream ecclesiastical bodies. This sociological appraisal finds echo not only in Frei but also in theological renditions such as that by J. I. Packer, who defended his willingness to sign the controversial 1994 document, "Evangelicals and Catholics Together," by contending that the church now faces a struggle between those "who honor the Christ of the Bible and of the historic creeds and confessions" and those "who for whatever reason do not," a division which in Packer's estimation "splits the older Protestant bodies and the Roman communion internally."[7] But perhaps the work that has more than any other set the tone of the discussion in recent years is James Davison Hunter's *Culture Wars: The Struggle to Define America*.[8] Expanding on Wuthnow's thesis, Hunter argues that the United States has become the battleground in a widespread war between an "orthodox" party committed to "an external, definable, and transcendent authority," and a "progressive" group who "resymbolize historic faiths according to the prevailing assumptions of contemporary life."[9]

Despite its seemingly undiminished popularity, the two-party approach is now under attack, with historians leading the charge. Critics point to the extraordinary "plasticity" of the model. The remarkable absence of any standard understanding among its users as to what the two parties in fact are makes the entire paradigm a rapidly moving target.[10] Moreover, critics of the two-party framework charge that it grossly misrepresents the great diversity displayed in American Protestantism from the late eigh-

5. George M. Marsden, *Fundamentalism and American Culture: The Shaping of Twentieth-Century Evangelicalism: 1870–1925* (New York: Oxford, 1980).

6. Robert Wuthnow, *The Restructuring of American Religion: Society and Faith Since World War II* (Princeton: Princeton University Press, 1988).

7. J. I. Packer, "Why I Signed It," *Christianity Today* 38, no. 14 (December 12, 1994): 36.

8. James Davison Hunter, *Culture Wars: The Struggle to Define America* (New York: Basic Books, 1991).

9. Ibid., 44–45.

10. Jacobsen and Trollinger, "Introduction," 2.

teenth century to the present. Thus, the simplicity that the model introduces into fund-raising campaigns, denomination takeover crusades, and
even classroom presentations comes at the expense of the complexity of
the subject matter. Jacobsen and Trollinger remark, "Not only were and
are there numerous Protestants who do not truly fit in either party, but
the fault lines within Protestantism are both multiple and constantly shifting, hence ensuring that conflicts did not and do not reflect a single bifur-
cated division."[11]

Considerations such as these have led many scholars to conclude that
although the two-party model has merit in certain, limited contexts, the
time has come to move beyond the constraints of this paradigm which for
too long has provided the cognitive tools for constructing the rhetoric of
"culture wars" that has dominated the discussion. Jacobsen and Trollinger
summarize the situation well by declaring,

> We must reject the notion that we can describe American Protestantism as
> falling along a single line spectrum that stretches from conservative to lib-
> eral, or from orthodox to progressive, or from any one pole to any other
> pole. American Protestantism is far too complex to fit onto this simple linear
> scale of difference.[12]

The chapters in this volume have been interested most directly in
the specifically *theological* dimension of this larger historical construct.
One theme running through these pages is the thesis, which has in recent years been gaining a wide hearing, that the labels "liberal" and
"conservative"—or "left" and "right" as they have commonly come to
be defined—were the product of a philosophical problematic that
emerged with the Enlightenment and, in turn, defined theology, both
positively and negatively, throughout the modern era but especially
since the mid-nineteenth century. With the waning of the modern
theological agenda, however, the commonly cited two-party dichotomy of "liberal versus conservative" is growing increasingly passé. Today, any approach that maps the *theological* landscape by placing thinkers and movements along a one-dimensional spectrum running from
left to right is suspect if for no other reason than because it is simply a
particular application of the two-party model. To reiterate a theme announced in chapter 5, proposing a bipolar theological continuum is
simply neither appropriate nor helpful.

11. Ibid., 9.
12. Douglas Jacobsen and William Vance Trollinger, Jr., "Conclusion," in *Re-Forming the
Center*, 471–72.

Not only does the two-party model require an oversimplification of a complex phenomenon, its use risks introducing certain dangers. For example, the practice of splitting the world into neat bipolar categories can open the way to associating one group with the forces of God and the right, while suggesting that the other group is veering dangerously in the direction of darkness, and then using this judgment as the basis for recounting the past and the present in a manner that sanctifies one's own party while calling into question the integrity or spiritual status of those deemed to belong to the other. As was noted above, this tactic marked a well-worn path during the height of the modernist-fundamentalist controversy. It has likewise been trotted out, dusted off, and pressed into frightening service in recent decades in several denominational, parachurch, and even academic societal conflicts, in which one or another particular group clothed themselves with the mantle of truth, demonized those whom they considered to belong to the opposing side, and then used this schema in the attempt to rally the majority of the membership.

The academic pursuit itself is not immune from this potential danger. For example, even as irenic and cautious a scholar as Marsden, whose goal is anything but that of providing the basis for a spiritual jihad, comes close to casting historical method within the context of a larger, cosmic struggle,[13] when in the afterword to *Fundamentalism and American Culture* he declares,

> We live in the midst of contests between great and mysterious spiritual forces, which we understand only imperfectly and whose true dimensions we only occasionally glimpse. Yet, frail as we are, we do play a role in this history, on the side either of the powers of light or of the powers of darkness. It is critically important then, that, by God's grace, we keep our wits about us and discern the vast difference between the real forces for good and the powers of darkness disguised as angels of light.[14]

Perhaps a more dramatic casting of this quasi-Manichean outlook in conflictual, even apocalyptic, terms may be found in James Davison Hunter's provocatively titled work *Before the Shooting Begins*, in which the sociologist speculates that the United States may be standing on the brink of a religious civil war.[15]

---

13. For this judgment, see Jacobsen and Trollinger, "Introduction," 5.

14. Marsden, *Fundamentalism and American Culture*, 229–30.

15. For example, Hunter ominously predicts, "When cultural impulses this momentous vie against each other to dominate public life, tension, conflict, and perhaps even violence are inevitable. . . . Indeed, the last time this country 'debated' the issue of human life, personhood, liberty, and the rights of citizenship all together, the result was the bloodiest war ever to take place on this continent, the Civil War." James Davison Hunter, *Before the Shooting Begins: Searching for Democracy in America's Culture War* (New York: Free Press, 1994), 4–5.

As unfortunate, potentially devastating, and perilously self-fulfilling as this kind of language can be, and as "un-Christian" as the combative spirit and uncharitable name-calling that often emerges from its use can become, for the purposes of this volume another, more directly theological danger is even more pressing. As has been noted repeatedly in previous chapters, despite their differences, both parties in the modernist-fundamentalist controversy were in fact modernists, insofar as the entire debate was largely framed by and waged according to modern assumptions. The continuation of a two-party model that polarizes the theological world into the competing alternatives of liberal and conservative actually serves to perpetuate the very modernist mindset that ignited the conflict of a former century. Gerald Sheppard states the point well, when he notes,

> What remains most useful about the two-party model is how it describes the survivals of modernity in a late modern situation. Because modern "conservatives" and "liberals" both "see" the world and the biblical text "objectively" through a similar set of spectacles, to use a commonplace premodern expression, they essentially agree enough to disagree. They thus situate themselves in symbiotic juxtaposition to each other, like "worthy" opponents who have squared off against each other face to face, while their lack of historical self-awareness allows them to assume that in that contest they are merely continuing a public struggle that has gone on through all human history.[16]

Sheppard later adds, "A common historical, referential grammar supported their conflict on political, ethical, and doctrinal matters. One side or the other could thus be deemed right or wrong. Conflict over 'truth' made sense."[17]

Perpetuating the use of the two-party model to describe the contemporary situation, therefore, not only entails an oversimplification of what has been and continues to be a far more complex phenomenon, it is also anachronistic—or perhaps more forcefully stated, theologically *dangerously* anachronistic. The attempt to fit a new and ever changing situation into the familiar categories of a bygone conflict decreases the ability of theology, and in turn the church, to engage constructively with the contemporary situation. Again, I cite Sheppard's poignant conclusion: "The two-party model misguides us by looking back nostalgically at older modern possibilities, just when we need to be the most sensitive to elemental changes in how we perceive reality within a postmodern, global culture and society."[18]

16. Gerald T. Sheppard, "'Two-Party' Rhetoric amid Debates over Scripture and Theology," in *Re-Forming the Center*, 447.

17. Ibid., 459.

18. Ibid., 447.

The postmodern condition calls Christians to move beyond the fixation with a conflictual polarity that knows only the categories of "liberal" and "conservative," and thus pits so-called conservatives against loosely defined liberals. Instead, the situation in which the church is increasingly ministering requires a "generous orthodoxy" characteristic of a renewed "center" that lies beyond the polarizations of the past, produced as they were by modernist assumptions—a generous orthodoxy, that is, that takes seriously the postmodern problematic. Therefore, the way forward is for evangelicals to take the lead in renewing a theological "center" that can meet the challenges of the postmodern, and in some sense post-theological, situation in which the church now finds itself.

"Back" to the Evangelical "Center"

Being at the "center" is not a new idea. Throughout its history the church has repeatedly been characterized by a "generous orthodoxy" that formed the center of theology, the church, and at times (for better or for worse) even society as a whole. Nor is the idea of constituting the center foreign to the evangelical experience, despite the tendency of evangelicals today to view themselves as marginalized from the center and for evangelical churches to attract those who, in sociologist Mark Shibley's words, are "socially and culturally dislocated."[19] On the contrary, in the heyday of the evangelical movement, i.e., the eighteenth and nineteenth centuries, evangelicals occupied the center in Britain and in much of the English-speaking world.

This was especially the case in the United States. Martin Marty recently reiterated Marsden's thesis that in the nineteenth century the center of American religious life was dominated by an evangelicalism that formed the antecedent of both mainline and evangelical Protestantism in the twentieth century.[20] Speaking of the wider, and predominately white, Protestant "center" that in his estimation persisted into the mid-twentieth century, Marty declares,

> Its members and alumni ran the universities, business and corporate life, and civic and political affairs in almost all but the hugely Catholic metropolitan areas. They overwhelmingly dominated *Who's Who in America* listings, had influence on what was in the textbooks and taught in the schools, gave birth to and

19. Shibley writes, "People who are socially and culturally dislocated disproportionately affiliate with evangelical churches, regardless of socioeconomic status. Contemporary evangelicalism therefore remains a 'church of the disinherited,' thought more in social and cultural terms than economic ones." Mark A. Shibley, *Resurgent Evangelicalism in the United States: Mapping Cultural Change since 1970* (Columbia: University of South Carolina Press, 1996), 132.

20. Martin E. Marty, "The Shape of American Protestantism: Are There Two Parties Today?" in *Re-Forming the Center*, 94.

then dominated many if not most voluntary associations on the philanthropic and reform fronts, made the news in the dailies and weeklies, and were the subjects of most curiosity for their ecclesial endeavors—not the least of all because they controlled the media that quickened and satisfied curiosities.[21]

Lurking beneath Marty's characterization of Protestant America, however, are certain dangers that the use of the language of the "center" can unfortunately occasion. Perhaps the root danger is that of reading the idea in "Constantinian" terms. Rodney Clapp characterizes the essence of Constantinianism as the view that sees the church as the sponsor of Western civilization[22] and as deriving its significance through its "association with the identity and purposes of the state."[23]

Evangelicals are susceptible to the temptation to understand the "center" along Constantinian lines, because the Constantinian ideal lies so deep within the Reformation heritage of evangelicalism. Although the Reformers sought to restore the gospel to the church, they perpetuated aspects of the approach to church and society developed in the era of the Christian empire and bequeathed to them by their medieval Roman Catholic forebears. Not only did the Reformers not challenge the Constantinian settlement, in John Howard Yoder's estimation, they actually opened the door to its expansion. The end result of their appeal to the territorial states in the cause of the Reformation, Yoder argues, was the elevation of the state as the incarnation of "the ultimate values of God's work in the world," and the demotion of the church to the status of being "an administrative branch of the State on the same level with the Army or Post Office."[24]

The Reformation infatuation with the Constantinian ideal is evident, for example, in Martin Bucer's *De Regno Christi*, which he dedicated to King Edward VI of England. In this work, Bucer called for a return to the faith and practice of the ancient church, which in his estimation was typified by the Constantinian era. According to Bucer, the church of Constantine's day was characterized by godly piety and healthy expansion. He declared,

> But if one considers how lost in iniquity all kinds of men are, so that always in every people many are called but few are chosen (Matt. 22:14), he will certainly find nothing wanting in the period of Constantine and the emperors who followed him, in regard to the happiness of the Church of Christ

21. Ibid., 94.

22. Rodney Clapp, *A Peculiar People: The Church as Culture in a Post-Christian Society* (Downers Grove, Ill.: InterVarsity, 1996), 17.

23. Ibid., 25.

24. John Howard Yoder, "The Otherness of the Church," *Mennonite Quarterly Review* 35 (1961): 291.

promised through the holy prophets, when churches were raised up all over the world and flourished in exceptional piety.[25]

The Constantinian ideal as reformulated by the Puritans was transported to the United States, where it produced in the nineteenth century a type of Protestant hegemony. In keeping with the widespread Americanized Constantinian spirit of the day, religious historian Robert Baird spoke of the United States in 1856 as "a Protestant empire," even "the most powerful of all Protestant kingdoms."[26]

When coupled with the Constantinian ideal, language of "renewing the center" can all too readily conjure up longings for some supposedly idyllic past age characterized by a glorious uniformity and the predominance of Christian principles, whether that era be nineteenth-century America, colonial New England, the Reformation, or even the patristic church prior to the Great Schism of 1054. No such age was truly and universally "golden," however, for often the past that today's utopians romanticize achieved uniformity at the expense of ignoring or even eliminating dissidents and prophetic voices speaking from the margins. Jacobsen and Trollinger offer a reminder that "Protestant America" in the nineteenth century was a time "in which all non-Protestants and even some Protestants (including for example, African Americans, members of peace churches, Pentecostals, and various 'ethnic' church communities) were deemed to be outside the religious and cultural mainstream."[27]

Furthermore, through its connection with "memories" of a day when "true Christianity" reigned, language of the "center" can be coopted into a new two-party paradigm characterized by a polarity between the "center" and the "margin." In this situation, certain persons all too readily assert that they alone are the legitimate heirs of the center to the exclusion of other, less pretentious voices, whose pedigree may in fact be just as long and whose claim to the "center" equally valid.

The call to renew the "center" articulated in these pages, therefore, does not entail the "returning" of evangelical Christianity to the political, social, and cultural center of the nation, a goal that is surely misguided. Rather, the "center" that is to be renewed is a *theological* center, and the quest to renew the center involves restoring a particular *theological* spirit to the center of the church. The renewing of this center, in turn, has as its goal primarily the re-

25. Martin Bucer, *De Regno Christi*, in *Melanchthon and Bucer*, ed. Wilhelm Pauck, vol. 19 of *The Library of Christian Classics* (Philadelphia: Westminster, 1969), 209.

26. Robert Baird, *Religion in America, with Notices of the Unevangelical Denominations* (New York: Harper and Brothers, 1856), 32.

27. Jacobsen and Trollinger, "Conclusion," in *Re-Forming the Center*, 474.

newal of the church, even though, of course, such renewal can and should naturally spill over into society, as Christians carry the gospel into the world.

Evangelicalism and Renewal

The language of "renewing the center" and the call to evangelicals to take the lead in such a renewal suggest that evangelicalism might well be understood as a renewal movement within the church.[28] Indeed, the evangelical movement has been, and should continue to be, about the task of continually calling the whole church to renewal. The message of renewal that evangelicals offer as their gift to the church is the ongoing reminder of the constant need for the transformation of the heart, understood both individually and corporately. Insofar as its message of renewal cuts to the heart, i.e., to the center, of the church's life and mission, evangelicalism has a rightful place at the center and its task is that of renewing the center.

There is strong historical precedence for viewing evangelicalism as a renewal movement within the church. This historical basis finds its genesis within the Reformation itself. Central to the Protestant movement from the beginning was an undeniable impulse toward renewal. Rather than intending to launch a new ecclesiastical structure, the Reformers had as their goal the renewal of the one church. The centrality of their renewing mission led the churches that emerged out of the Reformation to adopt as their corporate watchword the great Protestant principle, *ecclesia semper reformanda*.

The centrality of renewal born in the Reformation carried over into the Puritan and Pietist movements that gave rise to the evangelical awakening. The Pietists were above all a renewal movement within the wider church. As I delineated in chapter 1, the purpose of the *collegia pietatis* was to renew the church from within, that is, to bring the church to reflect once again its true identity.

The same renewing impulse is evident in Puritanism. As their name itself suggests, the goal of the Puritan movement was to purify, or complete the purification of, the Church of England. The Puritans believed that casting off the remaining vestiges of papalism and becoming truly reformed would mark the renewal of the English Church. When transplanted to the New World, the Puritan renewal program took the form of the attempt to establish what was to be a "city upon a hill." The New England Puritans were convinced that by founding a truly reformed church, which could act as a beacon pointing England and the European continent

---

28. For an example of a recent appeal to this idea, see "*CT* Predicts: More of the Same," *Christianity Today* 43, no. 14 (December 6, 1999): 37.

in the direction of complete reformation, they would serve the renewal of the whole church. This ethos imbued the various confessional groups that emerged within Puritanism, including the Presbyterians, the Congregationalists, and the Baptists, insofar as the intention of each was to bear witness to the need for renewal through reformation, as they had come to understand it from Scripture. The Puritan renewal impulse was summed up in the principle of "further light" articulated by Puritan leaders such as John Robinson.

The evangelical commitment to convertive piety that emerged from the blending of the Puritan and Pietist strands also embodied a renewing spirit. Of course, the evangelical message of the new birth was strongly oriented toward renewal, for it proclaimed the renewal of the human person through the regenerative work of the Spirit. Yet the fledgling evangelical awakening carried implicitly within itself the seeds of church renewal as well. The early evangelicals were convinced that the conversion experience not only renewed the individual believer, but that it would also have a renewing effect on the whole church. Such renewal would come about because the new birth uniting all evangelicals brings the truly regenerate together beyond the particularities of doctrine, polity, and ecclesiastical practice that divided them into separated and often competing confessional bodies.

By appropriating the vision of a renewal movement within the church, so prevalent in the genesis of the movement, contemporary evangelicals could gain a new sense of identity while fostering the kind of generous orthodoxy that could serve the whole church as it grapples with the postmodern, global context in which it now ministers. Evangelicals are well positioned to take the lead in the task of renewal because they embody the kind of dialectical relationship to the wider society that the church as a whole must come to know. Throughout their history, evangelicals have experienced both inclusion and exclusion, often simultaneously. They have been both participants in the establishment and marginalized by the establishment.

This seemingly self-contradictory situation was present already in the Reformation. Not only were the Protestants, who preferred the designation "evangelical" (*evangelisch*), alternately on the margin and at the center of ecclesiastical, social, and political life in the sixteenth century, they were as zealous as the Roman Catholics in pushing to the periphery the various Anabaptist groups, many of whom came to embrace a type of convertive piety two centuries before the evangelical awakenings.[29] Similarly, as was noted earlier, while evangelicals in nineteenth-century America

---

29. See Roger E. Olson, *The Story of Christian Theology: Twenty Centuries of Tradition and Reform* (Downers Grove, Ill.: InterVarsity, 1999), 414–28.

participated in the "Protestant empire," other traditions in which convertive piety had taken firm root, such as the African-American churches and the Wesleyan-Holiness-Pentecostal trajectory, were placed on the margins. Then, as the twentieth century brought the erosion of the evangelical Protestant domination of American culture, fundamentalists—and later evangelicals as well—came to view themselves as marginalized in the very society they firmly believed they had helped shape.

This juxtaposing of center and margin places evangelicals in a position to call the church to a dialectical relationship to the world, a relationship characterized by both "center" and "margin." Evangelicals stand as a reminder that the whole church is to be a people who are *in* the world, but not *of* the world (John 17:15–16). Christ's disciples are called to live and witness at the center of society and to take upon themselves the burdens of their world, while knowing that this world offers them no permanent home (Phil. 3:20; Heb. 13:14).

The crucial importance of this balance between center and margin for the vitality of the church and the advantage that evangelicalism has in carrying out this endeavor in the contemporary, pluralist context have been confirmed by recent sociological studies. Christian Smith, to cite one example, offers this succinct summary of the conclusions that emerged from his engagement with the current state of the movement:

> Evangelicalism thrives in pluralistic modernity, we suggest, because it possesses and employs the cultural tools needed to create both clear distinction from and significant engagement and tension with other relevant outgroups, short of becoming countercultural. And modern pluralism provides the environment within which that strategy works. By contrast, the classical American fundamentalist strategy of isolationist separatism, and the theologically liberal approach of radical accommodation appear to undermine those traditions' religious strength. Comparatively, distinction-with-engagement appears to be the most effective strategy for maintaining religious vitality in the American culturally pluralistic environment.[30]

The Shape of the Renewed Evangelical Center

Evangelicalism, therefore, has an ongoing mission to complete. One significant aspect of this mission is to continue its task of serving as a renewal movement within and toward the church as a whole. The task of "renewing the center" envisioned in these pages entails returning to the

---

30. Christian Smith, *American Evangelicalism: Embattled and Thriving* (Chicago: University of Chicago Press, 1998), 218.

center of the church the kind of generous orthodoxy, read through the lenses of convertive piety, that in fact lies at the heart of what it means to be the church and that has characterized the church historically, at least at its best moments. It means returning a truly evangelical theology to the center of the church for the sake of the church's mission as a worshiping community of people sent into the world with the gospel. But the question remains, What does the renewed center look like?

In speaking about the evangelical Protestant establishment that predominated in nineteenth-century America, Martin Marty declares, "It had some sort of center. Better not try to define it, as the would-be definers learned. Better to grasp its ethos, live with its semicoherence, and not ask too many questions about what held it together."[31] Marty's statement offers an appropriate note of caution against any attempt to suggest too detailed a description of the evangelical center that ought to be renewed in the postmodern, post-theological context. Nevertheless, the insights into the trajectory of the evangelical movement gleaned throughout this study allow for at least a broad-stroke picture of the generous orthodoxy that should characterize that renewed center. This trajectory suggests the pattern of church life toward which evangelicals can direct their efforts.

Gospeled in Focus

A renewed center that is truly evangelical must be characterized above all by a focus on the gospel. As has been noted repeatedly in the previous chapters, to be "evangelical" means to be centered on the gospel. Consequently, evangelicals are a gospel people. They are a people committed to hearing, living out, and sharing the good news of God's saving action in Jesus Christ and the divine gift of the Holy Spirit, a saving action that brings forgiveness, transforms life, and creates a new community. As a gospel people, evangelicals continually set forth the truth that the center of the church is the gospel and that the church, therefore, must be gospel-centered.

This evangelical focus on the gospel has characterized the church in its finer moments in every era. Yet, evangelicals hail the Reformation both for rediscovering the gospel-centeredness of the church and for restoring the gospel to the center of the church. For this reason, evangelical theologians and historians draw their appropriation of the name "evangelical" initially from the Reformation. Moreover, the Reformers, such as Luther, linked this gospel-centeredness with the church's Christological foundation, for in their view the presence of the gospel at the heart of the church entailed Christ's own presence in, and lordship over, the church. As Paul

31. Marty, "Shape of American Protestantism," 94.

Avis declares, "For Luther, the Church was created by the living presence of Christ through his word the gospel. Where the gospel is found Christ is present, and where he is present the Church must truly exist."[32] In this manner, for Luther and others the gospel served as the linchpin connecting ecclesiology and Christology.

Not only did the Reformers bind the church to the gospel, they also bound the gospel to the church at the center of which it stood. In their estimation the gospel was not some free-floating message that brought a kind of intellectual enlightenment to the individual knower who grasped it. Theirs was no gnostic gospel. Rather, for the Reformers the gospel was always the church's message. It was good news addressed by the community (through its representatives), to the community (or by extension to those called to participate in the community), for the sake of the community. As this message was embodied both in Word and sacrament in the presence of the community gathered to hear it, it became the vehicle through which the Spirit created the church. To cite Avis again,

> The Reformers characteristically thought of God as a speaking God (*Deus loquens*), of the gospel as a tale or spoken message, of the Bible not merely as a book but as preaching, and of the Church as the gathering of people who listen to the word of God being addressed to them.[33]

A renewed evangelical center must appropriate anew this Reformation understanding of the gospel-centeredness of the church. Yet the evangelical focus on convertive piety that has stamped evangelicalism since its birth in the eighteenth-century awakenings takes the Reformation insight a step further. Their commitment to convertive piety leads evangelicals to the conclusion that the gospel-centered church is not merely the product of the proclaimed gospel. Rather, the church is truly present when the gospel proclamation in Word and sacrament engenders the response of faith and a faith-filled, faithful response. Thus the truly evangelical church is a community of faith, understood not merely as the people in whose midst the faith is proclaimed, but as a community of people of faith and of faithful people. A true faith community, in other words, is not a community that merely identifies itself with "the faith," even if by "identification with the faith" is meant strict assent to orthodox doctrinal formulations to the point of reciting the creed in the context of weekly worship—although fidelity to the belief-mosaic of biblical Christianity is, of course, a dimension of what it means to be the believ-

32. Paul D. L. Avis, *The Church in the Theology of the Reformers* (Atlanta: John Knox, 1981), 3.

33. Ibid., 81.

ing community. Rather, the gospel-centered church is the community of faith in the sense that it is the assembly of a people in whose lives regenerative faith is present through the power of the Holy Spirit, whose energizing of Word and sacrament leads to the transformation of the lives of those gathered to hear and to participate.

Further, the evangelical commitment to convertive piety leads to the conclusion that the gospel-centered church is a Bible-centered community. Viewed from an evangelical perspective, a community characterized by generous orthodoxy is a people among whom the Spirit creates faith as they gather around the open Bible with the intent of being instructed and nurtured in their personal and communal faith journey. Kenneth Kantzer offered a helpful summary of the kind of Scripture focus that typifies the evangelical elevation of convertive piety: "God has given his word to the church, not to provide a topic for discussion, still less for controversy, but primarily that people may become acquainted with his means of forgiving sin (justification) and learn how to live in the daily power of Christ's conquest over sin (sanctification)."[34]

The Bible-centered dimension of the gospel-focused church ought not to be interpreted in an individualistic manner, however. Rather, even though Christians possess the great privilege of reading the Bible privately, discerning the gospel message is not merely a private, but also a community process. Michael Horton finds the genesis of this perspective within the Reformers themselves: "The best way to guard a true interpretation of Scripture, the Reformers insisted, was neither to naively embrace the infallibility of tradition, or the infallibility of the individual, but to recognize the *communal* interpretation of Scripture." This community focus, in turn, provides the context for evangelicals' openness to insights from the wider fellowship throughout history, that is, from "tradition." Horton continues: "The best way to ensure faithfulness to the text is to read it together, not only with the churches of our own time and place, but with the wider 'communion of saints' down through the ages."[35]

Doctrinal in Orientation

Neither the Reformation nor the constellation of streams that flowed into the evangelical movement at its genesis were greatly concerned about

---

34. Kenneth S. Kantzer, "Unity and Diversity in Evangelical Faith," in *The Evangelicals: What They Believe*, ed. David F. Wells and John D. Woodbridge (Grand Rapids: Baker, 1977), 61.

35. Michael S. Horton, "What Still Keeps Us Apart?" in *Roman Catholicism: Evangelical Protestants Analyze What Divides and Unites Us*, ed. John H. Armstrong (Chicago: Moody, 1994), 253.

full-scale doctrinal renewal. These were not doctrinally oriented reform movements in the strict sense. The concern of the Reformation was to return the gospel of justification by faith alone to the church; the intent of Puritanism was to restore a duly constituted church; and the burden of the Pietists was to place regeneration or the new birth at the heart of the church. Apart from these emphases, the precursors of evangelicalism were content to accept the orthodox doctrines hammered out in earlier centuries of church history. At the same time, with the Reformation, doctrine took on a new importance, insofar as doctrinal fidelity eclipsed the Roman Catholic emphasis on a succession of ecclesiastical officers. As Paul Avis declares,

> By making the gospel alone the power at work in the Church through the Holy Spirit, the Reformers did away with the necessity of a doctrine of apostolic succession, replacing it with the notion of a succession of truth. Correspondingly, the gospel of truth was held to be sufficient to serve the catholicity of the Church.[36]

Yet what finally gave impetus to the introduction of a concern for doctrinal renewal into the fellowship of purveyors of convertive piety was the modernist-fundamentalist controversy. At least initially, turn-of-the-twentieth-century fundamentalists viewed their cause as primarily that of maintaining orthodoxy in the face of the evaporation of commitment to the church's doctrinal consensus. A half century later, in the wake of what certain younger fundamentalists perceived as the unnecessary ghettoizing of the movement, neo-evangelicalism was born, with the goal at least in part to foster doctrinal renewal in the church. The architects of neo-evangelicalism believed that such renewal would result in an apologetic theology that could promote an engagement of orthodox Christianity with the modern context.

The lesson that emerges from the advent of neo-evangelicalism is that, just as the Reformers learned the importance of doctrinal fidelity in the rejection of the Roman Catholic magisterium, so also this side of the rise of modernism a gospel-focused church must be by its very nature doctrinally oriented. Indeed, the elevation of doctrine as a necessary (but not sufficient) aspect of the renewal of the center constitutes the "orthodox" component of the "generous orthodoxy" needed in the church. Yet the emerging postmodern situation suggests that evangelicals must rethink what it means to be a doctrinally oriented people committed to convertive piety, and hence what is involved today in calling the whole church to a generous orthodoxy that is truly orthodox. The need for such rethinking arises

---

36. Avis, *Church in the Theology of the Reformers*, 128.

at a time when doctrine and theology appear to be simultaneously both irrelevant and indispensable to the life of the church.

The perceived irrelevancy of theology among contemporary evangelicals has been amply bemoaned by David Wells in his 1993 jeremiad, *No Place for Truth, or Whatever Happened to Evangelical Theology?* In this work, Wells contends that theology has not only disappeared from the church,[37] but the concern for theology has been replaced by an antitheological mood.[38] Chapter 5 suggested the sense in which Wells's lament is correct. As he rightly complains, many Christians today, including a great number of evangelicals, are convinced that doctrine as such is of no consequence. This seemingly post-theological context challenges evangelical theologians to seek clarity about the place of doctrine as well as the role of theological reflection in shaping and nurturing the church's life, practices, and witness in the world.

Yet at the very time when some are dismissing theology and doctrine, others are noting that in the pluralist, postmodern situation doctrine and theology take on a new, crucial, even indispensable significance. Many theologians, representing a variety of confessional traditions and perspectives, now reject the modern axiom that ecumenism can only come through the watering down, or even the shedding of, the concern for theology, a postulate based on the now discredited presumption that doctrine only serves to separate Christians into various competing denominations. Against this widely held belief, a growing number of thinkers are convinced that not only ecumenical discussions but also interreligious dialogue require that the participants come to the table with a clear understanding of, and commitment to, the doctrinal core that marks their confessional group.

Moreover, in the eyes of many theologians the way forward for true church unity in the postmodern ecumenical context lies in a rediscovery of the orthodox doctrine that lies at the heart of all Christian traditions. This position has been articulated recently by the editors of *Christianity Today*. In looking to the future from a vantage point at the end of 1999 they declared, "Formal moves toward unity must be driven by more important reasons than ideals of unity or staving off secularism. True unity will be best served by the continuing retrieval of an orthodox consensus among Christians from all traditions."[39]

In articulating this bold assertion, these evangelicals were actually echoing a similar sentiment voiced by Roman Catholic theologian Yves

37. David F. Wells, *No Place for Truth, or, Whatever Happened to Evangelical Theology?* (Grand Rapids: Eerdmans, 1993), 95.
38. Ibid., 96.
39. "*CT* Predicts," 37.

Congar in the mid-1980s. Congar declared, "We all agree in affirming that the unity of the church can only be realized in the unity of faith."[40] While noting the inward and personal nature of faith, Congar asserted that faith has a confessional aspect as well. The unity of faith, he announced, "is not only that of the *fides qua*, the movement of personal gift and confidence in Christ, but that of the *fides quae*, i.e., the content of the truth—or truths—professed."[41]

As these considerations indicate, the pathway to the renewal of an evangelical center necessarily passes through a retrieval of orthodox doctrine. Yet, in the process of contending for orthodoxy, evangelicals dare not forget to qualify the noun by its proper adjective. If it is not prefaced by the word "generous," "orthodoxy" risks being modified by qualifiers like "dead," "narrow," or "uncharitable." Therefore, in their concern to keep orthodox doctrine at the heart of the church, harbingers of the new center must orient themselves around the grand consensus of the church throughout the ages and take care that they avoid dogmatizing points of doctrine beyond this consensus. But even in upholding the grand consensus, a yet more overtly expressed generous spirit must reign. This generosity of spirit emerges out of certain theological considerations.

The "generous" side of the renewal of orthodoxy arises from an understanding of the crucial difference between the truths of the Christian faith and the doctrinal formulations in which any one set of these truths comes to expression at any given point in history. Here, Congar offers a helpful reminder: "Every formula aims at expressing the truth perceived, but the perception itself already falls short of the reality."[42] He then helpfully points out that all statements of the *fides quae* are inherently inadequate, in that rather than being "copies" of the truth, such formulae are symbols of it. As Aquinas, quoting Isadore, declares, a theological or doctrinal statement is "a glimpse of Divine truth, tending thereto,"[43] or to cite Congar's (as translated) rendering of the characterization, "a perception of truth aiming at the truth itself."[44] In Congar's estimation, doctrinal formulae are always inadequate likewise because they are expressions of particular churches in their particularity. They are constructed by churches within the linguistic, historical, and geographical particularity of their own context.[45]

---

40. Yves Congar, *Diversity and Communion*, trans. John Bowden (Mystic, Conn.: Twenty-Third Publications, 1985), 168.

41. Ibid.

42. Ibid.

43. Thomas Aquinas, *Summa Theologica* IIa, IIae q.1 a.6 sed contra, trans. Fathers of the English Dominican Province (Westminster, Maryland: Christian Classics, 1981), 3:1167.

44. Congar, *Diversity and Communion*, 168.

45. Ibid., 169–70.

This realization of the "local" nature of all theology leads to another theological basis for a spirit of generous orthodoxy. The task of renewing the doctrinal center does not only look to the grand consensus of the church; it also reaffirms the "progressive" dimension of theological reflection, a principle that plays an equally important role in the historical evangelical trajectory.[46] Theology is progressive in that it is an ongoing discipline that repeatedly gives rise to new ways of looking at old questions, brings into view previously undervalued aspects of the Christian belief-mosaic, and occasionally even advances the church's knowledge of theological truth. Its progressive aspect bestows on theology, and consequently on the doctrinal formulations it authors, a certain proleptic character. Theological reflection becomes an anticipatory act, for it entails a partial yet nevertheless valid participation in a "knowing" that is ultimately eschatological. As a consequence, theological statements and doctrinal formulae always have a type of provisionality to them. In the end, they are attempts to conceptualize adequately and properly the complete cognition that belongs in its fullness to the day when faith turns to sight (2 Cor. 5:7), when seeing "but a poor reflection as in a mirror" gives way to seeing "face to face," and when knowing "in part" becomes knowing "fully" (1 Cor. 13:12).

A spirit of generous orthodoxy is also born from the realization that even while the church is oriented toward doctrine, its focus must always remain the gospel. The great insight of the Pietists in the context of Lutheran Orthodoxy was that doctrine is not the be-all and end-all of the Christian faith. Saving faith is not mere assent to orthodox doctrine. On the contrary, faith is directed toward, and entails the laying hold of, God's provision for human sinfulness freely available through faith in Christ. This legacy was in turn bequeathed to evangelicalism and has always formed its greatest contribution as a renewal movement within the one church.

Keeping the primacy of the gospel clearly in view is a necessary antidote to the temptation, common among doctrinally oriented traditions, to assert that right doctrine is essential to salvation. In defending his support for the "Evangelicals and Catholics Together" (ECT) document, J. I. Packer forcefully lays to rest this misguided assumption: "What brings salvation, after all, is not any theory about faith in Christ, justification, and the church, but faith itself in Christ himself."[47] Despite such warnings, evangelicals repeatedly run the risk of substituting *assensus* for *fiducia*. The Orthodox pastor Patrick Henry Reardon finds this danger

---

46. For an example of an evangelical statement of this principle, see James Orr, *The Progress of Dogma* (1901; reprint, Grand Rapids: Eerdmans, 1952).

47. Packer, "Why I Signed It," 37.

manifested in a manuscript in which Michael Horton challenges the ECT statement. In offering his response, Reardon echoes the principle articulated by Packer:

> Provided that I understand him, Horton is saying that, in order to be saved, I must have not only faith but also a correct doctrine . . . of justification by faith. Now herein lies a real difference between us. I am convinced that Horton's theology of justification is erroneous and abusive of the Word of God, but not for a moment would it occur to me to fear for his salvation on that account. Why? Because of his faith in Christ our Savior. You see, I believe that a man is justified by faith, not by entertaining a correct view on justification.[48]

Not only is the concern for orthodox doctrine subservient to the gospel of justification by faith alone, but theological reflection that seeks to articulate and maintain right doctrine is also the servant of the Spirit's work in the new birth and the transformed life. Theology, therefore, can never remain either on the speculative or the purely doctrinal level. Its goal moves beyond that of articulating and clarifying doctrine. It also has a practical intent. As Alister McGrath declares, drawing from both Calvin and Kierkegaard, "A theology that touches the mind, leaving the heart unaffected, is no true Christian theology."[49] To mind and heart, the evangelical tradition would add a third: theology must also move the "hand." Thus, a truly generous orthodoxy arises when orthodox confession leads via a transformed heart to generosity in life.

One task of this book has been to set forth an understanding of theology that can clarify the nature, purpose, and role of doctrine by connecting doctrine with the life-transforming work of the Spirit. To this end, chapter 6 moved beyond the categories offered by George Lindbeck to speak of doctrine—by appeal to the concept of the Christian mosaic of belief or the Christian interpretive framework—as that which facilitates the saving encounter with God in Christ and the ongoing transformative work of the Spirit in the believer and the community of faith.

Ultimately, this connection, which is closely related to the evangelical commitment to convertive piety, indicates why renewing the center involves an orientation toward doctrine. Understood as the constellation of beliefs that forms the Christian interpretive framework, sound doctrine plays a crucial role in the life of faith. Just as every experience is necessar-

---

48. Patrick Henry Reardon, "Editorial: Evangelicals and Catholics Together?" *Touchstone* 7, no. 4 (Fall 1994): 7.
49. Alister E. McGrath, *A Passion for Truth: The Intellectual Coherence of Evangelicalism* (Downers Grove, Ill.: InterVarsity, 1996), 79.

ily tied to an understanding of reality—an interpretive framework—that both facilitates it and emerges from it, so also the saving encounter with God in Christ through the Spirit, both at conversion as the beginning of the faith journey as well as in the ongoing life of faithful discipleship, is cradled by a particular belief-mosaic. And the belief-mosaic that effects and explicates Christian life and experience speaks of all reality in the light of the actions of the biblical God.

Doctrine, then, is the set of propositions that together comprise the Christian belief-mosaic. But the task of formulating, explicating, and understanding doctrine must always be vitally connected to the Bible, or more particularly, to the biblical narrative. Alister McGrath provides a succinct summary of this relationship. He writes, "Doctrine thus provides the conceptual framework by which the scriptural narrative is interpreted. It is not an arbitrary framework, however, but one which is suggested by that narrative, and intimated (however provisionally) by scripture itself."[50]

The necessary connection between Christian doctrine and the biblical narrative arises out of the genesis of doctrine itself. At the heart of the gospel is the biblical story of God's saving activity on behalf of sinful humankind. This narrative never comes merely as a recitation of a series of "brute" facts; rather, every telling of the narrative always takes the form of an *interpreted* story. Even the apostles and evangelists tell the story of Jesus in the context of its meaning, namely, that "God was in Christ, reconciling the world unto himself," to cite once again Paul's words (2 Cor. 5:19 KJV). Because of its character as interpreted story, the telling of the gospel narrative naturally gives rise to the constructive theological enterprise, as people of faith seek to understand the content of their faith. The result is the formulation of doctrines. These theological statements function as encapsulations of the belief-mosaic implicit in the narrative, but also as a type of shorthand for the narrative itself.

As I have repeatedly articulated throughout this study, all such doctrinal formulations must be continually judged by Scripture. To cite McGrath again, "The *sola Scriptura* principle is ultimately an assertion of the primacy of the foundational scriptural narrative over any framework of conceptualities which it may generate."[51] A renewal of the center, therefore, calls the church to the ongoing task of doctrinal retrieval and reformation, under the normative guidance of Scripture and Spirit, for the sake of the furtherance of the gospel of God's transforming grace freely available in Christ. Ultimately, dedication to this

50. Ibid., 113.
51. Ibid., 114.

ongoing task marks the church that is oriented around a generous orthodoxy.

Catholic in Vision

Finally, a renewed center that is truly evangelical must be catholic in vision. Since the composition of the Nicene-Constantinopolitan Creed in the fourth century, Christians have confessed their belief that the church is catholic. Chapter 9 focused on the significance of this affirmation within an ecclesiological context. What remains here is to explicate the sense in which an evangelical renewal of the center is likewise catholic in vision.

In popular parlance, the word "catholic" routinely refers to a particular institution, the Roman Catholic Church. Instead of this specific use, the following discussion will use the term in its more general meaning as derived from the Greek *katholikos*, namely, "comprehensive" or "universal in reach."[52] Thus, the renewal of the center advocated in this volume entails a rediscovery of a vision that is universal in scope. It is a vision that is comprehensive or directed toward the whole.

Stated simply, a catholic vision, understood in the sense of comprehensiveness, seeks to bring within its purview the church catholic. David Wells poignantly asserted, "There can be no theology worthy of that name that is not a theology *for the Church*."[53] The renewal of the center not only requires a theology for the church; it also demands a theology that seeks to draw the whole church within its vision. Such a theological program attempts to foster a renewal that encompasses the whole church.

As was noted above, a concern for the church as a whole lies deeply embedded within the evangelical heritage. The forebears of the evangelical awakening, from the Reformers to the Pietists and Puritans, did not limit their renewal interests but were concerned for the whole church of their day. Likewise, their goal was not the narrowly focused desire to erect a new ecclesiological structure; instead, theirs was the all-encompassing intention to ignite the reformation of the one church in its entirety (or at least in its Western expression). Furthermore, in calling the church to renewal they appealed to the whole church, in the form of the rich heritage of theological writings from the patristic era to the present that they readily admitted belonged to them as well as to their opponents. The leaders of the eighteenth-century evangelical awakenings,

---

52. For this definition, see *The Doubleday Dictionary for Home, School, and Office*, ed. Sidney I. Landau (Garden City, N.Y.: Doubleday, 1975), 112.

53. Wells, *No Place for Truth*, 292.

such as George Whitefield and John Wesley[54] in England and Jonathan Edwards[55] and Isaac Backus in New England, inherited this vision for, and attention to, the church catholic.

In the intervening centuries, evangelicals largely lost the catholic spirit that motivated their forebears at the genesis of the movement. In contrast to many of their predecessors, nineteenth- and twentieth-century evangelicals were often quite content to settle into either a very uncatholic sectarianism or into a kind of denominationalist/invisible church ecclesiology that dispelled any deep sense of responsibility to the wider church in its institutional forms, or at least institutional forms lying beyond the grand Protestant coalition.

In contemporary context, however, the language of a renewal of the center that is catholic in vision can no longer limit itself to self-consciously evangelical or even Protestant denominations. Rather, the quest for the renewed center must bring into its vision the church beyond what have almost invariably been the boundaries of recent evangelical interest. Yet any move to bring the Eastern Orthodox and Roman Catholic Churches into view, while seen as an intriguing prospect by some,[56] immediately raises red flags in the minds of many evangelicals.

For several reasons, attempts among North American evangelicals to cultivate mutual understanding and some kind of common cause with Eastern Orthodox churches[57] have not engendered great internal opposition, although those who are well appraised of the treatment of dissenters in lands where Orthodoxy is dominant often cast a more

54. See John Wesley, "Catholic Spirit," in *Forty-Four Sermons, or, Sermons on Several Occasions* (London: Epworth, 1944), 452–55. For commentators, see Albert Outler, "The Place of Wesley in the Christian Tradition," in *The Wesleyan Theological Heritage: Essays of Albert C. Outler*, ed. Thomas C. Oden and Leicester R. Longden (Grand Rapids: Zondervan, 1991), 76–95; "John Wesley's Interests in the Early Fathers of the Church," in *Wesleyan Theological Heritage*, 98–110; and Randy L. Maddox, *Responsible Grace: John Wesley's Practical Theology* (Nashville: Kingswood Books, 1994). For the use of the phrase "catholic spirit" by Wesley himself to mean "irenic" as opposed to "dogmatic," see Randy L. Maddox, "Opinion, Religion, and 'Catholic Spirit': John Wesley on Theological Integrity," *Asbury Theological Journal* 47, no. 1 (1992): 63–87.

55. Edwards' catholic vision is evident, for example, in his *A History of the Work of Redemption*, vol. 9 of *The Works of Jonathan Edwards*, ed. John F. Wilson (1774; New Haven: Yale University Press, 1989).

56. For an example of a three-party conversation, see James S. Cutsinger, ed., *Reclaiming the Great Tradition: Evangelicals, Catholics and Orthodox in Dialogue* (Downers Grove, Ill.: InterVarsity, 1997).

57. For an attempt at a somewhat more broadly focused mutual understanding, see Carnegie Samuel Calian, *Theology without Boundaries: Encounters of Eastern Orthodoxy and Western Tradition* (Louisville: Westminster John Knox, 1992). For a helpful engagement between the Anabaptist and Orthodox traditions, see Thomas N. Finger, "Anabaptism and Eastern Orthodoxy: Some Unexpected Similarities," *Journal of Ecumenical Studies* 31, no. 1–2 (Winter–Spring, 1994): 67–91.

critical eye. Relations with the Roman Catholic Church, in contrast, have historically been highly problematic for evangelicals. Historian John Wolffe notes that "particularly during the middle third of the nineteenth century, anti-Catholicism was, on both sides of the Atlantic, very much of the essence of evangelicalism."[58] For many conscientious evangelical Protestants, centuries of conflict with Rome, experiences with a dominating Catholic Church in lands where evangelical missionaries were active, and suspicions about what might motivate any conciliatory gestures from the Catholic side make any thought of rapprochement abhorrent.

Such reluctance is well-founded. Since Trent, the Roman Catholic Church has repeatedly claimed to be not merely one of many communities of faith, but to comprise *en toto* the church of Christ itself. Although Vatican II tempered Catholic ecclesiastical exclusivism, even after the changes of the 1960s the Church continues to claim a certain superiority over other Christian communities. Roman Catholic theologian Avery Dulles confirms this observation:

> The Vatican documents make it clear that the Church of Christ subsists in its institutional purity and completeness in the Roman Catholic Church, and nowhere else. Thanks to the efficacious promise of Christ, the churches in full communion with the Petrine See will always possess the objective elements of the total Christian patrimony: the saving doctrine of the gospel, the seven sacraments, and a legitimately empowered ministry.[59]

Nevertheless, the Council did take a great step by raising the possibility that conversations with Rome need no longer proceed on the assumption that Protestants are heretics who simply need to return to the true (i.e., Roman) church. Hence, Dulles concludes that according to the Decree on Ecumenism formulated at Vatican II, "The ultimate unity of Christians . . . is not to be conceived of as a simple movement of return of the straying sheep to the one fold of Roman Catholicism, but rather as a bold journey into God's future under the leading of the Holy Spirit."[60] As a consequence of this new spirit, the Roman Catholic Church has entered into well over a dozen official bilateral dialogues with various Christian groups.

58. John Wolffe, "Anti-Catholic and Evangelical Identity in Britain and the United States, 1830–1860," in *Evangelicalism: Comparative Studies of Popular Protestantism in North America, the British Isles, and Beyond, 1700–1990*, ed. Mark A. Noll, David W. Bebbington, and George A. Rawlyk (New York: Oxford, 1994), 179.

59. Avery Dulles, *The Dimensions of the Church: A Postconciliar Reflection* (Westminster, Md.: Newman, 1967), 28.

60. Ibid., 41.

Not only did mainline Protestants hail the new opening signaled by Vatican II, but some evangelicals have also joined the chorus. According to the Canadian Pentecostal ecumenist Ronald Kydd, the first official dialogue, begun in 1972, involved Catholics and participants from his own tradition.[61] In the aftermath of the Lausanne conference on evangelism, another official evangelical-Catholic encounter led to the publication of *The Evangelical-Roman Catholic Dialogue on Mission 1977–1984.*[62]

Arguably the most controversial development, however, was the informal, unofficial discussions that led to the publication in March 1994 of the document "Evangelicals and Catholics Together: Christian Mission in the Third Millennium" (ECT).[63] While responses within the Catholic Church were quite subdued, the reaction by other evangelicals was swift and acrimonious. Although some lauded the work, others were sharply critical. Even such sympathetic voices as Kenneth Kantzer urged caution.[64] The furor the document ignited among Southern Baptists resulted in two of the original signatories, SBC denominational officials Larry Lewis and Richard Land, reluctantly withdrawing their names.[65]

What drew the most fire were the declaration on justification by faith (which critics feared had compromised the distinctive Protestant position), and the statement decrying proselytizing (which critics, including some from non-North American contexts,[66] read as undercutting evangelization among nominal Catholics). But perhaps the biggest cause for concern was the tone of the document itself. In the eyes of many, the call for cooperation—as brothers and sisters—in a variety of causes from social concerns to world evangelism seemed too much like an endorsement of Roman Catholicism itself, which in the eyes of John MacArthur is nothing less than "another religion."[67]

In an editorial in *First Things*, signatory Richard John Neuhaus cited a response from an anonymous "respected evangelical theologian" that undoubtedly capsulated the thinking of many:

61. Ronald Kydd, "Evangelicals and Roman Catholics: New Hope for the Future?" *Ecumenism* 125 (March 1997): 22–23.

62. Basil Meeking and John Stott, eds., *The Evangelical-Roman Catholic Dialogue on Mission 1977–1987: A Report* (Grand Rapids: Eerdmans, 1986).

63. The text is printed in *First Things* 43 (May 1994): 15–22.

64. Kenneth S. Kantzer, "Should Roman Catholics and Evangelicals Join Ranks?" *Christianity Today* 38, no. 8 (July 18, 1994): 17.

65. "SBC Leaders Defect from Accord," *Christian Century* 112, no. 16 (May 10, 1995): 505.

66. See, for example, Agustin B. Vencer, Jr., "An International Perspective on Evangelical-Catholic Cooperation," *Evangelical Missions Quarterly* 31, no. 3 (July 1995): 278–79.

67. As quoted in Joe Maxwell, "Evangelicals Clarify Accord with Catholics," *Christianity Today* 39, no. 3 (March 6, 1995): 53.

I pray that what you and your colleagues have done is pleasing to God. I cannot praise or condemn it. I expect that this may change forever what generations of Bible-believing Protestants have thought was their mission in relation to Roman Catholicism. I pray that you are right. I tremble to think that you may be wrong.[68]

Activities since March 1994, however, have assisted in the process of defusing the tensions, toning down the rhetoric, and refocusing the direction of the discussion among evangelicals. These included a statement entitled, "Resolutions for Roman Catholic and Evangelical Dialogue," drafted by Michael Horton and revised by J. I. Packer, that appeared in the July–August 1994 issues of *Modern Reformation*; a meeting in Fort Lauderdale Florida in January 1995 involving several evangelical signatories and their critics;[69] and a second joint evangelical-Catholic statement published with an editorial by Timothy George in *Christianity Today* in December 1997.[70]

Whatever else might be said about the ECT document and the debate that came in its wake, the ordeal has awakened the evangelical consciousness to several urgent issues that few evangelicals had considered at length prior to 1994. Above all, the discussion has jarred at least some evangelicals into considering the question of the breadth of vision that characterizes neo-evangelicalism after more than a half century of existence. As I noted in chapter 2, the initial intent of the neo-evangelical movement was to provide a "third way" in the aftermath of the great turn-of-the-twentieth-century controversy within Protestantism. But the events since 1994 signal that the postmodern, global context has thrust upon the purveyors of convertive piety a new situation. No longer can evangelicals be content to limit the context in which they engage in the task of renewal to a church understood as bounded by the old-line Protestant denominations and the self-consciously evangelical groups. While not abandoning this aspect of their mandate, the postmodern condition challenges evangelicals to gain a vision of the church that is truly catholic, that is, a vision that is universal and comprehensive in scope. The globalized situation thrusts upon evangelicals the need to understand themselves as a catholic renewal movement, as a people committed to the renewal of the evangelical center within, as part of, and for the sake of the whole, global church.

68. As cited in Richard John Neuhaus, "A Sense of Change Both Ominous and Promising," *First Things* 55 (August/September 1995): 68.

69. For a report on this meeting, see Maxwell, "Evangelicals Clarify Accord with Catholics," 52–53.

70. See Timothy George, "Evangelicals and Catholics Together: A New Initiative," *Christianity Today* 41, no. 14 (December 8, 1997): 34–38.

By taking up this challenge, today's evangelicals are simply returning to their roots. In looking to the whole church as the context for the evangelical witness, they are merely retrieving the catholic spirit that characterized many of their forebears in the Reformation, in the Puritan and Pietist movements, and in the great evangelical awakenings. Moreover, when this ecclesiologically catholic vision emerges clearly in view, contemporary purveyors of convertive piety will be able to gain a vision that is catholic in the most comprehensive sense. Theirs will be a vision of a renewed evangelical center that engages with all of life and embraces all of creation under the rubric of the gospel of the biblical God who promises to renew and transform not only the human heart and the community of faith but "all things" in the glorious eschatological new creation.[71]

> "And he that sat upon the throne said, 'Behold, I make all things new.' And he said unto me, 'Write: for these words are true and faithful'" (Rev. 21:5 KJV).

71. Lewis S. Mudge, *One Church: Catholic and Reformed* (Philadelphia: Westminster, 1963), 73.

Scripture Index

OLD TESTAMENT

Genesis

1:1 317
1:2 210
2:7 210
3:15 271
3:20 271
9:1–17 271
12:3 271
14:17–24 267
14:18–19 273
20:1–18 267

Exodus

6:3 272
18:1 273
18:9–12 273
18:10–12 267
18:27 273
28:41 321

Numbers

22 273

Deuteronomy

32:17 274

Joshua

24:14 273–74

2 Samuel

24:1 274
24:15 274

1 Kings

17:7–24 273

2 Kings

5:1–19 273
5:17 273
5:18–19 273

1 Chronicles

21:1 274

2 Chronicles

11:15 274

Esther

4:14 7

Job

27:3 210
34:14–15 210

Psalms

104:29–30 210
106:37 274

Ecclesiastes

11:5 9

Isaiah

32:15 210
54:2 294
65:17–19 246

Amos

9:7 271

Zechariah

14:16 272

NEW TESTAMENT

Matthew

5:43–48 321
6:9 321
6:10 246
8:11 272
22:14 332

Mark

7:24–30 271
16:16 266

Luke

2:30–32 21, 271
4:25–27 273
7:9 271
9:49–50 273
13:23–24 267
13:29 267

John

1:1 247
1:3 284
3:16–18 266–67
3:36 267
14:6 266, 275
17:3 266
17:15–16 336
17:21 307

Acts

4:12 266, 275
7:6 128
10 257
10:2 267
10:4 273
10:34–35 271–72
16:31 266
17:22–23 273

Romans

1:18–23 256
3:23–24 267
5:12–21 285
6:23 267
8:14–17 323
8:29 323
10:9 266
10:14 267
10:17 267
11:32 267
13:11–14 23

1 Corinthians

1:23 22

7:31 246
8:4–7 274–75
10:17 321
10:19–20 274
12:13 302, 321
13:12 343
15:21 285
15:45 285
15:49 323

2 Corinthians

3:18 323
4:4 323
5:7 343
5:17 207, 217, 318
5:18–19 284
5:19 318

Galatians

4:6 323

Ephesians

2:15 321

Philippians

2:2 321
3:20 336

Colossians

1:15 323
1:15–16 284
1:17 247, 284

1 Timothy

1:13 267

2:4 267, 283
3:15 59

2 Timothy

1:14 178
3:15–17 143
3:16 75, 207

Hebrews

1:3 323
7:1–10 273
11:6 267
12:26–28 246
13:14 336

1 Peter

1:15–16 321
3:19–20 257
4:17 321

2 Peter

3:9 267

1 John

2:23 267
4:7–8 322
4:8 322
4:16 322
5:11–12 267

Revelation

21:1 317
21:1–5 281, 321
21:5 217, 246, 351
21:24–25 272
22:1–5 321

Author Index

Abbott, Walter M. 258 n. 46
Abraham, William J. 16, 175, 176
Ahlstrom, Sydney E. 38
Althaus, Paul 26–27
Andersen, Francis I. 106 n. 112
Anderson, James Norman D. 261
Anderson, Walter Truett 169 n. 81, 170 n. 84, 171 n. 86, 171 n. 89, 173 n. 103, 174 n. 106, 237 n. 69
Aquinas, Thomas 230–31, 342
Arecchi, Tito 236 n. 62
Armstrong, John 13, 165
Arnold, Matthew 46
Askew, Thomas A. 166
Avis, Paul D. L. 291 n. 11, 310 n. 84, 311 n. 88, 319 n. 114, 337–38, 340

Backus, Isaac 7, 23, 45–46, 347
Bainton, Roland 56
Baird, Robert 333
Barbour, Ian 219 n. 3, 219 n. 4, 247 n. 114

Barr, James 106 n. 112
Barrett, John C. 267 n. 101
Barth, Karl 111 n. 146, 253–54
Barton, Stephen C. 313
Baxter, Richard 301
Beale, David O. 72 n. 92, 78 n. 119, 79 n. 124
Bebbington, David 15, 44, 45 n. 88, 48 n. 97, 49, 65 n. 55, 66 n. 60, 250
Behe, Michael J. 219 n. 1
Bell, M. Charles 39 n. 62
Bellah, Robert N. 237 n. 71, 276 n. 124, 315, 316 n. 107, 317
Bentley, William H. 178 n. 120
Berger, Peter L. 243–44, 315 nn. 104–5
Berkhof, Louis 32, 37
Berkouwer, G. C. 299, 303 n. 55
Bilezikian, Gilbert 164
Blauw, J. 270 n. 109
Bloesch, Donald G. 25 n. 2, 41 n. 67, 111 n. 149, 117 n. 1, 132, 152, 153 n. 11, 290, 300, 301, 305 n. 66, 314 n. 101
Bohm, David 223 n. 14

Bonhoeffer, Dietrich 284 n. 147
Braaten, Carl E. 153, 158–59, 253, 263 n. 75, 301
Bradshaw, Tim 157 n. 33
Bray, Gerald 308 n. 80
Bromiley, Geoffrey W. 57 n. 14, 62 n. 42, 67 nn. 64–65, 75 n. 105
Brow, Robert C. 145 n. 158
Brown, Dale W. 41, 42, 43 n. 81, 62 n. 39, 62 n. 41, 62 n. 43, 64 n. 49
Brown, Delwin 146
Brown, Wesley H. 116
Browne, Robert 293
Brunner, Emil 212
Bucer, Martin 35, 311, 332–33
Bultmann, Rudolf 307 n. 78
Buswell, J. Oliver 124

Calian, Carnegie Samuel 347 n. 57
Callen, Barry L. 135, 136 n. 103, 141 n. 138, 144 n. 150, 147 n. 167, 150 n. 185
Calvin, John 30 n. 20, 30 n. 22, 31 n. 25, 34–35, 38

n. 52, 58–60, 298, 311,
317 n. 113
Campbell, Charles A. 190
n. 21
Campbell, Ted A. 38 n. 58,
50 n. 111
Camps, Arnulf 278 n. 131
Capps, Walter H. 259 n. 54
Carey, Eustace 302 n. 49
Carnell, Edward J. 123, 128
Carpenter, Joel A. 82
n. 138, 83, 90 n. 22, 179
Carson, D. A. 249, 252, 266
n. 98, 290 n. 8
Charry, Ellen T. 229 n. 39
Clapp, Rodney 332
Clark, Gordon H. 31 n. 24,
90, 111 n. 149
Clayton, Philip 235
Clowney, Edmund P. 289
n. 7, 299–300
Cobb, John B. Jr. 146
Cohen, Anthony P. 180
Cole, Stewart Grant 80
n. 132
Collins, H. M. 237 n. 68
Collins, Kenneth J. 45
n. 89, 48, 50 n. 112
Congar, Yves 258–59, 341–
42
Cray, Graham 167 n. 78
Culpepper, Robert H. 258
Cutsinger, James S. 347
n. 56

D'Andrade, Roy G. 180
n. 127
D'Costa, Gavin 252 n. 12,
259 n. 49
Daane, James 111 n. 146
Dale, J. 65 n. 58
Dancy, Jonathan 191 n. 25
Davidson, Donald 191 n. 29
Davies, Paul 240 n. 83
Davis, Stephen T. 141
Dayton, Donald W. 14
n. 13, 46, 51, 178 n. 118
de Saussure, Ferdinand
242–43
Dell, Robert S. 65 n. 54
Demarest, Bruce A. 32
n. 30, 44–45, 50, 77
n. 115, 118, 152 n. 7, 157,

225–26, 256–57
Denman, D. R. 106 n. 112
Descartes, René 186 n. 6,
187–89, 221
Dibelius, Otto 301
DiNoia, J. A. 252–53, 261,
262, 263, 265 n. 88, 269,
277, 279–80, 283
Dockery, David S. 118, 120,
124 n. 32, 126
Dorrien, Gary 67 n. 67, 99
n. 78, 138, 141 n. 136,
150
Dressler, Hernigild 258
n. 44
Dulles, Avery 297, 301
n. 41, 309, 312, 313, 348
Dupuis, Jacques 269 n. 108
Durkheim, Emile 276
Dyrness, William A. 179
n. 121

Eagleton, Terry 173–74,
217 n. 90
Edwards, David L. 267
Edwards, Jonathan 22, 49,
50, 347
Ellingsen, Mark 28, 51
n. 115, 65 n. 51, 79
nn. 125–26, 82
Erasmus 26
Erickson, Millard J. 18–19,
32, 81 n. 133, 82 n. 137,
88–89, 120 n. 8, 120 n. 10,
121 n. 12, 122 n. 20, 123
n. 29, 124 n. 31, 125
n. 33, 126 n. 43, 126
nn. 45–47, 128 nn. 57–61,
129 n. 63, 129 nn. 66–67,
130 nn. 69–71, 131 n. 75,
131 n. 77, 131 n. 79, 132
n. 80, 132 n. 81, 132
nn. 83–84, 133 n. 85, 133
nn. 88–91, 134 n. 92, 144,
152, 154 n. 16, 154
nn. 18–19, 155 n. 24, 159,
164 n. 65, 175–77, 183,
260 n. 61, 298, 300 n. 39,
302, 306
Estep, William R. 300 n. 39,
304 n. 60

Evans, Gillian R. 69 n. 80,
70 n. 81, 224 nn. 17–18

Fackre, Gabriel 132
Farley, Edward 320 n. 40
Farquhar, J. N. 283
Ferre, Frederick 172 n. 94
Feyerabend, Paul 236
Field, John 36
Findlay, James F., Jr. 289
Finger, Thomas N. 347
n. 57
Foerster, Werner 274
n. 118
Fonner, Michael G. 251 n. 7
Forde, Gerhard O. 32
Francke, August 63 n. 45,
64
Frank, Douglas W. 78
n. 120
Franke, John R. 8, 211
n. 79
Fredericks, James L. 278
n. 134
Frei, Hans 325–27
Freylinghausen, Johann
Anastasius 64
Fulop, Timothy E. 311 n. 90

Galloway, Allan D. 69
n. 80, 224 n. 17
Garrett, James Leo, Jr. 133–
34, 152, 159
Geisler, Norman L. 177
George, Timothy 152 n. 4,
182–83, 288, 350
Gillis, Chester 263 n. 73
Girdlestone, Robert G. 321
n. 118
Gnanakan, Ken 249 n. 1,
251 n. 7, 253, 264 n. 79,
268, 272
Goldingay, John 207 n. 75
Gonzalez, Justo 58 n. 16,
60, 67 n. 63, 67 n. 66, 68
Graham, Billy 90
Gregersen, Niels Henrik 219
n. 4
Grenz, Stanley J. 19 n. 17,
22 n. 18, 153 n. 11, 164
n. 66, 169 n. 80, 184 n. 2,

195 n. 44, 199 n. 63, 213
n. 83, 246 n. 112, 270
n. 111, 292 n. 12
Grudem, Wayne A. 19, 49,
77 n. 116, 153 n. 11, 154
n. 17, 154 n. 20, 155
nn. 22–23, 155 nn. 25–26,
156 n. 28, 158 n. 37, 162,
204–5, 216 n. 89, 226,
298, 299 n. 31, 306–7
Grunlan, Stephen 317
Guarino, Thomas 239
Guder, Darrell L. 312 n. 94,
320 n. 117
Gunton, Colin 212 n. 82

Haldane, Robert 66
Hall, J. H. 34 n. 36
Haller, William 36 n. 43, 38
Hampshire, Stuart 221
n. 10
Hanson, Norwood Russell
236, 242
Hanson, Paul D. 216 n. 86
Hart, Trevor 199 n. 63, 201
Haugen, Joel 235 n. 55
Hawking, Stephen 241
n. 88
Heard, Gerry C. 314 n. 100
Heavenor, S. 120 n. 11
Hebblethwaite, Brian 285
n. 149
Hefner, Philip 234 n. 54
Heim, S. Mark 251, 252,
257 n. 38, 265 n. 90, 266,
274, 279 n. 138, 281
n. 143
Heisenberg, Werner 239
Heitzenrater, R. P. 65 n. 57
Hendry, George S. 290
Henry, Carl F. H. 18, 25
n. 2, 53 n. 3, 81 n. 134, 86
n. 4, 87 n. 5, 87 nn. 7–11,
88 nn. 12–15, 89 n. 18, 90
nn. 23–24, 91 nn. 25–27,
91 n. 29, 92 nn. 30–33, 93
nn. 34–38, 95 nn. 44–45,
95 nn. 47–49, 95 nn. 51–
53, 95 n. 55, 96 nn. 56–
57, 96 n. 61, 96 n. 63, 97
n. 66, 97 nn. 68–69, 99

nn. 82–83, 101 nn. 86–87,
117, 127, 165, 245 n. 108,
255 nn. 33–34, 261 n. 65,
289, 325
Hensely, Jeffrey 245 n. 110
Hesse, Mary 223
Hick, John 252, 264–65,
266
Hillman, Eugene 277
Hocking, W. E. 263
Hodge, A. A. 72–77
Hodge, Charles 70 n. 84,
71–73, 74, 76, 77 n. 114,
204, 225
Hoffecker, Andrew 72 n. 91
Hogg, A. G. 264
Holdcroft, David 242 n. 94
Hooper, John 34
Hordern, William 129
Horton, Michael S. 339,
344, 350
Hoyer, Paul M. 29 n. 14
Hudson, Winthrop 293, 296
Hunter, James Davison
130–31, 327, 329

Inch, Morris A. 25 n. 2

Jacobsen, Douglas 326, 327
n. 10, 328, 329 n. 13, 333
James, William 194
Jantzen, Grace 279
Jastrow, Robert 241 n. 88
Jewett, Paul K. 152
Joachim, Harold H. 191
n. 22, 192, 193
Jodock, Darrell 210 n. 78
Johnson, Philip E. 219 n. 1
Johnston, Robert K. 111
n. 149, 142, 178 n. 118

Kantzer, Kenneth S. 25
n. 2, 26 n. 3, 53–54, 99,
339, 349
Kearsley, Roy 156 n. 27,
157 n. 35
Keesecker, William F. 31
n. 23
Kelsey, David H. 245 n. 109
Kendall, R. T. 39 n. 59
Kisker, Scott 45 n. 88

Klaassen, Walter 208
Klooster, Fred 111 n. 149
Knight, Henry H. III 179
n. 122
Knitter, Paul F. 251, 263
n. 74, 264–65, 266
Koivisto, Rex A. 142 n. 144,
297 n. 24
Kooiman, Willem Jan 60
n. 30
Kort, Wesley A. 191 n. 28
Kraemer, Hendrik 254–55,
257, 264
Krausz, Michael 191 n. 29
Kroeber, Alfred L. 211 n. 80
Kuhn, Thomas S. 171 n. 87,
192 n. 32, 236–38
Kuyper, Abraham 114
Kydd, Ronald 349

Lafleur, Laurence J. 221
n. 10
Lakatos, Imre 192 n. 31,
227 n. 31, 228
Land, Steven J. 179 n. 123
Lash, Nicholas 324 n. 125
Latourette, Kenneth Scott
302 n. 48
Lawson, Hilary 169 n. 81,
171 n. 85, 195 n. 43
Lehmann, Paul L. 285
n. 148
Leith, John H. 37 n. 51, 69
n. 77, 309 n. 81
Letham, R. W. A. 39 n. 64
Lewis, Gordon R. 32 n. 30,
44–45, 50, 77 n. 115, 118,
138, 152, 157, 225–26
Lightner, Robert 299
Lindbeck, George A. 198–
99, 202–3, 245, 268
n. 103, 271, 276 n. 126,
344
Lindsell, Harold 77, 90, 99,
100 n. 84, 108, 142
n. 144, 255 n. 33
Litton, Edward A. 297–98
Livingstone, David N. 219
n. 1
Locke, John 188
Long, Edward LeRoy, Jr. 29
n. 14

Lonning, Per 269 n. 107
Luckmann, Thomas 243,
244 n. 102, 244 n. 104
Luther, Martin 26, 30
nn. 16–19, 55–58, 59–60,
311–12
Lyotard, Jean-Francois 170
n. 83, 172–74, 283

MacArthur, John 349
Macchia, Frank 146
Machen, J. Gresham 78
MacIntyre, Alisdair 276
n. 125
MacIver, R. M. 172 n. 95
Macpherson, J. 66 n. 59
Macquarrie, John 307, 321
Maddox, Randy L. 135,
147, 347 n. 54
Markham, Ian 252 n. 10
Marsden, George M. 49
n. 107, 71 n. 88, 73 n. 98,
79 n. 127, 80 n. 131, 81
n. 133, 82, 106 n. 112,
182 n. 134, 288, 327, 329,
331
Marshall, Bruce D. 245
n. 108
Marshall, I. Howard 139,
157 n. 33, 159
Marty, Martin 326, 331–32,
337
Martyn, Henry 65
Matthews, Robert 236 n. 60
Maxwell, Joe 349 n. 67,
350 n. 69
Mayers, Marvin K. 317
McBeth, H. Leon 293 n. 17,
295
McClendon, James William,
Jr. 152, 153 n. 11, 215
McCree C. W. 47 n. 96
McCree, G. W. 47
McCullough, Donald W. 12
McDonnell, Kilian 322
n. 122
McGiffert, Arthur Cushman
70 n. 82, 189 n. 16
McGrath, Alister E. 69
n. 80, 153 n. 11, 167
n. 78, 199 n. 63, 220 n. 7,
224 n. 17, 245 n. 108,

258, 279, 344, 345
McKim, Donald K. 57 n. 12,
61 n. 35, 69, 72 n. 96, 76
n. 106, 77 n. 114
McLoughlin, William G. 51
McMullin, Ernan 219 n. 5,
239 n. 78, 242
McNeile, Hugh 310
Mead, George Herbert 276,
315
Meeking, Basil 349 n. 62
Meiland, Jack W. 191 n. 29
Melanchthon, Philip 36–37
Milbank, John 279 n. 137
Miller, Donald G. 300 n. 37,
302, 303–4, 312–13
Miller, Ed L. 111 n. 149
Miller, James B. 236 n. 61,
236 n. 63
Mohler, R. Albert 86, 99
n. 81, 100, 101 n. 86, 110
n. 144, 116, 289
Moltmann, Jürgen 322
Moorhouse, Henry 65–66
Moreland, J. P. 219 n. 1
Morgan, Edmund S. 37
n. 50
Morse, Christopher 153
n. 11
Mouw, Richard J. 72 n. 94
Mudge, Lewis S. 351 n. 71
Mulkay, Michael 238–39
Muller, Richard A. 68
nn. 71–72
Murphy, Arthur E. 193
Murphy, Nancey C. 182
n. 135, 184–85, 191 n. 26,
220 n. 8, 227–28

Nash, Ronald H. 25 n. 2,
120 n. 9, 121 n. 19, 255,
264 n. 82
Neff, David 25, 27
Neuhas, Richard John 349–
50
Newbigin, Lesslie 268–69
Nicole, Roger 135 n. 98
Nisbet, Robert A. 317
n. 111
Noll, Mark 51, 54–55, 76
n. 110

Ockenga, Harold J. 81, 85,
90
Oden, Thomas C. 131, 152,
300 n. 39, 305
Ogden, Schubert M. 266
n. 96, 266 n. 98
Okholm, Dennis L. 12, 13
n. 8, 14 n. 10, 14 n. 12,
199 n. 63, 251
Olson, Roger E. 14 n. 11,
26, 27 n. 9, 36, 42, 46–47,
78–79, 151–52, 183, 335
n. 29
Orr, James 79–80, 343
n. 46
Osborne, Grant R. 149
n. 176
Otto, Randall E. 157 n. 36
Outler, Albert C. 303, 347
n. 54
Owen, John 69

Packer, J. I. 261, 327, 343–
44, 350
Padilla, C. René 256 n. 35
Pannell, William 178 n. 120
Pannenberg, Wolfhart 55
n. 8, 74, 129, 195–98, 199
n. 63, 205, 210, 232–35
Parker, David 157 n. 34,
158, 167 n. 78
Patterson, Bob E. 86, 96
n. 62
Peacocke, Arthur 219 n. 4,
223, 236 n. 59, 239, 245
n. 111, 247 n. 114
Peel, Albert 36 n. 45
Peirce, Charles S. 193–94
Pelikan, Jaroslav 37 n. 48,
57–58
Perkins, William 38, 39
Perry, Tim 252 nn. 10–11
Phillips, Timothy R. 12–14,
199 n. 63, 251
Pinnock, Clark H. 18–19,
132, 134 n. 95, 135 n. 96,
136 nn. 101–2, 136
nn. 104–6, 137 nn. 108–
10, 138 nn. 114–15, 138
n. 117, 139 nn. 122–23,
139 nn. 125–27, 140
nn. 128–30, 141 n. 135,

141 n. 137, 141 n. 139, 142 nn. 142–43, 143 n. 145, 144 n. 150, 144 nn. 153–54, 145 nn. 155–59, 146 n. 160, 146 nn. 164–66, 147 n. 169, 148 n. 172, 149 nn. 176–81, 150 nn. 182–84, 152 n. 4, 160 nn. 45–46, 160 n. 48, 175–77, 176 n. 110, 245 n. 108, 257 n. 39, 258 n. 45, 260, 267 n. 99, 279
Piper, John 155 n. 25
Plantinga, Alvin 187 n. 9, 200–201
Plantinga, Cornelius Jr. 322 n. 121
Platcher, William C. 70 n. 83
Polanyi, Michael 240
Polkinghorne, John 228–29, 232, 235 n. 58, 241 n. 88
Popper, Karl 228, 236 n. 63
Price, Robert M. 139 n. 121, 141 n. 134, 150
Putt, B. Keith 131

Quebedeaux, Richard 130, 134
Quenstedt, Johann Andreas 62 n. 42, 67, 75
Quine, W. V. 191 n. 27

Race, Alan 252, 253 n. 18
Rahner, Karl 259–60
Rakestraw, Robert V. 144 n. 152, 147–48
Ramm, Bernard L. 18, 102 nn. 88–90, 103 nn. 91–93, 104 n. 94, 104 nn. 96–97, 105 n. 100, 105 nn. 106–7, 106 nn. 108–9, 106 n. 111, 107 nn. 113–15, 107 n. 117, 107 n. 119, 107 nn. 121–22, 108 n. 123, 108 n. 126, 108 nn. 128–29, 108 n. 132, 109 n. 133, 109 nn. 135–37, 109 n. 139, 110 nn. 140–43, 110 n. 145, 111 nn. 146–48, 111

n. 150, 112 n. 155, 112 n. 157, 113 nn. 158–60, 114 nn. 164–66, 115 n. 168, 115 n. 170, 116 n. 173, 219
Ratzinger, Joseph 271
Ratzsch, Delvin Lee 219 n. 1
Reardon, Patrick Henry 343–44
Reese, W. L. 221 n. 9
Reid, Thomas 71, 188
Reventlow, Henning Graf 74 n. 99
Reynolds, Edward 61
Reynolds, John Mark 219 n. 1
Richardson, W. Mark 142, 240 n. 86, 241 n. 89
Roennfeldt, Ray C. W. 141 n. 139
Rogers, A. K. 192
Rogers, Adrian 135
Rogers, Arthur Kenyon 191
Rogers, Jack B. 57 n. 12, 61 nn. 35–36, 69, 72 n. 96, 76 n. 106, 77 n. 114
Royce, Josiah 216, 316 n. 106, 317 n. 108
Rundle, Bede 188 n. 15
Runia, Klaas 251, 263 n. 76, 268 n. 105
Russell, Bertrand 219 n. 3
Rust, E. C. 106 n. 110

Samarthas, Stanley 264
Samuel, Vinay 262 n. 71
Sanders, John 19, 160 n. 44, 160 nn. 46–47, 160 nn. 49–50, 161 n. 52, 161 n. 56, 251 n. 4, 257 n. 40, 262 n. 69, 268
Satyavrata, Ivan 251 n. 7
Sauter, Gerhard 215 n. 84
Scaer, David 138
Schaeffer, Francis A. 77 n. 118, 131, 163
Schaff, Philip 34 n. 33
Scharlemann, Robert P. 171 n. 88
Schillebeeckx, Edward 259
Schineller, J. Peter 251 n. 7

Schmitz-Moormann, Karl 247 n. 115
Sernett, Milton G. 178 n. 120
Sharpe, Eric 264 nn. 80–81
Sheppard, Gerald 330
Shibley, Mark A. 51, 331
Sigountos, James G. 253 n. 17
Simeon, Charles 65
Simpson, R. T. 265 n. 92
Smith, Christian 83, 336
Smith, Timothy L. 44 n. 86
Smith, Wilbur M. 103 n. 91
Smith, Wilfred Cantwell 264, 265 n. 91
Smylie, James H. 71 n. 86
Solomon, Robert C. 195 n. 42
Spener, Philipp Jakob 40–44, 62–63
Sproul, R. C. 77 n. 117
Stackhouse, John G., Jr. 152 n. 3, 176
Stanesby, Derek 236 n. 63
Staniforth, Sampson 46
Stevick, Daniel B. 81 n. 134
Stewart, John W. 71 n. 89
Stock, Alex 215 n. 84
Stoeffler, F. Ernest 34 n. 34, 38 n. 57, 40 n. 65, 41 nn. 68–69, 42 nn. 71–72, 43 n. 81, 60 n. 34, 63 n. 46, 64, 67–68
Stone, Jon R. 175
Stott, John R. W. 267–68, 349 n. 62
Strong, Augustus Hopkins 260–61
Stroup, George W. 315 nn. 103–4
Sugden, Chris 262 n. 71
Surin, Kenneth 253
Swinburne, Richard 262

Tanner, Kathryn 180 n. 128, 180 n. 131, 181
Taylor, John V. 278
Telford, J. 46 n. 92
Thiel, John E. 187 n. 11, 190 n. 17

Thielicke, Helmut 284 n. 147
Thomas, Owen C. 202 n. 70
Tidball, Derek 167 n. 78, 288, 289
Tillard, J. M. R. 323
Tillich, Paul 297
Tinder, D. G. 296 n. 23
Tinker, Melvin 310–11, 319 n. 115
Tipler, Frank 241 n. 88
Tomlinson, Dave 166–68, 171–72, 178, 179, 181
Tomlinson, Hugh 170 n. 82, 171 n. 90
Toon, Peter 298 n. 27
Torrance, Thomas F. 222, 226–27, 231–32, 240, 241 n. 88, 303, 304
Touraine, Alain 180
Travis, Stephen H. 262
Troeltsch, Ernst 263
Trollinger, William Vance, Jr. 326, 327 n. 10, 328, 329 n. 13, 333
Trueblood, David Elton 245 n. 111
Turretin, Francis 68–69, 73, 76
Tyerman, L. 49 n. 103

Ullian, J. S. 191 n. 27
Uwoke, Tadakazu 62 n. 41

vam Beeck, Franz Jozef 274
Van Dusen, Henry 302–3
Van Engen, Charles 319–20
van Huyssteen, J. Wentzel 184, 185 n. 3, 190, 219 n. 4, 220 n. 6, 227 n. 30, 228, 232, 235, 237 n. 71,

244 n. 107
Vassiliadis, Petros 301 n. 43
Vencer, Agustin B., Jr. 349 n. 66
Venn, Henry 65
Villain, Maurice 302 n. 50
Volf, Miroslav 179 n. 123, 322 n. 122
von Weizsäcker, Carl Friedrich 244 n. 106

Wainwright, Geoffrey 300, 303
Warfield, B. B. 72–77, 256 n. 36
Watson, David 304–5
Webber, Robert E. 25 n. 2, 305 n. 66
Weborg, C. John 42 n. 74, 43
Welch, Claude 224–25
Wells, David F. 12–13, 19, 131, 139, 163–66, 173, 181, 182, 275 n. 120, 341, 346 n. 53
Wells, William W. 28
Wells, William W. 46 n. 93
Wendel, Francois 30 n. 21
Wesley, Charles 46, 65
Wesley, John 45, 48, 50, 65, 292, 347
Westblade, Donald 75 n. 102
Westphal, Merold 187 n. 8, 190, 200 n. 67, 201 n. 68
Whale, J. S. 312
White, Barrington R. 293 n. 16
Whitefield, George 44, 48–49, 291, 347
Wicken, Jeffrey S. 239

Wildman, Wesley J. 240 n. 84, 240 n. 86, 241 n. 89
Wiley, H. Orton 32 n. 29
Williams, Colin W. 301 n. 42
Williams, Donald T. 111 n. 149
Williams, J. Rodman 179 n. 124
Williams, Michael D. 299 n. 32
Williams, Raymond 243
Wimber, John 154–55
Wittgenstein, Ludwig 170 n. 83, 194–95, 237, 242
Wolffe, John 348
Wolterstorff, Nicholas 190, 200–201, 222 n. 12
Wood, W. Jay 71 n. 85, 186 n. 4, 187 n. 7, 187 n. 10, 188, 190 n. 21, 191 n. 23, 200 n. 65
Woodbridge, John D. 71 n. 87, 76 n. 107, 76 n. 111
Worthing, Mark William 241 n. 90, 246 n. 113
Wright, Christopher J. H. 270 n. 110, 272–73, 277 n. 127, 278 n. 132
Wuthnow, Robert 243 n. 97, 327, 327 n. 6

Yoder, John Howard 208 n. 76, 332
Young, Pamela Dickey 266 n. 97, 280
Young, Warren C. 119 n. 5

Zwingli, Huldrych 58 n. 20

Subject Index

accommodation 15, 106, 108, 111, 122, 143
African Americans 178, 336
Age of Reason 189, 222
American Baptist Seminary of the West 103
American Bible Society 295
American Council of Christian Churches 82
American Sunday School Union 295
Anabaptists 16
annihilationism 132
"anonymous Christians" 259
apologetic theology 18, 19, 20–21, 101, 114, 119–20, 157, 183, 205, 250
apologetics 92–93, 103–4, 109, 114, 135, 161
Apostles' Creed 213
Aristotelianism 67, 230
Arminianism 125, 139, 142, 144
assensus 41, 343
associational principle 293–94
assurance 38–40, 47–50
authentic Christianity 41, 42

authoritarianism 107
autonomy 146
awakenings 15, 16, 346–47

baptism 42, 47, 317–19
baptismal regeneration 41
Baptist Historical Society 295
Baptist World Alliance 119
Baptists 90, 293–95
basic beliefs 186–87, 190, 200–201
Baylor University 103
belief-mosaics 179–81, 205, 247, 343, 345
Bethel College 103, 159
Bethel Seminary 103, 119
Bible 14, 17
 authority 97–98, 107–9, 143
 autographs 75–76
 Calvin on 58–60
 communal interpretation 339
 as evangelicalism's formal principle 54
 human dimension 143
 inerrancy 65, 66
 inspiration 65, 66, 73, 74, 83, 97–98, 108–9, 121–22, 143

 Luther on 55–58
 in Lutheran Orthodoxy 66–67
 phenomena of 127–28
 Pietists on 62–64
 Puritans on 60–61
 in Reformed Scholasticism 67–69
 and science 104–6
 as self-authenticating 59, 115
 single meaning 74
Bible Institute of Los Angeles (Biola), 103
biblicism 15, 105–6, 109
Billy Graham Crusades 165
bipolar theological continuum. *See* two-party model
"born again" 42

Calvin, John 30–33, 34–35, 58–60
Calvinism, rejected by Pinnock 139, 145–46
Canadian Keswick Bible Conference 136
Canterbury Trail 13
center. *See* evangelical center
certainty 110, 136

certitude 110, 195
charismatic movement 154, 179
Chicago Call The (1977), 305
Christ as Word 59
Christian Century, The 90
Christian life 30, 32
Christian reconstruction movement 140
Christianity Today 11–12, 14, 15, 25, 27–28, 33, 49, 90, 151, 341, 350
Christians for Biblical Equality 125, 155
christocentrism 254, 266
church 214–16
    apostolicity 309–10, 319, 320
    bound by gospel 338–39
    catholicity 309–10, 319, 320, 346–51
    as community 313, 314–19
    gospel-centeredness 338–39
    holiness 309–10, 319, 321
    as local and universal 318
    marks 308–12
    unity 303, 309–10, 312, 319, 321
    as voluntary society 293–95
Church of England 36
"cognitive-propositionalist" approach 198
coherence 196, 233, 234
coherentism 191–93, 196–97, 205
collegia pietatis 41, 334
common sense 169
communal relativism 174
communitarian theology 21, 281
community 20, 214–16, 275–77, 281, 285, 313
    of hope 316
    and interpretation 339
    of memory 316
    and rationality 201
    and text 208
    and universality 283

complementarians 155
conditional immortality 145
Confessio Augustana 34
Confessio Belgica 35
congregationalism 293–94
Constantinianism 332–33
constructivist epistemology 171
consummation 22–23
context 168, 174–75
conversation 206–11
conversion 15, 17, 43, 45–47, 100
convertive piety 46–47, 53, 84, 144, 166, 176, 178, 250, 257, 335
core theory 227–28
correspondence theory of truth 169, 188, 190, 194, 198
Council on Biblical Manhood and Womanhood 155
Counter-Reformation 69
creation 270
"creative-love theism" 145
creeds 57, 61
critical realism 171, 242, 245
crucicentrism 15
cultural engagement 12
cultural pluralism 20
"cultural-linguistic" approach 198
culture 122, 168, 180, 210–11
culture wars 327–28

Darwinism 219 n. 1
deduction 187
deism 224
democratic capitalism 140
denominationalism 85, 296–97, 311
depravity 29, 94
Diet of Worms 56–57
discipline 34–35, 311
dispensationalism 78, 299 n. 32
doctrine 14, 53–54, 83, 166, 176, 340–44, 345

doubt 221
Dutch Calvinists 83

Eastern Baptist Theological Seminary 103
Eastern Orthodox Church 13, 301, 347
ecclesia semper reformanda 321, 334
ecclesiocentrism 266
ecclesiolae in ecclesia 41
ecclesiology 21, 33–37, 47, 126, 319–21
ecological values 173 n. 103
ecumenism 21, 209, 300–308, 341
egalitarianism 125, 155, 177
election 37, 38, 271
empiricism 188, 221, 222–23
Enlightenment 49–50, 70, 71, 112–13, 115, 159, 171–72, 182, 187–88, 212, 222, 226, 328
    foundationalism 200–201
    science 220–24, 225
    theology 189
entire sanctification 32 n. 29
epistemology 19, 20, 185
Erickson, Millard 18, 32, 88, 117, 118–34, 144, 151, 152, 153, 154–57, 159, 175–76, 177, 183, 298, 302, 306
eschatological community 247, 283, 316, 324
eschatological realism 20, 246–48
eschatology 20, 216–17, 284–85
Evangelical Affirmations 25 n. 2, 53 n. 3, 261
Evangelical Alliance 51, 295
evangelical boundaries 175–78
evangelical center 331–33, 350–51
evangelical establishment 18, 134, 162
evangelical left 129, 132, 176

evangelical modernists 182
Evangelical Theological Society 177
evangelicalism. *See also* neo-evangelicalism
boundaries 183
"classical" 51
cultural accommodation 165
definition 14–16
demise 12, 19, 91–92, 130–31, 163–64
disregard for institutional church 288
diversity 178, 179
ecumenism 304–7
first generation 18, 175
formal principle 54, 101
future 11–14
marginalized voices 178–79
material principle 53, 101
missionary impulse 250
and modernity 49, 336
as mosaic of local theologies 179–81
and postmodern context 181–83
as Reformed 26–28, 178
as renewal movement 334–36
reverence for Bible 64–66
and scientific model 225–28
second generation 18, 117–18, 147, 153–54
sociological perspective 15
and storytelling 202
theological roots 16
third generation 19, 153–54, 156, 161, 162, 168
Evangelicals and Catholics Together 327, 343–44, 349–50
evangelism 285–86
evidences 136–37
evidentialism 96, 103–4, 109–10, 115, 141
evil 145
exclusivism 252–58, 268

experience 39, 46, 47, 49–50, 70, 147, 153, 198, 202–3, 292
experimental religion 53
extra ecclesiam nulla salus 253

facts 225, 226
faith 338
and science 240
fall 94, 270
fellowship 281, 306, 323
fiducia 41, 343
first principles 230, 248
Formula of Concord 62
foundationalism 19, 20, 185–90, 199–200, 221, 223, 226
free church 310
free-will theism 160
Fuller Theological Seminary 90
fundamentalism 12, 15, 17–18, 78, 81 n. 134, 83, 87–88, 102, 108, 112, 120–21, 159, 165–66
Fundamentals, The 54, 78, 79–80
further light 335

Garrett Theological Seminary 119
gathered church 36
general revelation 121, 127, 256–57
"generous orthodoxy" 21, 325–26, 331, 340, 342
globalization 170, 174, 179, 249–50
God
author of Scripture 98
holiness 163–65
impassibility 154
incomprehensibility 113
knowledge of future 146
love 164–65
nature 162
openness 145–46, 159–62
as pure relationality 146
rationality 95
sovereignty 146
transcendence 95

trinity 282
as unity of truth 197
universal saving activity 270–71
good works 31, 39
gospel 17, 25–26, 43, 57–58, 250, 337–39, 343
bound to the church 338–39
and justification 27
universality and particularity 266–67
grace and nature 259
Graduate Theological Union 103
grammar 198–99
Great Awakening 45, 51, 346–47
Greek philosophy 145, 160, 162, 196, 234
Grudem, Wayne 19, 49, 77 n. 116, 153 n. 11, 154–59, 168, 204–5, 216, 226, 298, 306

hard exclusivism 257, 258, 262
hell 145
Helvetic Consensus Formula 68
Henry, Carl F. H. 18, 85–102, 114–15, 117, 119, 120, 127, 130, 136, 147, 151, 153, 156, 157
heritage 209
hermeneutics 106, 209–10
Hispanic evangelicals 178
historical-critical approach 74
history 22–23
holiness 31
holiness movement 78, 179, 336
Holy Spirit 48, 110, 247, 282
Hour of Decision, The 136
human freedom 145–46
human government 29

identity formation 278
idolatry 274

illumination 63–64, 107,
     142, 144, 149
imago dei 96, 213, 282, 322–
     23
implicit faith 258–59
imputation 27–28, 43, 48
incarnation 59
inclusivism 144–45, 252,
     258–63
individualism 314
induction 77, 187, 226
inerrancy 123
     Erickson on 127–28
     evangelicalism on 83
     among fundamentalists
          79–80
     Grudem on 156
     Henry on 98–100
     Pinnock on 137–38, 141–
          44
     Ramm on 108–9, 112
     Warfield on 73–77
instinctus divinus 259
"integrative theology" 44
interpretation 144, 216,
     202–3, 239, 317
interpretive frameworks
     202, 203–4, 315
InterVarsity Christian Fel-
     lowship 136
intratextual theology 199
intuition 147
invisible church 21, 36–37,
     38, 297–99, 308, 310,
     323
Islamic fundamentalism 173
     n. 103

Jesus Christ
     bridge between creation
          and new creation 284–
          85
     finality 280–83
     as revelation 107, 109
     uniqueness 253–55
justification 17, 26–30, 31–
     32, 41, 43, 48, 57–58,
     340, 349

knowledge 210, 343
koinonia 323

L'Abri Fellowship 136
laity 40–41
language 242–44, 246–47
language games 170, 194–
     95, 198, 237, 242
Lausanne Covenant (1974),
     255–56
law 29
     and gospel 31
     and grace 29
     and sanctification 30–33
     third use 29 n. 14, 31
liberalism 17, 78–79, 104,
     108, 196
     Grudem on 158
     as new foundationalism
          202–3
     on science 224–25
lifestyle enclave 315
linguistics 194, 242
local church 293
local theology 19–20, 174,
     343
logic 227
logos 95, 227
Lord's Supper 317–19
lost 257–58, 261–62, 268
Luther, Martin 26–30, 34,
     55–58, 60
Lutheranism 26, 28, 30, 32,
     33, 41–42, 62, 83

Madras Christian College
     264
mainline Protestantism 91,
     301
mapping 188
marginalized voices 178–79,
     333, 336
marks of the church 34,
     309–13, 319, 321
Mars Hill Fellowship (Se-
     attle) 164
Marxism 173 n. 103
McMaster Divinity College
     140, 143
mechanistic worldview 223,
     236
Mennonites 83
metanarrative 19, 172–74
metaphors 122, 161

metaphysical realism 188,
     190, 194–95
method of correlation 120,
     126
Methodism 16, 45, 48
Middle Ages 26–27, 229–32
miracles 109
mission 319–21
moderate Calvinism 125
Modern Reformation 350
modern theology 91–92
modernism adopted by
     evangelicalism 130
modernist-fundamentalist
     controversy 329, 330,
     340
modernity 14, 92, 163, 168
modest foundationalism
     188
Moravians 47
multiple realities 170
myth 172, 173

narrative theology 101, 148,
     216, 315
National Association of
     Evangelicals 25 n. 2, 53
     n. 3, 82, 165
National Council of
     Churches 82
natural religion 224
neo-evangelicalism 16, 54,
     85–86, 101. *See also*
     evangelicalism
     as culture-affirming 123
     as foundationalism 204–5
     fundamentalist roots 17–
          18, 81–83
     irenic tradition 116, 155
     post-fundamentalist char-
          acter 16
     shift to right 159
neo-orthodoxy 94, 137
neo-Protestantism 196
new birth 292–93
new creation 246, 270, 284
New International Version,
     inclusive language ver-
     sion 155
New Lights 292
New Orleans Baptist Theo-
     logical Seminary 136

"new paradigm" story 173
    n. 103
Nicene Creed 213
nonbasic beliefs 186–87
North American Baptist
    Conference 16
Northern Baptist Theologi-
    cal Seminary 90, 119
Northwestern University
    119
notae ecclesiae 309–13, 319,
    321

obedience 31, 33
objective revelation. *See*
    propositional revelation
objectivity 20, 170, 220,
    235–37, 241, 245–46
ontology 20
open-ended exclusivism
    258
openness of God 145–46,
    159–62
ordo salutis 47

parachurch 21, 136, 288–
    90, 295–300, 308
paradigms 174, 237
Pentecostalism 149, 154–55,
    179, 336
perfection 30
perseverance 139
personal ethics 87
personal testimonies 202
physico-theology 241
Pietism 17, 40–43, 44, 46,
    94, 133, 150, 196, 334,
    343
    on Bible 62–64
    ecclesiology 291, 340
    in Princeton theology 72
pilgrimage 18, 134–35, 150
Pinnock, Clark 18, 117–18,
    132, 134–50, 151, 153,
    154, 157, 159, 160, 175–
    76
pluralism 252, 263–66, 279
postconservative movement
    129
post-evangelicals 166–68
postfoundationalism 195,
    200

postmodernism 14, 19–23,
    131, 168–75, 182
    and post-evangelicalism
    167–68
    and science 236–39
post-postmodernism 22
pragmatism 191, 193
predestination 37
presuppositionalism 96,
    103, 115, 122, 126, 141
Princeton theology 17, 70–
    80, 84, 99, 134, 137–38,
    189
progress 173 n. 103
progressive creation 106,
    125
prophecy 109
propositional revelation 63,
    84, 94–95, 96, 101, 112,
    127, 134, 148, 156, 161
Protestantism 26, 290, 333,
    336
psychology 123
pure church ideal 36
Puritanism 17, 23, 33–36,
    44, 46, 334–35
    on assurance 38–40, 48
    on Bible 60–61
    ecclesiology 291, 340

quantum theory 236

Ramm, Bernard 18, 85–86,
    102–16, 117, 120, 124,
    126, 129, 130, 151, 153,
    157, 167, 219
rationalism 18, 70, 93, 101,
    115
realism 19, 20, 169–71, 188,
    229, 244
reason 94, 212, 230
reconciliation 320
Reformation 16, 17, 26, 55,
    340
    and Constantinianism 332
    ecclesiology 36–37
    and science 222
Reformed epistemology
    200–201, 214
Reformed tradition 31–32,
    33

regeneration 17, 31, 42–43,
    44–47, 133
Regent College 140
relativism 70
relativity theory 236
renewal 334–36
repentance 30
Re-Thinking Missions 263
revelation 93–97, 107–8,
    126, 156–57. *See also*
    propositional revelation
    in all religions 249
    as analogical 122
    as communication of in-
    formation 100
"reverent agnosticism" 268
revivals 16, 22, 43, 44, 78
righteousness 27–28
Roman Catholic Church 26,
    37, 298, 301, 346–50
    ecclesiology 309–13
    evangelicals converting to
    13
    on exclusivism 252
    and inclusivism 258–60
    on Scripture 55–57

sacraments 317–19
salvation
    explicit Christian focus
    262, 279
    of lost 132, 144–45, 175,
    261–62
    universal and particular
    aspects 251, 266–67,
    283, 284
sanctification 17
    and assurance 39
    and law 30–33
    and regeneration 43
    Wesley on 48
Sanders, John 19, 159–62,
    168
schism 126
scholasticism 17, 196
    Henry as 94
    Lutheran 41
    Protestant 47, 66–69, 74,
    84
    Reformed 67–69, 134
science 20, 69, 102, 172–73,
    219–28, 238

and the Bible 104–6, 157
and faith 240
as interpretation 239
and new creation 247–48
and religion 219 n. 3
and theology 225–28,
    239–41, 244
Scopes "monkey" trial 85
Scots Confession 35
Scottish common sense real-
    ism 71
"Scripture principle" (Pin-
    nock), 143–44
Second Helvetic Confession 68
sectarianism 296
separatism 81, 126
signs of grace 39
simul iustus et peccator 29
sin 113–14, 304
skepticism 70, 212
social cohesion 276, 281
social construction 19, 20,
    241–42, 243–44, 315
    n. 104
social contract 314
social ethics 82, 87–88
sociology of knowledge 123,
    238–39, 243
sola fide 26–28, 30
sola scriptura 17, 55–57, 61,
    66, 74, 206, 345
soteriology 27, 42–43
Southern Baptists 349
Southwestern Baptist Theo-
    logical Seminary 119,
    131
special revelation 121, 127,
    256–57
Spirit 209–11
    Pinnock on 148–50
    testimony of 63, 108, 121
    and Word 58–60, 61, 62–
    63
stories 202
structuralism 243
subjectivism 107, 115, 196
symbols 171, 180, 276

systematic theology 123–24,
    126, 152–53, 158

testimonium spiritus internum
    63, 108
theistic evolution 106
theocentrism 266
theology
    as academic discipline
        182–83
    and the church 164, 182–
        83
    as communitarian 214–16
    as conversation 206–11
    as eschatological 216–17
    goal 344
    irrelevance 341
    as local 211, 343
    and meaning-making 180
    metaphorical nature 122
    as progressive 343
    public nature of 232–35
    as science 20, 71–72, 225–
        29, 231, 233
    task 156
therapy 12
Tomlinson, Dave 19, 166–
    68, 171–72, 179
Toronto Blessing 149
tradition 55, 57, 208, 315
traditionalists 151
transcendence 95
Trent 248
tribes 174
Trinity 212–13
Trinity Evangelical Divinity
    School 25 n. 2, 53 n. 3,
    137, 154, 159
true church 34, 297–99,
    308–12
Truett Seminary 119
truth 20, 174, 193–94. *See
    also* correspondence the-
    ory of truth
    coheres in God 233
    as eschatological 197, 234

as historical 197
two-party model 21, 326–31

universal church 312
useful fictions 174

Vatican II 258, 312, 348–49
Vineyard fellowship 154–
    55, 156
visible church 21, 36–37,
    297–99, 308, 323
voluntary society 293–95,
    314

web of belief 191, 205
Wells, David F. 12–13, 19,
    131, 139, 163–66, 168,
    173, 182, 341, 346
Wesleyans 32 n. 29, 83,
    147, 179, 336
Western Seminary 119
Westminster Confession of Faith
    37, 39, 61, 73, 206
Wheaton College 89–90
Willow Creek Community
    Church 164
women in ministry 155, 177
Word and sacrament 311,
    312, 318
Word and Spirit 206–7
World Council of Churches
    300
World Evangelical Fellow-
    ship 51
World Missions Conferences
    263, 302
worship 272–73
Wycliffe Bible Translators
    136

"young earth" proponents
    125
Young Men's Christian As-
    sociation 295
Youth for Christ 136

Stanley J. Grenz (D.Theol., University of Munich) is the Pioneer McDonald Professor of Theology and Ethics at Carey Theological College and professor of theology and ethics at Regent College in Vancouver, British Columbia. A leading voice on the North American theological scene, he has over twenty books to his credit, including *A Primer on Postmodernism*, *Created for Community*, and *Revisioning Evangelical Theology*.